JEM ROBERTS was born in Ludlow in 1978, gained his first professional writing gig as a teenage games journalist, and has over twenty years of magazine toil under his belt. As a comedy performer, he has inflicted his noises on audiences from Edinburgh to Glastonbury Festival, solo and with his troupe, The Unrelated Family. His love of *I'm Sorry, I Haven't a Clue* led to his first officially authorised book, *The Clue Bible,* in 2009, and a lifetime's obsession meant that the ultimate guide to *Blackadder* had to follow, with 2012's *The True History of The Black Adder*. In 2014, he became the official biographer of Douglas Adams, with *The Frood* marking his third release from Preface Publishing. *Soupy Twists!* is his fourth work of comedy history. Also published by Unbound in 2018 is *Tales of Britain,* the first British folktale treasury in over thirty years, which Roberts performs all over the UK.

JEMROBERTS.COM

BY THE SAME AUTHOR

The Clue Bible: The Fully Authorised History of I'm Sorry, I Haven't a Clue

The True History of The Black Adder

The Frood: The Authorised and Very Official History of Douglas Adams

Tales of Britain

SOUPY TWISTS!

JEM ROBERTS

The full official story of the sophisticated silliness of Stephen Fry & Hugh Laurie

Unbound

This edition first published in 2018

Unbound
6th Floor Mutual House, 70 Conduit Street, London W1S 2GF
www.unbound.com

All rights reserved

© Jem Roberts, 2018

The right of Jem Roberts to be identified as the author
of this work has been asserted in accordance with Section 77 of the Copyright,
Designs and Patents Act 1988. No part of this publication may be copied,
reproduced, stored in a retrieval system, or transmitted, in any form
or by any means, without the prior permission of the publisher, nor be
otherwise circulated in any form of binding or cover other than that in
which it is published and without a similar condition being imposed
on the subsequent purchaser.

While every effort has been made to trace the owners of copyright material reproduced
herein, the publisher would like to apologise for any omissions and will be pleased to
incorporate missing acknowledgements in any further editions.

Cocktail illustrations, p.v and p.267 © Darrell Maclaine-Jones

Text design by PDQ

A CIP record for this book is available from the British Library

ISBN 978-1-78352-451-8 (trade hbk)
ISBN 978-1-78352-460-0 (e-book)
ISBN 978-1-78352-450-1 (limited edition)

Printed in Great Britain by CPI Group (UK)

SURREY LIBRARIES	
Askews & Holts	10-Oct-2018
791.4502 ENT	£16.99

For Jo, and Jo.

TIME *hath, my lord, a wallet at his back,*
Wherein he puts alms for oblivion,
A great-sized monster of ingratitudes!
                        Shakespeare, *Troilus and Cressida*, Act 3, Scene 3

Let fame, that all hunt after in their lives,
Live regist'red upon our brazen tombs,
And then grace us in the disgrace of death;
When in spite of cormorant devouring Time,
Th'endeavour of this present breath may buy
That honour which shall bate his scythe's keen edge,
And make us heirs of all eternity.
                        Shakespeare, *Love's Labours Lost*, Act 1, Scene 1

You cannot step into the same river twice, for fresh water is always flowing past you.
                        Heraclitus

Your Cambridge was built of people, not of bricks and stone and glass, and those people have severally dispersed into the world. They will never be assembled together again. The circus has long since folded its tents and stolen silently away and you are standing on the village green wondering why it looks so shabby and forlorn . . . Now pop off out of my sight. You smell of mortality. I don't need you to remind me of my age, I have a bladder to do that for me . . . If you have been, hello.
                        Professor Donald Trefusis

CONTENTS

Preface: Be Nice!	1
The First Bit	5
The Next Bit	63
The Main Bit	119
The Last Bit	239
A Bit of a Fry & Laurie Guide	269
Unseen Extracts from the Fry & Laurie Archive	273
Notes	365
Index	369
Supporters	383

CONTENTS

Preface: Be Nice!	1
The First Bit	5
The Next Bit	63
The Main Bit	119
The Last Bit	239
A Bit of a Fry & Laurie Guide	269
Unseen Extracts from the Fry & Laurie Archive	273
Notes	365
Index	369
Supporters	383

PREFACE: BE NICE!

'I think it was Donald Mainstock, the great amateur squash player, who pointed out how lovely I was. Until that time I think it was safe to say that I had never really been aware of my own timeless brand of loveliness. But his words smote me, because of course you see, I am lovely in a fluffy moist kind of way and who would have it otherwise?'

'Say please, don't make me say it twice, Let's all get some manners here, let's try to Be Nice, 'Cause I'm a good ass motherliker.'

How unauthorised biographers manage to sleep at night, knowing their subject actively does not wish them to do their job, I do not know. However, writing officially authorised biography also has its difficulties, and never more so than when chronicling the doings of massively beloved famous artists, who just happen to have never quite developed the rhinocerine thick skin that tends to be a by-product of years of fame and fortune. A few celebrity demagogues never need thick skin, they create their own universe with them at the centre of it, but to delight in engaging with the wider world, while being deeply bruised by its buffets, is an unfortunate cocktail of traits.

Stephen Fry's numerous dramas on Twitter and elsewhere, not to mention Irish threats of blasphemy charges, have shown the perils of being heralded as a spokesman for almost everything – don't presume safety in nuance. Fry is the most sensitive of souls, almost unavoidably exposed on all sides by his sheer desire to honestly engage, and be himself. The immediacy of social media intensifies a tug of war and love with the public that has always been part of the Fry & Laurie story – from the very start, their positions of undeniable privilege have put them on the back foot, paradoxically requiring them to fight their corner harder than most comedians. Even the most blindly committed adorers of the two gentlemen will concede that Stephen & Hugh haven't always been the most reliably breezy of fellows. In differing ways, and no matter how much laughter they have generated together and apart over the last four decades, neither colleague habitually eyes existence with absolute equanimity.

They are not, therefore, the kind of chaps anyone would imagine lightly taking the decision to hand their life stories over to a third party. Luckily for them, *Soupy Twists!* is a celebration of laughter, offered in tribute to one of the funniest double acts of all time, while both colleagues are still around to be dreadfully embarrassed by the attention. This is not a whitewashing hagiography, but nor, thankfully, is it a dustbin-raking exposé – it is the story of the creation of a singular cocktail of humour by two friends, and as such its real area of fascination stops around twenty years ago, as Fry & Laurie began permanently to follow their own solitary paths. As much as possible, the duo's story is told by themselves and their closest collaborators and friends, and hopefully by the end we will know our two heroes better than ever; they will speak with candour and amused honesty, but let the armchair psychiatrists do their own work.

As to those collaborators, friends, and other crucial creatives who steered *Soupy Twists!* into your grasp – not to mention the many benefactors listed at the back of the book, as they are mentioned there, but thank you . . . For Unbound, deep gratitude must go to John Mitchinson, Mathew Clayton, Georgia Odd, Jimmy Leach, Mark Bowsher, Philip Connor, DeAndra Lupu and Anna Simpson. I'm indebted to the kind staff at the BFI, the BBC Archive and Cambridge University Library. But after the main men, the greatest roles have been played by the ever-gladdening Jo Crocker and Elizabeth Fergusson, who represented Fry & Laurie respectively, and ensured that any of the proceedings could proceed, with extra thanks to Fergusson's successor Joshua Woodford.

I was delirious with pleasure in managing to gain audiences with Paul Shearer, Emma Thompson, Kim Harris, John Lloyd, Jon Canter, Nick Symons, Roger Ordish, Robert Daws, Fiona Gillies, Richard Curtis, Brian Eastman, Deborah Norton, Jon Plowman, Maurice Gran, Jo Laurie and of course, Jo Crocker. Further thanks-awfullies for numerous suggestions and fan memories go to Tom Boon, Paula Clarke Bain, Dave Lee, Darrell Maclaine-Jones (especially for designing the cocktail icons), Steve Medcraft, Andy Tubb, anyone whose comments helped, plus Pam and all the *House* fan base. But above all, of course, for putting up with all this necessary nosiness and cheek-reddening celebration, everybody's thanks go to Stephen & Hugh.

Haters, by and large, are by definition going to hate. But Stephen has a particular favourite tale which has always encapsulated his ideal, and it is one we should all hug to ourselves and aim to live by: 'There's a wonderful story that I always treasure of a young undergraduate who gets elected to a junior fellowship of an Oxbridge college at the turn of the last century. As he arrives at the seniors' common room, there's an ancient old don who says, "Welcome, welcome young man. A word of advice – Don't try to be clever. We're all clever here. Only try to be kind, a little kind . . ."'

THE FIRST BIT

'When I was nine – oh, fewer years ago now than I care to remember! – my mother told me that in life one could either be an elf or a pixie. What she meant by that, I fully suppose you may be able all too readily to guess . . .'

'You know what makes me REALLY mad? It's this belief that I'm John the Baptist.'

AMERICA – Hollywood Boulevard, Tuesday 25 October 2016, 2:30pm PST. Outside the Pig'n Whistle British Pub, a new star is unveiled, as a permanent tribute to the talents of international heart-throb and one-time highest paid TV actor in the world, Hugh Laurie. Six years earlier, Hugh was on hand to unveil the star for his ex-girlfriend Emma Thompson, and this time, the duty has fallen to his comedy colleague and best friend of over thirty-five years, Stephen Fry – who has travelled the relatively short distance from his new home in Los Angeles.

He expounds, 'That he is preposterously talented, not just as an actor in all weights – lightweight, middleweight, heavyweight and super heavyweight – but as a musician, novelist and athlete, is beyond dispute. That he is repulsively handsome and quite intensely blue-eyed is also a matter of public record. But he's also a star, that's what we're here to celebrate – an ineluctable, ineffable star. But what is a star? I'm a very literal-minded person, so I wanted to look up as many attributes of a star as I possibly could, and while the dictionaries and encyclopaedias make several and varied claims, they are all agreed on one thing – *a heavenly body*. I think that's fair, Hugh has exactly that. He's slightly knock-kneed, and his nipples are too far apart, but otherwise almost perfect . . . And so we come here to the epicentre of the entertainment capital of the world, the very eye of the galaxy, where it is the tradition in this marvellous town to reward stars by bringing them right down to earth – so far down to earth, that now Hugh will spend eternity having chewing gum and dog poo trodden into him. And very likely worse. The world was at his feet, and now the world's feet are at him . . . But there are two other qualities that no source that I've consulted tells me are necessary for a star. Nowhere does it say that a star should be filled with wisdom and kindness. And yet above all things, Hugh Laurie is wise and kind. Nowhere does it say, either, that a star should hide any of its light, but these are lights that Hugh does hide, and I'm happy to bring them out in the open . . . And I can say, like Dr Watson of his Holmes – "the kindest and wisest friend I ever knew" . . . I celebrate and congratulate him from my heart. My dear friend.'

Hugh has been shifting uneasily throughout, pulling his unique features this way and that with every gag and compliment. When asked to describe his colleague for a TV documentary the previous year, he had only offered, 'If I was describing him to a police constable, I would say tall, physically imposing, funny, big-hearted fellow. I suppose the nose is the other distinguishing feature, but I wouldn't want to harp on that.' But at the conclusion of Stephen's tribute, in front of the LA elite, the two colleagues embrace, their place as one of the most extraordinarily successful – and missed – UK double acts of all time indisputable, over thirty years after they first 'came out' on TV as a true partnership. The road to the Hollywood Boulevard has been a long, and laughter-filled one, but as Laurie stresses, it has been a far from carefully planned journey: 'I feel like we were both just falling downstairs together for ten years – just two blokes with no idea of where we were going to land . . .'

M'Colleague and I

For two comedy colleagues to ever fall in love at first sight is a rare thing indeed. Peter Cook & Dudley Moore first sized each other up in a restaurant alongside the other two *Beyond the Fringe* players, while acts including French & Saunders and Morecambe & Wise experienced antipathy to their partners on first encounter – perhaps Vic Reeves & Bob Mortimer are one of the few duos who claim an instant bond and rapport. And so it's no great dereliction of drama to say that Stephen Fry & Hugh's Laurie's path to their initial collaborative spark was not an explosion of spontaneous comradeship that would last them the rest of their lives. Legendarily, there's still some intrigue as to how it was they first caught a glimpse of their future in each other's gaze at all.

Perhaps it's telling that they each became aware of the other by being in their respective audiences, equally knocked out by the shows they paid to see. Neither production was in Cambridge, but that other Great University city, the Petri dish of the majority of British Comedy stories, Edinburgh. Between his first two years at Cambridge University, in 1979 Fry had travelled up to the Scottish capital and marvelled at the rudimentary comic antics of the Footlights club in *Nightcap*, managing to mumble vociferously deflected compliments behind stage afterwards, and during the following equally hot and busy August of 1980 Laurie had caught Stephen's first and only play, when it was staged by Cambridge's Mummers Club, and repaid the good crits, to an equal flurry of defensive cries of 'Nonsense!' and 'Tummy rubbish!' It was only back down south within cycling distance of the Cam, some time in the Michaelmas term of the same year, that any meaningful (albeit apparently unmemorable) contact between the two hilariously tall young men took place.

One common thread which holds together both versions of the tale of 'How Fry & Laurie Met' is the indispensable involvement of Emma Thompson. 'They would have probably met five minutes later anyway,' she protests. 'I like to think that I was responsible for the entire Fry & Laurie phenomenon . . . But they were destined always to be friends.' In Stephen's oft-told version of events, Emma took him out to the suburbs, to Hugh's place at Selwyn College, where he was playing a satirical song about American IRA supporters on a cheap guitar from Woolworths:

Give money to an IRA bomber / Why yes, sir, I'd consider it an honour, I'm always game for a worthy cause / If it doesn't involve breakin' laws,

*Take my money and do what you will / But if anyone asks you I never
    said kill,*
Everybody must have a cause . . .

. . . And within no time at all the pair found themselves working on the script for that year's Footlights pantomime. Hugh refutes almost every element of this memory, insisting that it was he who made the journey to Stephen's place at Queens', where their eyes met over crumpets and chess – and that he *never* owned a cheap Woolworths guitar.

'Isn't it extraordinary that all my life up to university and beyond, I had dreamt of the idea of being in comedy, in radio, in television, as the most exciting, enthralling thing that could ever happen to me,' Fry says, 'and now when I look back on it, that feeling is still there, except I've committed the unpardonable error, the insult to that dream, of forgetting so many of the details! Believe me, it's not that I'm casual about it or take it for granted, it was a joyous and explosive period of my life.' Ever the most muscular thrower of caution to the winds where anecdotes are concerned, Fry has often been chucklingly traduced as a chronicler of the facts. General facts, yes, no public figure could be said to have such incredible retention of an endless database of Quite Interesting nuggets and detailed libraries of knowledge on everything from baroque sonatas to snooker, but, Laurie smirks today, 'His memory is absolutely pathetic. He delivers his memories very confidently, but that's not the same as accurately. I think he's actually slightly deluded a lot of the time – there is some gigantic narrative engine in his head accommodating all sorts of obstacles and making sense of things as best he can. It's a pitiful spectacle, really . . . Shall we check this whole prison thing? There's a governor of some borstal somewhere saying, "Nope, there's been no Fry here, I've been through the records." "But he's talked about it on *Wogan*, for God's sake, it's on national record!"' 'I am sometimes accused of having a good memory, but it is only good for useless things,' his colleague admits. 'Hugh's is both compendious and useful.' As Stephen conceded in his first volume of memoirs, 'Memory is a most inaccurate and unstable entity, and autobiography can never be the same thing as history.'[1] He adds, 'The spectator sees more of the game – my friends and family probably better know than I do why I behaved in certain ways, and certainly the effect of it, and all I can do is remember what I did.' Nevertheless, this independent investigation has its work cut out, particularly with someone like Fry, who has always been entirely honest about his dishonesty – his debut semi-autobiographical novel was, of course, *The Liar*. 'When people say I am industrious, I say, "Ah, that's because I am lazy." I fight like the dickens to counteract that. Similarly, I try to be honest because I know I am fundamentally dishonest. At core I am a shiftless figure and I have to use a bit of energy to stop myself from being that, whereas there are many who are at core honest and industrious and do not have to expend any energy in order to be those things.'

'It's the layers of the onion, isn't it?' he told the *Telegraph* in 1997. 'The onion is its layers. One can be gamesome and paradoxical with it forever . . . I do often think, "Christ, Stephen, you're either a chameleon, a complete hypocrite or you have no identity whatsoever."' Nonetheless, his romantic reimagining of this all-important first collaboration is still the most logical and pleasing, to open the story of the comedy careers of Fry & Laurie. But one crucial fact which remains the same in all versions of this origin story is that at this time, Hugh was the boss, the President of Footlights, and something of an old hand at the comedy game, at the tender age of twenty-one: 'I basically gave Stephen his first job and I constantly remind him of it . . .'

A Chump in Oxford

James Hugh Calum Laurie had no trace whatsoever of show business in his blood, but what he did have, courtesy of his parents, was a ready-made complex, with twin ideals to try to live up to – his father's stoic heroism, and his mother's strict Presbyterianism, instilling a taste for humility bordering on fetish which was only heightened by a privileged education. 'I wouldn't say my father was uptight, but upright and pathologically shy. I suppose I get a lot of my character from him, also my mother. Humility was the quality she admired above all. Comfort was the work of the devil. Dad wasn't joyless, he had a strapping Presbyterian hardiness. My mother took it even further. She was a complicated personality and we had our good times and bad.'

Patricia Laidlaw met fellow anglicised Scot William 'Ran' Laurie in the Sudan during WWII, where the young district commissioner's brawny good looks and tales of triumphing for his country under Hitler's nose in the 1936 Berlin Olympics won her hand, and they were married in 1944. Patricia wrote about life as a district commissioner's wife in articles which were published in *The Times,* about which Hugh admits, 'I must say, I was surprised by how good the stories were. You spend so long thinking of your mother as the provider of socks and toast and Marmite. I suppose all children grow up with that egocentricity, but that makes it hard to imagine her having a life of her own.'

Similarly, Ran's achievements were not spoken of in the home, and Hugh only discovered his father's proud past one day when taking a boat out on a loch, he sniffed to Patricia whether Father 'knew how to row'. The look on Mrs Laurie's face no doubt spoke volumes, but the full extent of the stupidity of Hugh's question was only borne in on him when an idle mooch in the attic turned up a gold-plated Olympic medal, hidden away in an old sock. 'There were no frames, no glass cases, in fact hardly any rowing memorabilia was on show in the house. It was astounding humility of a sort that people would barely comprehend nowadays. Humility was a cult in my family.' With his rowing partner Jack Wilson, Ran had proudly won gold for Britain, which was no surprise for anyone who had seen them rowing for Cambridge while at Selwyn College earlier in the 1930s – on return to Blighty, the pair also won gold at Henley in 1948. In time, with his successful sporting career drawn to a close, the nearly forty-year-old Ran, with three children to support – an eldest son, Charles, and two daughters, Janet and Susan – retrained as a doctor, and settled down as a GP in Oxford, with particular care for the factory workers on the Blackbird Leys estate.

The arrival of a fourth child on 11 June 1959, several years after the family seemed complete, may not have been wholly predictable – but the blue-eyed youngest, for all the parental pressure put on him, remembers family life at the Lauries' as far from morose: 'I had a wonderful if uneventful upbringing. My parents were very loving, but there's no question they were suspicious of ease and comfort. My mother was the first person I can think of who was into the idea of recycling. In about 1970, she was collecting newspapers from the whole village, bailing them up and taking them to a paper mill . . . Humility was considered a great virtue in my family. No show of complacency or self-satisfaction was ever tolerated. Patting yourself on the back was definitely not encouraged, and pleasure or pride would be punishable by death.' However, he continues, 'I can remember laughing more than I remember making people laugh. My father, mother, sisters and brother I always thought of as being tremendously funny – meals were very enjoyable, because we used to laugh a lot. I suppose by ten I started to give as good as I got, as it were . . . That was good fun, but I don't think I was the one doing Liza Minnelli impressions at breakfast or anything. I am now, obviously, but I wasn't then.'

'It's the fate of many siblings to feel that they are the least favourite. My sisters and brother would firmly argue that I was the blue-eyed boy who could do no wrong and that I irritated them greatly for that reason. But of course I didn't see it that way at the time. I don't suppose anybody does really . . . I was, and still am, a great fantasist, and I spent a large amount of time on my own.' When not mooning around risking maternal censure, Hugh would try and make himself useful by aiding his father: 'I went on house calls with him. Usually I would sit in the car while he was inside lancing a boil or whatever. I mostly remember being at home answering the phone for him, in the days before answering machines. Being my father's son, I sounded like him, and before I could say, "This isn't the doctor", they would jump in and say, "Doctor, thank God! It's all exploded, I can't stop it!" And with no obvious juncture for me to step out of the way, I would, you know . . . let's just say I'd reassure them. As far as I remember, I never lost any patients.'

At seven years old, Oxford's Dragon School was chosen for Hugh as prep for Eton at the age of thirteen – following in Ran's footsteps – and was the site of his earliest experience of getting laughs from an audience with his rubbery little face. His first laugh, he thinks, probably 'was something foolish. It was playing a moron. I just seem to have a face that lends itself to idiocy, and I think I probably exploited that. I think I've probably wrung everything I could out of it . . . I was a bit of a class clown, but not frantically so. I did know by age nine or ten, after winning a prize at school for acting, that funny was something I could do reasonably well. And, of course, it was just a way to show off to girls and be noticed by all. That's how these things start; you try to make a girl laugh and then forty years later you still wonder if you're any good or not.' That first prize for performing obviously struck a deep chord within: 'I can remember when I was nine there was a school drama competition, I won a prize – I can't remember what I won, a book token or something. But I do remember my parents being in the audience, and I happened to be looking at their faces as my name was read out; not in anticipation, 'cause I didn't know I was going to win this thing . . . And my name was read out: "And the winner is . . ." They didn't know I was looking at them, and they looked at each other and smiled, and it was a really significant moment for me. It just felt like the first time I'd seen them take a real . . . that I'd done something that really satisfied them, something that really pleased them, that they were proud of.' Early signs of parental unease must have been made equally clear, however, when he attempted to make a petrol bomb at the age of ten, and burned himself badly. Within a year or two of starting at Eton, young Hugh was seen to be heading further off the rails.

Eton College is perhaps the most famous school in the world outside of a J. K. Rowling book, the ultimate privileged playground of future prime ministers, world leaders and all sorts of villains – but other old boys include George Orwell and many notable actors. Hugh was simply following the family tradition, this duty taking a huge chunk out of Dr Laurie's salary. Fry claims that the Laurie family tree has a shorter route to proper aristocracy than his own, with 'very grand Scots' blood and ancestral homes north of the border (of little relevance to a younger son), but Hugh insists, 'I went to a very posh school with some very posh people, but I'm not especially posh myself . . . I suppose I'm middle-class. And I don't think I'm alone in that. We're few, but we're organised.' Hugh's generation at Eton wasn't over-populated with embryonic Establishment figures. Not until he was ready to leave would little David Cameron and cronies arrive, and Laurie never wanted to be a world leader anyway – he and his peer group fancied themselves rebels. Beginning a lifetime nicotine addiction by hiding in the toilets sharing cigarettes, this gang volubly supported the Baader-Meinhof group and made a pact to kill themselves before the age of forty, lest they become just another bunch of grey Old Etonians. In a joyously silly *Telegraph* article written in 1999, Laurie described his younger self as a 'scraper-through of O levels, mover of lips (own) while reading, loafer, scrounger, pettifogger and general berk of this parish', and rued his adolescent attitude: 'I spent a large part of my youth smoking Number Six and cheating in French vocabulary tests. I wore platform boots with a brass skull and crossbones over the ankle, my hair was disgraceful, and I somehow contrived to pull off the gruesome trick of being both fat and thin at the same time. If you had passed me in the street during those pimply years, I am confident that you would, at the very least, have quickened your pace . . . My history teacher's report actually took the form of a postcard from Vancouver.'

This early teenage slump was not lost at home, either: 'I was lazy. I lied, about everything, all the time. I was a fussy eater. Once Mum caught me with two pieces of liver in my pocket and sent me back to the table to eat it. It took three hours and then I caved in. I gave up on the piano. That was a battle I won. I went on a hunger strike and didn't eat for three days.' That Hugh had an instinctive musical skill was apparent, but like many a musician, formal lessons strangled any early desire to make music – not least when the teacher turned to 'Swanee River' and dismissed it as a worthless 'negro spiritual'. With that avenue of expression stifled, Hugh's idleness and cheek increased, to his mother's evident dismay. 'I was an awkward and frustrating child. She had very high expectations of me, which I constantly disappointed. Long after I had stopped being a child, I heard from my sisters that I was the apple of her eye, her golden boy, but I didn't realise it at the time . . . She had moments of not liking me – when I say "moments" I use the word broadly to cover months. She was contemptuous of the goal of happiness, of contentment, comfort. She disliked even the word "comfort" . . . I didn't kiss my mother as a child. It struck me in my mid-twenties that it's a standard thing to kiss your mother, and then we started doing it by agreement. Is that usual? I suspect it is.'

However, remembering his Eton days many years later, Hugh admits, 'Generally, I would dearly love to be able to appear a much more tortured soul than I am. I just sort of plodded through Eton, enjoyed it. I'd love to tell you I burned the place down – the odd youthful petrol-bombing anecdote comes in useful on these occasions – but such was not the case. I was a bit of a square.' Hugh has in the past credited any turnaround in his adolescent attitudes to two not entirely unconnected discoveries – P. G. Wodehouse, and The Blues.

'About thirteen' seems to have been a magical age for Hugh. It was at that age that a copy of The Master's *Galahad at Blandings* fell into his grip, and 'From the very first sentence of my very first Wodehouse story, life appeared to grow somehow larger. There had always been height, depth, width and time, and in these prosaic dimensions I had hitherto snarled, cursed, and not washed my hair. But now, suddenly, there was Wodehouse, and the discovery seemed to make me gentler every day. By the middle of the fifth chapter I was able to use a knife and fork, and I like to think that I have made reasonable strides since.' By his late teens Hugh found a second literary love: espionage thrillers, particularly the works of John Le Carré and Len Deighton, which fuelled daydreams of spying for his country.

Also when 'about thirteen', a chance radio knob twiddle from his brother Charles while driving wrought an even deeper tremor in the Laurie bosom, as the sound of Willie Dixon singing 'I Can't Quit You Baby' poured out of the radio. 'I knew that this was for me when I was very young. I can remember the first blues song I heard on the radio, and saying to my brother, "What is that?" It was like I'd always known it was there, and I heard this thing, and the hairs on the back of my neck went up, and a love was born which has stayed with me until this day.' Discovering the works of Doctor John, Professor Longhair, and other highly qualified blues legends gave Hugh a passion to drive him – although his own musical exploits at this time ran to playing percussion in the Eton orchestra, having given up on French horn. The theatrical opportunities at Eton gave Laurie more scope, and thirteen was also 'when I realised I quite liked being onstage. I knew especially I liked making people laugh – and girls, most especially. I was scared to death of girls at that age, but onstage – as a king in a school play, for example – I would actually be seen by them, which is to say I wouldn't be completely invisible, as was my normal condition.'

The kindling of these passions did not entirely inspire Hugh to rally around and become an instant credit to the Lauries, however, and the crunch arrived at fifteen: 'I was quite bad, I was nearly thrown out and had a ghastly traumatic meeting with my parents who came to take me away, and gave me a talking to at a service station on the M4, which I can never drive past now without thinking of the shame and embarrassment. But by the end of it I suppose I became square, and House Captain. I became Establishment – oh, God!' One fillip of House Captaincy was the right to stay up late watching TV, and Hugh picked a premium period to be tuning in to the comedy zeitgeist: 'The Pythons were just immense. To see a new Python show, that was a pretty great pleasure, but in a strange kind of way an even greater pleasure was to buy the records and sit around with a group of friends and just play those sketches over and over again until you knew every breath.' Passing his exams also introduced Hugh to another lifelong pleasure – motorbikes: 'My Dad gave me my first bike at sixteen. I soon fell off and was in a wheelchair for weeks. I haven't fallen since.'

Cheer Oh, Cambridge!

Sport, however, was Laurie's métier, and it was sport that took him to his father's old college, Selwyn, eighty-five miles east of his home, in the enchantingly crumbly medieval city of Cambridge. In the summer before taking the journey there was one further instance of the rebel teen's reclamation: effecting a citizen's arrest. 'I nabbed this chap on Kensington Church Street. He was running out of a leather goods shop, loaded with stuff, and I brought him down to the pavement, held him there until the police arrived. You can't get much more creepy.' Perhaps this was one of the experiences which gave Hugh a dream of working for Queen and Country as part of the Hong Kong Police. 'I sent off for the brochure. Young men in Land Rovers with creases down the front of their shorts and shiny peaked caps. It seemed to be a terribly glamorous and exciting life,' he admits. 'They were looking for good men and true to go and serve in the colony, and I suddenly fixed on this romantic idea of myself . . . I'd smoke a pipe and be rather acerbic, but ultimately I'd have a heart of gold and I'd unite young lovers on the bridge, or whatever it might be. And I got the brochures, and sure enough, the uniform was very smart, it was all shaping up well. And in actual fact, now I slightly regret not taking that course. I'll tell you why – in 1997, all those blokes who would have been in my position retired on full pension at thirty-five!' This *Serpico*-style fantasy was a very real ambition, but first things came first – ROWING.

'My father had high hopes for me following him into medicine,' he says. 'I wanted to, and I had an interview at the London Hospital in Whitechapel, which is where my father had studied, and in fact I came very close to going there. I forget now why I didn't do so, probably I was too stupid, or too lazy, to commit to the necessary eight years of study. I wanted to, and was going to choose the right subjects at school, but in the end I copped out. Medicine is awfully hard work and you have to be rather clever to pass the exams.' But there were other ways to follow in footsteps, and Hugh enrolled at Selwyn College in 1978 to study Archaeology and Anthropology. To this day, he will maintain that his irrelevant degree in the subject – despite giving him material for an apparently hilarious monologue about a Bantu hut – means that he has about as much knowledge of archaeology and anthropology as anyone reading this. The lecturers in those subjects were strangers to him, their lecture halls a Laurie-less place – for the duration of each one, Hugh could almost invariably be found down on the river Cam, honing his skills as an oarsman.

At the age of eighteen Hugh's obsessive training had turned the strapping six-foot-two-er into a taut man of muscle, with a raging metabolism which could not even be believed when evidenced. He positively inhaled steaks, turning every calorie he habitually consumed into muscle to force a boat through water faster than a student wearing a slightly darker shade of blue, due to the misfortune of attending Oxford rather than Cambridge. In 1977, with James Palmer (technically his first double act partner, but in this case a rowing duo), Hugh had already won the British national rowing title, and the two had represented their country at the Junior World Rowing Championships in Finland. But to triumph alongside seven fellow students plus cox in the annual spring Boat Race against Oxford was his ultimate dream, the very reason he was in Cambridge at all.

And so, the doctor's prognosis shortly after his arrival at Cambridge that the sore throat he had been complaining of was actually glandular fever could not have been a more dismaying curveball. Given strict warning not to indulge in any exhausting rowing business until given the all-clear, Hugh was in an awful quandary – what was he going to do? Study? *Work?*

Of course the malady changed his life in unimaginably fortuitous ways, and this random twist of fate was summed up by Laurie with an apt metaphor: 'With rowing you're facing backwards, moving away from the direction you're facing. When you look at other people's careers, it's very easy to see things as being constructed, planned, devised, how they clearly got from A to Z to a series of calculated decisions. In actual fact, I think we're all facing backwards, stumbling from place to place, from one thing to the next and it only takes shape in retrospect . . . Which is how I went from wearing dresses to talking to mice to solving medical mysteries. At no point did I ever have a plan. I was simply facing backwards, doing my best along the way.'

A girl called Allison is the one we have to thank, allegedly. Hugh was drinking away his blues in a student bar, entertaining his peers with a particularly stoic but cutting display of wit, when the laughter led to the perhaps inevitable Cambridge cry: 'You're so funny, you should join Footlights, actually!' 'I think I made a girl laugh in a bar,' he remembers, ' . . . So many stories start that way. That might be the title of my autobiography.'

'So I went along to the Footlights, and as I walked in the first thing I saw was these rows and rows of photographs of all my heroes, essentially. I realised I was in a hallowed space.' The Cambridge theatrical club Footlights had just celebrated its ninety-fifth year. Despite mid-run flashes of fame thanks to comic alumni Richard 'Stinker' Murdoch and Jimmy Edwards, it was only in the previous two decades that the club had become infamous as the nursery of comedy legends. In the late 1950s, Miller presaged the era of Cook, Bron, Bird and Fortune, Frost's worship of them gave way to the advent of Cleese, Chapman, Brooke-Taylor, Oddie, Kendall, Hatch and Lynn, then Idle and Garden hoofed about with James and Greer. A long dearth of big names followed, and the club's reputation for cheesy light entertainment even led members like Douglas Adams and John Lloyd to stage their own revues outside of the club's jurisdiction in the early 1970s, unlike their friend, President Jon Canter. But by Hugh's arrival, there had been an upturn of fiercely ambitious young jokers – with names like Geoffrey McGivern, Griff Rhys Jones, Clive Anderson, Rory McGrath and Jimmy Mulville – all vying to get the last laugh in a series of hotly tipped shows. 1974's *Chox* and 1977's *Tag!* were pitched as huge hits in waiting, with big West End openings, but their flops led to much of the generation accepting uniform offers from BBC Radio LE (under the management of David Hatch) to start providing content to make listeners laugh. One member of the *Tag!* cast, Martin Bergman, was still kicking about, however, and had just relinquished the role of Footlights President to ambitious young actor Robert Bathurst when Hugh plucked up the courage to attend an audition. Smart and smiley, Bergman had all the hallmarks of a budding Frost within this generation of Footlighters, while Bathurst specialised in solidly posh characterisations. This being Hugh's first term, the club was staging its now traditional seasonal pantomime, and so instead of working on his rowing, Hugh found himself vying for a role in the 1978 show, *Aladdin*.

The title role had already been cast, and Aladdin was sitting right next to Bergman – they were childhood friends, having both attended West Hampstead Primary School. Emma Thompson was a bedazzling north Londoner, who had grown up on the fringes of show business as daughter of actors and *Play School* presenters, Phyllida Law and Eric Thompson. By the time Emma was at school, she had a little sister, Sophie, and her father had embarked on his greatest work, translating – or rather, inventing – scripts for French animation *The Magic Roundabout*, the most popular children's programme of the generation. Sophie was said to be the most precocious actress as the sisters grew up, but theatre had always been in Emma's blood, and she worked with professional companies even before qualifying for a place studying English at Newnham College – the women-only college, just two minutes from Selwyn. 'She was the most obnoxiously talented person, and still is, that I've ever come across,' Hugh says. 'Everything she did just oozed talent. She said talented things, she wore talented clothes, she rode talented bicycles, she made talented spaghetti, it was really, really irritating.'

'Hugh Laurie!' was next called to the stage, and Thompson sized him up: 'He was gigantic, a fucking giant. He trained and ate all the time. He looked a bit like Indiana Jones, wearing a lot of khaki.' With one look, she jabbed Bergman in the ribs, and none-too-subtly mimed one firm prophecy – 'STAR!' Back when the term 'cultural appropriation' meant little more than complaining about the Elgin

Marbles, the enormous fresher Laurie was up for the part of the Emperor of China – a role he essayed with a dumbshow of extreme diffidence, the mighty Emperor meekly trying to catch someone's attention to order a cup of tea. The result was universal hilarity from the Footlights members present, and a warm welcome into the cast, and the club, to both Hugh and Emma's delight. 'They had a very strong tradition and a high expectation, and I sort of tumbled into it. And I loved it! I absolutely loved it – the pleasure of making people laugh is a very great one, and an addictive one.'

This was a whole new not-so-secret society for Hugh to belong to, with their own basement clubroom beneath the student union, nestled just behind the iconic Round Church. 'Emma claims that she sort of spotted me,' he recalls, 'and we became . . . friendly, as a result. We got on very well!' 'He was always so funny,' Emma insists to this day, 'the funniest person I've met. I remember once driving back from some Footlights performance and hearing on the radio that somebody had been kidnapped and driven off in a Ford van. We were in a Ford van, so he did a lot of struggling and thrashing around on the front seat to see if we would be stopped. And I laughed so much I had to stop for a wee.'

This first college romance was short-lived. Emma's oft-quoted description of Hugh as 'lugubrious, like a well-hung eel' may betray its own depths of familiarity, but once 1979 rolled around and Hugh was given the glandular all-clear, he was back on the river and his girlfriend's role seemed largely to be to help drag his exhausted heavy body back home and fill it with food. Friends complained that Hugh was borderline narcoleptic, and could sleep, and sleep deeply, almost anywhere. 'I was in full-time training for rowing, that's what I did the whole time,' he protests. 'The physical demands of that meant that any time I wasn't doing it, I would just fall asleep . . . It could just have been that she was immensely boring. No! Plainly not.' 'I think he quite rightly fell for my much more beautiful friend Katie Kelly, with whom he went out for some years,' Emma adds. 'But it was a natural ending, we were much better suited as friends . . . I know Katie did tons of work for Footlights, she was an unstoppable force of nature.'

Clearly no parting could be more amicable, and by the last term of their first year, Hugh and Emma were both key parts of the cast of the

1979 May Week Revue, *Nightcap*, alongside Bergman, Bathurst, Nick Mills and Emma's new boyfriend, English student Simon McBurney – a unique actor whose comedy exploits also included forming a double act with *Nightcap* contributor Sandi Toksvig, a tiny bombshell of razor-sharp wit who took the same subjects as Hugh, but managed to bag a First. In May, just before *Nightcap*, Toksvig & McBurney had dared to travel down to London to grace the stage of The Comedy Store on its infamously raw and rowdy opening night, a feat which must have earned them highest levels of awed respect in the Footlights coterie. As Hugh had learned, revues were the result of terms' worth of smaller more relaxed shows still called 'Smoking Concerts', put on by individual members and entitled things like *Death in the Aisles*. With only one freshly opened comedy club in the country, there were few other places where comedy could ferment.

The May Week Revue was always the *raison d'être* for Footlights' existence, the showcase which sent undergraduate comics pelting into the stratosphere, or obscurity. The influence of the Mulville/McGrath generation was still obvious, but a decision was made to aim for a more low-key format for *Nightcap*. The set consisted of a bar, where cast members would relax when not appearing in sketches – Hugh accompanied Bathurst in a number of two-handers, one in which they played crazy old-time prospectors, and a slightly clumsy item involving two heterosexuals who proudly 'come out' and proclaim their sexuality. These shows had a well-defined path to tread every year – opening at the ADC Theatre, just around the corner from the Footlights clubroom, often taking in Oxford and Nottingham as a traditional build-up to the all-important Edinburgh Fringe run. Moderately warm notices were received across the board, but Emma was always singled out as the ultimate find among the cast, radiating talent so brightly that what should have been nauseating simply took audiences' breath away. So well-received was Thompson's comedy debut that she was quickly offered a contract from one of the country's grandest talent agencies, The Noel Gay Organisation. With its roots in the success of songwriter Reginald Armitage – composer of classics like 'Run Rabbit Run' and the musical *Me and My Girl* under the name of Noel Gay – by 1980 the agency was the kingdom of his son

Richard, who already represented John Cleese and Rowan Atkinson, and was fascinated to see this fresh seam of gold coming through from the Footlights.

Performing in Edinburgh was all so new to Hugh that he only has the vaguest memory of the fellow Cantabrigian friend of Emma's who came backstage to gush about the show. If anything, all Hugh could remember of this truly first meeting was ejaculating 'Blimey!' at the rarity of meeting somebody taller than he was, but this tall and tweedy visitor was just another stage door johnnie for now.

Row, Row, Row Your Punt . . .

By his second year, Hugh was of course fully fixated on nothing but rowing, but no matter how good a fool he played onstage, the invitation to appear on BBC TV was not one any game nineteen-year-old could turn down. The late-night strand *Friday Night, Saturday Morning* was an ever-changing format, broadcast live with different hosts for each episode – it had already made headlines thanks to an inept turn from former PM Harold Wilson, and a celebrated face-off between two Pythons and two Christians over the blasphemy of *The Life of Brian*. But only one week after that historic altercation, on 16 November 1979, it was the Footlights' turn to take the reins.

A few weeks earlier, John Lloyd and his co-producer Sean Hardie had debuted their own TV sketch show, *Not the Nine O'Clock News*, bringing Oxford men Rowan Atkinson and Mel Smith together with Pamela Stephenson and Chris Langham (and latterly ex-Footlights President Griff Rhys Jones), and although that first series had its own problems, Lloyd seemed to have nothing to worry about from these younger competitors. Bergman hosted, in full 'fresh Frost' mode, the central treat in store being a typically horizontal chat with Footlights god Peter Cook. But much of the show's hour consisted of excerpts from *Nightcap*, introduced, pre-credits, with Hugh's TV debut – a special appeal:

```
HUGH:      Hullo! I'd like you to remember, as you
           sit in front of your cosy fires watching
           me, that there are some people less
```

> fortunate than yourselves. Some people
> who not only can't see me, but can't hear
> what I'm saying either. Please send your
> donations here to the BBC, and help those
> people who haven't got a television set.[2]

Hugh wasn't one of the primary writers, but bagged a number of roles, from the editor of 'The Daily Con' in the opening tabloid satire, to an American film star in a mockumentary celebrating Barry Norman's career – and no doubt many fans of vintage comedy were outraged by the closing sketch, which ruthlessly ripped into Denis Norden's *Looks Familiar* and aged comics like Arthur Askey, with Hugh as Northern turn Colin Hasbeen, whose only shtick is a stream of variations on the line 'I went to Bournemouth once, it were shut!'

This flash of teenage fame was all just larks to Laurie. As 1980 rolled around, he also made his Radio 4 debut in a more straightforward broadcast of *Nightcap* in March, but only one date was emblazoned on Hugh's soul – 5 April, when he would earn his Blue by taking on Oxford in the annual Boat Race. His hometown adversaries had triumphed for the previous few years, and 1980 had to be Cambridge's turn. Had Hugh never achieved fame, this Oxbridge clash would still be remembered as one of the closest, hottest and most dramatic in the event's history – the victors eventually passed the post first by only the smallest margin in the century. But they weren't Cambridge.

Exhausted and demoralised, Hugh had to face it, he hadn't managed to equal Ran's golden sporting achievement, and salt was quickly administered a month or two later, when Laurie & Palmer came nowhere much in that year's Henley Royal Regatta. Ran was characteristically supportive, his mortified son recalls: 'His consoling summary of the whole experience was "Any idiot can win." And I thought, "What? Surely you've got that wrong." But that's sort of brilliant – that winning doesn't teach you anything, that's something you simply experience. Whereas losing, and what you do with that, and how you develop and learn from that, is everything, that's where it gets interesting. As it happens, I don't think he actually ever lost a race.'

Despite being jokingly presented with footage of the 1980 Boat Race TV broadcast on chat shows over the years, the agony of those close-run defeats has remained fresh and deadly for Hugh ever since – everything he had worked for was snatched from his grasp in the last agonising minute. And so, with a third and final year looming, Hugh had to find something else for his whole life to be about.

The comedy business had gone noticeably cold, and that year's revue, *Electric Voodoo*, had a very different line-up – for the first time in Footlights history, the girls outnumbered the boys, with Toksvig and the club's first woman President Jan Ravens leading a cast with only two men, including future comedy producer Nick Symons. 'It was certainly a horse of a different hue,' Laurie remembers. 'They wore primary colours and danced and sang, which confirmed my preference for black curtains, cigarettes and sitting still.' Nonetheless, Hugh still travelled beyond the border to see the show in Edinburgh, alongside Emma, who had also absented herself from Footlights for a while to help look after her ailing father – Thompson suffered a stroke at the age of fifty, and only survived for a further couple of years. The exes made the most of their time at the Fringe, dropping in on Emma's fellow English student thespian, who had written a play which was doing great business – *Latin! or Tobacco and Boys*. It wasn't the first time Hugh 'clocked' Stephen onstage – he recalls *Volpone* being his first sight of his future colleage – but it was the first time Hugh played the fan, the tables turned as a blushing Laurie ventured to offer his congratulations to the author and actor after the show. More cries of 'thanks awfully' and 'do you really think?' and 'now shush' were elicited, but Fry had other things on his mind, and the moment passed. Laurie, however, made a crucial mental note of this saturnine playwright's potential value when he inherited Footlights' top job at the start of his third year.

'I happened to be President – or as they would now say, "Chief Executive Officer" – of the Footlights Club, and these were my chicks, as it were. I was in charge of the ship at that time.' With rowing diminishing in importance, and Hong Kong still a distant possibility, Hugh had his work cut out steering the comedy club that autumn, even with Katie to back him up, with Smokers to stage and even another television outing on the horizon.

This was a second bite of *Friday Night, Saturday Morning*, this time with Oxford Revue guests The Hee Bee Gee Bees, and McBurney replaced with ex-Footlighter Rory McGrath (he having already starred in Radio 4 sketch show *Injury Time* with his generation of Footlighters – plus Thompson, expanding her comedy portfolio without even graduating). This follow-up episode, almost exactly a year on from the last, presented a weirder hash of material written for the format. Hugh performed a monologue as an American lecturer with the most strangulated transatlantic vowels imaginable, giving a talk on 'Philosophistics, and the Symbology of Ideas' – seeing this performance in Edinburgh is one of Stephen's very first memories of his colleague-to-be: 'I remember being impressed by his accent.' Hugh also partnered Emma as a *Mr & Mrs* contestant who loudly proclaims that his hobby is 'beating her up' (if that sounds unacceptable, you do not want to hear about McGrath's turn as a Rastafarian). Hugh also made a uniquely troglodytic appearance as a 'suedehead' (a skinhead with a bit more hair) in an interview on gang warfare, and played Matthew in a Malcolm Muggeridge-baiting Last Supper sketch, in which McGrath's Jesus suggests that Matthew pay the bill by cheque:

MATTHEW: No waysville! I got caught out like that with that picnic we went on, I ordered one sardine sandwich and ended up paying for the whole bloody multitude![3]

Being already positively a veteran of BBC radio and live TV broadcasting at twenty, Hugh's place as President seemed natural. A crucial thing about the Footlights, appreciated by few, is that it has always been entirely student-led, nobody is in charge from one year to the next, and each generation only has the example of their forebears to prove to them that they have what it takes to sculpt a brilliant comedy show to take up to Edinburgh in the summer. But in the autumn of 1980, it was the Christmas pantomime – for which Hans Christian Andersen's *The Snow Queen* had been selected as a break from the usual Grimm fare – that hung heaviest on Hugh's broad shoulders. He was director, producer, actor, guitarist and head writer for the show, and may even have had some essays to try to write. It was looking a bit thick. One timely groan of agony in Emma's presence triggered her casual suggestion that her friend Fry could be just the chap to help extricate young Laurie from the soup. 'I knew of Stephen's existence long before he knew of mine,' says Hugh, 'I had watched him in many plays, as a straight actor. It so happened that I ended up in this position of some power – or at least responsibility – I had to put this show together . . . Heaven be praised, we made each other laugh. Such a lot. And continue to do so. I just knew he was the man for me! As it were.'

Not Normal for Norfolk

The tweed-influenced presumption that Stephen John Fry is as Anglo-Saxon as Alfred the Great has always been a fair one, but one he is quick to derail: 'One of the interesting things about being English is that people who are said to be exemplars are often curiously hybrid, as I am . . . It's this quality, the ability of England to open itself up, to absorb and mutate rather than advance by revolution and spasm as other countries do, that makes it fascinating.' The Fry clan certainly gives Stephen a long legacy of impeccable Englishness – one ancestor, John, signed Charles I's death warrant, and his father's brother George even penned a book, *The Saxon Origins of the Fry Family*, refuting claims from the chocolate-making Quaker Fry line that their roots were Norman: 'unlike so many so-called English families, the Frys did not come over with the Conqueror, they were there to meet him when he arrived.'

Young Alan Fry was as English as they come, but when he enrolled at London University to read Physics he met Marianne Neumann, a History scholar whose family were Hungarian-Jewish. Stephen describes their attraction as instant and deep, their long marriage an inevitability, particularly given the great approval of Marianne's father Martin for this brilliant young German-speaking English son-in-law. If there is any genetic propensity for hobnobbing with the famous, Stephen was surely to take after Martin Neumann – prior to WWI, he claimed to have charitably and innocently provided a young and cold Adolf Hitler with a warm coat from his second-hand clothing business, and once drawn into the Great War's fighting, shell shock saw Martin referred to Sigmund Freud for psychiatric evaluation. Between the wars, he joined forces with his brother to found a sugar refinery in Czechoslovakia, and their success in refining sugar beet earned them an invitation to Suffolk in 1925, to show the Brits how it was done. This was the one stroke of luck that saved Martin's branch of the Neumann family from the horrors of the Holocaust, and his daughter was given a thoroughly British education.

Alan and Marianne were quickly wed, and Alan embarked on establishing himself as a fiercely respected technician and inventor. Marianne's teaching career was not ended by the arrival of their first son Roger, but with a second arrival on the cards, the young family faced a thorny quandary when Alan was offered a prestigious position abroad. 'I've always loved America deeply, rather obsessively,' Fry enthused on *Larry King Live*, 'I think because my father was offered a job at Princeton, to develop what would become semi-conductors and microprocessors, which was what his thesis had been as a student. He thought very hard about it, my mother was pregnant with me at the time, and he eventually decided to stay in Britain. And when my mother told me this, I projected this figure, this "Steve Fry", who was me but kinda American, and who grew up wearing jeans and driving a car by the time he was sixteen, and chewing gum, and a whole different world. I grew up in a very traditional – I wouldn't say *Downton Abbey* – but a quite countrified life in England. So I had this obsession with this other me that could have been – would I have thought differently, felt differently?'

On 24 August 1957 the Frys' second son was delivered in the leafy north London environs of Hampstead, but the family soon decamped further out of the metropolis, to the Buckinghamshire town of Chesham. Little Stephen's earliest memory is of being curled up under his mother's chair as she marked history essays and the BBC Home Service marked the hours in woodiest tones and pips. This warm infancy, clinging to his mother's skirts ('a woman more cheerful than Pickwick, Pollyanna and Mrs Tiggywinkle on a sunny day in Happyville') and fearing the distant figure of his scientist father, who puffed his pipe in Holmesian disapproval at his younger son's antics, was soon broken by the necessity of attending Chesham Prep, a mixed-sex school where little Stephen got his first girlfriend, and, notably, tripped and broke his cute button nose in such a way that it would never grow straight again.

Fry is quick to point out that it wasn't only his nose which was not growing straight, and one of his greatest pleasures at this time was to play a game called 'Rudies' with his friend Timothy. They would secretly pull down their shorts in class, sitting bare-bottomed while appearing perfectly respectable from the teacher's view, and then rush out into the countryside to have weeing contests, or enjoy a number two in nature. While a personal memoir can indulge in detailing childhood peculiarities, it would seem intrusive to take the same liberty here, were this behaviour not powerfully telling about Stephen Fry, and his deceptively urbane brand of humour. Stephen was a polite, respectable boy, already showing precocious signs of prodigious development, and when stood next to his brother Roger, the pair of them were paragons of solid, middle-class English boyhood. But then as now, Stephen gloried in the freedom that came from private – or not so private – rebellion, of transgression, and a refusal to be pigeonholed as the upstanding product of privilege that he appeared to be. This simmering subversion hiding behind an impressively Establishment façade is key to the way his comedy fuses the sublime with the outrageous; but it caused Fry problems then, and it can do so to this day. He closes his memories of 'Rudies' with 'Getting caught, I think now, is what it was all about to me.' His bucking of the norm was notable when Roger and Stephen were treated to a pantomime outing, and Buttons' invitation for a little volunteer to come onto the stage sent him into paroxysms of arm-flailing desperation, while Roger tried to hide under his chair: 'Two boys, eighteen months apart in age, bred in the same conditions and by the same parents. There are many more Rogers in the world, praise be, than Stephens.'[4]

Stephen's passion for subversion glaringly manifested itself in one crucial way – his struggles, and triumphs, with language. From the age of seven, he developed an obsession with collecting and memorising facts, screwing reams of *The Guinness Book of Records* into his brain, but as he rushed to share this knowledge with family and friends, a communication problem became apparent. 'My problem was eventually diagnosed by a keen-eared master. I was speaking too quickly, far too quickly; I talked at a rate that made me unintelligible to all but myself. The words and thoughts tumbled from my mouth in an entirely pauseless profusion.' A course of elocution training followed, and 'When excited, I was still likely to revert to rushing streams of Stephenese at moments of high passion . . . But something wonderful and new had happened to me, something much more glorious than simply being understood. I had discovered the beauty of speech. Suddenly I had an endless supply of toys: words. Meaningless phatic utterance for its own sake would become my equivalent of a Winnie-the-Pooh hum, my *music*.'[5]

By this time, the Fry family was completed by the arrival of little sister Jo, and Alan had set himself up as an independent inventor, establishing Alan Fry Controls Ltd., developers of all sorts of electronic gadgetry, from Ford Capri systems to Sellotape dispensers – and the perfect base for the company had been found by one of Martin's employees, in Norfolk. This impressive country house near the village of Booton was chosen largely because the stable block could house Alan's laboratory, but the home itself was less high-tech. Fry paints a bucolic sepia-tinged picture of rural life, with orchards and vegetable gardens providing food for housekeeper Nanny Riseborough to turn into delicious meals, shared duties on pumping water into the house, and only real fires to heat the enormous rooms. Even with Roger at home and little Jo to play with – she already worshipped her funny, wicked older brother – it was something of a lonely life for a stimulus-starved boy who otherwise devoured books and sneaked as much time in front of the television as he dared, given that the set lived in his father's study.

'When Stephen was small he did virtually nothing except glue himself to the television set while our other children were out and about, doing things,' his father complained. 'On a fine summer's day he'd draw the curtains and frowse away six inches in front of the black-and-white screen. As a result he has an encyclopaedic knowledge of films and television from the sixties.' Comedy was a particular magnet for the young Fry, and programmes now forever wiped, like Alan Bennett's cerebral sketch show *On the Margin*, and episodes of Cook & Moore's *Not Only . . . But Also*, made crucial impressions – the work of Pete & Dud all the more so via their vinyl releases. 'They really are the background to almost anything which happened in British comedy after them,' Stephen says. 'There was an extraordinary chemistry between them as a pair – I mean, everybody remembers the joy of them setting each other off giggling, it's just fabulous how natural and close to the surface their comedy seemed . . . A new tradition was born, because it was nothing whatever to do with Variety, as it was called then, it was just a whole new way of being funny, a different way of being comic. And one that obviously I owe everything to.'

Stephen's struggles with his parents for TV allowance were over when the time arrived for him to be sent away to prep school like Roger before him, with little of the homesick trepidation one would expect of more 'normal' boys.

Approaching Genius

To this day, the South Gloucestershire village of Uley is as perfect an English idyll as could be imagined, and Stouts Hill School (now holiday accommodation) was its jewel – a crenelated educational stronghold to rival Hogwarts. When Stephen arrived, he joined a small but friendly force of schoolboys who brought the village to life, even if the Uley sweet shop was officially out of bounds. Sweets were Stephen's primary addiction, from Sugar Puffs to sherbet dips, the fuel of years of criminal misbehaviour, under the watchful eye of two imposing figures – Stouts Hill's thrusting young Headmaster-in-waiting, Anthony Cromie, and Martin Neumann, who had passed away, but seemed to young Stephen to be forever looking down at his grandson's wickednesses.

In general, Fry already had a reputation for being 'too clever by half' (to which his pert reply tended to be 'how stupid would you like me to be, sir?') and this prodigious swank was not hindered by one of his regular burglarious intrusions on Cromie's office, where he discovered an eleven-plus result which labelled him 'Approaching genius' – which the master had annotated, 'Well that bloody explains everything.' 'It will seem boasting wherever I go with this,' Stephen wrote, 'but I was not in the least pleased to learn that I had a high IQ. For a start I didn't like the "approaching" part of the phrase (if you're going to be a freak, be a complete freak, no point at all in going at it half-cock) and secondly I wriggled in discomfort at the idea of being singled out for something over which I felt I had no control.'[6] Conspicuous intelligence is a double-edged sword, and so began what Fry calls 'The bass-line to the badly produced dance-track of my life: "How come you know everything, Fry?"'

Stephen already identified as 'The Odd Boy', a natural aesthete who spurned all sporting activity partly due to acute asthma which would forever plague him, but largely due to an instinctive rejection of all that was deemed acceptable, respectable, sporting and *healthy*. Before reaching double figures, Stephen had self-diagnosed an inescapable 'otherness', be it as a homosexual, a Jew, an intellectual, or any number of possible classifications which marked him off from his classmates. This was largely why he would skulk around school while all the other fellows were getting muddy, and if he wasn't losing himself in Sherlock Holmes adventures, or the works of Wodehouse (he even sent the octogenarian Master a fan letter, and received a signed photograph in return), he was finding new ways to risk a beating.

'Of all the school rules I liked most to flout, the breaking of bounds gave me the greatest pleasure. Perhaps there's a metaphor there, I do hope not, all this psychology grows wearisome.' The steep Uley high street was only five minutes' jog from school, and was strictly *verboten* to pupils who had to make do with the tuck shop – but Stephen had risked and received three strokes on at least one occasion within a short time of arrival at Stouts Hill. The one key punishment which stayed with the schoolboy, however (to the extent that it was dramatised for Sky's *Little Crackers* series, with Fry playing his own teacher), involved a joke shop, contraband sweets, and a little friend. This friendship held despite the bigger boy's random cruelties, such as claiming to be an orphan to gain sympathy, to which he could only shrug when rumbled, 'I say these things . . .'

Off games as usual thanks to a self-induced asthma attack, young Stephen was bewitched by a comic advertisement for joke shop tricks. Skint due to his own profligacy, he gathered the necessary coins to send off for the fake spiders and itching powder from his schoolmates' clothes in the changing rooms, taped them inside an envelope with his address, and hunted for a stamp. His investigations into Cromie's study, however, yielded such an exciting cache of confiscated sweets, the whizz-popping kind only found in the village shop, that he dropped the envelope and forgot about anything but filling his filling-filled mouth with them, and stuffing his pockets into the bargain. When the all-too-familiar roar of 'send for Fry Minor!' reached him later that day, he was stunned to discover his master positively twinkling with begrudging respect. In Fry's own reconstruction of the scene, Cromie told him, 'You are going to go very far . . . Whether to the Palace of Westminster or to Wormwood Scrubs I can't quite tell. Probably both, if I know my Fry . . . You'll go far because you have the most colossal nerve. For sheer, ruddy cheek, I have never met anyone to match you.'[7] The master had found Fry's envelope, and presumed that it had been deliberately inserted into his correspondence to blag a free stamp, and was so impressed with this gall, he chummily decided to send the joke shop order anyway . . . Until, that is, a prefect discovered the sweets on the massively relieved Fry Minor. Fry's despicable attempt to finger 'Bunce' for the crime of stealing off to the village shop failed at the first fence, despite his little friend's brave attempts to take the blame, and that ruse only intensified the disappointment in Cromie, and the punishment meted out – eight strokes, with threats of exclusion and expulsion on the cards.

Stephen's time at Stouts Hill was more usually contented, and he did manage to complete his time there without expulsion, gaining his first theatrical experience with a small role in a production of *Oliver!* But despite failing his first scholarship exam, at the age of twelve he left Gloucestershire and was sent north to begin a new period of his life in the tiny occasional-county of Rutland, at Uppingham – a stolidly middle-middle-class Victorian public school.

Before the start of his first term, however, a life-defining discovery was made back home in Booton. Stephen's unquenchable thirst for the written word was fed, out in that secluded part of the country, by a mobile library which stopped at the end of a lane not far from the Fry home, and one day he had a specific request. A few days earlier he had become transfixed by a broadcast of the 1952 film *The Importance of Being Earnest*, when a singular line clasped him in an embrace which never let go – 'I hope, Cecily, I shall not offend you if I state quite frankly and openly that you seem to me to be in every way the visible personification of absolute perfection.' His keen brain instantly memorised the sentence, and he tried it out on Nanny Riseborough, hugging himself at the new avenue of verbiage which had been opened to him: 'I had simply no idea that language could do this. That it could dance and trip and tickle, cavort, swirl, beguile and seduce, that its rhythms, subclauses, repetitions, *clausulae* and colours could excite quite as much as music.'

A pleasure in language for its own sake, for wordplay and linguistic subversion, is a kind of polite, personal rebellion – the refusal to be caged by cliché, a freedom nobody can take away from us. For Stephen, language became his sport, his instrument, and his weaponry. 'There are those who loathe puns, anagrams and wordplay of any description,' he once wrote. 'They regard practitioners as trivial, posey, feeble, nerdy and facetious. As one such practitioner, I do understand the objections. Archness, cuteness, pedantry and showoffiness do constitute dangers. However, as a non-singing, non-games-playing, -dancing, -painting, -diving, -running, -catching, -kicking sort of person, words are all I have. As the old cliché has it, they are my friends. I like to say them, weigh them, poke them, tease them, chant their sound, gaze at their shape and savour their juiciness, and, yes, play with them. I take pleasure in their oddities and pleasures and contradictions . . . It saddens me that the French talk of the *jouissance* of language, its joyousness, juiciness, ecstasy and bliss, but that we of all peoples, with English as our mother tongue, do not.'[8]

Despite any misgivings the mobile librarian may have had for introducing a pre-pubescent lad to Oscar Wilde, Stephen inhaled his Complete Works, and along with it, the tragedy and injustice of Wilde's fate – confirming to his mind the already nagging presentiment that he was not like other boys. This all came into clearest focus on the second day of his fourth term at Uppingham, when Fry fell instantly and extravagantly in love. The identity of the golden object of his devotion is nobody's business – Stephen has given the idealised fair-haired, blue-eyed beautiful boy numerous names in myriad fictionalised forms – but the effect on Fry Minor cannot be sidelined: it may well be that a romantic arrested development took root at this time which has never fully been dispelled. The singularly tall teenager was pubertally an abashedly late bloomer, but Fry's own first sexual experience took place when a game of strip poker with a prefect led to a behind-the-bike-sheds initiation: 'I bear him no grudge and cannot believe he did me any harm. He didn't make me queer, he didn't make me a bugger or a buggeree, so all's jake as far as I'm concerned.'⁹ Fry's pragmatic attitude to public school sexuality, allied to the Ancient Greek ideal of youth, and love between men and boys, would become a bit of a theme in his work, and the life-changing importance of this first love remained something of an obsession. Fry maintained a close friendship with his desired school friend, and achieved a consummation of his all-pervading passion, but nothing affected him like the end of the affair. 'I had always been Bad, both publicly and privately', he admitted. 'Bad in terms of "mobbing" and "ragging", showing off in front of the other boys, daring to go those extra few yards towards trouble and punishment, and Bad in the realms of secret wickedness. But now I didn't care. I just did not care. My behaviour in the first year may have been judged to be purgatorial, now it became unequivocally infernal.'¹⁰

Between academic excellence and behavioural malignancy, at Uppingham Stephen was, like any teenager, an open vessel for all manner of stimuli to pour into. Hair was sprouting everywhere in the early 1970s, and music from groups like The Incredible String Band lingered on the air in many pupils' studies, mingling with the incense, and the ever-present fug of fresh toast. Although The Bonzo Dog Doo-Dah Band sadly called it a day in 1972, the anarchic art school jazz/rock outfit headed up by Neil Innes and Vivian Stanshall had brought together music and silliness like no band ever before. Innes would soon be co-opted into the extended family of the already hot Monty Python, but it was the ginger geezer Viv who held Stephen spellbound when he bought a copy of *Tadpoles* at the study sale of his exceedingly cool friend Rick Carmichael (nephew of Ian, Bertie Wooster in BBC TV's *World Of Wooster*). Stanshall's deep, fruity cocktails of scatology and absurdism in musical epics like 'Rawlinson End' had a marked effect: 'When I first heard the joke "Scrotum, the wrinkled retainer" I laughed so much I honestly thought I might die of suffocation . . . for me it was as delicious as anything could be delicious. With Stanshall, it was as if a new world had exploded in my head, a world where delight in language for the sake of its own textures, beauties and sounds, and where the absurd, the shocking and the deeply English, jostled about in mad jamboree. It was Stanshall's voice, I think, that delighted me more than anything. It had two registers, one light and dotty . . . the other a Dundee cake of a voice, astoundingly deep, rich and fruity . . . as well as great gutsy trombone blasts of larynx-lazy British sottery, to use a Stanshally sort of phrase.'[11]

'The Bonzos were my bridge between rock music and comedy,' Fry wrote, 'but comedy was more important to me by far than rock music . . . Not just the modern comedy of the Bonzos and Monty Python, nor the slightly older comedy of Cook & Moore, much as I adored those geniuses. I also collected records with titles like *The Golden Days of Radio Comedy* and *Legends of the Halls* and learned by heart the routines of comics like Max Miller, Sandy Powell, Sid Field, Billy "Almost a Gentleman" Bennett, Mabel Constanduros, Gert and Daisy, Tommy Handley, Jack Warner and most especially, Robb Wilton.'[12] Besides his youthful aversion to sport, Fry was well aware that he lacked any ability to dance the slightest syncopated step or, famously, to sing a single note – and his voice breaking did nothing to alleviate this talent black spot. However, he continued, 'If I learned all the comedy, I could repeat it, perform it, which was as close as I could come to singing or dancing . . . I could repeat back the comedy I had learned, word for word, intonation for intonation, pause for pause. Then I might be able to try out some of my own.' Despite his musical neuroses, Stephen was briefly in a band which played Bonzo covers and old rock & roll. 'I can't remember what I actually did to justify my presence in the band, apart from a little incompetent hammering on the piano when Rick was playing the guitar or singing. I suppose I just arsed about entertainingly.' This fascination with the funny led to Fry's very first comedy double act: 'Richard Fawcett, a boy of my term, shared this love of comedy. He was a fine mimic too, and an astoundingly brave and brilliant actor.' Both had appeared in an Uppingham production of *Macbeth*, in which Stephen's Weird Sister's repulsive depravity was emphasised by the boy swathing himself in offal, which began to stink long before the run ended. Fry also played Mrs Higgins in *My Fair Lady*, receiving his very first crit, that she: 'would grace any drawing room'. Fry & Fawcett spent hours listening and re-listening to comedy albums, mimicking Cook & Moore sketches, 'pointing out to each other why this was funny, what made that even funnier, trying hard to get to the bottom of it all, penetrating our passion, wanting to hug it all to us in heaping armfuls, as teenagers will . . . Fawcett also shared with me a passion for words and we would trawl the dictionary together and simply howl and wriggle with delight at the existence of such splendours as "strobile" and "magniloquent", daring and double-daring each other to use them to masters in lessons without giggling.'[13]

Stephen apologetically admits that becoming famous was certainly a deep-rooted ambition by this time – he even begged his family to join him on Robert Robinson's interminable TV swot-fest *Ask the Family,* to his father's forbidding disdain. But partnering up with Fawcett eventually led to Stephen's first ever comedy gig – a Christmas party at which the duo planned to entertain their house, Fircroft, with a sketch cribbed from Benny Hill, of all comic inspirations. 'Richard and I rewrote a skit in which a vicar is being interviewed unaware that his trouser flies are widely undone. Richard was the vicar ("I like to throw open my portals to the public"), I was the interviewer ("I see your point, yes I do see your point"). We rehearsed this endlessly and were astonished, as the curtain descended on our dress rehearsal, to hear Frowde, the housemaster, call out, "Trousers down, trousers down!" We looked at each other, utterly baffled as to his meaning (as I still am).'[14] A sudden ban on innuendo forced the pair to improvise something different, but the full filthy sketch was staged that night in the dormitory, no-holds-barred. Fry clearly had the bug: 'Richard and I had by this time become so obsessed with comedy that we wrote to the BBC, who had just started a new series called *Open Door* designed to allow victims of injustice, support groups and others to air their grievances, but we somewhat misinterpreted its aims and believed it to be a chance to Perform On Telly and Become Famous . . . In our letter to the BBC, we pompously elaborated our pitch. Comedy, we observed, with the arrival of Monty Python, had entered a modernist phase. Would it, like the other arts, disintegrate into modes of abstraction and conceptuality? How could a "new comedy" be formulated? All that sort of thing. We planned to show the progress of comedy over the last twenty years and compare it with the progress of music, painting and literature. Would comedy disappear up its own self-referential arse, we wondered? Ridiculous, I know, but there you are. It was enough at least, to get us an interview in Lime Grove, Shepherd's Bush. Nothing came of the meeting, but I still have the producer's card.'[15]

It was an entirely different trip down to London which spelled calamity for Fry Minor. As the youngest member of the Sherlock Holmes Society, Stephen had been given special dispensation to attend the 1972 Society gathering on the Saturday night of a bank holiday weekend celebrating the Queen and Prince Philip's silver wedding, travelling with his good friend Jo Wood, and both promising to be back in Uppingham by Monday teatime. He attended the event – but then the two friends wandered into a Soho cinema, and time disappeared. 'We were completely mesmerised by an utterly new world and all its possibilities. Art had gripped me, poetry, music, comedy, cricket and love had gripped me and have me in their grip still, but – cinema! Films have a peculiar power all their own.' *Cabaret, The Godfather, A Clockwork Orange* and the less obviously seminal *Fritz the Cat* blew the public schoolboys' minds, and in those days it was possible to sit in the cinema watching movies on a loop, which they did . . . until they realised Monday had come and gone. 'When we returned to Uppingham,' Fry wrote, 'still blinking at the light and at the dawning realisation of our madness, all was up. In my case the camel's back had been snapped completely in two by this final straw and I was instantly expelled, not even given the chance to say goodbye to a single friend.'[16]

Stephen had been sent home before, and Alan and Marianne sent their troublesome middle child to numerous experts who diagnosed 'developmental delay' – perhaps even a bipolar disorder – and prescribed Lentizol. Alan took time out to coach his wayward son in his specialised subject – and Stephen's worst – mathematics. This time spent together, and the breakthrough the student experienced, did much to soften Stephen's fearful antipathy to his father, and ignited a lifelong passion for teaching. But with this expulsion returned the inevitable, deeply disappointed paternal disapproval. All Stephen got out of his father on the way from Rutland to Norfolk this time was 'We will discuss this whole sorry business later'.

Interviewed by *The Times* in 1988, Alan Fry admitted of his by-then successful middle child, 'I don't think Stephen and I have ever agreed about anything. We've always had a turbulent relationship. I was conscious in his early years of getting in his way because I've always had a big spread of interests; everywhere Stephen looked, there was Father telling him how to do it . . . We were always trying to cajole him into doing things ordinary little boys did, blissfully unaware that ordinary little boy he was not. When he was about thirteen he announced that he wasn't going to marry because it was silly, that he was going to be a writer, and that he'd always have plenty of money. As I was struggling to pay the school fees at the time, I was very cross indeed.' Thankfully, the 'sorry business' was firmly in context for Stephen's family by 1988. 'For a variety of reasons he left most of the schools he ever set foot in,' Alan continued, 'which was distressing for his mother and me because we very much wanted him to fulfil whatever it was he had it in him. Although we are very different, we both find it difficult to conform; I was never any good at working under people. Stephen found at school that he didn't like being forced into this mould of schoolboy. His mother always had a simple faith in him, but . . . he turned out alright in the end.'

My Whole Life Stretched Out . . .

Maths aside, Stephen had already flown through his O levels, but was told on his arrival at the Paston School in North Walsham that he was too young for A levels, and would have to re-take his exams. Refusing to take the blow to his ego, he barely turned up for school, hanging out in the cool quarters of North Walsham or Aylsham, playing pinball and smoking while Glam Metal blared out of the jukebox. Paston soon acquainted the adolescent with the door, and it was left to the Norfolk College of Arts & Technology to try to achieve the impossible, and straighten Fry out. Taking A levels in English, French and History of Art, the dandy sixteen-year-old Fry expended far greater energy learning about adult life than studying these subjects. He left the family home and found a bed on the top floor of a hostel in King's Lynn, working at the Castle Inn bar and riding around town on a moped. He even found a girlfriend, reporting total satisfaction with the heterosexual apparatus, and yet never ultimately estimating his tastes as any less than 90 per cent homosexual for the rest of his life. He also found a collective of similarly bright minds, intellectuals who gathered at bohemian hangout 'Just John's Delicatique' and irregularly published a magazine called *The Failiure Press*, for which Stephen provided teasing crosswords.

The acting bug was still surging through the student's veins, and defined his ambitions. 'Drama was taken care of at Norcat by a talented enthusiast called Robert Pols. He cast me as Lysander in *A Midsummer Night's Dream* and Creon in a double bill of Sophocles' *Oedipus* and *Antigone*. Somewhere inside of me, I was still certain that I was going to be an actor. My mother used to explain to me that really I wanted to be a barrister, which, as she pointed out, is much the same thing and I had played along with this idea. In my heart of hearts however, and in hers too I suspect, it was acting that mattered.'[17] But this flurry of excitement and Coming of Age still triggered an equal and opposite reaction in the adolescent Stephen. Very like Hugh's synchronous oath never to live past forty, this was the time that Stephen sat down to reaffirm his arrested development by writing his future self an excoriating poison pen letter, not to be read until the ancient age of twenty-five, and stressing, 'This is me now, the real me'. Poetry was (and remains) one of Fry's most jealously guarded private outlets, and an 'Untitled Epic', lightly fictionalising his own life hitherto, was a bottomless pit into which he poured his woes: '*Passions to passions, lust to lust shall pass: Life's a bugger and a pain in the arse . . .*'

Before his final term, believing that 'My whole life stretched out gloriously behind me,' Stephen made his first serious attempt on his own life. Fortunately for us all, he had chosen exactly the wrong combination of pills to do the job effectively, and his brother Roger became the hero of the hour by overhearing his little brother's prodigious vomiting from the next room, and raising the alarm. Delivery from oblivion did nothing to alleviate Fry's downturn, and, cloaked in shame and simmering with teenage anger, he never even turned up to his final exams. Instead, the summer of 1975 was to be a hedonistic saga, revisiting many of the sites of his 'Untitled Epic', and maybe even reuniting with his lost love at the Reading Festival, or some other happening at Stonehenge. The lack of funds for such an expedition, however, suggested the same solution to Stephen as it always had done – he would take what he needed. A hidden wad from a host's grandmother here, an array of credit cards from a close family friend there, all carried off with the lofty swagger that Stephen Fry had been impressively perfecting all his life – that charming, erudite English outer shell that could assure anyone that they were talking to somebody who *belonged*, who was who they said they were, and that everything would be fine. 'The next few weeks passed in a kind of cacophoric, if there is such a word, buzz,' Fry wrote, 'which is to say a state of joylessly euphoric wildness, what a psychiatrist would call the upswing of manic depression . . . I know that I went to London and transferred my possessions, such as they were (books mostly) from my rolled up sleeping bag to a brand-new suitcase. I stayed for a while in the Imperial Hotel in Russell Square, applied for a job as reader of talking books for the blind and made regular visits to the American Bar of the Ritz Hotel where I had become friends with the barman, Ron, whose passion was Renaissance painting. He could remember P. G. Wodehouse sipping a cocktail in the corner, and F. Scott Fitzgerald leaping over the bar, drunk as a skunk.'[18]

Stephen has never really painted these weeks of nomadic crime as anything akin to a Bonny & Clyde-style spree. The lowest point was the occasion of his eighteenth birthday, spent on his own in a hotel in the Cotswolds, where he fished a stranger's credit card out of their jacket, and made himself vastly ill on a bottle of Scotch, while his family marked the day in silent heartbreak back home in Booton. It was unquestionably the best thing that could possibly happen when a few days later he checked in to The Wiltshire Hotel in the concrete town of Swindon to find himself accosted by The Law. To add to his crimes, just that day Fry had nabbed a brand-new watch from a nearby jeweller, and no game had ever been more up. With a charming smile, young Stephen assured his accusers, 'Yes. Yes, I'm afraid that you are absolutely right', and went along with the officers to the police station (which was laughingly only next door) obeying not meekly, but with jokes ('I hope I get special consideration for being easy on the legwork!') and smiles all round. 'I was so happy,' he recalled, 'so blissfully, radiantly, wildly happy that if I could have sung I would have sung. If I could have danced I would have danced. I was free. At last I was free. I was going on a journey now where every decision would be taken for me, every thought would be thought for me and every day planned for me. I was going back to school. I almost giggled at the excitement and televisual glamour of the handcuffs.'[19]

The Nice Cop and Even Nicer Cop who arrested Stephen did not have to work hard to get past his fake names and pretences – his name was written in his books, and he was on the Missing Persons list. He pleaded guilty to all charges, and was placed on remand at the misleadingly cuddly sounding Pucklechurch Remand Centre (now HM Prison Ashfield), just north of Bristol and near enough to the schoolboy paradise of Stouts Hill for irony to register. As predicted, these two periods of remand, while the paperwork was being dealt with, were perfectly suited to Fry's institutional training. He thrilled at the task of polishing the prison floors, was quickly cast in the 'Professor' role among his fellow inmates, and regained an equanimity he had not shown for a very long time.

By the time his day in court came, the sincerely contrite teenager faced the judge, and was told, 'You have led a very privileged life, young man. You have been expensively educated and you have repaid the patience and devotion of all those around you with dishonesty and deceit. Let us be clear, the crimes you have committed have not been schoolboy japes. They have been very serious offences indeed. In the light of the probation officer's report, however, and various other representations it is the sentence of this court that you be placed on probation for a period of two years.' Having completed over three months in prison, Stephen was allowed to go home to his fearful but forgiving family, and to finally put these life lessons to good use.

This he did with an immediate force. When the time came to register for fresh A levels at Norwich City College, he received the news that his chosen subjects were all completely taken with a determined display of self-knowledge: 'If you admit me on to those courses I will get A grades in each subject,' he informed the staff. 'I will take S levels in all subjects and get Grade Ones . . . I will go to the library, take out past papers and, if I have to, take a job in the evening to be able to pay one of your staff to invigilate while I sit the Cambridge Entrance. I will be given a place to read English at Queens' College. If you take me on, this is what will happen.'

And this is what did happen, of course – Fry had long inculcated an unrivalled databank of astonishing knowledge, an appreciation of art high and low, and could dazzle people from any background by sharing this wisdom, but only now did he have the work ethic, the plan, and the drive to put these singular blessings to good use. After the tearfully joyous news of his successful acceptance on an English Scholarship at the medieval college of Queens' was phoned through to him at 'Just John's' by his proud and emotional mother, Stephen was changed. He enjoyed a period teaching at a prep school in Yorkshire, eschewing corporal punishment and perfecting the art of pipe-smoking, cricket umpiring and beard ownership, took to sporting the most geriatric tweeds, and arrived in Cambridge in the autumn of 1978 – to learn, to improve, and above all, to act.

. . . Belts Off, Trousers Down, Isn't Life a Scream?

'The funny thing about Cambridge is there's a strong feeling that you're in a place that is part of history and the cultural landscape of your country, and that you're not going to be worthy,' Fry says. 'It's not the most perfect meritocracy in the world, and it certainly wasn't then, there was a far higher proportion of people from expensive public schools, but then there were lots of people also not. A friend of mine said he thought everyone was called Ashley, which he thought a very unlikely name for public school people, then he realised they were saying "Actually" . . . And then of course there are other people there who just seem to be there because they went to Eton and are good at rowing . . .'

This new old world of quads, porters, dons and dusty libraries, with the punt-peppered Cam twinkling its way through the centre, could not have been more perfectly attuned to Stephen's character, and he was instantly at home in the creaky corridors of Queens'. Those charged with overseeing the broadening of the student Stephen's mind were shrewd enough to quickly recognise a singular intellect – it was said of him that he possessed a fine brain, though his mind was 'nugatory', a rum distinction, with insinuations he has gone far in his career to disprove. But like Hugh, Stephen maintains that only the smallest minimum of his time was spent in lectures or seminars studying his subjects: 'The chances of failing a degree were fabulously remote. It was perhaps a part of the institution's arrogance that it is believed anyone it selected for entrance was necessarily incapable of failure . . . if you preferred to spend your time pulling an oar through the water or striding about in tights roaring pentameters, why then that was fine . . . A relaxed atmosphere of trust pervaded the University.' His exam technique was down pat, and he received esteemed Firsts for Shakespeare papers writing to his own formula – but Fry was far more interested in speaking the Bard's dialogue onstage than deconstructing it on paper. 'I was always confident about my voice and my ability to speak verse and to inflect and balance speech properly . . . The few prizes I had won at school were for poetry reading or recitation of one kind or another . . . if I had faith in my potential I certainly had no particular sense that it would be on comic roles that I should concentrate. Quite the reverse. Theatre to me meant, first and foremost, Shakespeare, and the comic roles in the canon – fools, jesters, clowns and mechanicals – didn't really suit me at all.'[20] One of the University's most respected theatrical groups was BATS, based in Stephen's own college of Queens', and the dramatis personae of their productions became his primary peer group. In his first year, he found himself cast as the foolish old King Alonso in *The Tempest*, and realised that his apparent maturity – although only a year or two older than contemporaries due to his dramatic adolescence – gifted him all the aged roles going. Fry's deep booming tones were unrivalled on campus, but during long runs boredom would inspire his somewhat mannered senile characterisations to become ever more obtuse, with wavering noises at the close of every line which eventually developed into not so much a catchphrase, as a catchnoise. Soon, if Stephen's gargantuan presence in a room was not enough, friends could easily identify him by the bombastic bleating noise which heralded his entrance – 'BEHHH!'

Making cast members laugh was one thing, but as for Footlights and their big show, 'If you were cool it was an event to disdain. "Apparently the Footlights are crap this year," you would say to your companion as you wrinkled your nose at a poster for the event. There has never been a year in which this has not been said . . . If you were normal, such cynicism did not occur to you, and the May Week Revue was another fun fixture on the Cambridge calendar. I was neither cool nor normal, but simply too busy with *The Tempest* and other things to be able to attend.'[21]

Stephen made one particularly meaningful connection within Queens' shortly after his arrival, when he met a blue-eyed, blond-locked Classics student with a fierce intellect to complement his own. Kim Harris came from a more moneyed background than Stephen, introducing his fellow fresher to unknown luxuries as their closeness blossomed into a full relationship, and they became barely separable, living together for the rest of their time at Cambridge, as they indulged in their shared adoration of chess and Wagner, and exquisite living. Fry has always pleaded guilty to charges of snobbery, but only the kind that looks up – his hero Alan Bennett called that kind of upwardly mobile snobbery an 'amiable vice', and while Stephen was happy to be elevated to finer tastes, looking down on others was always considered out of the question.

Kim recalls, 'I first met him at a Freshers' drinks party and immediately assumed he was a junior don with Basil Rathbone somewhere in his family tree. He was slightly older than the rest of us, and acted it. Already this cheerful, freakishly articulate, immensely tall but slightly stooping, kindly, courtly scholar-gent seemed perfectly at ease in the courts and cloisters of Cambridge, exhibiting a kind of Englishness I'd never seen outside of National Trust guides, Derek Nimmo and insecure assimilationists. He was all I could have hoped for in a Cambridge friend – civilised, bright, funny, and best of all, kind. Fizzing with a thrillingly benign energy, he could talk about anything, and had an endearing way of endorsing and enhancing your enthusiasms. I was keen on chess at the time and he liked to see how quickly he could solve *The Times* crossword . . . Behind his suave and composed exterior there lurked, I was soon to discover, a sneaky, cheeky wee demon, a system-bucking, angle-shaving little imp – let's call him Little Stevie – who well before leaving short trousers had worked out that most of those *in loco parentis* over him hadn't the faintest clue which end was up. They were all improvising. And so would he . . . There were those who found his adolescent troubles cool and rebellious. Then there were those, like me, who thought Little Stevie needed a hug.

Little Stevie's plausible casing – the mature and civilised Stephen – was interested in quality, success, achievement and talent. Little Stevie was more interested in fame, even notoriety . . . When Little Stevie came out to play there was always fun to be had. Because Little Stevie liked to tease. He was never cruel. Stephen was – and remains – the least sadistic of men . . . But he did like to tease and loved to play. There was double bubble watching his little toasting fork blunt itself on Hugh Laurie's unyielding decency.'

Despite both studying English, it was not until 1979 that Stephen first caught a glimpse of Cambridge's brightest young thing Emma, essaying the role of Gwendolen in Tom Stoppard's *Travesties* – meeting future bosom pals by paying to see them act was *de rigueur* among this group. When young Stephen was over the border in Edinburgh that summer, playing the lead role in in a sci-fi-themed production of *Oedipus Rex*, this new friendship led to him getting that dose of *Nightcap* which further alienated him from any comedy ambitions. As the punter recalled years later, 'This was to my shocked mind as perfect a comedy show as I had ever seen. It had never occurred to me that the Footlights would be this good. So good indeed I instantly abandoned any dream I might have had of next year dipping my own toe in the waters of sketch comedy. I knew that I could not for a second hold my own with these people. Cool as I wasn't, I had nonetheless absorbed the predominant cool person's view that the Footlights Club was peopled with self-obsessed, semi-professional show-busy show-offs. What was so extraordinary about *Nightcap* was how technically perfect in delivery, writing, timing, style and confidence it was, while managing to project a wholly likeable awareness of the absurdity of the whole business of student comedy . . . The drama I was doing at Cambridge suddenly seemed ordinary, worthy and desperately unexciting.'[22] Fry's approving verdict was therefore sincere when given to Laurie that evening – but nowhere near as ecstatic as his reaction to the winner of that year's Fringe First award, the comedy rocket fresh out of Oxford, Rowan Atkinson, giving his three-man one-man show at the Wireworks Theatre. Being crushed into a pâté of mirth by this extraordinary performer, seeing such funny young comics streaming out of Oxford as well as Cambridge, once again suggested to Fry that comedy was not something he had the talent to take seriously. And so his second year proceeded in much the same way as the first, with ever-growing theatrical duties and pleasures to get stuck into, an estimated twelve plays in an eight-week term. Besides BATS, Stephen joined Emma in the Cambridge Mummers company, touring Europe over Christmas as Duncan in *Macbeth*, while exclusive Cambridge dining club Ye Cherubs became the first of many to call Fry a member. Another momentous occasion came when a letter to his sister Jo was shared with his parents, and they were at last fully apprised that their son was gay – although, of course, they insisted they always knew, and considered this coming-out-by-proxy an enormous relief.

Stephen's desire for fame had not evaporated, and towards the end of his second year in 1980, a dream opportunity to get his face on television cropped up, only months after Hugh's TV debut: *University Challenge* was in town. 'I had watched this religiously since I was a child and could hardly have been more desperate to be picked for the team . . . When a handwritten note arrived in my pigeonhole to tell me that I had been picked I was almost as jubilant and irradiated with joy as the day in 1977 that my mother had telephoned to break the news of my scholarship to Queens'.'[23] As near to simultaneously with Laurie's defeat in the Boat Race as dammit, Fry travelled up to the Granada Studios in Manchester for a series of jubilant appearances, winning for Queens' with a brilliant display . . . Until the Grand Final came around, against Merton, Oxford – and once again, Cambridge lost. In fact, this last defeat came from a close tie-breaker, the best of three, with Stephen's team having won by a record-breaking margin the first time, and the injustice of the outcome was no less poisonous for Stephen than Hugh's defeat had been for him: 'I have rarely been so devastated or felt so cheated. It hurts even now that our team can have answered so many more questions correctly than the opposition and yet have lost.'

This frustration aside, Fry's prodigious hat size was a well-known phenomenon among his contemporaries in Cambridge, and soon writing joined performing in his list of study-snubbing occupations. Before his last summer break he was asked to come up with something for the opening of a new theatre, the Corpus Playroom, which triggered a few evenings of pipe-sucking amid flurries of typewriter-clacking (Fry had taught himself keyboard proficiency at school by obsessively typing out the entirety of P. G. Wodehouse's *Frozen Assets*) which resulted in *Latin! or Tobacco and Boys*, originally credited to 'Sue Denim'.

A necessarily simply staged two-hander written as half of a double bill, *Latin!* saw Stephen reaching selectively back into his own rich history, to tell a farce-tinged tale of totally forbidden love at an English public school. Taking the central role of young schoolmaster Dominic Clarke, Fry's opening innuendo-riddled monologue, perhaps inspired in part by Rowan Atkinson's own show-stopping class register sketch, was warmly received by the audience-cum-class:

DOMINIC: Right, settle down now. Hughes! Face the front, boy. Silence at the back! All right then — Cartwright, what have you got in your desk that's more interesting than me, hm? 'Just stuff, sir.' Well I'll 'just stuff' you if you're not careful. Don't snigger, Standfast, it's unsightly... When do you think Common Entrance is, hm? A year's time? Because it's not, Madison, it's in two weeks... and you can't remember the simple fact that *pareo* takes the dative. Two weeks, Spragg, and you still think *gradus* is second declension. Well it's not good enough, I'm afraid... and sit up *straight*! If I have to tell you again you will suffer. Boys who rub me up the wrong way, Elwyn-Jones, come to a sticky end. No need to smirk, Cartwright...

The conclusion — in which Clarke's no-less-perverse colleague Brookshaw reveals that the younger master has eloped to Morocco with Cartwright, his underage millionaire orphan schoolboy lover — perhaps seems more problematic today than on the play's debut:

triumphant ephebophile heroes being surely a tougher sell to a twenty-first-century audience, although there was a minor revival in 2009. Clarke's protestation of arrested development, a desire to attain a kind of permanent boyhood, is one sentiment shared by the playwright, but *Latin!* was provocative invention. Fry admitted: 'The writing of *Latin!* was an experiment in the techniques of theatre and comedy, combined with a not entirely disgraceful undergraduate desire to shock ... the theatre-going public were quite anaesthetised ... pederasty on the other hand could still, I hoped, set a few ganglions quivering.'[24] Joe Orton's work was one obvious progenitor in the field of sexually amoral comedy, but *Latin!* was never an easy plot to pull off. Fry's performance nonetheless carried the nihilistic themes elegantly, and audiences were so approving and numerous, the play moved to the Trinity lecture theatre for a further week, then to Edinburgh. Stephen had a whole raft of important acting jobs for the remainder of that college year – he bagged some work as an extra on *Chariots of Fire*, technically his first film appearance (albeit with Eton standing in for Cambridge), he played another Shakespearean King in *All's Well That Ends Well*, with Emma in the cast, and was chuffed with his first professional notice for playing his hero Oscar Wilde in the biographical play *Have You Seen the Yellow Book?* The critic from *Gay News* took to Fry's Wilde, and the way he 'carried the lilt of Irish without the brogue' – a review which the actor kept in his wallet for many a year afterward. Returning to the role of Dominic Clarke, however, was a wise move – this year, it was Stephen's play which bagged the Fringe First award from *The Scotsman*. So festooned with garlands was the playwright that it's small wonder the after-show praise of Thompson and her tall friend with the startling blue eyes and triangular blushes on his cheeks was so easily waved away. Nonetheless, watching Fry as Clarke berate his virtual class made a real impression on young Laurie.

By the time he returned to ever more heavenly quarters with Kim in his third and final year in 1980, then, Stephen Fry was already a celebrity in certain theatrical circles, and he needed to feign no humble surprise when the new Footlights President got word through to him that his writing skills could be a great help with that year's panto. Emma had already commissioned him to toss off a couple of sketches for an epochal comedy show staged away from the club: *Women's Hour*, Cambridge's first all-female revue, boasted Thompson (with shaven head, thanks to a pact with McBurney), Toksvig and Ravens in its cast, but took its material from anywhere. Stephen obligingly contributed a book review show parody, and a monologue for Emma as a horsey gymkhana mother which Kim recalls began, 'Here comes Marjorie on Heat . . .' While adding gags to *The Snow Queen* seemed like rather a fun project, however, he admits, 'I wasn't sure about this comedy business, I thought it was perhaps beneath me, especially as I intended to stay on in Cambridge, to get a doctoral thesis and quietly grow tweed in the corner . . . I'd sowed my wild oats and it was time to grow sage. But she persuaded me, and so I went round to see this Hugh.'

Did Hugh then arrive at Stephen and Kim's beautiful rooms, A2 in Queen's? Or did Emma, Kim and Stephen intrude on Hugh and Katie as he sang his IRA song? It doesn't matter – but what does matter is that it was on this meeting that Fry & Laurie (crucial binding ampersand finally in place) first made meaningful creative contact, and instantly began collaborating on funny material.

'About six hours passed,' Fry wrote, 'and Kim, Katie and Emma had been staring at us, as if they'd witnessed Troilus meeting Cressida or Romeo meeting Juliet. It was love at first sight – it was, I have to say, not erotic love, but comic love at first sight. An instant collaborative relationship was formed . . . You read about people falling suddenly in love, about romantic thunderbolts that go with clashing cymbals, high quivering strings and resounding chords and you read about eyes that meet across the room to the thudding twang of Cupid's bow – but it is less often that you read about collaborative love at first sight, about people who instantly discover that they were born to work together or born to be natural and perfect friends.' 'It was pretty instantaneous,' Hugh concurs, 'luckily for us, being English, it was concealed by the need to actually do something, we agreed that we were going to do this show, and we had to start writing there and then. We made each other laugh, we played chess until the sun came up, and we've barely had a cross word. I think we might have had three – one of them was "of", I cannot remember what the other two were. That's not really natural, is it, never to have a cross word? It feels odd.'

A Tall Story

'My overwhelming emotion when Stephen started writing for the Footlights was one of relief that I wasn't going to have to steer this ship on my own as both President and producer,' says Hugh. 'I didn't want it to be shiny-faced undergraduates singing songs, capering about and being larky, I wanted it to be grown-up and mature, and Stephen had that in spades, in fact he had it in every suit. *Gravitas* was the word and Stephen had more suitcases of *gravitas* than any undergraduate I had ever met. Exactly the same as he does now . . . He was covered in tweed. Tweed socks, tweed handkerchief, a tweed pipe. I'm exaggerating of course, but only just . . . His greatest quality is that he has the grace to find himself ridiculous, which not many people can do.'

The tradition of Cambridge comedians being unfeasibly tall, from Cook and Cleese to the giant Adams, is a fitting subject for glibness, but the six-foot-four Norfolkian Fry and only marginally shorter Oxonian Laurie did stand out in their crowd, eyes meeting over everyone's heads, and there was something discernibly complementary about Hugh's goggly eyes and Stephen's bent nose. Whatever it was, Fry wrote, 'The moment Hugh and I started to exchange ideas it was starkly and most wonderfully clear that we shared absolutely the same sense of what was funny and the same scruples, tastes and sensitivities as to what we found derivative, cheap, obvious or stylistically unacceptable. Which is not to say that we were similar. If the world is full of plugs looking for sockets and sockets looking for plugs, as – roughly speaking – the Platonic allegory of love suggests, then there is no doubt we did seem each to possess precisely the qualities and efficiency the other most lacked. Hugh had music where I had none. He had an ability to be likeably daft and clownish. He moved, tumbled and leapt like an athlete. He had authority, presence and dignity. I had . . . Hang on, what did I have? Patter and fluency, I suppose. Verbal dexterity. Learning . . . I suppose I had the edge on playing authority figures. I wrote too. I mean I actually physically wrote lines down with pen and paper or typewriter. Hugh kept the phrases and shapes of the monologues and songs he was working on in his head and only wrote them down or dictated them when a script was needed for stage management or administrative purposes.'[25]

Presenting himself in the club's underground lair, tall, lissom and pipe-smoking like a bastard son of Graham Chapman, Stephen was at home in Footlights, Kim by his side, in no time at all – as evidenced by the Smoker running orders from the time. On 29 October, Hugh and Katie presided over a show with one spot by Kim, and the name 'Fry' appears co-credited with Emma on a sketch she performed with Hugh called 'Cakes' – technically the first comedy sketch with Fry & Laurie input, its content forgotten by both. Less than a fortnight later, Stephen and Kim held their own Smoking Concert with their names all over the list – they wrote and appeared in three two-handers, 'Died Again', chess sketch 'The Master Game', and 'Doctor Doctor' – while sketches from the imminent return to *Friday Night, Saturday Morning* were tried out, and there was a debut from ambitious fresher Neil Mullarkey, a future Comedy Store stalwart. Kim says, 'Stephen and I had seen Hugh perform in a Smoker and had duly sunk to our knees to accept him as our Lord and personal saviour. He made everyone else onstage look like meat in the room and his accent (American) was pitch perfect. Not a hair out of place nor a false quantity in sight. He was also known to us as the author of the previous panto's biggest woofer. Curtain up on *Cinderella*, Act two. The Ugly Sisters, played with vast aplomb by Simon McBurney and Nick Symons, are nursing massive hangovers. Oversize tam-o'-shanter ice packs battle with their wigs. "I never thought I'd see the day: one frigid old bag on top of another."'

Fry's keyboard dexterity was a godsend for Hugh, and *The Snow Queen* was soon down on paper and ready to rehearse. Fittingly, Fry & Laurie's first script collaboration had more of a sketch format than most pantomimes, the plot unfolding via a series of barely connected character vignettes – indeed, there were actually five writers credited, with Katie also pitching in, along with Kim, who made an outstanding Dame. The last credit went to Paul Shearer, a slip of a Computer Science student who had been active in Footlights for a long time, co-producing a Smoker with ex-President Jan Ravens, and specialising in straight man roles which allowed others to bounce their madness off him. The main characters Gerda, Kay and the Snow Queen herself stumble into the plot eventually, but the programme's scene breakdown provides a tantalising idea of the undergraduate silliness that went into the festivities – a 'loose adaptation' which made even Disney's *Frozen* seem faithful:

SCENE 1   Somewhere in space, the Mighty Marvo and his niece Semolina work their dirty magic.
SCENE 2   In the remote Scandinavian village of Happyvjk (Twin town Godalming), the inhabitants prepare for their jubilee.
SCENE 3   Gerda gets stuck with the paper chains and is made to make a match.
SCENE 4   Meanwhile, in the forest, Fagend and his henchmen plan the Happyvjk Heist.
SCENE 5   Dame Tibo tries to pave the way with a ½ bot. of Welsh sherry (Non U) but love will out and Gerda and Kay are into each other.
SCENE 6   Marvo's marvellous mirror finally completed, space echoes to his loud rejoicing. But for one tiny error, we could spend the rest of the evening in the bar...

With Hugh as Marvo, Katie as Semolina and Stephen popping up as the non-singing, non-dancing Montmorency Fotherington-Fitzwell, Ninth Earl of Doubtfulworth, this first collaboration at the ADC Theatre is remembered as an absolute scream for this fresh young gang – the *Cambridge Evening News* concluding, 'A pantomime with a difference is rare enough. This one augurs well for the Footlights' current team, which writes with flair and acts with vigour in presenting virtually an intimate revue.'

Accordingly, when 1981 dawned and the students trooped back from Christmas hols, they returned to proper sketch comedy, with further Smoking Concerts geared towards finding the best shape for that year's big show. In February, Hugh and Katie presided over *Memoirs of a Fox* (the title a play on Siegfried Sassoon's novel, *Memoirs of a Fox-Hunting Man*), with Tilda Swinton joining Emma, Stephen, Hugh, Kim and Paul, and featuring alongside Hugh in a sketch set in an American courtroom which is run like a quiz show, complete with imperfect accents – but by the next Smoker in May, presaging the big show itself, Swinton was gone. She was one of a few famous-actors-in-waiting attending Cambridge who never took the Footlights path, Simon Russell-Beale being another – Fry performed alongside the talented thespian in *Volpone* and was hilariously upstaged, but Simon had no interest in performing sketches. Many of the coming stars of recent years had all moved on – Bathurst, Toksvig, and McBurney, who was on the verge of establishing the world-beating Théâtre de Complicité alongside the Snow Queen, Annabel Arden.

This last Smoker did heavily feature one new name: Tony Slattery. A working-class Londoner, the youngest in a large Irish family, the dashing Slattery had represented his country at judo in his teens, and was in his second year of a Modern and Medieval Languages scholarship, his head now fully turned by the smell of the greasepaint. In Edinburgh the previous summer the young scamp had reduced Fry to a giggling mess with his outrageous silliness in a Jacobean drama which played in the same venue as *Latin!* and Stephen easily indoctrinated Tony into the club as soon as he was at liberty – before long, Fry recalled, his lewd antics had the distinction of making at least one punter literally wet herself laughing.

Footlighters tended to slog their guts out for years to get into the prestigious May Week Revue, but Fry and Slattery simply exploded into the existing club dynamic, and with the addition of one more name – Penny Dwyer, a friend from the Mummers – Hugh had his cast for The Big One. Those few months from mid-autumn 1980 to the birth of *The Cellar Tapes* seem to more than qualify for the term 'halcyon', or perhaps even 'salad days'. Hugh, Stephen, Emma and friends would meet up and head to that most American and excitingly new of establishments, a fast-food bar called The Whim, where they would fuel themselves with Whimburgers and plot out the show that would present their comic generation to the world. Back down in the clubroom, Hugh would play and sing at the piano as his friends looked on admiringly, licking the Whim grease from their fingers before getting down to work. 'I'll have a go at any musical instrument,' Laurie shrugs, 'if it's designed to be played, I take the view that it must be playable. Generally speaking, instruments are very slightly easier than they look – with the exception of the harmonica.'

The core performers amassed by Hugh soon bagged their first professional booking – coincidentally to Stephen's background work on *Chariots of Fire*, it was decided that the Royal Command Performance of the film would benefit from a spot of Cambridge jollity at the party, and although they were asked to perform for nothing, the boss put his foot down, Shearer remembers, 'Hugh had fought fiercely to get us our £50 fees, and when we arrived at the Dorchester ballroom, there were four huge palm trees which had been hired for the night – and their fee was higher than ours!' Taking to the stage in a faux-slow-mo pastiche of the film's famous race scenes, the ordeal turned out to be a miserable baptism of fire for the youngsters. 'Because all the guests had taken so long drinking, instead of being after-dinner entertainment, we were very much mid-dessert, which was just disastrous – people getting up, wandering round, being served, the room wasn't exactly settled – and we were just shoved onto stage with a couple of microphones, and it wasn't a good place to perform. I remember looking down at Lindsay Anderson who was facing away, and at one point he briefly turned around, then decided his pudding was more interesting.' As leader, Hugh showed a fierce loyalty to his friends, and when one equally appalling gig for the Emmanuel College May Ball led to heckling, Laurie dragged the loudest 'bijou revolutionary' outside and shook him until the entire marquee quaked, yelling 'Don't you DARE insult my friends!' Laurie remembers, 'I sometimes still wake up sweating over a show we did in a marquee somewhere, a festival, and we did what we thought was a rather good and pithy forty-five minutes, and were congratulating ourselves in the dressing room, cracking open a bottle of beer, when a bloke stuck his head through and said, "That was great, shall we say second half in ten minutes?" And we had no second half! We had about twelve minutes to concoct a second half, and the fact that we survived that without getting arrested I look back on with some pride.'

There was actually one more project of historical note predating *The Cellar Tapes* – Hugh joined Stephen in a Marlowe Society production of *Love's Labours Lost*, taking the role of the King of Navarre in his one Shakespearean experiment. Stephen got to be as loud as he liked as an outrageously Hispanic Don Armado, while Hugh's opening speech, which begins this book, now provokes shivers with its uncanny aptness for such a bunch of promising superstars. Perhaps the most important thing the two undergraduates got from this experience was their first proper joint comedy sketch. 'Hugh and I had both seen and found hilarious John Barton's *Shakespeare Masterclasses* on television,' Stephen explained, 'in which he had painfully slowly taken Ian McKellen and David Suchet through the text of a single speech.' Stephen took it upon himself to lampoon this textual pedantry, with Hugh as his keen young student trying to get out more than just the word 'Time' from his *Troilus and Cressida* excerpt, and the 'Shakespeare Masterclass' sketch was born:

STEPHEN: Hello, good evening, and welcome to the third in our series of 'Shakespeare Masterclass — An Actor Prepares'. Last week if you'll remember, we were concentrating largely on the body. Well tonight it's the turn of the voice, and we'll be doing some vocal work. Well here's our space — where's our actor? Well, we're very lucky to have with us in the studio this evening, Hugh. Hello, Hugh!

HUGH: Hi!

STEPHEN: Hi! What have you prepared for us this evening, Hugh?

HUGH: I have a speech from *Troilus*, 3-3, ah, it's the Ulysses speech...

STEPHEN: Okay, give it a go... (Hugh prepares) Woah, woah woah! Hugh Hugh Hugh, where do we gather from?

HUGH: Oh, the buttocks!

STEPHEN: Always the buttocks, Hugh, gather from the buttocks, thank you...

One remarkable thing about this first sketch is how long it takes until the first identifiable joke appears – and how many laughs Stephen & Hugh could get out of an audience, just by feigning a clearly phoney sincerity. The 'Masterclasses' would prove to be a winning format, with Stephen's unctuously patronising expert misleading young Hugh on all sorts of topics, from music to comedy. Although Hugh, as Footlights President, was the more experienced comic performer of the two, somehow Stephen's extra inch and a half and gravity of bearing made him a natural authority figure over the more easily gauche-seeming Laurie – besides, his name came first alphabetically. 'Fry & Laurie' were, in effect, established then.

'Hugh was determined that the Footlights should look grown-up but never pleased with itself or, God forbid, cool,' Stephen wrote. 'We both shared a horror of cool. To wear sunglasses when it wasn't sunny . . . Any such arid, self-regarding stylistic narcissism we detested. Better to look a naive simpleton than jaded, tired or world-weary, we felt . . . What right had we got to moan and moon and mooch about the place looking tortured?'[26] Despite this ever-present self-awareness, moaning, mooning and mooching was to play its part in the creation of *The Cellar Tapes*, due to a combination of pained perfectionism and the sheer pressure of following in the biggest footsteps. When Fry first descended the steps to the pine-panelled dungeon of the Footlights clubroom, one of the first things to meet his gaze was the monochromatic glare of Miller, Cook, Cleese and Co. – 'There were pictures of them on the wall in the clubroom, all in duffle coats, and that classic sort of sixties student look . . . It was very interesting, that whole sense of a connection, of the continuity of the Footlights all the way through. And of course, you believe when you're there that it's over, you think, "Those were the glory days, and we're just an embarrassment." And one doesn't realise that it's going to go on twenty years after you.'

A Cellarful of Noise

When the running order of the undergraduates' final show began to take form, there was very little to suggest any kind of thematic continuity – just as there never had been in almost any other Footlights revue. Hugh came up with the name, a play on Bob Dylan's *The*

Basement Tapes alluding to the club's subterranean HQ, but besides the subterranean-style stage design created by a pre-*Grand Designs* Kevin McCloud, which added a confined element to the skits, it meant nothing, particularly when allied to the aesthetics of espionage drama which the President applied to the poster and programme – spools of magnetic tape and mugshots of the cast, suggesting a clandestine cabaret, something Top Secret to tease punters with, the product of Laurie's adoration of spy thrillers. The programme also contained more levity than most, with the two main writers determined not to be helpful with biographies:

STEPHEN FRY: Fry shrinks from personal publicity of any kind. He is an intensely shy and private young man.

HUGH LAURIE: 'I get up at 5:26 every morning, two hours before Kingsley Amis, and make Mary a pot of tea. I read all the papers in the world seven times, have a more frugal breakfast than Malcolm Muggeridge, and answer the 40,000 letters I receive each day. I'm in bed by 9:00 with a bucket of tea and Sonia. I'm reading Proust at the moment and I think television is a corruptive influence.'

One banker was regretfully scratched from the running order by Hugh when its author leapt at the chance to trouser a real BBC credit. Comedy whizz-kid John Lloyd had left Cambridge several years earlier, but still popped up at Smokers to see how the younger bucks were getting on, and a quickie about a gents toilet patron kicking someone in the groin to use their gasp as a hot-air dryer seemed perfect for the latest series of *Not*. Even his name appearing on screen as 'Steven Fry' could not mar the realisation of such an ambition for Stephen, but Hugh was less pleased when his colleague shared his good news, as it meant they could no longer use the sketch.

This rare admonishment showed that Laurie was still in charge, but Shearer noted that the two tallest members of the cast had already begun to show a discernible authority in every meeting. 'They formed a very strong creative partnership quite early on, and had an idea of what kind of material the show would favour . . . Stephen had a wonderful parodic style that could turn to all sorts of literature, Hugh had a fiercely angry streak about so many subjects, he kind of introduced a political strand to it. Emma was already earmarked for stardom and had a fantastic range. Penny had a very gentle way of performing, and worked well with Emma.'

As with the 'Masterclass' double-hander, theatrical and literary parody was undoubtedly the main ingredient in the show – Stephen wrote a sketch, 'My Darling', which allowed Emma and he to mercilessly mock the clipped vowels of the 1934 film of Victorian melodrama *The Barretts of Wimpole Street*. There was further send-up of Victoriana in his own solo spot, 'The Letter', a pun-packed play on *Dracula* with Stephen as a prototype Gelliant Gutfright. 'The Letter' had the longest life of any spoof on offer, resurfacing in charity shows decades later, and still liable to be dusted down by Fry when the need arises to this day. If he takes to the stage in a louche velvet jacket holding a leather-bound volume, it's fair to presume what narrative is to follow (note the first appearance of a surname of historical importance, taken from Labour politician Baron Melchett):

> The day the letter arrived, I was due in court on the intricate case of Melchett vs The Vatican, which was coming to a delicate and potentially explosive stage. The letter then came as a welcome diversion, and I tipped the delivery boy out of the window with more than ordinary generosity. Even then, I fancy I gave a momentary shudder as I unfolded the letter, but it was a cold morning, and in accordance with Mr Tulkinghorn's instructions with regard to Melchett vs The Vatican, I was naked. The letter read as follows: 'If Mr John Lawson-Particle will travel immediately to Transylvania, as the honoured guest of Count Dracula,

to personally advise His Excellency on a matter of great legal delicacy, Mr Lawson-Particle will be handsomely remunerated. He is to bring on his journey no garlic, no crucifixes, no wooden stakes. Neither is he to look up in a dictionary, the word "vampire".' It seemed innocent enough . . .

Even the most modern extended sketch, a domestic scene in which two mind-meltingly mundane suburbians, Alan & Bernard, display their ignorance in a game of charades, was as much a pastiche of Alan Ayckbourn as a standalone sketch. Dwyer played Alan's deeply suffering wife, and Slattery Bernard's equally miserable son, Ben, but the majority of the dialogue belonged to Fry & Laurie:

```
STEPHEN:   Ben wants to be an actor, don't you, Ben?
HUGH:      Lot of actors out of work, Ben.
STEPHEN:   Just what I tried to tell him, Alan, and
           would he listen? No thank you.
HUGH:      Tell you what though, Sue and I happen
           to be fairly chummy with one of the
           usherettes at the Peterborough Key
           Theatre, we could put in a good word for
           you? You never know, it's worth a try,
           isn't it?
STEPHEN:   There you are, you see, Ben? Thanks a
           lot, Alan. I must say I never knew you
           were a man of the theatre!
HUGH:      Oh, yes, we always go up and see the
           Ayckbourn, you know?
STEPHEN:   Oh, he's marvellous, Ayckbourn, isn't he?
           Well, I've never actually seen any of his
           things, but...
HUGH:      Brilliant, Bernard, quite, quite
           brilliant. I've taken Sue to see all of
           his plays twice. It really is uncanny,
           it's almost as if you were holding up
```

	a microscope... Sue, I was just telling Bernard how much you adore Ayckbourn.
PENNY:	I don't.
HUGH:	Oh, Sue, you're such an old reactionary!

The self-satisfied small-mindedness of Alan & Bernard – types Fry & Laurie would come to label 'horror men' – would make them tempting characters to return to, and the unattractive personas (Hugh the most unbearable, right-wing, bitter and cold, Stephen an equally clueless streak of smugness) would mutate into platitudinous businessmen Gordon & Stuart.

These lengthy playlets were supplemented by quickies and sketches by others – Harris's chess number and the astonishingly prescient Thompson monologue in which 'Juliana Talent' receives an award for theatrical brilliance, and blesses her 'luck' – that she was born so very talented. The spy recruitment and US courtroom sketches were also included, but shed by the time the revue reached TV. The primary other ingredient was music, and particularly political satire in song, the comic form in which Stephen found Hugh immersed on first collaboration. These sections of the show were the least funny, but capable of delivering a real punch, particularly Slattery song 'I Want to Shoot Somebody Famous', inspired by the recent murder of John Lennon, and the closing piece in which the cast took on the persona of a White Power choral group – although musically, the standout number was misanthropic blues number 'Everybody Hates You', performed by Tony and Hugh, with help from musical director Steven Edis. Supporting material came from a number of students including Mullarkey, Toksvig and her new writing partner Nick Symons, but this additional material aside, by common accord, a rare credit went into the proofs for *The Cellar Tapes* programmes – 'Written by: Stephen Fry & Hugh Laurie'. Jan Ravens had done sterling work as the long overdue first Footlights President of a non-male gender, and had a great career ahead of her, but as director of the revue, she has gone on record admitting, 'It's basically the Stephen & Hugh show! They were quite a formidable force, both kind of in their opinions, and also, they were so good, that it was difficult to give everybody else a fair crack of the whip.'[27]

Slattery aside, these six individuals also had to complete their three-year degrees while the show took form, Fry knocking up two dissertations, on Byron's *Don Juan*, and 'aspects of E. M. Forster' which landed him 'a dull, worthy and unexciting' 2:1. As for his new writing partner, when all the hard work was done and *The Cellar Tapes* debuted at the ADC Theatre on 3 June (not May) 1981, the President took to the stage and began: 'Ah, good evening, ladies and gentlemen. Welcome to the May Week Revue. We have an evening of entertainment, of – I got a Third by the way – sketch comedy, music and . . .'

There are no memories of anything going wrong that first night, nor indeed any other night on this virgin run. Stephen remembers a kind of blissful blur of pleasing an appreciative crowd: 'All these moments were more pleasurable and thrilling in this theatre, on this occasion, before such an enthusiastic audience, than anything I had ever done before . . . Hugh and I looked at each other after the curtain fell. We knew that, come what might, we had not disgraced the name of Footlights.'[28] The ADC Theatre was just the beginning, of course – they were embarking on the well-worn path to Edinburgh, which included Oxford (the one place the local press were less than effusive, and the venue treated the cast so shoddily Hugh wrote a furious letter); the Robin Hood Theatre in the tiny Nottinghamshire village of Averham; and even a return to Uppingham for Stephen, the rebel returned, reformed. But before any of that, Stephen & Hugh's lives took a jolting detour.

Word had been rife in showbiz circles that the 1981 show had brought together the strongest line-up since the 1960s, and before that first week was over, offers were percolating through to the cast from the BBC, from Granada and even old boy Martin Bergman, who had lined up a tour of Australia, just as the *Cambridge Circus* team had toured down under eighteen years previously. But unbeknownst to either colleague, one particularly famous face popped up to Cambridge to test out their wares – at his agent's request, Emma's Noel Gay stablemate Rowan Atkinson had been sent ahead as a scout, and returned to Richard Armitage in London to urge him strongly to see for himself what an opportunity was his for the taking. Accordingly, before the Cambridge run was over, *The Cellar Tapes* cast were ushered into the presence of the immaculately tailored, cigar-smoking pre-eminent show business Svengali, and asked the most significant question of their lives: 'Do you see yourselves doing this kind of thing professionally? As a career?'

THE NEXT BIT

'In my dreams I've played snooker with Stephen Hendry. I've sung with Barbra Streisand and I've been to bed with Anneka Rice. In reality I've played snooker with Barbra Streisand, I've sung with Anneka Rice and I've been to bed with Stephen Hendry. Sometimes life is even better than a dream.'

'I was Princess Anne's assistant for a while, but I chucked that in because it was obvious they were never going to make me Princess Anne, no matter how well I did the job. It was a question of who you were, rather than how well you did, you know, and I hate that.'

'It was all so sudden, strange and overwhelming', Fry wrote. 'Since I had met Hugh and started writing sketches with him and on my own I had dared hope that I might perhaps apply one day to BBC Radio for a job as a scriptwriter or assistant producer or something along those lines. About my future as a comic performer I was less sure, however. All the facial mastery, double takes, clowning and fearless assurance that Hugh and Emma displayed onstage and in rehearsal came much less naturally to me. I was voice and words; my face and my body were still a source of shame, insecurity and self-consciousness. That this Richard Armitage was prepared, keen even, to take me on and shepherd me into a genuine career seemed like astonishingly good luck.'[1] 'Acting is not an English thing to do,' Hugh adds. 'It's not a thing that school teachers ever advise kids to look into or take seriously. In fact, generally speaking, they probably frown on it: "Sure, you want to play around with it, but then grow up and get a proper job." Which is something I plan to do very soon.'

The usual route for successful Footlighters was to receive a tap on the shoulder from someone in BBC Radio LE, and to start out as a producer, but Fry shrugs, 'I think they knew I'd be hopeless as a staff producer.' Nonetheless, until Armitage's offer, the two friends really were sworn to their chosen fates – cosy academe, and the Hong Kong Police. But, as the likes of would-be-lawyer Cleese had decided before them, why not give show business a try, to see how far it might take them? The drudgery of reality would always be there to return to – and so, without too much anguish, they agreed to join Emma and Rowan on the Noel Gay books. Rowan's right-hand man, Richard Curtis, remembers, 'There used to be a slight rivalry between Oxford and Cambridge, but because Stephen & Hugh were a year or two below, it was very benign when we overlapped in Edinburgh, they were very sweet and it didn't feel like a competitive thing, so we became friends.'

'A year and a half earlier I had been on probation,' mused Fry. 'For almost all of my youth I had been lost in the dense blackness of an unfriendly forest thick with brambles, treacherous undergrowth and hostile creatures of my own making. Somewhere, somehow I had seen or been offered a path out and had found myself stumbling into open, sunlit country . . . Sooner or later, I was convinced, I would be found out, and the doors of show business would be slammed in my face, and I should have to set about answering my true vocation as a teacher of some kind.'[2] Hugh was even more sceptical, and for decades to come, would complain, 'Sometimes I feel I've chosen the wrong career. I don't have the mental equipment for it really. That sort of "to hell with it" attitude that actors and performers need. They need an element of, "I don't care what people think, what will be, will be."' This lacking element, however, was present in his new colleague, and that gave Laurie the strength to give comedy a try. 'I don't think I would have gone through this career without him. I'll take the bull by the horns and say I love him.'

The Bubbly Water People

Stephen & Hugh had taken a bold move together, but were still only at the start of their tour. Before it began, they bade a very fond farewell to the familiarity of Cambridge: 'I'd hate you to think we were like characters in some Edwardian schoolboy novel – "And so the three chums marched off to the tuck shop for a pound of Mrs Godfrey's best bull's eyes and two bottles of frothing ginger pop . . ."' Fry says, 'But I did enjoy myself at university. Especially since it was such a close squeak getting there, after expulsions, prison and probation and all. Part of the pleasure of being at a university is the feeling that the place belongs to you, and there is a corresponding irredentist melancholy in returning and seeing the place usurped by new waves of the young. The ancient universities are remarkable places, to be sure . . . but even if Cambridge had been all brutalist concrete with horrible drip-marks and sour smelling catwalks, I would still have had a wonderful time, because of friendship.' They decamped to north London, Stephen joining Kim in his house in Hadley Wood, while Hugh lodged with Katie in Hampstead – Paul Shearer recalls, 'When we all first came to London, there was a very large bedsitter in Hampstead, above William Hill the bookies, which had six bedsit rooms, and a rolling population of people. Nick Symons found a room in there first, then me, then Katie got one, so Hugh stayed there a lot. We all used to pile into the kitchen and play poker, including Stephen when he was visiting.'

When the show finally arrived at St Mary's Church Hall, Edinburgh, the cast all felt like old hands, and were closer than ever – Emma took particular delight on tour in trapping Stephen in dressing rooms so she could threaten him with her naked breasts and rapacious come-ons, sending the poor flower into hyperventilating paroxysms of camp discomfort. Stephen also made a shaky radio debut, performing one sketch and being interviewed by Brian Matthew for a Fringe round-up on Radio 2: 'performing the sketch was fine, but as soon as I had to speak as myself I found my throat restricted, my mouth dry and my brain empty. This would be the case for years to come. Alone in my bedroom I could say things to an imaginary interviewer that were fluent, amusing and assured. The moment the green recording light was on I froze.'[3] This diffidence would of course be comprehensively overturned before long, and came despite glowing reviews all round, *The Times* trumpeting, '*The Cellar Tapes* is just about the most entertaining, the most delightful, the most thoroughly good-time show that I have seen for years . . . their satire has enormously improved.' But there was even less excuse for Fry to lack confidence after the excitement of the last show of the festival.

By 1981, the true roots of 'Alternative Comedy' had long been dug up and kicked around since the fabled meeting where Alexei Sayle, Pauline Melville, Keith and Tony Allen and others had lit the fuse, but what remained was a crucial sentiment across the generation that new comedians had some responsibility to get laughs without the unthinking racism, sexism, homophobia and general bigotry which had fuelled whole swathes of British comedy for decades – even the satire of university clowns, from the Pythons and The Goodies to the *Not* team, although well intentioned, sometimes failed to live up to the ideals of this new generation. In this radical environment, one group always ripe for kicking was the toffs of the Cambridge Footlights. Therefore, despite the good reviews, *The Cellar Tapes* gang were not expecting to triumph against the anarchic comic forces which surrounded them in Edinburgh.

It was an even bet all round on who was more stunned when news trickled through that the all-new highest accolade given at the Fringe, sponsored by Perrier, had their names on it. Not content with being Fry & Laurie's fairy godfather within Noel Gay, Rowan Atkinson was also on the panel for the Perrier Award, and as the Footlighters took their final bows amid wild audience approval, the timid comic hero struggled onto the stage, and held up his hand for silence: 'Um, ladies and gentlemen. Do forgive me for interrupting like this. You must think it most odd. You may know that this year sees the institution of an award for the best comedy show on the Edinburgh Fringe. It is sponsored by Perrier . . . the bubbly water people. The organisers and judges of the award, which is to encourage new talent and new trends in comedy, were absolutely certain of one thing, that whoever won, it wouldn't be the Cambridge bloody Footlights. However, with a mixture of reluctance and admiration, they unanimously decided that the winner had to be . . .'

Rowan shook Hugh's hand, presented him with a cheque for £1,000, and the crowd reached new heights of hysteria. The news had been announced, but through the spotlight-dazzled mists of memory, Stephen only remembers the moment as a completely random bombshell, the most unexpected cherry on the most delicious cake, to close one of the most celebrated shows ever to run at the Edinburgh Fringe. Certainly, one young punter never forgot the buzz that night – nineteen-year-old street performer Eddie Izzard, who saw Fry & Laurie's triumph as one of the greatest spurs to his incendiary ambition to join them in the comedy limelight.

Hugh had less of a mountain to climb, and blushed to recall, 'Part of the prize was a week-long run at a theatre in London where we got good reviews. As a result neither of us had to work down a coal mine for ten years before getting a big break. I'm afraid there have been no real jobs . . . I've never had to pay any great price for what I do, and I sometimes feel a bit guilty about that.' This prize week in The New End Theatre (an ex-morgue in Hampstead, where they followed on each night from Steven Berkoff's *Decadence*) flashed by, and as autumn arrived, Bergman shepherded everyone onto a plane for an incarnation of the show down under – provocatively renamed *Botham: The Musical*, after the cricketer's recent jubilant Australian tour, which saw England retaining the Ashes. Sadly the cast was now sans Slattery, who returned to Cambridge to inherit Hugh's Presidency of a Footlights now bloated with new blood – Morwenna Banks, Richard Vranch, Steve Punt, and others who would herald a wave of new comedies as the decade progressed. Penny Dwyer also turned down the Australian tour, and indeed, a theatrical career, concentrating on her work as a metallurgist. In the early 1990s she told the *Daily Mail*, 'I loved the messing about side of it, but when we started to take ourselves seriously I was less happy. And no, I don't feel any pangs . . . it was another world that I have no part in now.' Dwyer's career path gave her a key role in the construction of the Channel Tunnel before she sadly died, after a long illness, in 2003.

As another Noel Gay artist and Thompson's co-star in *Injury Time* – which also gave Fry an uncredited cameo – Robert Bathurst was the perfect man to beef up the cast, and the new five-piece ensemble had a glorious time in the Antipodean sun, socially if not theatrically, and as Emma observed of Stephen & Hugh, 'By the time we came back, they were married.' Kim insists, 'They were born to be a double act, remarkable in every way. Everyone knows that politics is showbiz for uglies. But that goes double and cubed for British comedy – a galore of grotesques in the main. Q: Imagine an erotic encounter with a British comedian of either or any sex. What's the most romantic thing you could say? A: "Put your wallet away. This one's on me." This was never true of Stephen & Hugh who I thought mould-breakingly dashing.'

Returning to a snowy London, the heavily bronzed quintet were soon set to work on yet another evolution of their show, this time a refreshed arrangement of Smoker material staged by Armitage at the Lyric Theatre, Hammersmith – now retitled *Beyond The Footlights*, although the company would tour the UK under the name *A Sense of Nonsense*. 'Every now and then we got ambitious,' Hugh admits. 'I remember I once had this idea, onstage, I liked the idea of having one really substantial set piece that was complex – it was set on a cruise ship, and the idea was that we had a length of PVC piping that stood in for the rail, and one person could hold this as if leaning on it, then another could join them and also apparently lean on it, then the first person could disappear and the rail stays where it is, a constant throughout the sketch. The idea was that the audience would be blown away by our incredible "Cirque de Soleil" mime skills, but of course, we weren't trained mime professionals, and it was absolute bollocks. It never worked, it was just a piece of piping that was wobbling all over the stage, but I kept trying to get everyone to do it, I put people through hell trying to make it work, and it never did.'

Before their tans were faded, and despite allegedly returning home with empty pockets, the cast popped out one December evening for an Italian meal at la Sorpresa in Hampstead, and had a chance meeting with Footlights royalty. The restaurant was Peter Cook's local, just over the road from his home, and he sat at the bar working his way through a stack of newspapers apparently without a care in the world – although he was recently separated, and entering a particularly low period. Nonetheless, when Bathurst blithely invited him to join his young disciples, he was absolutely delighted. When chucking out time came round, Pete even shuffled over the road with them to the bedsitter in Baker's Passage, where, Shearer recalls, 'He entertained us all by being Peter Cook – he was very funny about Nancy Spungen at the time, as I remember.' He also drank them dry, sending Stephen off to find a bottle of Armagnac intended for a family Christmas present. 'God knows how sycophantic, drivelling and hysterical we were,' Fry says, 'yet he didn't show any signs of alarm or irritation . . . Peter never hoarded his wit, never kept it back for a more important occasion. His wit was anyone's.'

The God of Comedy would forge a real bond with Fry in particular in the coming years, and he was not the only hero that Fry's burgeoning fame would lead him to befriend, besides being stablemates with Cleese and Atkinson. Bonzos icon Vivian Stanshall had been through hell and back by the 1980s, but he and his family found a lasting helpmeet in Stephen, who would help get his typically outré maritime musical *Stinkfoot* off the ground in Bristol in 1985. But perhaps Fry's closest new friendship was with the newly minted best-selling author Douglas Adams, who had kept as close an eye on his Footlights inheritors as his friend John Lloyd, and was just ahead of Stephen in the queue for the UK's first Apple Mac. Hugh allegedly goggled when he thought his friend had spent thousands of pounds on a coat, and admits, 'Stephen was one of the first people I knew to buy a computer – I couldn't even use a typewriter; I prefer to write in pencil, but he loves gadgets and all high-tech stuff. Gradually I was converted and I follow him in that. But when I started driving a motorbike again, and absolutely fell in love with bikes, he did the same.' Once young Fry discovered the joys of Macintosh computers, he and Adams became like schoolboys together, ringing each other's doorbells for long evenings of playing with the latest code, games and gadgets. Adams had a rather sad history of falling out with his closest male friends, and Fry was no different, but during this glittering entry into metropolitan society for Stephen, his even taller new friend Douglas joined the 'charmed by Fry' club. He loosely based a minor character in *Hitchhiker's Guide* lore, Murray Bost Henson, on Stephen, and marvelled at his growing ubiquity, as if there were 'a whole cupboardful of Stephen Frys, all *doing things*.'

This shoulder-rubbing with comedy greats was not just extra-curricular, and from the start Armitage made sure his young charges were working with the best. Oxford graduate Jon Plowman was not the comedy boss he is today, but at the start of his career he was given the job of directing *Beyond The Footlights,* while another name whose place on a comedy credits list would become a guarantee of quality was Geoff Posner, who approached *The Cellar Tapes* team and asked to film the revue as the graduation piece for his Studio Direction course – he passed with flying colours, and became an unparalleled director of live TV.

Nonetheless, Posner's recording was disregarded when it came to putting *The Cellar Tapes* on screen, and as the gang decamped for the first time to the BBC rehearsal rooms in the now long-demolished vast carbuncle known as the 'North Acton Hilton', they were honoured with the attention of legendary producer Dennis Main Wilson, a nicotine-steeped veteran who had steered the Goons to greatness at the start of a career constructed from comedy classics. Although his taste for BBC hospitality meant that he was easier to work with in the mornings, he regaled the youngsters with tales of comedy yore, and Fry insists, 'He gave us the impression that as far as he was concerned we were cut from the same cloth as Spike Milligan and Tony Hancock. Such attention and respect from one so august could only make us glow . . . Dennis saw us as respectful inheritors of the Golden Age mantle and the new "Alternative" comics as vandals and interlopers who were of no account.'[4] Fry, Laurie and Co. hung on his every word and matched his every puff as the two-hour-plus revue was hacked down to forty-five minutes, broadcast on BBC2 on 20 May 1982. Only the very best was laid on for the production, with John Kilby directing and Hugh having the honour of Ronnie Hazlehurst orchestrating his music, while Tony and Penny were sent for to rejoin the team.

Opening with another take on the *Chariots of Fire* pastiche, showcasing the baby faces of the new generation, this 'best of' broadcast marks the arrival of Fry & Laurie before the viewing nation. As with Posner's recording, there was no live audience, lending the proceedings a perhaps unwelcome surfeit of *gravitas*, but as a snapshot of household names before the celebrity world claimed them forever, it remains priceless, and was well received. Sadly the same could not quite be said for *Beyond the Footlights*, which did reasonable business at the Lyric Theatre, but received only middling reviews, certainly for anyone but the universally feted 'Emma Talent'. Stephen tended to have second priority, with *The Stage* heralding 'a tall, languid young man with a polished, highly attractive personality, a pleasant speaking voice and a gift for investing every oddball he portrays with exactly the right degree of nuance'. While Michael Billington in the *Guardian* was doubly prophetic when he wrote, 'Even if it doesn't set the town ablaze, it introduces one to some highly talented performers and shows a particular gift for literary parody and for pricking the excesses of the privileged Cambridge life,' noting that Fry 'has the omniscient repose of a natural butler.' Less successfully prophetic was Irving Wardle in *The Times*: 'There is nothing in this show that tempts you to predict a glittering theatrical future for any of the five members of the company, but jointly their personalities and separate skills do form an effective company, and – an unusual merit in Oxbridge revue – they spend at least as much time in making fun of themselves as in having a jolly good old sneer at the world outside. A strong sense of unjustified privilege runs through the show, as in Hugh Laurie's description of the ideological torment he went through before accepting a whacking grant from the UGC. They even have a heartfelt blues on lacking anything to feel blue about . . . The specialist in top dogs is Stephen Fry, a harmless lanky figure who seems built for nothing but pouring out dry sherries.' None of this guesswork, however, matched the uncanny puff-piece written by James Seddon in, of all places, the *Mirror*, when an article to publicise their TV debut proclaimed Fry & Laurie to be a 'double act on the fringe of a great future'. In a piece which may as well have been penned by Richard Armitage himself, this appreciative item went on to equate Fry with Cook and Laurie with Cleese, quoting Main Wilson as saying that they had created the best revue since *Beyond the Fringe*, and assuring readers 'the names mean nothing now – but just wait'.

A Bit of Bennett & Eastwood

The headline of this flattering bumph caught our heroes amidships, as, despite their ever-growing friendship and partnership, they had never identified themselves as a double act. When Armitage brought his new recruits together and asked them whose footsteps they felt keen to follow in, Hugh pulled a few faces and came up with three equally outrageous names – Clint Eastwood, Peter Ustinov, and a dash of Mick Jagger. That trinity threw up its own imponderables, as he admits, 'I sing like Peter Ustinov, and I play the piano like . . . actually, no, Clint Eastwood does play the piano very well! It seems to me that I was cheating in my answer because the whole point was to pick one person, and there was I trying to get three people in one. Actually, the Mick Jagger thing was incorrect, I don't think the strutting frontman was something I could ever pull off – I have great admiration for people who can do that, who want to be at the front of the stage cavorting, but it's not quite my thing.' Fry had a stronger idea, to his agent's surprise – he may have been expected to nominate Cleese or Cook, but instead, he admitted it was Pete's humble ex-colleague Alan Bennett he most admired. 'Bennett's miniaturism, his frailty combined with his verbal touch and literary, almost academic, frames of reference appealed to me more as a role model. History has, of course, shown that his kind of career path was as unattainable for me as Cook's and Cleese's, but a man's reach should exceed his grasp, or what's a heaven for?'

If Stephen & Hugh had any intentions of making it as a duo, it was still only within the framework of a sketch troupe – a Cleese & Chapman, rather than a Morecambe & Wise. Armitage had answered the call from Granada TV, and agreed with Scottish producer Sandy Ross that *The Cellar Tapes* cast would form the ideal basis of a team for a new sketch show he was preparing for the Manchester region, assisted by trusted researcher Jon Plowman, who had been getting them into shape in *A Sense of Nonsense*. 'We were extremely lucky,' said Hugh, 'because *Not the Nine O'Clock News* was a great success, and very quickly other television companies were desperately scrabbling to get their own version of it, so suddenly young people doing sketch comedy became a very sought after . . . *product* is such an awful word, but that's probably how television executives would have described it. We were sort of caught up in that scrabbling.' The fourth and final series of *Not* was in production, and Stephen quietly fretted that it would be the last hurrah for Oxbridge comedy: 'I am not by nature a pessimist but I did wonder if the door had closed on types like us. Comedy is, as everyone knows, all about timing, and I feared that in the career sense our comic timing was way off . . . What punk had done for music the Alternative comedians were doing for comedy. The classic "Ah Perkins, come in, sit down" comic sketch would be swept away along with the tuck box and the old school tie. This is how it seemed to us in our darker moments.' If ever an Oxbridge swank could be discerned in their linguistically stylish comedy, both Stephen & Hugh seemed to react to their shot at fame in equally despairing ways. 'I used to have a lot of confidence,' Hugh admitted. 'I used to think "I know I can do this; I can stand on a stage with virtually nothing and no idea of what I'm going to say or do, and know that it will be alright, I can make it work." And as soon as I started doing it for a living, it all changed, I don't know why. One of the strange things that happened was that hitherto I had always thought of audiences as being female in character, and when I started to do it professionally for some reason they became male. They became competitive, an adversary that had to be conquered, and I imagined rows of men with their arms folded saying, "Go on, then!" I have to confess I'd get very aggressive. Stephen and I would absolutely seethe with rage if we hadn't triumphed.'[5] 'I know how infantile and silly such fears may sound,' Fry concludes, 'but in comedy confidence is paramount. If the performer is unsure then the audience is on edge, and that's enough to strangle laughter before it is born.'[6]

Perhaps it would help that they were to be joined in the new enterprise by the prince of 'punk comedy', the most exciting new performer of the decade, Rik Mayall, who had broken through on another recent attempt to take on the might of *Not* (albeit co-created by Sean Hardie), *A Kick Up the Eighties*. Stephen had seen Rik in action, and this only exacerbated his inferiority complex, knowing he had none of Rik's 'physical charisma, devastating self-assurance and an astoundingly natural appeal that radiated out at the audience like a thermonuclear shockwave . . . You didn't question it, analyse it, applaud its cleverness, appreciate its social meaning or admire the work behind it, you simply adored it, as you might any natural phenomenon. Whatever gifts I possessed appeared shrivelled, pale and underdeveloped. In the comedy shower-comparison test I failed, and it hurt.'[7] It seemed everyone, from Wood & Walters to Cannon & Ball, wanted to work with this unstoppable rebel – but sadly Stephen & Hugh weren't to get their chance, as Rik decided to pull out of the deal to concentrate on his new sitcom, *The Young Ones*. This was a disappointment, as was Tony Slattery's decision to join Chris Tarrant in new show *Saturday Stayback* rather than rejoin his old pals, while Robert Bathurst was not considered, and would appear in many comedy pilots until he made his name in shows like *Joking Apart* and *Cold Feet*. Ross discovered fellow Scot, St Andrews graduate Siobhan Redmond to be a versatile credit to the cast, while other bookings considered included Alfred Molina, poet Liz Lochhead and the wildcard, Chris Langham.

When the Footlighters arrived at Plowman's flat to discuss the nature of this new comedy show (which Stephen wanted to call *Trouser, Trouser, Trouser* but was quickly overruled), they found that Rik had at least recommended an understudy who would prove a considerable consolation – 'a dark-haired spectacled young fellow of earnest aspect' called Ben Elton. Ben had taken over from Alexei Sayle as The Comedy Store compère, developing a machine-gun-like delivery to deal with hecklers, and having ever-so-slightly hero-worshipped Mayall since meeting the cool long-haired second year as a fresher at Manchester University, he was overjoyed to have been crucial in getting Rik's vision down on paper as chief scriptwriter on *The Young Ones*. Less pleasant was his failed bid to step into Peter Richardson's shoes as Mike 'Thecoolperson', and so this consolation, playing a key part in an all-new sketch troupe, was very welcome – he'd made it clear to Ross, if they wanted his scripts, they had to have him as well. Elton was from a family of German-Jewish academics who came to Britain to flee Nazism – but being born and brought up in Catford and attending state schools before attending a red-brick university, there was unquestionably a surface divide between Ben and his new colleagues: his south London vowels and rapid-fire patter a marked contrast to their style – but that wasn't a problem. After all, Stephen pointed out, 'Very few of the first wave of Alternative comedians could claim to have got their education from the streets or the school of hard knocks; as an old lag *I* might be said to be the most real and hard of any of them, a thought preposterous enough to show that the idea of there being a group of working-class comics threatening Castle Poncey was really quite misguided.' But despite the dyslexia which often surfaced in his wild writing, where Elton unintentionally pinpointed Fry & Laurie's Achilles heels was in his sheer industriousness as a writer.

'Our slow, mournful and insecure rate of writing had been trumped and trampled on,' Fry wrote. 'For every one page of uncertain and unfinished sketch comedy we held apologetically up for judgement, Ben produced fifty. That is no exaggeration. Where our comedy was etiolated, buttoned-up and embarrassed, his was wild, energetic, colourful and confident to the point of cockiness. While we would read ours out with a sorrowful cough and somehow framed in self-deprecating inverted commas, Ben would perform his, playing every part, with undisguised pleasure and demented relish. Despite our complete sense of humiliation and defeat we did laugh and we did unreservedly admire his astonishing talent and the unabashed zest with which he threw himself into performance.'[8] 'Ben was just a whirlwind,' Laurie confirms, 'he sort of blew us away, really. We had one thing written on the back of an envelope, and Ben would just smack down this forty pounds of quality com.' Emma had it even worse, admitting, 'It was difficult, Ben wrote so much great stuff, and Stephen & Hugh felt a bit drowned out, I think. Trying to get my own monologues in there was like pulling teeth.'

Pre-empting *The League of Gentlemen* by a couple of decades, Ben's disparate material fitted together in one setting – a Didsbury street where the cast of sketch characters could interact. The tall pipe-smoking patrician figure of Fry particularly fascinated him, inspiring the nickname 'Bing', and the crafting of a character who was a prototype General Melchett, Colonel Sodom – a bluff patriarch expertly personified by Stephen, let down by his main characteristic of explosive flatulence. Hugh received shorter shrift as Mr Gannet, a mild-mannered nobody whom Laurie conveyed in a kind of apologetic one-note daze. The character did, however, dovetail nicely with one bit of Fry & Laurie sketch action for the first episode – the first of a long line of losers for Fry to cruelly stamp on:

STEPHEN: Well, I won't mince around the bush any longer, Gannet... what do we pay you these days?
HUGH: Seven and a half thousand.
STEPHEN: Pounds?
HUGH: Yes...
STEPHEN: How would you react to a cut in salary, then?
HUGH: Obviously I wouldn't be too happy about it, but you know, if it's for the good of the firm.
STEPHEN: Yes, so, what would you say to a cut in salary, for the good of the firm, of — a figure from the air — seven and a half thousand pounds a year?
HUGH: Somewhat harsh...[9]

At the conclusion of the episode, Gannet is arrested by WPC Thompson, whose cries of 'Take a look everybody – a police officer arresting a white man. Let's see what Polly bloody Toynbee's got to say about this one' are a perfect example of how astonishingly, perhaps depressingly, contemporary the programme still seems in the twenty-first century. Those first twenty-five minutes passed in a blur of Brut-swigging chauvinist 'Wallies', skin-creeping Christian teenagers and egregiously right-on neighbours, but while the second episode maintained the intent of allowing every sketch to lead naturally onto the next, the Didsbury street was abandoned. Elton created a second standout character for 'Bing', however, in the form of private medic Dr De Quincy, once again treating everyone with patrician disdain, and now charging for every heartless barb.

These attacks on BUPA and their ilk signified surges in political awareness which took hold on long smoky evenings of passionate polemic from Ben in Manchester's Midland Hotel. It was one thing to be uncomfortably aware of white-male-Oxbridge privilege, but even better to use that position to score points on behalf of those who don't belong to any exclusive clubs – particularly in an era when Thatcherites were only just beginning to roll their sleeves up and begin their attacks on British 'society' (which, of course, they insisted did not exist). As a child, Stephen unquestioningly supported his family's Tory activism, and even sent a fan letter to Enoch Powell – but Elton's brand of compassionate humanism was a key part of Fry & Laurie crossing the political floor entirely. The terms 'left' and 'right wing' have always been unhealthy political jargon, which can overwhelmingly be replaced with the terms 'humane' and 'inhumane' – good comedy always naturally tends towards the humane. 'I remember Ben and Stephen sort of morphing into each other,' Plowman says. 'As time went on, Ben started to wear tweed jackets and Stephen became much more right-on, it was interesting, they found new styles and became happier as human beings.'

With the first of the three try-outs heavily Elton-led, the third became the closest thing we have to a prototype *A Bit of Fry & Laurie*, framed as it was by another contemptuous brush with Alan & Bernard – this time displaying their ineptitude at tennis, and with Emma and Paul taking Penny and Tony's places as their long-suffering counterparts. The episode also featured the US courtroom sketch, and the first appearance from an ethnic minority who would become a minor theme in Fry's work – the speakers of the nondescript European language of Strom. This tongue, carefully constructed out of absolute bilge and delivered in flat accents, was a perfect way for Stephen to revel in the most free kind of linguistic music, and the cast were soon able to converse quite freely in the fantasy tongue. Strom's inventor Fry says, 'It was all about a sound that pleased us – one of the rules, a silly one, was that it should always be spoken in a very English intonation and accent, so there wasn't a kind of Balkan or Serbian swing to it.'

The recording of *There's Nothing to Worry About!* was an instructive time for Stephen & Hugh up in Granadaland. Fry's only previous experience of live studio comedy had been attending a Norwich recording of forgotten sitcom *Backs to the Land* as a teenager – but this audience did not seem too keen to volunteer their presence via laughter, which undermined the shows all the more when they were finally broadcast in early summer. No response to this TV sketch debut was more harsh than that of Armitage, a man who at the best of times was described by Stephen as having 'the aspect of a rather cross owl who has just washed his feathers and can't do a thing with them.' Despite the show's reassuring title, the agent complained for weeks that 'a foul-mouthed cockney street urchin with a sewer for a mind' had taken his promising young Footlighters and given them fart gags and leftie jokes to perform – his only comfort was that the ill-received shows would not be seen outside of the North West regions. A proper series was nonetheless commissioned on the strength of the three pilots, but Stephen admitted, 'It was made obvious to us that high up in Granada a problem with our writing had been identified. In the case of Ben it might have been over-productivity and a lack of self-censorship; in the case of Hugh and me it was exactly the opposite – crippling constipation and a kind of apologetic, high-toned embarrassment that must have been excessively irritating.'[10] Plowman is typically diplomatic when he says, 'They worked really slowly as writers, they really crafted what they did.' But grizzled Scots Executive Producer Steve Morrison was more forthright, ordering the young comics to 'Go out and create! I want Ayckbourn with edge!' One scheme was to give the young bunch a week's comedy workshop with Second City stalwart Bernie Sahlins, which proved anathema to everyone: 'Hugh and I were pretty appalled at the idea of "building a scene" through improvisational dialogue in the approved American way. When we wrote together we sometimes did improvise, inasmuch as we made a sketch up out loud as we went along before committing it to paper. I suspect that if we had been accused of improvising we would have frozen in horror midway and would never have been able to continue.'[11]

The full run of six episodes was to be retitled *Alfresco*, in reference to the freedom offered by the latest lightweight recording equipment, normally the preserve of news reporting, which allowed much of each episode to be filmed on location, but that was not the only change – after two years of collaboration, Paul Shearer moved on. 'It was fine,' he insists. 'In terms of the mix of blokes, I was really too similar, and my role, both in that and later on, has been to be the straight man, and they wanted a different mix of sketch performers.'

So the summer of 1982 was to be spent writing as many sketches for a rejigged line-up as they could squeeze between Elton's offerings, Hugh pacing the floor as Stephen tapped away at the keyboard of the brand-new 32K BBC Micro computer he had picked up at the Arndale Centre.

Compact and Bijou: A Commercial Break

BBC Micros did not come cheap, of course, and it was not Noel Gay's job just to guide their talent towards artistic expression, but to make money for them, and from them. A trio of regional comedy pilots was no money-spinner, and both Stephen & Hugh were kept ticking along with extensive loans from Armitage's company – eventually, the debt had to be faced.

Beer turned out to be the initial answer, and both colleagues swallowed pints of it on sets at the same time as they swallowed any pride they may have had in never taking the same shillings as the likes of Lautrec, Welles and Cook, exploiting their value to the not famously savoury advertising industry. Hugh visited the Kestrel brewery, pretending to be a job applicant for the lager's Chief Taster, while Stephen dressed in ridiculous military moustaches to star in an obtusely odd commercial for Whitbread Beer (and in good company too – he first met Tim McInnerny on the same set). A vast expanse of book could now be expended on pontificating about the aeons-old debate, whether St Bill Hicks' hallowed diatribe about any artist who ever does an advert ('You're off the artistic roll call, every word you say is suspect, you're a corporate whore') has ever been more than an entertaining rant, or if he was correct, making the artistic roll call a very short and drab list of names. The fact remains that the £25,000 or thereabouts which entered Fry & Laurie's accounts in those early days allowed them both to breathe sighs of relief and get back to concentrating on laughs. Few of their heroes turned down similar offers, although their new friend Ben made a strong stand against taking any advertising pay cheques, which he would never renege on besides one gratis ad for fairtrade chocolate. He wrote a sketch to conclude the new series in which he played a footballer who was only interested in attracting commercial deals, a satirical point he could make with no moral quandaries, but Stephen & Hugh would never have that level of freedom to mock again. In the years to come the colleagues would appear together and apart in a whole multitude of ad breaks both at home and in any country that asked particularly nicely, unsubtly hinting to viewers that they might like the look of a Polaroid camera, a glass of Schweppes, an Extra Strong Mint (Stephen again moustachioed as a naked Phileas Fogg, powering his balloon with minty breath), a Vauxhall Cavalier, a pint of Heineken (Stephen even appeared in a print campaign as the 'smooth-talking bar steward') or – most obviously – the building society Alliance & Leicester.

This last job came along in 1987, when both Fry and Laurie had more of a profile to cash in on, and could claim some control of how they were to be seen promoting the product. They posited a couple of characters – Hugh as Peter Mostyn, the straight man, who knew that the financial institution in question would see him right, and Stephen as an unnamed preposterous loser ('I don't remember Stephen's character having a name, but why don't we pretend it was Beauregard? No particular reason'), who preferred to bank with competitors 'Sproggit & Sylvester', and always suffered as a result, while blindly sneering at Mostyn's prudence. For several years, this commercial took many forms: a chat at a railway station, a party at which the characters' sisters, nephews and grandfathers (all played by the colleagues) have their own financial issues, a child 'Fry & Laurie' miming to the pair's voices, or perhaps most warmly remembered, the occasion when Mostyn had cause to visit his silly friend's miniscule new home – described by the loser as 'compact and bijou'. Their roles were reversed in a campaign for Panama cigars which launched around the same time, with Stephen this time the smarter of the pair, patronising the simple-minded Hugh to underline the tagline 'Anyone who doesn't buy Panama must have a cigar missing'.

In addition, many comedians pay their mortgages with corporate events which never get thrust into the public's gaze, and Fry & Laurie accepted their fair share, recording special sketches for advertising companies and training firms, and also popping along to the studios of Video Arts, the company set up by John Cleese and Antony Jay in the 1970s which really created the whole world of corporate comedy in the first place, belting out training films which have paid the rent of almost every notable name in British comedy at some point, from Douglas Adams to Ricky Gervais. 'I secretly called the whole project *How To Make Money by Stating the So Fucking Obvious It Makes Your Nose Bleed*', Fry says. 'They were fun films to make, however, and to be around John Cleese, a towering inferno from my early teens, still made me rub my eyes with disbelief.'

These on-screen appearances were only the tiniest tip of the biggest iceberg. It was very early on in Fry & Laurie's careers that they first entered the clandestine world of the recording booth, and made these studios their homes, their kingdoms, their patches. Whole supermarketsful of products would be promoted via the unique vocal cords of Fry & Laurie, be it Hugh's ripping turns as the 'Hunger Monster' for Shreddies, or Stephen's wilfully incongruent intonations for Old El Paso Mexican food. Fry's rich, warm tones have become an inescapable part of the audio world of commercial TV, with Hugh's crisp, puckish delivery no less ubiquitous, and theirs have long been the voices that ad executives yearn to employ for almost any campaign – they could easily have spent every working hour of the last thirty-five years ensconced on the other side of the Plexiglas from directors and company reps, reading copy into a microphone. Both colleagues have a very strong comeback to anyone who sees this line of work as demeaning or in any way unworthy of a couple of great comedians, and coming from such performing perfectionists, it's a tough line to dismiss – they *enjoy* them. The challenge of shaving half a second off a phrase recommending a certain kind of low-calorie spread, while still carrying the same tone of joyful sincerity, was a kind of game which Stephen & Hugh prided themselves on playing at the very highest level. In 1989, Hugh characteristically came clean to the *Independent*, admitting, 'It's an absolute definition of money for old rope, of course. You turn up, drink a cup of coffee, say, "soft, long and very, very strong", and go and buy a shirt with the money.' But Stephen has expanded further: 'Of course one does things just for money, everyone knows when you do a commercial you're not doing it as a statement of personal belief, but if it's a fun film, and you try to choose a commercial that's made by good, nice people and is for a product you'd be perfectly happy to be associated with, obviously you do those in order to earn time to do other things . . . We've never pretended to be so morally pure as to have nothing to do with advertising. If you're on ITV you're as implicated in advertising as if you appear in adverts. It's rather silly to pretend you're not. I have a huge admiration just for the bloody-mindedness of someone like Ben, who has been offered towering sums to make adverts. But he sees it as a kind of obligation to his particular audience not to . . . I know that I am supposed to be ashamed of advertising work and feel that it's either beneath me or some kind of sell-out, but I cannot bring myself to apologise or regret . . . I just find it fun. I don't have that vanity about my image. I will continue to do commercials because they are so enjoyable – not because I need the money, because I don't. Some of them are less good than others, which is a pity, but generally speaking . . . I should do more of it, because the last thing I want is to be this figure of probity, some sort of oracle. Probably all through my life at regular periods I will smash and foul that image, and quite happily go and do something just so people don't say that about me. We weren't put on this Earth to satisfy somebody's tick boxes of what represents respectable or not respectable. I understand some people find doing commercials a bit below one, but I like to be below myself.'

The hows and the whys and the d'you-mind-if-I-don'ts aside, the voiceover work enjoyed by these young bucks, besides making them uneasy bedfellows with the red-brace-wearing 1980s bogeymen (the yuppies, advertising executives and general capitalist lackeys who were espousing their wish to Rule The World, as outlined by Tears For Fears), did not just pay for paisley shirts and shiny new CDs, and large houses, and perhaps some cars . . . but the colleagues' recording careers also gave them their one true neologism. One day, handed a sheet of copy loaded with plosive consonants, Ps and Bs, Hugh ventured to the recording assistant that the bare microphone would need a foam guard to combat explosive sounds, and asked, 'Shouldn't we have a spoffle on for this?' Years later, when a similar problem arose, entirely different technicians quickly volunteered the need for a 'spoffle', to Hugh's amazement. 'Spoffle' is now the industry standard term for a foam pop-shield. Stephen's comparable achievement, cited as the first person to use in print the derogatory term for actors – 'luvvie' – is less of a source of pride, though he does also venture to claim credit for popularising the comedic non-simile, having come up with the drunken Melchett line, 'You twist and turn like a . . . twisty-turny thing!'

Trouser Trouser Trouser!

Paul Shearer's replacement in the sketch show was a logical booking for the notably Scots production – Robbie Coltrane had just begun to carve a place for himself in the world of 1980s comedy, working with Rik Mayall on *A Kick Up the Eighties* and haunting Kevin Turvey spin-off *The Man Behind the Green Door*, and grabbing two key roles in the first ever *Comic Strip Presents* film, *Five Go Mad in Dorset,* into the bargain. A big, brash Glaswegian several years older than Stephen & Hugh, this bullish new element in the team perfectly plucked on their 'toff' complexes, with Fry's only coping mechanism an over-compensatory habit of flirting with Robbie, rubbing legs against his and groaning with ill-received ecstasy. But as ever, outward appearances belied the lack of any need for inverted snobbery – Anthony Robert McMillan was a member of an eminent old Scottish family, educated at the Scottish equivalent of Eton, Glenalmond College, before rebelling, enrolling at art college and naming himself after jazz legend John Coltrane to begin his acting career. Early November 1982 was an epochal period in British comedy – after nearly twenty years as a three-channel nation, Channel 4 was launched to give UK TV a much-needed kick, and there on the first night was Robbie and his Alternative cohorts burying Enid Blyton. One week later, after a tough day filming around and about the streets of Manchester, the cast piled into Stephen's room at the Midland Hotel and saw the first episode of Ben's new sitcom *The Young Ones* broadcast on BBC2 – with a kind of stunned hysteria. Fry's observation – 'When Ade Edmondson as Vyvyan punched his way through the kitchen wall in the opening five minutes it felt as though a whole new generation had punched its way into British cultural life and that nothing would ever be the same again'[12] – could not be seen as exaggeration, and once again, as their series took shape, Fry & Laurie were both aware of fighting a losing battle against the anarchy erupting from the Comic Strip gang.

Alfresco unwisely disposed of the linking narrative concept, and there was less effort put into the segues between sketches – the third episode of seven was even largely composed of footage re-edited from the try-outs, while a few sketches were rerecorded. If anything, it seemed to take longer for the new show to find its way than the first trilogy, and besides some very silly regular items (Elton and Laurie forming a duo as Mr Butcher & Mr Baker, two E. L. Wisty-like Londoners swapping bad puns as they mooch around canals), the resultant shows were stodgy and confusing. The very first item had Hugh in Gannet form trying to buy perfume for his mother, who is actually his grandfather, because he wants to go to bed with them, and bizarrely dark skits like this were blended with historical sequences which had money spent on them, but little comedic power justifying the expense. Elton had a passion for history – his uncle G. E. Elton was one of the most respected historians in Britain – and sketches featuring Restoration fops or the French Resistance seemed great fun to record, but rarely led to a knockout comic idea, and soon cut to some other set-up entirely. Including songs from witty new wave band Squeeze seemed like a boon, but five minutes of Redmond singing a number about nuclear destruction against a backdrop of corpses hanging from trees did nothing to dispel the mood of crushing misery instilled from the grubby and mournful animated opening credits onwards. Fear of WWIII was a definite preoccupation at the time, so it's unsurprising that it was a recurrent theme, but rarely with hilarious results – at least until the series began to warm up, and Fry & Laurie found themselves in a situation which would become familiar: Stephen as the shady government figure coaching Hugh the spy on an operation (in this case, to go over to Russia and steal it, bit by bit, smuggled over to Britain in bin bags). It feels fair to say that the more Fry & Laurie influence there was in each episode, the better *Alfresco* became, and soon tropes familiar from their work began to bristle. Alan & Bernard were their most obvious contributions, the only other regular items in the series (albeit wandering darkly off-model, with Alan claiming to have burned Sue's tongue off with an electric toothbrush, and inviting Bernard to insert fruit up him), but there was also a pastiche of *Tales of the Unexpected*, 'Tales of the Barely Credible' introduced not by

Gelliant Gutfright, but by Coltrane as Orson Welles, featuring Hugh and Emma as a couple called John and Marjorie. Most glaring of all, however, was the first prototype shop sketch which allowed Fry to run totally lunatic linguistic circles around customer Laurie – although Mr Dalliard's predecessor seems to have been a Mr Spanking:

HUGH: Good afternoon, I'd like a pair of trousers.

STEPHEN: A trouser! A trouser for Sir, yes indeed. A fine leg, if I may be so bold, is deservant of a fine trouser – and if Sir will pardon the liberty, so fine a legging as Sir's is rarely met twice in one lifetiming. Spanking. Spanking! A selection of our trouser for Sir.

HUGH: And perhaps a pair of shoes as well.

STEPHEN: Sir will find we rarely part with a trouser but that a gentleman's shoe-ing completes the sale. Spanking! An exhibit of our gentleman's winter shoeing to complement the trouser for Sir.

HUGH: Perhaps not so much winter—

STEPHEN: Ah, oui! With madam our bosom companion and helpmeet for a punt on a summer's even. Spanking! An exhibit of gentlemen's shoeing for the clement clime, with Sir's fine leg and trouser always borne in mind.

HUGH: Mm. As for the colour...

STEPHEN: Sir requires a colouring? A colouring for Sir? Is Sir quite sure? However, Sir is no doubt the best judge of his own leg, and a fine legging it is indeed. Spanking, a mid-season-any-time colouring for Sir's trouser, the trouser for Sir. And Spanking, bear in mind that this must

> consistently reflect upon the quality and
> character of Sir's clement clime shoeing
> for a summering punt of the even with
> madaming... and er, what side does your
> plonker hang?[13]

The punchline may not have been promising, but it was certainly clear that rather than having shot their bolt with their early material, the new sketches Stephen & Hugh were creating together were gaining confidence and a unique flavour of their own all the time.

Sandy Ross had talked his friend John Lloyd into script-editing a couple of episodes, but besides having two ludicrously ambitious shows to launch at the same time – *The Black Adder* and *Spitting Image*, John decided he was wasting his time on the Granada show: 'Script editors have no power at all; you can say, "I know what to do with this, this is too long, this is too clever, this bit is frankly weird. Let me get my teeth into this, I can do this." Sandy's a very nice guy, still friends, but at the end of the day not really a comedy guy, not his manor – it was, "Don't rock the boat, these are stars!" It was probably the greatest sketch show cast ever, and they were so self-certain even as young people, you couldn't change a damn thing! They would sort of band together to defend their work against me, but they didn't really agree amongst each other. They just paid me to turn up.'

This obvious unevenness did not help distinguish *Alfresco* amid the plethora of new comedy shows springing up from the 1980s generation when it aired in the summer of 1983. 'It was pretty much, I won't say a disaster, it was just a sort of damp nothing, didn't really work', Fry feels. Those that reviewed the programme did so briefly and dismissively, and audiences were not much more enthusiastic – ITV would never be the right home for this new generation of comedians. But luckily, despite their growing joint manifestation in the *Alfresco* scripts, Fry & Laurie had a very pleasant meeting at the BBC with a singularly ribald executive called Jim Moir, guaranteeing them their very own pilot – alongside Emma. 'I suppose the BBC were just thinking, you know, "We could take a chance on these two, they're probably not going to spend too much money,"' offers Hugh. 'Which I don't think we did, we used a few wigs, we ran through the wig store, our wig budget was substantial.' They were both paid the eerie fee of £666.66p for writing and performing, John Kilby was back calling the shots as director and producer, and they had agreed on the ideal concept for their breakaway vehicle.

There was nothing especially new about the 'mockumentary' – sketch shows had always lampooned serious broadcasting, but the cogency of the TV spoof Fry & Laurie wanted to present to the world was its greatest strength. They would present *The Crystal Cube*, a kind of uber-patronising *Tomorrow's World* format which allowed them to throw in anything that amused them. It was, Fry explained, 'a mock-serious magazine programme that for each edition would investigate some phenomenon or other: every week we would 'go through the Crystal Cube' . . . We produced our script in what was for us short order but would for Ben have constituted an intolerable writer's block. It was rather good. I feel I can say this as the BBC chose not to commission a series: given that and my archetypical British pride in failure it hardly seems like showing off for me to say that I was pleased with it . . . Aside from technical embarrassments there is also a good deal wrong with it comically. We were awkward, young and often incompetent, but nonetheless there are some perfectly good ideas in it struggling for light and air.' 'We loved *The Crystal Cube*,' Hugh agreed, 'we just thought this was something that no one had ever done before, and there were all kinds of great comic possibilities, as we saw it. The BBC I think hated . . . would that be too big a word? No, I think that was about right, they *loathed* it.'

With the supposed first episode focusing on genetics, Stephen, Hugh and Emma topped the pilot with a monochrome reimagining of *Logan's Run*, the 1976 movie – 'Tomorrow' – preceding a studio-based anchoring of the half-hour complete with Coltrane and Shearer, and a host of supporting eccentrics like John Savident, stealing the show as a facetious bishop. Emma was in Esther Rantzen mode as anchor Jackie Meld, Stephen appeared as Dr Adrian Cowlacey, practising clinician at St Thomas' Hospital, while Hugh furthered his American accent ambitions as Max Belhaven of The Bastard Institute, California:

STEPHEN: Imagine a society divided into three categories, or 'classes', if you like. An upper category of administrators and rulers, a middle category of professional people, and a lower class of workers and manual labourers. A self-perpetuating system, each kept to their own social place. Sounds like some kind of crazy dream, doesn't it? Or does it?

HUGH: Much of what you're about to see has never been seen on television. In particular, we will be showing you the results of a unique human experiment revealed to the public for the very first time. It's all part of genetics, the science of the future — today. Come with us now as we take a look through the Crystal Cube.

TITLES, APPLAUSE

EMMA: The ideas in the film 'Tomorrow' derive almost exclusively from the work of one man, the mid-Victorian scientist, theoretician and, some would say, prophet, Harris Edgeley-Woad. Woad was born and brought up in a working-class home, which his parents had specially built in the grounds of their Gloucestershire estate...[14]

Although this last gag was deemed recyclable a few years later, the concept and execution of *The Crystal Cube* was perhaps better than the quality of the jokes, and the pilot concluded with a human clone running amok, and mass violence — and all was silence, from the BBC. A second stab at *Alfresco* was already under contract, but otherwise this promising try-out spelled the end of the colleagues' association with Thompson as a trio, and perhaps their hopes of ever getting a BBC series.

All three would, on the other hand, manage to perfectly insinuate themselves in the middle of an episode of the hottest sitcom of their generation, and chief provider of inferiority complexes, *The Young Ones* – the second series of which Ben had been busying himself with while travelling up and down to Manchester. One day, chatting in the Granada dressing rooms as the queues amassed outside to be in the audience for *University Challenge*, that arena of Stephen's first TV nightmare, an idea formed. Fry had gained some revenge by stepping into host Bamber Gascoigne's chair for one brief send-up in *Alfresco* series one, but as Ben and Stephen talked (neither are willing to entirely give up credit for the inspiration) the idea arose for Rik, Vyv, Neil and Mike of Scumbag College to appear on Bamber's quiz in the new series. The resultant episode, *Bambi*, almost acts as a fulcrum in the whole history of British comedy, so thickly peopled with comic legends was the recording in the spring of 1984. Griff Rhys Jones played the title role, with Mel Smith not far behind, while Tony Robinson as Dr Not-the-Nine-O'Clock-News struggled with a stampeding elephant, series regular Coltrane as his fellow physician, and the arrival of Ben, Hugh, Stephen and Emma as Scumbag College's inbred rivals 'Footlights College, Oxbridge' could not have been more apposite. Fry wrote that the episode 'Almost made manifest the deep insecurities we had, that we were the snobby public-school types, and they were literally above us and kicked through to us, and it was like a living representation of what they were doing to the old guard.'[15] The colleagues' turns as the insanely privileged Lord Snot and Lord Monty provide a kind of apex of their inverted inferiority complexes, particularly given the presence of series regular Alexei Sayle, the Marxist-Leninist stand-up who portrayed random members of the Balowski family. Despite having featured in the execrable Chris Tarrant series *O.T.T.* and having years of advertising voiceovers ahead of him, Sayle passionately believed that the Comic Strip group were morally superior, their duty being to mock and suppress the Oxbridge set, as they had done in their first series – and he was dismayed to find five of them in on the joke. 'I thought, "These are the enemy!"' Sayle ranted, 'I was out there sawing through the brake cables of Stephen Fry's car, saying "These people are the devil and you're inviting them onto my show!" Of course nobody else knew what I was talking about, you know – "Stephen's lovely! Emma's gorgeous!" I was a twat to go on about it really, but that's how I felt.' 'When I first met him,' Fry wrote of Sayle, 'I was made acutely aware that I represented everything he most despised: public school, Cambridge and, due to that manner that I have never been able to shake off, Establishment . . . I was desperate to be proud of being no class . . . bohemian-class, eternal-student-class, artist-class. I missed all those by a mile and continue to this day to reek more of the Garrick Club than the Groucho Club, but that has never stopped me trying, in my doomed, futile and pointless way, to be free.'[16] Potential unrest was averted by Sayle only having one very separate scene as a biscuit-oriented train driver, and *Bambi* went on to become one of the most fondly remembered comedy half-hours of the decade. This waltz into the lion's den marked a rite of passage for Fry & Laurie, giving them firm footholds with the coolest comedians of their generation, and proving that they could hold their own against the best.

Incidentally, the late summer of 1983 saw another epochal moment for Fry, when the movie *WarGames* was released – in one key scene, the aerospace scientist McKittrick, played by Dabney Coleman, fumes at a disdainful General Beringer, 'I don't have to take that, *you pig-eyed sack of shit*!' This term of abuse utterly captivated Stephen, and it would become almost a motif in his work.

Everything Bright and Breezy

Not all Stephen & Hugh's early exploits paid off – one which heavily involved them both was a film, *Gossip*, which could have signalled different career directions from the off, had it not been a criminal disaster. As early as the summer of 1982, Fry had been deemed a writer trustworthy enough to rework and anglicise an existing screenplay, a romantic satire of early Thatcherite yuppiedom, and Hugh was to have a supporting role. However, despite a quarter of the script being filmed, dud financing from a shady foundation based in Lichtenstein spelled disaster when no payment materialised, and the production was closed down, to the dismay of producer/director Don Boyd.

It was immediately clear, as Fry & Laurie embarked on their media careers, that there was a gulf between the two friends' abilities to say 'no'. Stephen's credits as a writer and actor, in print, radio and television, soon began to mount up with ferocity, in stark contrast to Hugh's modestly expanding portfolio, although *Alfresco*'s second outing needed compiling – which makes Fry's output even more impressive, perhaps even 'Eltonian'. It may not be inconsequential that this ballooning of work from Fry came as he set up life on his own, amicably taking leave of Kim and his new chap in Chelsea for the solo life in Bloomsbury. Stephen has written about how the gay scene of the time was anathema to him, with its body fascism and strobing clubs heaving with sweaty bodies and thudding music, and once he was back to his bachelor ways, he concluded, 'All you need know is that I, my 128 kilobyte Macintosh, ImageWriter bitmap printer and small collection of floppy disks were all very, very happy together. What possible need could I have for sex or human relationships when I had this?'[17]

This mention of abstention from the pleasures of the groin alludes to the most infamous cliché for journalists to use as a hook on this saturnine young upstart-cum-throwback for years to come. The admission arose from Fry's bountiful articles, features and reviews which slid neatly into newspapers and magazines week after week – lost titles like *The Listener*, *Tatler* (for which he even took a salaried role as a kind of coverline pun editor), and by the end of the decade, despite the Tory bent, the *Telegraph*. Both colleagues admitted a soft spot for that periodical, but Fry made his political position clear, in print: 'It's not as if I have rejected, along with Conservative loyalties, all the other characteristics of my caste. I retain a love of country that, while not jingoistic, a cruel man might call sentimental; I remain as emotionally reserved and spiritually constipated as any proud Briton; I share a love of sport, the countryside, pageant and all the tweed, twaddle and tweeness that one associates with traditional England . . . I have no quarrels with foxhunting, Ascot, the monarchy or Bernard Manning; I prefer the *Daily Telegraph* to the *Independent* and I go a bit funny when I think of Churchill . . . I do however draw the line at the Conservative Party.'[18] Hugh did once pen an amusing item on the Henley Regatta for the *Telegraph,* and enjoyed it so much he wrote another one for them on Wodehouse fifteen years later, but Stephen rather outpaced him. Fry's most memorable article, commissioned by Jonathan Meades for *Tatler*, was on the subject of 'Things I Do Not Do', and he happily elected to share his new-found abandonment of what he termed 'rogering blindly away all the time' in an entertainingly immature cascade of revolted prudery about those 'tufted areas', which would haunt him beyond the decade. Being asked about his stance on sex was as much of a bore as hacks' tiresome overuse of the adjective 'tweedy' (even when Stephen joined Hugh in a short-lived love for motorbiking, with attendant leathers and macho aftershave). But despite his eventual exhaustion with the subject, from 1982, for a period of fourteen years, Stephen maintained his celibacy. He was married to the Mac – and, indeed, to Hugh.

Fry's love affair with print rapidly palled, and reviewing books (often under a variety of pseudonyms) proved a particularly painful job, the role of 'The Critic' being ultimately anathema to his artistic spirit. Eventually, with trademark candidness, he would groan, of the press: 'It's like opening a piece of used lavatory paper reading newspapers, just so unpleasant, the *smell* . . . I would hate to do it myself and I hate reading other people doing it . . . I absolutely agree one hundred per cent that it has to be done, but I can't bear the sight of it. I just find it so demeaning. I mean, professionally, to pick up a pen and make someone cry.'[19] On one level, Stephen still clamoured for more fame, but growing the thickness of skin required to live in peace with the critics remained a mountain to climb.

It was, however, his prowess at the word processor that landed Fry with the true plum job of this period. Richard Armitage had a particular soft spot for his young polymath, and invited Stephen to his grand Essex country pile one weekend, with a sensitive but sensational offer. Nearly fifty years earlier, 'Noel Gay' had enjoyed a rollicking hit with the vaguely Wodehousian musical caper *Me and My Girl*, which led to a film and screwed songs like 'The Lambeth Walk' and 'The Sun Has Got His Hat On' into the national consciousness. It told the tale of cockney barrow boy Bill Snibson, who is identified as the heir to the Earl of Hareford and has to balance the need to live up to the snobbish expectations of his aristocratic family with his love for cockney sparrow Sally Smith – and as a period piece, it stood up well enough. But Armitage wanted to revive his father's musical with a sharper new book and modern stage techniques, and make it a hit all over again. Stephen would be the one, alongside director Mike Ockrent, to make Bill and

Sally's zingers zing anew. Very little hesitation was shown before his acceptance, and he started work almost immediately.

Fry was not only at home in the opulence of Armitage's grounds, he had also been spending an increasing amount of time with stablemate Rowan – the two were working on a rudimentary Mr Bean movie that would never see the light of day, and Stephen would accompany his senior comic on what the latter termed 'bank raids' – performing comedy for ex-pats in the Middle East for astonishing rewards – though Fry insists for him, the pleasure was all in partnering such a comedy titan: 'I was the famous other man in his "one-man show", like Angus Deayton or Richard Curtis. So I'd be the blind man on the beach and various other characters, plus I'd have the chance to do my *Dracula* monologue or a few other things, so I had my little moment. But it was fantastic fun; I just love Rowan's company.' In these early days, Stephen had goggled at the riches Rowan's rubber face had brought him – and the *fame*, which made a walk through London together almost impossible, Stephen never being the public draw.

He tapped away at a faithful but fresh script for his agent – expunging the regrettable instance of the word 'niggers' here, adding extra Gay numbers such as 'Leaning on a Lamp-post' there, and generally slipping in a new line in quality innuendo:

JAQUIE: I thought we might meet this morning, as Mummy said I should take you in hand. To teach you about art and literature and life. Are you familiar with any of our great novelists? Dickens? Thackeray? Do you like Kipling?
BILL: I don't know, I've never kippled.
JAQUIE: Bill, you and I are soulmates, I can look deep into your eyes and see what you're thinking.
BILL: Then why don't you slap my face?
JAQUIE: I'm on a ship with you – sailing away. I'm abroad.
BILL: You're telling me!

JAQUIE:	Italy! Beautiful Florence. Just we two making love.
BILL:	What, you and Florence?
JAQUIE:	You kiss me on the piazza.
BILL:	I never do![20]

But it was impossible for Fry to guess that *Me and My Girl* would be the job that would give him that lifestyle he had hitherto only experienced as an admiring guest. Emma Thompson partnered with Robert Lindsay as the musical spread joy from the West End to Broadway – although she shook off Sally before the transfer, admitting, 'I thought if I did the fucking Lambeth Walk one more time I was going to fucking throw up.' Stephen would, however, benefit from going along for the ride, falling in love with New York, and, as the money kept coming in from hit productions all around the world, he could even afford an apartment there. It would be tacky to specify a figure, but as an estimate, the international income from the musical would at one point bring the writer a weekly income equivalent even today to three or four reasonable annual wages, and by the time he hit thirty, it would be safe to describe Fry as 'financially arrived', in a decade of Mammon.

If You Have Been . . .

The musical reboot did not open until 1985, and of course, before it could happen, there was another helping of *Alfresco* to go out, in the spring of 1984, up against not just *The Young Ones'* finest half-hours, but airing on Saturday nights at 11 p.m. opposite Fry & Laurie's Footlights forebears, Jimmy Mulville, Rory McGrath and others, in *Who Dares Wins* on Channel 4. But, never was a show more changed, third time lucky. Over the autumn and winter Ben, Stephen & Hugh formalised equal credit for the scripts, with Emma providing 'additional material' – and, along with the rest of the cast and new producer John Temple, a completely fresh format was hammered out. There would still be regular blocks of sketches recorded 'al fresco', and Fry & Laurie's evolving style would be evident in many of them, including sketches in which Stephen's walrus-faced officer dares Hugh's gritty adventurer to undertake a suicide mission, duelling Regency dandies, librarians who give away the endings to all books (including WWII non-fiction), a game show presented by Stephen that challenged contestants not to say the word 'bottom', and one item in which Hugh showed a particular flair for portraying a cold-hearted German, when two Gestapo figures storm into Stephen and Siobhan's bedroom:

HUGH: Ah, I see that we share a taste in pictures! You are fond of Matisse?
STEPHEN: Look, who are you, what do you want?
HUGH: Such courageous strokes of the brush. Courageous and yet... cunning. What were you doing, please, at 8:30 yesterday morning?
STEPHEN: I was having breakfast.
HUGH: Lie number one! Mott?
ROBBIE: You finished your breakfast at 8:26, and you left the house at 8:27...
STEPHEN: The newsagent's! I stopped off at the newsagent's!
HUGH: Ah! The newsagent's. News. Agents. And what did you purchase at the newsagent's, Mr Ram, was it twenty filtered tippings perhaps, or a bar of nourishing nougat covered in thick, thick chocolate? No, I think not...
STEPHEN: Um, I can't remember.
HUGH: Come, come, Mr Ram, don't play games with me. I'm not very good at them...[21]

The sketch becomes a spoof of a then-popularly-annoying commercial for the *Guardian*, the victims tortured into explaining why they buy the newspaper. There were, however, fewer sketches this time, to allow for a new framework, positively a sitcom in itself, with the cast playing distorted versions of themselves to represent British society in a *Beano*-inspired comic world where they hang out in a 'Pretend Pub'. With the Scottish contingent behind the bar, Bobzza the management, Siozza the rebellious worker, Bezza made his inferiority complex manifest as the flat-cap-raising proletariat, under the heel of the posh set, Ezza the ditzy Sloane ranger, Lord Stezza the 'Snooty'-ish kindly aristocrat, and Laurie as Huzza, the bitter middle-class Tory, whose constant anger erupted in perfectly wrought lines, blisteringly delivered: 'I suppose you think it's somehow amusing to go around saying things that are funny . . .'

Above all, this format for typical comic scrapes (such as the Pretend Pub being slated for destruction so that Thatcher could spell out 'MAGGIE IS MAGIC' in motorways, and the gang always trying to appease their sinister unseen boss, Dr Network) was an exercise in deliberately paper-thin artifice, as the name of the pub suggested, with cartoony make-up scrawled on the cast, deliberately incorrect special effects, and plots constantly undermined by the performers pre-empting punchlines and commenting on the script. Maybe the cocktail of clashing concepts seemed to be overdoing things somewhat, but *Alfresco* series two certainly achieved a uniquely post-modern sense of anarchy. In the final episode, Lord Stezza jeopardised the show's future by apparently accepting the role of James Bond from his friend 'Tubby Brussels Sprout', leading Huzza to wrongly proclaim, 'Well everybody, this is it. The end of our careers!' By this finale it really did feel, at last, that a workable vehicle had been found for this mix of young comics, and the audiences were volubly loving it . . . just as the team reached the end of the road.

If it wasn't for their subsequent stellar successes, *Alfresco* would be forgotten now, although Jon Plowman notes, 'It is still to be found on some of the cheaper airlines!' There was a slight fillip for Redmond and Shearer when they bagged roles supporting Robert Lindsay in dystopian radio comedy *Nineteen-Ninety-Four*, produced in Manchester by Nick Symons and with Hugh and Stephen providing back-up silly voices as a favour to Nick, while Emma of course also joined Lindsay and was swept up in a musical whirl of success, Robbie had greater roles ahead of him, and as for Ben, nobody had more irons in the fire.

In particular, Elton wanted to expand *Alfresco* into a totally different sitcom style, offering *Young Ones* producer Paul Jackson a new challenge in lieu of series three. Despite the talent-packed cast typical of Jackson's work, *Happy Families* remains one of the BBC's most criminally underrated comedies, dark and filmic long before its time, and it remains unfairly unreleased in any form. Ben envisaged an episodic narrative designed as a vehicle for Thompson's versatility, casting her as a whole family of characters in a kind of gender-switched *Kind Hearts and Coronets*. Emma's West End commitments led to Jackson rightly insisting that Jennifer Saunders could be equally versatile, embodying all the female members of the Fuddle family, but one vestige of *Alfresco* remained – the return of the blithely offensive omnisexual bastard Dr De Quincy – now a country GP who diagnoses the Fuddle matriarch with a terminal disease requiring her grandson, obnoxious hero Guy (Saunders' new husband Ade Edmondson), to travel the world bringing his sisters home. Stephen featured in every episode, but Hugh only popped up twice as Jim, the doctor's live-in 'friend', fellow doctor and misogynist. Although their relationship is never spelled out, this does have the distinction of being the only time Fry & Laurie played a same-sex couple, endearingly referring to each other as 'pimple' and 'plumplops' – but it was a minor role for Hugh in a series cast with an embarrassment of riches.

Nonetheless, as filming proceeded in the idyllic Staffordshire village of Denstone, near the heaving metropolis of Uttoxeter, the chemistry between the pair stood out enough for Jackson to approach with an utterly terrifying offer of regular work on a new TV show which would debut at the end of the year – an offer which required a great deal of mulling over. Hugh had of course made his live TV comedy debut at nineteen, but the idea of being resident double act on the planned Channel 4 show, *Saturday Live,* hit them both as something of a watershed for their 'act': 'We conferred nervously with each other in the bar that evening,' Stephen wrote. 'The new world of youthful stand-up comedy was going to be represented on this "edgy", "alternative" and "ground-breaking" show . . . Hugh and I wondered if we would stick out like sore and inappropriately tweedy thumbs. Despite our characteristic fears and forebodings we decided that we should do the show. In the end, somewhere at the bottom of our churning wells of nonsense we knew that we could and should do comedy together. It was a kind of destiny.'[22] 'Doing what we do, which is vaguely creative, it has to be so personal and I couldn't imagine doing it with someone I didn't like or I wasn't friends with,' Hugh says. 'It would be so inhibiting. There's a lot of trust involved. The key to relaxation is you have to feel completely at ease. I don't think we've ever had a serious disagreement about the things that we do together. We sulk a bit, very rarely, but we never argue. Partly that's because we're scared of arguments. We each spend so much time running ourselves down that it would be pointless having the other person do it too.' As their careers brought them closer together, so they moved closer together too, finding an old house in Camden to share with Katie and Nick Symons. Stephen wrote, 'It looked, to Hugh's approving eye, like the kind of house the Rolling Stones might have rented in 1968.'

Meantime, there was more to life than TV, and as with print, Hugh certainly dabbled when it came to radio. Besides *Nineteen-Ninety-Four*, in the busy year of 1985 there was a role in Simon Brett's Radio 2 thriller *So Much Blood*, plus two years later he joined an extraordinary line-up including Morwenna Banks and Rory Bremner for Moray Hunter's weird political series *The Party Party*, around the time both colleagues popped up in sequel *Nineteen-Ninety-Eight*. But to offer a similarly comprehensive list of Fry's radio credits just for the 1980s would see us through to the index. Of any medium, it is the entirely aural/cerebral universe of Radio 4 where Stephen has perhaps seemed the most native. 'My voice, I think, owes more to the BBC microphone and the dusty, slow-to-warm-up Mullard valve than to the accents and tones of my family, friends and school fellows,' he says. 'I believed from the earliest age that I would be quite content to work in radio all my life. If I could just be a continuity announcer or regular broadcaster of some kind, how happy I would be. My dislike of my facial features and physical form contributed to this ambition. I had, as the tired old joke goes, a good face for radio.'

His earlier reticence in front of a live mike quickly dispelled, one of Fry's first audio jobs was for Radio 1, of all incongruously funky media. There was a time when the station broadcast more than just the current chart hits, and comedy was once a cornerstone of their output. David 'Kid' Jensen helmed a regular magazine show named *B15* after the number of the studio in the bowels of BBC Broadcasting House, and very early in 1982 Fry was hired to create a spoof of the station's news strand *Newsbeat* called *Beatnews*. This he did in the guise of Bevis Marchant, a strident reporter who was in his element bombastically covering the Falklands War, which began only a few weeks into his time on the show – and only lasted a few more weeks, as letters pelted in complaining about this young upstart's mockery of the hostilities. There were, however, a couple of students out there who had been hooked to Marchant's media satire: Chris Morris and Armando Iannucci, who would credit Fry's inspiration in this, and other radio projects, when they created *On The Hour* a decade later. Besides becoming something of a satirical go-to for the BBC (he played a Johnson-esque figure on *Newsnight* for the 1982 General Election, in a monologue about 'the great choosing'), two years after *Beatnews* Fry would have more satirical radio success as another media-satirising mock presenter – David Lander, the voice of Radio 4's *Delve Special,* created by Tony Sarchet. Roger Cook had launched the radio investigative reporting show *Checkpoint* in 1971, and Lander was a direct pastiche of the crusading journalist, risking regular beatings by delving into a variety of criminal activities. Alongside some of the hottest new names in comedy, including Harry Enfield, Dawn French and Tony Robinson, over three years Fry played Lander as straight as possible, supporting the naturalistic approach, and when Roger Cook moved to TV, David Lander was to follow in 1988 – *This Is David Lander* airing on Channel 4 after the BBC's factual department turned it down. 'I don't think Lander's nasty exactly,' he said at the time. 'He's just so steeped in the lore of being an investigative journalist: he's presumably trained at the BBC in some kind of training scheme, watched various television interviewers, believes in it and is humourless, essentially because he's so concerned with it and believes he's a crusader of some kind. There's a pomposity about him, and also a condescending quality, which snaps neatly into my character.'

Stephen's brief sojourn on the BBC's pop station had also attracted the attention of Radio 4 producer Ian Gardhouse, right-hand man of *TW3* titan Ned Sherrin, who had carte blanche to create a series of magazine shows for the world's greatest spoken-word station. Soon Fry's was a regular voice on programmes with names like *Late Night Sherrin, And So To Ned, Extra Dry Sherrin* and *The Colour Supplement,* which coalesced into the still-running *Loose Ends,* in 1986. 'Each week I performed a kind of monologue as a different character: an estate agent, an architect, a journalist – I cannot remember the whole gallery. Their surnames usually came from Norfolk villages, so I do recall a

Simon Mulbarton, a Sandy Crimplesham and a Gerald Clenchwarton.' As the most comfortable of the young Turks around Ned's green baize table, Fry got through a lot of material, so his greatest creation would be suggested to him by Gardhouse – a fusty old academic challenged to sit through an evening of modern TV: 'I tapped away that Friday afternoon and came in the next day with a piece written in the persona of a Professor Donald Trefusis, extraordinary Fellow of St Matthew's College, Cambridge, philologist and holder of the Regius Chair of Comparative Linguistics . . . Trefusis' age and perceived wisdom and authority allowed me to be ruder and more savagely satirical than I could ever have been in my own vocal persona. The British are like that, especially the middle-class Radio 4 audience: a young snappy, angry person annoys them, and they shout at the radio for him to show some respect and get the spiritual and intellectual equivalent of a haircut. But let the same sentiments exactly, word for word, be uttered in high academic tones . . . and they will roll on to their tummies and purr. For the next four or five years I fed *Loose Ends* on an almost exclusive diet of Trefusis.'[23] It would be crass to pinpoint any one inspiration for the great philologist, though Stephen ventures, 'He was a composite of people real and not, but I guess there is Tony Spearing, the English fellow and Medievalist – very precise, sweet and smiling, with sudden bursts of wisdom. He used a very extraordinary tense – a modal future conditional, as an imperative, so instead of "shut up!" he'd say, "you will be shutting up?" or "you will be providing the essay tomorrow, I believe?" which meant that you *will*. He seemed like a font of wisdom, but also had eccentricity and an anti-establishment contrarianism that I liked. But there's also an unquestionable level of fantasy with Trefusis, a kind of academic father I dreamt of having – a bright, cheerful, festive figure.' The other returning character, a one-time near-lover of the Professor and a great favourite of Sherrin, was Fry's vocal dragging up as Rosina, Lady Madding, 'a kind of crazed old Diana Cooper figure' – but Trefusis would remain Stephen's most faithful alter ego even beyond Ned's radio sphere. To this day, Fry says, 'I think there is nothing more appealing than that type, in everything from Father Brown to Doctor Who – the eccentric older person who still has a spring and a kind of irreverence, but a deep wisdom about them.'

While wireless is the theme, one key element of the Fry persona we have barely touched on is his hot-blooded passion for games, as a proud member of the species *homo ludens* – he even presented a radio documentary on gamesmanship in 2003. It seems astonishing that the linguistic battleground of *Just a Minute* saw no effort from Fry until as late as 1992, but besides a whole array of forgotten programmes of wireless gamesmanship, Stephen lucked his way onto the real jewel of Radio 4's panel game slot, *I'm Sorry I Haven't a Clue*, at the tender age of 29, filling in for an indisposed Barry Cryer, which made him then the youngest contestant by far – and he is still a cherished part of the extended *Clue* family. But although *Clue* is the ultimate antidote to panel games, on radio and TV, Stephen was soon proving himself among the cream of contestants on the real thing, and he began to tick off the titles of every major quiz that could slot into his personal organiser. Hugh's few panel game appearances over the decades have, comparably, borne some element of the poor chap being hounded behind a desk with a cattle-prod, which is a shame, as his natural wit generally proved worth the booking.

Lapdogs to a Slip of a Girl

The preceding whistle-stop early career summaries may have given the impression of Hugh sitting at home twiddling his thumbs, but his work rate was perfectly natural for a young actor and comedian – it was Stephen's work ethic that was remarkable, so delighted was he to be in such demand and finding it difficult to turn any offer down, having found a legal way to fill his wallet with credit cards. In an interview with *GQ*, Laurie mused, 'The biggest difference between us is that Stephen can duel and I can't. I dread any competitiveness. I find it completely inhibiting. Stephen's fine with that, he can perform under pressure.' To which Fry suggested, 'I think I'm rather more of a lion, circa 20 or 30 AD. When Christians were in plentiful supply. I've always thought he was a panda, probably because he's not naturally aggressive.' 'Stephen is really better at putting himself about, agreeing to put himself in the firing line,' his colleague concurred. 'My reaction is always to say, "No, don't do it, you're mad, people will tear you to bits, or they'll think such-and-such about you!" He is much more open. He thinks, "Well that's too bad, but I'll do it anyway."'

Perhaps this was the spirit that saw Fry alone rejoining Slattery and Shearer in an ITV documentary in 1983 to mark the Footlights' centenary, recreating corny Cambridge material which involved not only miming to 'Cheer Oh, Cambridge', but *actually dancing*. Besides dominating in print, radio and TV, Stephen had not relented his first avowed intent to be an actor, and theatre remained another medium which meant the world to him. In 1983 the Lyric had staged a new production of *Latin!* starring Simon Russell-Beale as Dominic, and the year after, Stephen was back onstage also playing a schoolmaster, paying his own tribute to Alan Bennett's original characterisation of Tempest in his 1968 play *Forty Years On* – although Stephen may not have landed the role if his playwright hero hadn't respected his jitters by hiding under the seats in the stalls for the duration of his audition.

With that long run over and *Happy Families* in the can, Fry was to receive another irresistible offer of work, once again from Elton. He invited the by-then-infamous Thatch-basher to not just any of the myriad ancient London clubs which approved of his respectable aura, but the Carlton Club, the very heart of Tory connivance. As a snarling Lord Hailsham earwigged, these 'two Jewish comics pretending to be *flâneurs* of the old school', as Fry had it, conferred on Ben's new stroke of luck – taking over from Rowan as Richard Curtis's co-writer on the finally greenlit second series of *The Black Adder*. From Armitage's point of view, Ben had managed not only to besmirch the promising sketch careers of his young Footlighters, he was now moving in on his prize clown's turf. Stephen, however, was so firmly in his agent's good books with the sterling work on his father's musical, he was able to reassure him that Elton, with his historical obsessions and love of wordplay, would only strengthen the Atkinson vehicle – a programme Fry had viewed with disappointment in its eccentric first series. Elton had loved the medieval sitcom, however, and when he met Curtis at a *Spitting Image* writers' meeting under the approving eye of John Lloyd, their mutual appreciation turned the corner for what would become the greatest sitcom in British history. Their first four scripts are still considered by Lloyd to be the best he's ever read.

With the Elizabethan period selected for its familiarity and sexiness, Ben was quick to repay his pal Bing's support with a plum role –

the dashing anti-hero's nemesis, a Lord Burghley figure – 'all forked beard, forked tongue and fur-lined cloak' – rival for the Virgin Queen's attentions. Lord Melchett was as written to measure for Fry as Dr De Quincy had been, and despite being younger than the star of the show at the age of 28, the pervy old sheep-with-fangs he brought to life became an eminent part of the chemistry of the cosy Family Regina, amusingly stuffed into the smallest throne room in TV history. While rehearsing and recording these six half-hours, slowly learning the extent to which producer Lloyd was keen for the cast to tinker with the writers' text, Stephen was to gain a close-up masterclass on comedy from two friends.

Rik Mayall had already made an explosive cameo in the first series, and Stephen & Hugh had mingled extensively with Mayall and Atkinson the previous summer, when the Hampshire village of Nether Wallop attempted to stage an eccentric arts festival to rival Edinburgh, which was televised as *Weekend In Wallop*. Musicians like Bill Wyman and Squeeze pianist Jools Holland had mixed with actors Michael Hordern and Jenny Agutter, Stephen & Hugh threw in the 'Shakespeare Masterclass', an inebriated Lloyd, Peter Cook and Mel Smith worked out an act for the latter pair as a brace of raving lesbian synchronised swimmers, Rowan performed his Geordie football coach monologue, Rik gave a special Kevin Turvey lecture, and Billy Connolly closed the show.

Stephen's comedic inferiority complex took a surprising turn when placed between the parallel supernovae of Rowan and Rik – the latter an explosion of balls-out confident swagger, the former quiet and exacting, 'as if his comedy comes out of him like . . . some excrescence that is not of his personality, but an extra limb that he has, that no one else has, and it's phenomenal to watch. I would never say one was greater than the other.' Fry claimed to have just modestly stood back and marvelled, particularly with Miranda Richardson at his elbow giving a career best performance as a firecracker Queen Bess, but the creaky, creepy character of Lord Melchett remained an indispensable part of the fresh chemistry. During filming, Stephen also claimed to have developed a crush on make-up artist Sunetra Sastry, but he shook off this rare dose of heteronormativity and allowed the star of the show to move in – becoming Best Man at Sunetra and Rowan's wedding a few years later.

And as for Hugh? By the final episode of *Blackadder II*, 'Chains', recorded in July 1985, he got his own tailored show-stealing character – Prince Ludwig the Indestructible, a villainous German in a period where Spain was Britain's greatest enemy. The surprise of this psychotic guest appearance was slightly lessened by his stepping in for a small role in the previous episode, 'Beer', as Simon Partridge, one of Blackadder's boozy party guests, but this double appearance instantly marked Hugh out as a special member of the exclusive *Blackadder* club. 'I had the strong feeling at the time that someone had backed out at the last minute . . . But of course it was thrilling, because by that time Stephen had been doing the second series, Melchetting and all that stuff, and I had pangs of jealousy! And it was a real thrill to get a ticket onto that ocean liner . . . It was something of a feather in the cap to play two separate characters in the same series, so I was more than delighted.'

Blackadder II debuted on 9 January 1986, with a relatively approving reception from critics and viewers alike, but when the series was repeated at the end of summer the following year, presaging Blackadder's third incarnation, audiences and approval ratings began to positively soar. By this time, Stephen & Hugh had of course found more ways to present themselves before the nation's comedy connoisseurs. Youthful British comedy in the 1980s was essentially swayed by two great producers – Lloyd on one side, with his painstakingly crafted and exclusively cast productions, and on the other, Paul Jackson – not an Oxbridge man, but with TV in his blood, having worked his way up from assistant floor manager to helming shows including *The Two Ronnies,* before becoming the man to bring the Comic Strip generation to the nation's TVs. Jackson's productions famously gave exposure to the widest array of young comics imaginable, but his new scheme for Channel 4 would be unrivalled as a springboard for burgeoning talent. *Saturday Live* very consciously took inspiration from US show *Saturday Night Live*, with a different guest host each week in its first series, and regular sketch performers, which included Rik & Ade with the latest evolution of their double act, The Dangerous Brothers, and 'The Wow Show' – Stephen Frost, Mark Arden, Lee Cornes and Mark Elliott. Jackson knew Fry & Laurie would be a crucial addition to this roster, but this was still, for them, the ultimate step forward: the first time their exclusive ampersand-linked duo would be foisted onto the public – and completely live, to boot.

You can forgive the pair for fretting that another double act wasn't particularly what British comedy needed at the time. Morecambe & Wise were the nation's favourite duo, but Eric's death in 1984 had ended that era, while Ronnie Barker was only a couple of years away from retiring, removing the Two Ronnies from circulation. Mainstream fare came courtesy of Little & Large and Cannon & Ball, while the new wave boasted Rik & Ade, of course, Arden & Frost as The Oblivion Boys and Gareth Hale & Norman Pace, two ex-teachers who were about to reap great rewards with their own saucy sketch show on ITV (before facing the oblivion that came with the cultural amnesia that curses nearly all ITV comedy). Far out in the field were Mel Smith & Griff Rhys Jones, whose spin-off series *Alas Smith & Jones* was already on its third outing, but their model of show business was not to Fry & Laurie's taste. Smith & Jones' show supported a great many talented comedy writers, and their new independent production company Talkback supported a great many more, including Stephen & Hugh, who were not averse to recording the odd radio advert for them. When Mel & Griff realised there was money to be made from owning the means of production for their adverts, they created Talkback, sparking a trend for comedians to set themselves up in business which eventually revolutionised the comedy industry, spawning companies like Hat Trick, Tiger Aspect and many more. Stephen told one journalist, 'We've always rather fought against the – naming no names – Griff Rhys Jones & Mel Smith style of corporate comedy, with a huge office and grey carpetry and cappuccino machines . . . it's not for us. The one thing we didn't want was a regular job and an office to go to.' Fry & Laurie's closest double act contemporaries were Dawn French & Jennifer Saunders, who had taken on a considerable amount of the burden of blazing trails for women comedians among the right-on but still male-dominated Comic Strip set; the two pairings were to work together regularly over the years – one of Hugh's first solo comedy outings was a guest spot in series two of *Girls On Top*, playing poor Tom, the unsuspecting object of radical loser French's lust.

Saturday Live was designed as a bear pit, with Elton as warm-up and regular satirical ranter, Jackson in the control room, and Geoff Posner keeping everything together on a studio floor filled with fairground rides, giant inflatables and hordes of achingly cool kids with regrettable hairdos – while the stages would see a stream of stand-ups, bands and novelty acts trying their best to hold the hepped-up crowd's attention. As the scope of Jackson's plans became clear, and despite Hugh's live TV experience, Stephen and he knew they had their work cut out to take their place among this gaggle of duos: 'Hugh was convinced that they were more interested in how their hair looked on screen than in anything we might be saying or doing to try and amuse them.'

'The problem with being a duo rather than a solo performer is that you speak to each other, rather than out front to the audience,' Fry wrote. 'We had in the past written a certain number of sketches, the "Shakespeare Masterclass" for example, in which the audience could be directly addressed, but for much of our time we played characters locked in mini-dramas with a fourth wall between us and the watching world.'[24] The friends made a decision to try out their sketches in the most honest environment they could find which, several years after the launch of The Comedy Store, turned out to be the Jongleurs club in Clapham. Having been impressed by the daring of a young Julian Clary, the tweed-bedecked duo did their best to sell their sketches in their allotted time before the headliner – Lenny Henry – stepped up to the mike. 'When Hugh & I left the stage after our fifteen minutes and puffed out our usual "Christ they hated us" (Hugh) and "It wasn't so bad" (me), we stayed back to watch Lenny. I remember thinking how wonderful it must be to be known and loved by an audience. All your work is done before you go onstage . . . That night at Jongleurs we sweated blood as we treated the audience to our exquisitely wrought phrases, cunning jokes and deft characterisations, only to be rewarded with vague titters and polite but sporadic applause. Lenny came on, did a bird call, boomed a hello and the building almost collapsed . . . He was relaxed and he made the audience relax. Hugh and I might have hidden our nerves and anxiety as best we could, but from the beginning we were working the audience rather than welcoming them with any confidence into our world. A tense audience might admire our writing and performing, but they are never going to give us the great rolling waves of love they sent out to Lenny. Later, when we were familiar figures and went onstage to gusts of welcome, I would remember that night at Clapless Clapham, as I always thought of it, and thank my lucky stars that I no longer had to prove myself in quite the same way.'[25]

Lenny would play a similar blinder as the very first host of *Saturday Live* when it was piloted in December 1985, with further presenters as memorable or incongruous as Peter Cook, Tracey Ullman and Michael Barrymore. Besides a few items which would quickly bite the dust, like weekly soap opera spoof 'Rich', a few filmed inserts slightly lowered the pressure for performers and crew – The Dangerous Brothers' stunts generally required pre-records, while a *Beverly Hills Cop* parody featured Hugh's take on a Steven Berkoff villain. Otherwise, and always for Stephen & Hugh, it was a case of flying by the seat of numerous pants. 'By about Wednesday we were sweating blood,' Fry says, 'by Thursday we were vomiting, by Friday our bowels were completely loose, and by Saturday we were just simply barely alive.' Ben would wander round using his unique brand of curtailed slang, fretting that this week the team were in 'DHT' (Deep Humiliating Troub'), but of any comic present, the effect on Hugh seemed the most marked. Everyone was nervous, but Hugh's deep humility manifested itself as the darkest, most hopeless pit of despair, barely ameliorated by his partner's chivvying, but resulting in a singular obsession with getting every beat right when it was their time in the spotlight. There were live flubs to be ridden, of course, and extra laughs to be gained from dealing with mistakes, but Hugh wanted the barest minimum left to chance.

No matter how loud and obnoxious the crowds were, Fry & Laurie stuck firmly to their guns, refusing to go for easier laughs in the ultimate low-fi comedy arena which forced them to use often basic costume and scenery – Stephen beginning one nun sketch by knocking on a table to signify somebody at the door. Occasionally Elton and 'Junior Boy' Enfield joined them in a sketch, with some material repeated from *Alfresco*, but generally – whether sending themselves up as two effete poets, returning to Dr De Quincy's sadistic bedtime manner, or confusing the cool crowd with some other deliberately obtuse concept – the Fry & Laurie brand of silly, cerebral sketch comedy was beginning to bed in with a young audience. Some repeated motifs began to occur: such as the highly unlikely TV shows presented by Hugh under his advertising moniker of Peter Mostyn (including live surgery, and in the second series, 'Taking and Driving Away With . . .' in which the pair were mortified to be out in the LWT

Studios car park failing to smash a carefully primed car window live on air), and there was a new line in Masterclasses.

Most famously, a 'Piano Masterclass' in series two was the spur for Stephen to face his deeply rooted horror of singing, courtesy of a Hungarian hypnotist, who uncovered a painful buried memory of a humiliating music lesson at school, and encouraged Stephen, in his hypnotic state, to relax enough to adequately perform the closing song. Fry's own memory of the event was flawed (it was he, not Hugh, who spoke the trigger phrase, 'Play it, bitch!') but the basic joke, of a raunchy pop song being performed by this tweedy young man, relied heavily on Fry's growing public image, delighting the crowd. The same trick was used in a sketch in which Hugh played a lascivious glamour photographer trying to coax Stephen's coquettish and very tweedy model into removing his dog-tooth thornproof.

Next, the 'Comedy Masterclass' came in handy for all sorts of benefits and shows. This time, 'the actor Hugh' was being put through his paces as a stand-up, and of course ended up as a waving, tongue-waggling idiot:

STEPHEN: Hugh, you've proved that you're a master of dramatic comedy by the way you handled your Bottom in my *Dream*, but tonight we're going to be concentrating much more on audience skills, alright? So you've done your exercises, you're fit and you're ready to go... on your feet, then.
HUGH: I am on my feet.
STEPHEN: No, this is comedy, Hugh, always on the *balls* of your feet for comedy, that's very important. Alright, good. Now, because we're going to be doing some joke work, some gag work, I'm going to give you a simple joke, and I want you to deliver it, alright?
STEPHEN WHISPERS IN HUGH'S EAR, HUGH LOOKS NONPLUSSED, AND APPROACHES THE MIKE.

HUGH: I won't say it was a small town, but the speed limit signs were back to back.

STEPHEN: Good, relax, off your balls. Okay, Hugh, I wonder if you knew this, in all comedy there are only two jokes, did you know that?

HUGH: That wasn't one of them, was it?

STEPHEN: No, it was <u>both</u> of them, Hugh! Because the two jokes are firstly, a blurring and a slipping of moral categories, and secondly, logic gone awry. That's what they were laughing at. Alright? So bear that in mind, and let's try again.

HUGH: Can't I try it with another joke?

STEPHEN: What's wrong with this one, Hugh?

HUGH: Well, I don't think it's very funny... Why do I say that I'm *not* going to say it's a small town, and then say it's a small town?

STEPHEN: Never analyse comedy, Hugh. Never. Don't try and break it into little pieces, it's beautiful, it's lovely as it is, don't smash it up.[26]

Mid-sketch post-modern deconstruction was becoming a Fry & Laurie speciality, their arch cleverness a fine contrast to Rik & Ade's mindlessly violent brand of silliness which belied the pre-watershed start time – and the latter duo made good use of this difference in a crossover sketch in which the two Footlighters' idea of comedy, a weedy flower arranging dance, was spoiled by the nasty, rowdy Dangerous Brothers' intrusion, even though they had been 'banned' from the show for being too explosive and sexy. In addition, botty obsession remained a mainstay of Fry & Laurie's output, as Stephen admitted to an audience of teenagers on Channel 4's *Open to Question* in 1989, 'Because Hugh and I have slightly sort of Oxbridge manners, rather patrician accents and so on, people often think "Oh, it's those poncey two!" you know, and they don't notice that a lot of what we do is quite rude. I must say, we get away with a lot more rudeness – Ben Elton is always complaining to us that he has virtually never sworn on television . . . I find bottoms very funny.' Ultimately, however, he concluded, 'You can only write what makes you laugh. It's the only way to do it. You may then find nobody else in the world laughs, in which case you've got the wrong job.' The duo openly mocked the yoof-ful crowds by offering them pre-sketch choices between satire and filth, and took more risks than anyone else on the staff, often allowing a sketch to reach a conclusion with no clear punchline, hoping Posner would be on hand to signal to the audience that their item was over.

This first series, extending into the early spring of 1986, also saw the arrival of two key business buddies, a pair that the colleagues could slip into at any point: greasy marketing executives Gordon Inglis & Stuart Marsh. Corporate executives had been legitimate targets for many years, but the decade of greed Stephen & Hugh found themselves in saw such red-brace-twanging drones reaching new heights of cultural ubiquity, and general revulsion. As with Alan & Bernard, both were decidedly unctuous and unpleasant, but Hugh's bitter, stupid Stuart was by far the worst. They were first seen egregiously pulling up their shiny grey suit pants at a presentation for 'Chocolate Goodies UK PLC', competing for the respect of their employer in a vein of larky chauvinism, in-jokes, desperate Americanisms and idle brags:

HUGH: 1985 was a good year. It was a good year for chocolate, and a good year for this company, and we've had some good times because of it. But tonight is a sad night. It's a sad night because we're losing a friend, but more than that, we're losing a *colleague*. Gordon Inglis, who joined us, what? Eighteen months ago from Leicester, is leaving us to head up a high-powered team, as you might expect,

	with our US division, based out of Ohio. Now one thing our US cousins ought to know about Gordon — apart from don't ever play squash with the guy, right? Haha, no — is Gordon is a guy who knows more about brand profiling of chocolate confection than even I do. Gordon?
STEPHEN:	I first met this loony when our boss John Dowling brought Stuart here to head up a brand of high profile top-end countline confection bar on the housewife-impulse-buy-indulgence end of the snack market. That project, as you know, became the Chocolate Knob — still, I'm happy to say, brand leader...
HUGH:	Alright, we've told some stories, we've had a few laughs, but you know, everywhere, there has to be a bottom line. People, they talk, don't they, about the love between a man and a woman, and for sure, that's got its place, no one would deny that. But you know, there's another kind of love, a love between colleagues that's based on respect, respect for performance. I'm not a homosexual, never have been...
STEPHEN:	Neither am I.
HUGH:	I think our records show that. But I have to tell you here tonight, John, with your permission, that I love this guy. I love this big, crazy, flyaway roister-doister, I love him! Gordon, I love you.
STEPHEN:	Stuart, you're giving me a lump.
HUGH:	Christ I'm going to miss you. Get over here!
STEPHEN:	You bastard...

THEY COLLAPSE ONTO THE FLOOR IN A PASSIONATE CLINCH.[27]

The punchline smacks of pervy slash fiction, but this was the only time anything like that went on with Inglis & Marsh. Their competitive camaraderie was to develop in further appearances, Gordon always trumping Stuart's pathetic little executive boasts, leading to outright war when he won the Golden Dick award for sales excellence, and proved his desert by flogging it to the pitifully envious Stuart.

The one remaining ingredient in *Saturday Live* was of course the presence of Greek kebab shop owner Stavros, as embodied by Harry Enfield and co-created by his plasterer friends. By now, Stephen & Hugh were successful enough to afford to enter another partnership – as homeowners. With Katie and Nick, they moved into a house in St Mark's Rise, as part of the vanguard of gentrification of the Hackney district of Dalston. When they realised how much work the house needed, they called in an expert plasterer, Martin – and it was only remarkable coincidence that the two flunkies he brought with him were fledgling comic powerhouses, Paul Whitehouse & Charlie Higson – the latter moonlighting from his day job as rockstar 'Switch', in the band The Higsons. These drop-outs from the University of East Anglia shared a nearby council flat with Harry, who had caught Fry & Laurie's attention with a storming Comedy Store appearance a month earlier, after years of his trying to make it in the double act Dusty & Dick. The banter shared by these plasterers once again pricked Stephen & Hugh's inverted inferiority complexes. 'They were quite extraordinarily funny,' said Stephen. 'I brought them coffee, as you do when you have the builders in, and I chatted with them in what I hoped was a friendly and unpatronising manner but just couldn't get over how much they made me laugh . . . Hugh and I believed that, excellent as Paul and Charlie were with the bonding, skimming, rendering and so forth, they really should have a stab at making their way in comedy.'[28] Or, as Hugh put it, 'They were so funny that it actually made me think, well either they're really really funny or I'm just simply not, and I ought to now become a plasterer.' Of course, the colleagues were misled on two counts – with the admitted exception of Paul, who had a cosy Welsh lower-middle-class background, their seemingly hardcore new friends were not much less well-to-do than themselves, both Higson and Enfield having attended prep schools, and Harry descended from a family of Hampstead intellectuals, famously derided by Virginia Woolf. Additionally, their banter was not totally natural, as Whitehouse & Higson knew full well who they were working for, and were keen to impress. 'It was very kind of them to say that they thought we were the funny ones,' Higson says, 'but that wasn't how it felt from where we were, painting their walls. We were there as we were painting, doing comedy routines to each other and doing funny characters, taking it up to eleven in the hope that they might say, "Why don't you come onto one of our shows?" We did overdo it probably, and tried to sell them some sketch ideas.' They didn't need to impress Stephen & Hugh, though – by providing Harry with characters and material, they became part of the extended *Saturday Live* team, joining the hip backing band for Stephen's musical nightmare, and their own comedy careers were underway – they could even afford to buy the Dalston house from Fry & Laurie a few years later.

Valid Arenas and Valid Arenas

Stephen & Hugh envied Harry his returning characters, whereas they made a point of usually offering something totally other for the show, ever returning to 'the blank sheet of paper and accusatory pen, or rather the blank screen, flashing cursor and accusatory keyboard. The sketches that seemed to work best in the insanely hot, loud and unstable atmosphere of the studio were the ones, as we had imagined, where Hugh and I talked out to the audience.'[29] Even given the fact that Fry & Laurie's spots were considered unusually lengthy for comedy sketches, five minutes' apparent work a week does not seem overly taxing, but *Saturday Live* filled their lives for the opening months of 1986, and the rest of the year saw intriguing developments.

When work had ended on *Blackadder II* the previous summer, Richard Curtis had thrown a bash at his Oxfordshire home, with *Live Aid* as the main attraction, shown on a TV wheeled out under the shade of an old apple tree in the back garden. The party's host was close friends with Charity Arts founder Jane Tewson, both equally horrified by Ethiopia and the Sudan's famine, as the sainted Bob Geldof had been – and on 4 April 1986, the live show *Comic Relief Utterly Utterly Live*, warm on the heels of a hit single by the resurrected Young Ones and Cliff Richard, was the result of their endeavours to find other entertaining ways of raising emergency funds. A decade earlier, John Cleese had set the trend for the marriage of comedy and charity in the *Secret Policeman's Ball* shows for Amnesty, but this new benefit on the scene aimed to ape *Live Aid*'s level of excitement and impact. Though only Stephen found a role in that first live show – fittingly stepping into John Cleese's shoes in a new version of Python's 'Merchant Banker' sketch with Geldof and Midge Ure – he and his colleague would quickly opt in to being voluble spokesmen for Comic Relief in its future permutations, helping to relieve suffering in Africa and the UK. The arguments were always rife – whether celebrity charity events are a desperate ploy to absolve governments of responsibility, if taking part was a career move rather than genuine compassion, and predictably, Alexei Sayle came down solidly on the 'yes' side on both issues – but he was in a tiny hardcore minority as the comedy fraternity embraced Curtis and Co.'s plans to establish the national institution of Red Nose Day. 'The phrase that's often used is it's a "sticking plaster operation",' Stephen told the *Open to Question* audience. 'My view is that if you're walking down the street and a man is bleeding, then a sticking plaster is a very useful thing. If people are starving, you don't go immediately to Hyde Park Corner and stand on a soapbox and make a speech about it, you grub around in your pockets for some money to give them something to eat . . . While there is real suffering, it's very hard to walk the other way, no matter how sound the political reasons for doing so are.'

Also in that year, the sacking of the colleagues' friend Jools Holland from Channel 4 music show *The Tube* for using the phrase 'groovy fucker' on a live teatime trailer, led to *The Laughing Prisoner*, a suitably odd hour-long pop-musical tribute to mind-bending 1960s TV caper *The Prisoner*, with Stephen popping over to Portmeirion to play a mercurial Number 2, and Hugh as a corporate lackey – both sharing writing credit with Holland and his fellow 'Groovy Feller' Rowland Rivron. At the end of the year came guest spots on gloriously puerile vicious media satire *Filthy Rich & Catflap*, for which they gave their 'N'Bend' & 'P'Farty', two supercilious art critics, as a reunion with *Saturday Live* pals Rik, Ade and scripter Ben ('Knobend & Poofarty?! What a script. Get out.').

Both of these appearances went out in the new year, while for our two colleagues it wasn't all adverts, and they of course had separate gigs, with Hugh earning a few acting roles, once again appearing with Dawn French, in the video for Kate Bush's *Experiment IV*, and inheriting one highly atypical role from Elton. *South of Watford* was an LWT documentary strand which went out only in the London region, each episode looking at a different element of modern youth culture, and for a time Hugh became its third presenter, sandwiched between Ben and John Lloyd. His duties included a very trippy interview with outrageous performance artist Leigh Bowery (which provided an outré clip for *Saturday Live*'s stuttering-sample-packed opening credits), and explaining Sigue Sigue Sputnik. Stephen, meanwhile, matched Hugh's solo sitcom cameo with a one-off part in his new friend Simon Callow's show *Chance in a Million*, and managed to record a third series as David Lander for Radio 4, with Enfield once more – before popping onto the most popular chat show of the day, *Wogan,* to announce to visibly charmed guest host Kenneth Williams his imminent departure for America, nursing *Me and My Girl* on Broadway.

Douglas Adams offered free use of his Manhattan apartment for the occasion, and Fry's friends all flew across with him to bate their breaths for the opening night critical verdict. The musical's instant wild trumping of its West End success was a welcome surprise for all, and perhaps the final vindication of Richard Armitage's pride in his father's music. With his big name clients and young protégés all going great guns, Armitage must surely have been very contented at the end, though it was a sudden one – word came through to Stephen & Hugh in November that their agent had died of a sudden heart attack at home. Armitage had been, if not the architect, then certainly the chartered surveyor of their unexpected careers in show business – the man who had believed in Fry & Laurie from the start, and his Footlights stars were to remain loyal, if not to Noel Gay, then to Armitage's assistant Lorraine Hamilton, who founded her own still-running talent agency in a cupboard in the Noel Gay building.

Armitage completed one momentous task in his final months – contacting the chaps with instructions for them to return to BBC Television Centre, all sulks from *The Crystal Cube* expunged, for a fresh assault on Auntie's comedy Everest. Falstaffian executive Jim Moir was still as keen as ever to harness the unusual wit that was making the more cerebral adolescents titter every Saturday evening on the 'cool' channel – and before the year was out, a pilot for a Fry & Laurie BBC2 sketch show was theirs. 'The nice BBC people gave us another chance,' Fry says. 'This time, we thought "This could be our last chance to crack, or at least have a proper go at, sketch comedy."'

'We just decided that we were going to write them all,' Hugh says. 'All the other sort of sketch shows that were around at the time were all more or less being written by the same people, and so we felt that the thing we have going for us, if we have anything, is that this is personal, this is our personal view of the world, it's not a corporate machine that's just sort of generating thirty minutes of a sketch from here and a sketch from there, and these two guys will put on funny moustaches and do it.' There was a whole stable of keen gagsmiths they could have turned to, the Jon Canters, Laurie Rowleys and Colin Bostock-Smiths, but Hugh was determined that any certain failure they faced would be their blame, and nobody else's. Fry & Laurie would stand alone. 'The advantage of writing your own material', Fry told *TV Guide* in 1990, 'is that you learn when you've run out of ideas. If we're sixty and still doing stupid sketches and saying "bottom" a lot, it's going to look a little strange . . . If we had said, "We are funny people, please write us some sketches!" why would anybody want to do that? You'd have to be as good as Rowan Atkinson to get someone to write for you, and I never felt I was as good as Rowan, and I'll never feel that. But I knew what I could do, I knew my limits, and I could write for them. And Hugh's the same – his limits are wider than mine, because he can sing, and do all kinds of other things I can't do, but nonetheless that's the huge advantage of writing for yourself.'

The writing wasn't the only thing Hugh was adamant about – despite his many critiques of audiences, he told Stephen that taking their sketches on the road was a necessity. And not only that, but they could not throw in any of the recycled material from previous tours – no 'Dracula', no 'Shakespeare Masterclass' – they would prepare for their TV try-out by forging fresh material and honing it in live venues, and live tour impresario Phil McIntyre made the necessary arrangements. 'I remember it as simultaneously exhilarating and terrifying,' offers Hugh, 'which is usually the way it goes, you don't get exhilaration without terror, they are two legs of one pair of trousers. We tended to concentrate on an undergraduate audience, campuses and things. I can look back on it now, because we survived it and nobody stabbed us in a comic rage of dissatisfaction, as a thrilling time, but of course, I was probably thinking, "Oh, tonight's the night we actually are finished, we'll get called out and challenged and have our comic licences revoked." Not that we had comic licences, this was our attempt to get them.'

'Although we were not really well known and certainly nothing like as famous as Harry and Ben were becoming,' Stephen wrote, 'There was a sizeable enough demand for us in college and university towns, it seemed, and a tour was arranged. We wrote and stared out of the window and paced up and down and bought Big Macs and looked out of the window and went for walks and tore at our hair and swore and watched television and bought more Big Macs and swore again and wrote and screamed with horror as the clock showed that another day was over and we looked at what we had written and groaned and agreed to meet again first thing next day whoever turn it was agreeing to arrive with some coffee and Big Macs.'[30] It was clearly going to be a bit of fun.

THE MAIN BIT

'Well, I thi— oh, Christ, I've left the iron on!'

'My father was a Conservative, my mother voted Labour, so I suppose, by rights, I should be a Liberal Democrat. But in actual fact, I'm a Nazi.'

The BBC was now pledged to offer 'a bit of Fry & Laurie' by the end of 1987, but work was not to sag for our two colleagues in the meantime. The second *Saturday Live* outing, with no Rik & Ade and Ben installed as permanent host, began the new year. This run included Fry's hypnotised singing and desperate car burglary, plus one brand-new sketch painstakingly constructed by Stephen & Hugh for the show, requiring little set-up besides a shop counter and a telephone. It was called, quite simply, 'The Hedge Sketch':

STEPHEN: Good morning, sir. Can I help you?
HUGH: Hello. I'd like to buy a hedge, please.
STEPHEN: A hedge! Well, we have three sorts, sir. What sort of hedge would you like?
HUGH: Well, what sorts have you got?
STEPHEN: We have the Royal, the Imperial and the Standard hedge.
HUGH: Could I have a look at the Imperial, please?

STEPHEN:	Certainly, sir. May I ask, is the hedge for you?
HUGH:	No – it's a present.
STEPHEN:	Ah! For your wife perhaps?
HUGH:	I'm not married.
STEPHEN:	Right – well I'll just ring down to the stockroom if you wouldn't mind waiting?
HUGH:	Not at all – I'm in no hurry.
STEPHEN:	(ON PHONE) Hello, stockroom? Have we got any Imperial hedges left? Oh thanks. (TO HUGH) He's just having a look. (PUTS DOWN PHONE) Ah, you appear to be in luck, sir, stockroom tells me we've got one Imperial hedge left.
HUGH:	Right! I'll take it then.
STEPHEN:	Certainly, sir. How would you like to pay?
HUGH:	Cash, if you don't mind.
STEPHEN:	Cash will be perfectly convenient, sir.

... Or rather, of course, this doggerel is precisely how boring 'The Hedge Sketch' would be, were it performed 'properly', rather than the constant muddle in which the two performers found themselves: forgetting lines, swapping roles, never getting it right, and concluding once again with one of those unashamedly awkward not-quite-endings which Geoff Posner had to be sharp to telegraph to the audience. 'The sketch that goes wrong' was not an original idea – the chaps had a another 'fake prompt' item, and Richard Curtis wrote an earlier 'Prompt' sketch for Tim McInnerny and Helen Atkinson-Wood of the Oxford Revue – but 'The Hedge Sketch' was mainly a triumph of performing skill, a Two Ronnies-esque display of dexterity, which, once mastered, could be performed by the two with minimum prep.

Excitedsville, Idaho!

As with so many comedy shows, it took a second series to really nail down what made *Saturday Live* tick, and there's no question it was the defining comedy arena of a generation. It was a necessity of the times that the show was anti-establishment through and through, albeit via the conduit of some terribly well brought up comedians, and one sketch even saw Stephen, Hugh and Harry playing monopoly with former GLC leader Ken Livingstone, giving him a platform to complain about the council's abolition. Other special guest stars included Rowan, who remained speechless in an ecclesiastical sketch with Stephen & Hugh; and Emma, who performed watershed-baiting stand-up and reunited with them for another Victorian drawing room sketch, in which Hugh's request for Emma's hand in marriage is complicated by her father Stephen's lust for him. This was the last sketch the trio would perform together on TV, but Thompson had been busy on her own account since *Alfresco*, with her Coltrane reunion in *Tutti Frutti* in the can and a Channel 4 special *Emma Thompson Up for Grabs* preceding her 1988 BBC2 sketch show, *Thompson*: neither of which had any input from her old friends. Despite being packed with inventive sketches, the latter was so viciously blasted with critic venom for its blend of proud theatricality and highbrow humour it spelled the end of Emma's TV comedy career. By then, however, she had met Renaissance Theatre firebrand Kenneth Branagh and the two briefly became either the new Golden Couple of Theatre, or the nucleus of a cabal of 'luvvies' ripe for mockery, depending on your stance. *Spitting Image* certainly took the latter option, and within a few years the satirical juggernaut started by John Lloyd would include Stephen and, eventually, Hugh, in their latex group, privileged toffs revolting in their individual surfeits of talent and, in Stephen's case, an obsession with botties – as mocked by the booming vocal dexterity of Harry Enfield.

Fry drew from his recent sojourn in America in a *Saturday Live* sketch mocking the multitudes of Brits who see the USA as the epicentre of all existence, a particularly common source of irritation in a decade defined by Coke-versus-Pepsi, MTV, Michael Jackson, and baseball caps worn quite the wrong way round. The pair subverted their tweedy reputation by bounding out, whooping in appallingly loud 'sports' wear:

STEPHEN: How ya doing out there, are you all right? Bloody glad to hear it, that's great, great news!
HUGH: Simon and I are very excited at the moment!
STEPHEN: BLOODY excited! (BOTH WHOOP A GREAT DEAL)... I gotta tell you, it's great to be back home, Peter and I have just got in from the States.
HUGH: The <u>United</u> States!
STEPHEN: Yeah, the United States of America! I love the United States... I quite like the UK too... The UK is OK, but let's face it, you've gotta travel an awfully long way in this country to get yourself a decent game of softball...
HUGH: I mean, wake up, Channel 4, wake up to what's going on in the US of States, for Christ's sake!
STEPHEN: Yeah! Go for it! Because let's face it, that's where it's all happening... We're so Excitedsville, Idaho!
HUGH: ... There's a word for that, isn't there, all that stuff you can only get over there, what do they call it?
STEPHEN: Was it something like 'grap'?
HUGH: Grap! That's right, yeah! Because they're always saying it's amazing how we British swallow any old grap the Americans throw at us...[1]

British Amerophiles were to become a regular target in *ABOF&L*, and in 1992 Stephen complained to Clive James, 'I get terribly depressed about the English obsession with America. I mean, it is a marvellous country, let me lay that on the record fair and square, a superb country, delightful, full of charming people, literally charming...! But! This country is stocked from John O'Groats to Land's End, with these absurd sort of disc jockey types for whom America is one huge masturbatory fantasy . . . And these wasted little people in their baseball hats who live in Newport Pagnell.' Hugh goes so far as to say, of their manifold ass-based American jibes, 'It wasn't about America or Americans, it was about British people, and more specifically, ourselves. And it's worth remembering that America was a very different force in the world then. When I grew up, Americans really were the master-race, there was no denying it, they were the fastest, they had the Heavyweight Boxer, the World Tennis and Golf and Everything Else Champions, they went to the moon, for fuck's sake! They were just such a dominant force that how everyone in the world responded to America was an important thing in everyone's life, and now, weirdly enough, they don't have any of those things . . . I always had this theory that people's response to America back then was related to their relationship with their own father. People who got on well with their father generally liked America, and those who resented anyone having dominance over them tended to dislike it. When I was a troublesome, rebellious youth, I remembered getting into a terrible argument with this woman about the Baader-Meinhof gang, I thought that global anarchy was the way to go. But that was adolescent rage.' 'America just cast a huge shadow culturally,' Stephen adds. 'And Hugh and I used to get amused by the rather feeble and pathetic sight of English people trying to be American . . . We were annoyed by the early wave, which is now a tsunami, of people saying "Oh, but American TV is *so* much better!"'

As the resident *Saturday Live* rep company, Stephen & Hugh played alongside many special guests, but none more special than the man who formed perhaps Stephen's greatest double act – Meat Loaf & Fry. 'I think the writing was the combined effort of Ben and me. I may be wrong,' Stephen says. 'Meat Loaf and I didn't rehearse much; it was like running along a high wire without a net as I recall. But Mr Loaf was very amiable and smart.' This ragged two-hander, once again playing on a great transatlantic divide, saw the enormous musical guest attack Stephen with a knife, intent on mugging him – but not until the erudite victim translated his violent jive talk, not unlike Cook & Moore's 'Bo Dudley', but with a sweating, hollering rock star reading idiot boards, and holding a blade to an Englishman's throat. Sadly, Meat returned home to the US of Stateside shortly after, and Stephen henceforth had to make do with Hugh.

Gordon Inglis had won the Golden Dick, but in March, Fry selected the Silver Dick as the appropriate award to present at that year's *Secret Policeman's Third Ball*, when Hugh and he were given the honour of joining the exclusive roster of Amnesty comics at the London Palladium. Besides offering their 'Hedge Sketch', the two performed a kind of cruel travesty of the handing over of the comic torch which had always characterised those benefit shows – the winner being the man who had started the whole thing in the first place, but who had begged off the latest show to begin work on *A Fish Called Wanda*. Having introduced the recipient with glowing words and assurances of sexual desire, the two young bucks let rip on special guest 'Jim' Cleese, as the poor man wept and clawed at their trousers:

HUGH: They took your highly entertaining heart-warming comedy classic *Fawlty Towers* off the air after only twelve episodes, what was that about?

STEPHEN: It was really beginning to get good, Jim... it had the makings of something.

JOHN: Yes, well there were in fact only ever supposed to be the twelve episodes.

HUGH: And the twelve were fine, Jim! There was lots in there which I thought eventually maybe may have turned into something.

STEPHEN: Yes. You know, one minute you're a rising star and then some TV executive decides to make you a nobody with a flick of his pen.

HUGH: Just cuts you off!

JOHN: Er, I don't think that...

STEPHEN: It was around that time, wasn't it, Jim, that you were in the middle of a rather messy divorce with the woman who was chiefly responsible for writing your scripts? And it was from then on that things started to go wrong for you, wasn't it?

HUGH: Now they tell me Michael Barrymore doesn't even bother to do you any more... For heaven's sake, I hate to see a *very* old man cry. I mean, we still love you! We want to see you come back!... What was it that finally finished you off, Jim? Was it the hair weave, or the move to the SDP? Which was it, d'you think?

STEPHEN: Was it growing that rather odd beard, I wonder, or perhaps it could have been those strange psychiatric group therapy sessions? Did you find, Jim, that once you stopped being mad, you stopped being funny...?

Cleese's imminent greatest solo movie success was to show the young pretenders who was boss, of course (with no hard feelings – Stephen even had a cameo, being punched by Kevin Kline in *Wanda's* airport denouement), but that this pair, neither even thirty, could so relish tearing one off the Pope of Comedy like this, was another indicator of their assured place in the comedy double act firmament.

Inevitably, with this fame came an instant hostility from some quarters, and those voices of doubt, dissatisfaction and derision that took up so much room inside Fry & Laurie's heads were not only inside there. The *Daily Mail* of course found itself particularly affronted by a pleasingly tweedy old-fashioned English urbanity belying, in their view, a vain, publicity-hungry, left-wing, 'openly gay' humanist – positively a *Daily Mail* reader's worst nightmare, and the reason Fry is still targeted in the most poisonous terms to this day. He also picked his adversaries well when a dispute with Bernard Manning was turned into column inches, Stephen being quoted in *Woman's Own* as part of a musing on 'PC humour': 'The real joke is Bernard Manning going on about how fat and ugly his mother-in-law is. I defy anyone to find me anyone uglier and fatter than Bernard Manning. When I hear him I think, "Hang on, has this man seen himself?" It's the arrogance of it.' To which the tabloids demanded a Manning response: 'I've never seen Fry's act. He has the wit and charm of an unflushed toilet. I was making people laugh when he was still in his nappy. He wasn't brought up at Eton – he was eaten and brought up! He should have seen me in the Army in 1947 when I was twenty stone lighter.' 'For all the horror of some of his jokes, he is I think a supremely good and gifted joke teller,' Stephen was to insist on *Open to Question*, however, and this faux-spat was not typical – Fry & Laurie quickly became almost universally popular with the comedy old guard, even those who probably had the *Mail* delivered daily. Fry puts this down to 'a great British love of the traditional and the tweedy and the well-spoken, if you like . . . there's a massive audience out there of people who may not understand a single joke, but say, "I could hear every word, it was wonderful, so clear and so polite, and nobody said 'cunt', and it was lovely, thank you for that." So we were sort of aware that on one hand we'd be hated by the cool sort of punk comedians who were coming up, and on the other hand loved by a rather strange constituency of *Daily Mail* readers.' Fry also guested on an early edition of ITV discussion programme *Central Weekend* (co-presented by David Lander inspiration Roger Cook) for what the production team had planned as an all-out war between comedy's old guard Barry Cryer, Neil Shand and Michael Bentine and new comics Stephen, John Lloyd and Ben Elton, which turned out to be a honeyed love-in from start to finish, and allowed Fry to use the word 'fuck' on commercial television allegedly eighteen times in three minutes.

A Roarer, a Rogerer, a Gorger and a Puker

Stephen was to return to New York shortly after the winter's run of live performances, but Hugh was certainly not left high and dry at home in Blighty. 1987 saw perhaps the two most crucial arrivals in Laurie's life, Fry excepted – one was a life partner, the other a long-dead Hanoverian monarch.

Naturally, many of the names dropped hitherto in this narrative became firm friends of our colleagues in the 1980s, and a new comedy aristocracy was established, the secret society depicted at play by Helen Fielding in her first novel *Cause Celeb,* and indeed by her ex Richard Curtis in *Four Weddings and a Funeral.* Curtis's gifted maestro Howard Goodall was one of these troops of friends, partying many times with Fry

& Laurie and their wide circle, and in 1987 he split with his girlfriend, a striking petite brunette theatre administrator called Jo Green. Her close friend Jon Canter recalls that Hugh's limpid blue pools, ripped physique – and of course, wit – gave Jo a sudden and steely determination to turn the comic's head, and in no time at all Jo and Hugh became a not terribly secret 'item'. In a sheepish and rare moment of candour to *GQ* magazine in 1993, Laurie volunteered that 'Kate went away to Kenya to work for a year and I started fooling around with Jo, who had just been left by her boyfriend . . . the accepted form is that before climbing inside a girl's pants you say, "Look, I'm with this other girl, let me go and speak to her." But I didn't, I missed out that stage. So instead of saying to Kate, "It's over. Can I have your assigned chit?", I had to say, "Look, I'm having an affair." Kate was rightly upset.' While loving and losing is painful, perhaps it's some consolation if the affair leads to a relationship which lasts over thirty years, and from that time on Jo would become a crucial corner of a Fry & Laurie triangle. Curiously, despite Hugh not getting on the bill for the previous year's Comic Relief show, Jo *was* in it, as the poor victim of Lenny Henry's soul singer Theophilus P. Wildebeest, pulled up onstage for an erotic encounter.

Elton & Curtis were sure that Lord Blackadder needed a new descendent, in a new era, for the third series, and had been mulling over the subject when they went to see Robbie Coltrane's one-man show about Samuel Johnson in April, and the idea of Blackadder burning Johnson's Dictionary started a Georgian ball rolling. Edmund Blackadder was always tantalisingly close to the seat of power, and who would that have been in the Regency period? Not the Mad King George, but what about his fat, fornicating heir? *Blackadder the Third* would be as blithely historically incorrect as any other series if not more so, but even so, by the time he became Prince Regent, the future George IV was a massively obese alcoholic pushing fifty, and he had never been svelte, exercising a rapacious appetite for booze, food and enormous women. Tim McInnerny would have been far too skinny for the part, but had left the series for fear of being typecast as Blackadder's dense foppish sidekick Lord Percy anyway. Ben & Richard had imagined the Prince as a yobbish nob, as thick as he was boorish and conceited, and Ben for one knew that Hugh could deliver that in spades. 'I don't think we'd done enough research,' Curtis admits, 'I mean, Ben always knew about the history, but we never considered anyone other than Hugh.' Many years later, Laurie was to say with typical self-effacement, 'I was conscious of filling the great Tim McInnerny's shoes, and in comic terms, he takes a size twenty-two. He's very big-footed, comically. I suppose George was sufficiently different, rather than being a sidekick of Blackadder's, the dynamic was different.'[2] Hitherto, Hugh was known for playing frustrated middle-class Tories, young innocents and anyone with a ridiculous foreign accent, but his promotion to the height of aristocracy, a performance built on the inbred tones of Lord Monty, was so successful, it would give the actor his own typecasting problems in years to come.

His arrival as part of the sitcom's central cast was to ratchet up the divide between writers and performers more than ever, and despite his personal affection for Elton & Curtis, Laurie was soon picking holes in the scripts with greater abandon than any previous cast member, groaning, 'Do you think they actually read it back once they've written it?' and similar grumbles of despair. The effect on the perfectionist Atkinson was to pull *Blackadder* production into a new era of obsessive 'plumpening' (Lloyd's term for the intricate embellishment of the scripts), as Ben eventually complained, 'They got into over-analysis, but you'd have two actors, Hugh and Rowan, and I know they'll forgive me for saying it, but they were both very, very intense people. The two of them together could get very gloomy about things and talk themselves into a great deal of a "This is awful, we're awful, who are we kidding?" sort of world. Particularly Hugh, but I think Row would always go along for the ride.' Ever the peace-bringer, Curtis shrugs, 'They were a pretty high-level bunch of fiddlers all round, and Rowan was always sort of dissatisfied, and Tony always willing to try anything, so we just had to accept that the script was always going to take a battering.'

John Lloyd was particularly aggrieved by Hugh's flagrant self-flagellation, and remembers the frustration of Laurie's new girlfriend: 'Jo often used to say, "Not only does Hugh think he's unattractive and untalented, he also thinks he's short!" He wears his heart on his sleeve; he doesn't conceal anything. If Hugh is nervous or depressed you see it, it's all over him.' This is a trait Fry has also had cause to rue: 'I can't help it, but whenever I smile it looks smug and complacent – the very opposite of Hugh. Hugh looks pissed off. People go to a party and they say, "What's wrong with Hugh? What have I done to offend him?" And I go, "No no, that's just how he looks – hangdog and pissed off, but he's fine, don't worry." Whereas people probably think, "What's Stephen looking so pleased about?" And in fact I'll be crying inside, and miserable, but it looks smug.' 'There was a lot of time with Hugh in rehearsal going "I'm fucking useless, I'm hopeless! I can't do this!"' Lloyd continues, 'and I used to say, "Hugh, you're one of the best actors I've ever worked with! I don't understand how you're not a Hollywood star!" and as he does, Hugh said, "Oh, I'm rubbish." He's one of those rare people who can play completely silly and downright evil and everything in between. That's very, very unusual.' 'Hugh's Prince Regent should be celebrated more,' Elton adds, 'I mean, a truly brilliant performance of a foppish Regency idiot', and co-writer Curtis agrees: 'When Hugh plays stupid, there is nothing behind the eyes. I think we took Percy, who hadn't been clever, and scooped out the final teaspoonful of brains . . . That utter thickness was something that was fun to put Blackadder against, different from Miranda's sort of dangerous childishness.' 'It's that utter sort of gullibility,' Atkinson muses, 'the perfect sponge for whatever anyone says. Anyone can take him in any direction at any one time. He has no resolution of his own. In the hands of The Black Adder, he is complete putty.'

The ramping up of *Blackadder* 'plumpening' increased when Stephen returned for his guest appearance in the planned closer at the start of July, a month after recordings began and, as *Blackadder* was always recorded out of broadcast sequence, some weeks before the series would be complete. A few years after Laurie played the soldier in *Alfresco*, it was Fry's turn to step into Wellington's boots, as a deafeningly loud, violent bully pledged to end George's life in a duel. The placeholder line 'The King, your father, is mad' instantly stood out as a wasted opportunity to Stephen, who proffered the alternative, 'Your royal father grows ever more eccentric and at present believes himself to be a small village in Lincolnshire with commanding views of the Nene Valley.'

The other development to come from this climactic cameo was a masterclass in comedic violence. Slapstick had played next to no part in

Fry & Laurie's careers hitherto, save the occasions when proximity to Rik & Ade had made it inevitable. The Dangerous Brothers had given Hugh a good bashing on *Saturday Live*, but that was nothing to the pasting dished out to the disguised Prince by Wellington and Blackadder in 'Duel and Duality'. Stephen had long envied his partner's physicality, but the bone-china-smashing gymnastics performed for *Blackadder* showed off Hugh's skills like never before. Perhaps comparison to Buster Keaton seems hysterical, but Laurie surely would have excelled in silent comedy, possessed as he is of such a unique hangdog physicality. 'As anyone who's done that kind of slapstick knows,' says Stephen, 'the skill is not in the person punching or throwing a slap, it's always in the person receiving it, and Hugh is an absolute genius at being hit. And something about those enormous blue lagoons of eyes and their sorrowfulness makes it all the funnier, because he doesn't really understand why he's being hit. Both Rowan and I had a great time punching, kicking and generally yelling at him. Very enjoyable.' 'There is something funny about Stephen being cruel,' Thompson adds, 'because it's his purpose in life to be kind, so when he lets that cruelty out, there's something terrifically compelling about it, and very funny, for me in particular.' Hugh complains, 'I remember him arriving to do the violent stuff, the slapstick stuff, with some trepidation, because I'd done things with Stephen before, physical things, where he's had to act punching me, and his acting . . . well, how can I put it? He's punched me, basically, he's just punched me. There were scenes where you had to judge your distance quite carefully, and be looking at the marks on the floor, thinking "well, he's got quite a lot of reach, if I just dip forward here I could catch one in the chops."'[3] Henceforth, Hugh abuse would become a minor motif in their double act, particularly when he had the gall to sit at the piano and play. 'I don't know what the hitting was supposed to express,' Hugh adds. 'It's not really the gist of our relationship. I just liked falling over, and he liked making me fall over, and that seemed to be reason enough. It's not *very* profound, is it?' Stephen adds, 'For some reason hitting me wouldn't be funny, perhaps because people really want to do that.'

Hugh's murder at the hands of Stephen would not, of course, prevent George's return in another incarnation, and the last episode to be recorded on 20 July, 'Amy and Amiability', would earn *Blackadder* its first BAFTA. With that new career high achieved, Hugh was free to finally rejoin Stephen to put plans for their own vehicle into operation.

Things had been moving along with their BBC2 pilot, and they were gifted Roger Ordish as producer/director – a dream job for Ordish, away from his more familiar turf, working on the damned and *verboten* children's show *Jim'll Fix It*. Ordish had started out in comedy himself, and recalls, 'I was absolutely delighted, I very much wanted to do that kind of thing. I was in an appallingly bad ITV sketch show in 1965 called *Broad and Narrow* with my group from Trinity College, Dublin – Ralph Bates, Bill Wallis, Chris Serle – I'm glad it doesn't exist!' Facilitating the comedy of a couple of young Footlighters was a breath of fresh air, and he was happy to tell 'the boys' that their programme (simply agreed upon as being entitled *A Bit of Fry & Laurie*, with 'bits' of Stephen and 'bits' of Hugh co-mingling) had a Boxing Day broadcast slot, and would be recorded in the first week of December. 'Stephen was housesitting Douglas Adams's house in Islington, and we had our first meeting there,' Ordish continues. 'I was very impressed with his Apple Mac computer, and it was very jolly – he recorded my voice saying things like "Get on with it!", which was supposed to repeat on the Mac when they were sitting there not writing.'

They were encouraged not to be hampered by the twenty-nine-minute format, but even with the tour prep, it's a wonder that Stephen's creative vein wasn't pumping out hot air at this stage, as mid-1987 perhaps formed the apex of Fry's slightly scary fecundity. Behind the mike for a final run of *Delve Special* he met young radio producer Dan Patterson, understudy to Paul Mayhew-Archer, and a long-standing fan of all Stephen's comedically sesquipedalian achievements, who relentlessly urged on the star the sheer rightness of having his own radio programme, not just performing others' scripts or having a few minutes with Ned Sherrin. In *Saturday Night Fry* (almost known as 'Fry on Saturday', or more obtusely 'Room to Room') Stephen would have his own green baize table to populate, and looking back, Fry says, 'Though I shouldn't say so, I really am very proud of it . . . I was genuinely inspired. All my love of radio, a love that went back to my earliest memories, was poured into the construction of the scripts.' Stephen's rate of appearances in Broadcasting House had not slackened, and his voice was a Radio 4 staple by the time his own show was piloted during the Christmas season, having been recorded on a hot Saturday in July, the cast reading from scripts personally formatted and home-printed by the word-processor-loving man with his name in the show's title. 'Dan left it completely open, so I started writing the first one, and I thought, "Hang on, this is radio, it takes four times as many words to write as TV, plus I don't have Hugh!" I wrote what I thought was an hour-long show, but it was probably not more than twenty minutes, because it was just all words, a few sound effects and music cues.' And so, a proportion of each episode was scripted by jobbing writers Ian Brown & James Hendrie (creators of cult comedy *The Mausoleum Club*, in which Fry had guested earlier in the year), who usually provided a strand inspired by Roger Ordish's other TV show, retitled something along the lines of 'Stephen Will Do His Level Best to Comply with Your Wishes'. Nonetheless, the majority scripting of a solo series at this time was still a remarkable feat even by Fry standards. 'Ian and James played with the way I spoke sometimes, this ridiculous "Tush and sixpence!" idiom, and I let that in, because it was self-mocking.'

The bulk of the series followed several months later, five half-hours written in one dizzying week, but that first episode was to be the final time Stephen, Hugh and Emma worked together as a trio (albeit with a world-beating cameo from Barry Cryer). With their own joint TV show hoving into view, there could have been a slightly awkward chemistry to Hugh being a hired actor to play sidekick in his partner's own show, but of course the part of 'Hugh' was designed for no other person, and he happily slipped into the role of kickable sneak that his best friend marked out for him. What *Saturday Night Fry* does provide, however, is an idea of exactly what it was Laurie brought to their writing partnership, via its absence. Unchecked by Hugh's stronger desire to avoid the brickbats of elitism, Fry's imagination roved through dozens of literary spoofs, among the realistic mockumentary strands and general 'did I just hear that?' Radio 4 distortion. The multisyllabic narrative which poured forth from the unchecked Fry mind stopped just short of a Stepheñese gabble, and brought us such unforgettable names as Frillidy Waistsplendour, Bennifer Thruss, Suckmaster

Burstingfoam, and (thanks to a real friend of his mother), Hecate Carbide. The eventual show title also suggested a suitably tenuous theme tune, with Louis Jordan's 'Saturday Night Fish Fry' blasting out to presage the programme's numerous classical extracts which faded in and away – a punchy sig tune which allowed the host to intone not just 'Hit it, bitch!' but, by the final episode, a truly oleaginous phrase picked up from the US children's show *Romper Room*, which had aired on Anglian TV when Fry was small: 'Please, Mr Music, will you play . . . ?'

The Arse of the World's Mind

Dan Patterson was thrilled with the pilot, and was to become an eager booker of Stephen for years to come, but in the meantime, the student unions and bearable hotels of Britain awaited our colleagues, as they hit the road. They were performing material unfamiliar to any of the audiences, and even writing new stuff on the go, thanks to the proliferation of cheap soaps from Down Under. At first, when crowds began yelling for 'More!' they had nothing to hand, but an afternoon of mocking *Neighbours* gave them a perfect closer – the student audiences watched the same awful daytime TV, so just standing in the wings singing the soap opera's famous theme caused eruptions every night. This fresh finale rounded off a specially written hour or more, with only 'Piano Masterclass' familiar from TV (albeit with a new ending: no singing for Stephen), eventually being replaced by a 'Ballet Masterclass' in which Hugh, with a blatant excrescence forced down the front of his tights, had to communicate that he had muesli for breakfast via the medium of dance (incorporating the unfollowable punchline 'We were washing my foreskin'). Some items were to make their way to TV, however, including a dialogue about the evils of estate agents, and two sketches in which Fry took his natural place as a schoolmaster dealing with Laurie as either a sexually ignorant parent (With Fry as a Mr Casalingua – 'house of language', a favourite codename), or a poetic schoolboy responsible for disturbing doggerel:

STEPHEN: Explores? You think that's what the poem
           explores? Explores? I mean, is it a poem

> or a jungle expedition? Explores! Dear me. 'Scrotal threats embalm a blood-crusted canister unhorsing a question of flowers', I mean, what's the matter boy?... I can't understand you. You're an intelligent boy, you know my door is always open to problems from 10:30 to 10:45 during morning break. If ever I see you and ask how things are going, you tell me they're going fine: but now I discover you want to 'crawl lumpenly back up the mother's womb and scrape the walls bare' — how can things be going fine?

This extract was dropped before the sketch debuted on TV as 'Prize Poem', while other sketches were never to be broadcast, including a directionless dialogue in which Fry's crusty military type tries to tell Hugh's yes-man what's wrong with the country, and a sketch with Hugh as an American shrink, unravelling Stephen's dream about turning into a shade of blue and being bowled out by popular TV quiz host Bob Holness (for whom Stephen was of course to develop a bit of a thing – another upshot of the overdose of daytime TV). Fry also presented a kind of alternative *Dracula*, this time based on *The Exorcist*:

STEPHEN: It is with heavy heart and trembling fingers that now I take up my pen to unfold to you all the tale of horror; strange, dreadful, incredible — yet true, that you are about to hear. It was early on the Wednesday after Rogation Sunday that Mrs Miggs announced a visitor awaiting me at the Rectory. I was at the font, cleaning my teeth. Upon her announcement I dressed quickly. First in the vestry, and then in the pantry: I was just fixing my collar in the study,

> when Mrs Miggs ushered my visitor in... She looked interestedly about the room and its contents. Years of celibacy have left me pretty much to my own devices, and these she examined with evident curiosity. 'Rector,' she breathed... 'Do you, do you believe in – in the devil?' 'My child, if you believe in heat, you must believe in cold, if you have light, you must have dark, if you have joy, you will have despair, if you have boys, you'll end up in court. For all good there is evil.' 'Rector, it is my son. I believe he is possessed.' Her words filled me with a nameless – a nameless... something... That evening, as the sun set slowly in the west, I strode towards the hall, armed and ready for the great fight ahead of me. What a glorious midsummer's evening it was. I paused only to pick a buttercup. Why people leave buttocks lying around, I've no idea...

It should not be particularly shocking by this stage that the rector's hours of sweaty writhing with the possessed boy lead to the punchline '. . . And that, your honour, concludes the case for my defence', but whether the punchline made the tale beyond the pale for TV or not, only the 'buttercup' pun was gleefully recycled for *ABOF&L* and folded back into further performances of *Dracula*.

Another item which did make it to their pilot script was a cod TV discussion show about the concept of 'Honour', which most closely foreshadowed sketches in which Stephen bombarded Hugh with rapid diatribes on the beauty of language, the humour arising as much from the sound of the words streaming from Fry's mouth, as their actual meaning. 'Stephen has the most terrific facility with the English language,' Hugh muses, 'I mean, he can cast a good sentence. He takes a genuine poetic pleasure in the feeling of a good sentence.' 'I thought language for language's sake was funny,' his colleague concurs. 'That simply saying certain words at speed and with a kind of rhythm could be entertaining.' One key gripe of Fry's – aired both in his column and in the 'Language' sketch – was the use of clichés, when English gives us so much constant scope for originality, be it 'Hold the newsreader's nose squarely, waiter . . .' or some other neologistic sentence, and his urging to always avoid, pervert or otherwise overleap linguistic cliché was an inspiration to many. The fixation on the music of language was also evident in one of their greatest skits, a debate about the misuse of the lovely word 'Gay' which bristled with unexpected stresses ('Oh, it's one of the great *words*') and carefully honed rhythms which turn Fry & Laurie's voices into two perfectly complemented comedic instruments, every bit as much as Cook & Moore's rapport aped jazz syncopation.

STEPHEN: I want to talk tonight about honour. About the meaning of the word honour, about the possibility of honour and perhaps even more alarmingly, the future of honour. To help me in this quest, I have Rowley Francis, editor of Honour magazine, a man who puts in his passport under 'occupation', 'Gentleman of Honour'. Good evening, Rowley, and perhaps more interestingly, welcome.

HUGH: Up your crack you fat runt.

STEPHEN: ... Good. Okay. Now, Rowley. Darling. Let's collect, collate, refine. Let's take stock, add flour and put it into the cauldron of ideas in front of us. Let's do it now. Please... I'm going to hurl this one right at you... do we need, I wonder, honour – as you've defined it, Rowley, not as anyone else has defined

> it, or undefined it, we can't afford
> closed minds now, not at this stage...

This wilfully befuddling item closed with a song about Honour from Hugh which made roughly as much sense as Stephen's own vocal peregrinations, and although the whole piece was recorded in front of BBC cameras on Tuesday, 8 December, it was dropped in favour of a different Laurie song which had also been written for the tour, and remains a classic comedy number by most standards: the heartfelt piano ballad, 'Mystery'. Delivered in Sammy Davis Jr-aping style, this love letter to a complete stranger arguably became Hugh's signature tune, even featuring on his 2006 *Inside the Actor's Studio*. 'Mystery' provided a rare musical moment in the eventual series, alongside a return to lampooning obsessive Amerophiles with the soulful 'America', establishing the tradition of the unmusical Fry putting a stop to his talented partner's music-making displays with a fist. Stephen would appear as a musical frontman, but he stuck to his celebrated *sprechgesang* as the obvious half of 'light metal' icons The Bishop & The Warlord, while a curly-bewigged Hugh got to play out his tongue-waggling guitar hero dreams.

The tour came to a close with only one prickly moment, perhaps presaging worse to come several years later, by Hugh's memory: 'We had one falling out on tour – Stephen disappeared for a day; I'm not sure which town but he wasn't there for the soundcheck, and he'd just vanished. It turned out he'd got on a train and gone to another town – at least he hadn't gone to the continent. But he'd got upset about something and just pushed off, and it wasn't clear that he was coming back. It was something I'd said inadvertently – I didn't even know that I'd upset him! – but I think it was something to do with America, I'd suggested he was more intent on life in America than he actually was, and he took offence.' 'It wasn't an argument so much,' his colleague argues, 'I simply went away! We were in the Castle Hotel, Taunton, I think, and I wasn't getting through to him, and rather than have an argument, I did what I always do, and ran away! And of course Phil McIntyre, who was producing, said "Don't EVER do that again!" But Hugh and I never had heated words, never have. Hugh's always said his family was one of sulks rather than rows, my family was one of neither.

My parents never had a row, and still, they're both still bouncy, full of life and fun, and they chat away to each other without a dark word. When I was at school, and "taken out", as it were, by another boy whose parents lived near, I remember being *horrified* by parents having rows with each other, in front of their children! It made me shrink inside like a salted snail, because I'd never seen it.'

Unlike subsequent comedians, who had hit TV shows and then made a fortune taking them on the road in the 1990s, Fry & Laurie never toured again, despite the entreaties of Phil McIntyre. Their live experiences did stand them in good stead for a crucial date on the 1987 calendar, however, as 7 June 1987 saw the debut of a new comedy benefit, presented by Fry at the Victoria Palace Theatre. The necessity for a new fundraiser was all too obvious for Stephen's generation in the mid-1980s, as the horror of AIDS became more apparent with each passing tragedy. He may have needed no personal spur, but Fry knew what it was to lose close personal friends to the illness, and The Terrence Higgins Trust – named in memory of one of the UK's first AIDS victims – had been created in 1982 to help sufferers, and above all, to promote awareness and understanding, and there could be no better beneficiary. The Hysteria Trust was created to aid the charity, and Stephen's revue, named *Hysteria Hysteria Hysteria*, was a key part of that. Deciding on a formal dinner jacketed style for the proceedings, 'Piano Masterclass' included, some of Stephen & Hugh's closest collaborators were invited to join the cast, Atkinson and French featuring in a specially written and very silly guide to safe sex, and the *Who Dares Wins* team making the first of two appearances, while much of the evening was filled with stand-up plus *Spitting Image* cameos and cabaret oddities Fascinating Aida and Kit & The Widow, while Harry Enfield pleased *Saturday Live* fans with fresh Stavros. This first show had the feeling of a try-out, and was not televised, but there would be more to come. Despite Fry's passionate candour about his sexuality in the *Hysteria* shows, it wasn't until June 1988, when he gave a short speech in Ian McKellen's celebration of gay theatre, *Before the Act,* that Stephen was celebrated in the public eye as 'out and proud'.

There was one final live date in Fry & Laurie's 1987 diaries, and it was a world removed from the student unions they had grown used to. The 1987 *Royal Variety Performance* was back at the London Palladium, with big names including Tom Jones, Shirley Bassey and Les Dawson performing for HMQ and Prince Philip, and two other double acts – Cannon & Ball and Hale & Pace – also on the billing. 'Comedy Masterclass' was dusted down and lightly cleaned up for the occasion, with less emphasis on 'balls', Fry explaining to the *Mirror*, 'We don't necessarily believe Her Majesty would take any offence, but we would hate to cause her any embarrassment.' With no offence taken, this would mark the first of many occasions that both comics would perform for royalty, both publicly and behind securely closed doors.

Shortly after, Stephen & Hugh piloted their first programme as a double act over the second Tuesday and Wednesday of Advent, at first pre-recording sketches including the return of Gordon & Stuart, 'Prize Poem', and their very first recorded *ABOF&L* sketch, 'Police PLC', which poured invective over Thatcherite plans to privatise every public service in Britain. Despite this satirical opener, Stephen was affronted when he gingerly sent John Lloyd a sample script, not long after John's split with Helen Fielding, with a view to him coming on board as script editor: 'I was exhausted and broken-hearted,' Lloyd recalls, 'so I wouldn't have been in a particularly good mood. I said to Stephen, "The problem is, it's not about anything." And he got rather cross, and said, "Does everything have to be political satire now?" I said, "No it's not that, Stephen, a lot of the sketches are very clever, but Python had something to say about the state of the world." I liked it when Stephen & Hugh got onto the Spies, and businessmen particularly, they absolutely nailed that part of the culture. I'm sure they would despise me for saying that's better satire than pointing out that the Prime Minister's got a big nose.' 'There were certain things that we felt needed satirising – not politicians in particular. There's this idea that topical comedy is satire, and I don't think it is. It was not apolitical,' Hugh was to protest. 'We have political obsessions that we tend to write about. We wrote a great deal about the whole idea of a "value" being placed upon everything, even people, that distorts real value.' Stephen certainly could not be accused of political impotence – it was around this time that Labour leader Neil Kinnock read an article Fry had penned for *The Listener* entitled 'Licking Thatcher', and saw to it that the comic was approached with a view to becoming one of his speech writers – an occasional job he performed as one of a number of party duties, not just for Kinnock, but his successors, up to Gordon Brown. However, disclaiming any blame for damage done to society by the New Labour experiment, Fry wrote, 'Once Tony had won in 1997 let's just say it stopped being fun. Writing for the underdog is infinitely more challenging and amusing . . . I cannot claim that a single paragraph, sentence, phrase or word of mine made the slightest impact on British politics. It probably only served to annoy more people who found "Labour luvvies" instinctively repellent than it attracted to the party.'[4] There are few phrases more repugnantly redundant than 'champagne socialist' (and besides, Stephen is allergic to anything but the pink kind), and both colleagues actively tried to protest the Conservatives' stranglehold on power in some way. While not forgetting for one moment the privilege and wealth these young guns were enjoying, Stephen wrote, 'Thatcher's Britain seemed to us to be something that needed searingly to be indicted, the searinglier the better . . . our educations and upbringings had been received under Labour and Edward Heath's more liberal and consensus-based dispensations. The new callousness and combative certainty of Thatcher and her cabinet of vulgar curiosities were alien to the values we grew up with, and it smelt all wrong.'[5]

Another pre-recorded sequence for the pilot reflected the more personal politics of art criticism, with Stephen & Hugh originating the revolting, pointless sprawling figures of Simon Clituris (or 'Flituris' in the series) and co; commenting on the comedy on offer and thereby deflating any real criticism in advance, while getting laughs into the bargain. This was not a wholly novel ploy – on radio, *ISIRTA* was known to cut to pretentious critics after particularly dodgy sketches, who would then pull it apart, to which Fry says, 'I'm not in the least surprised because I think Hugh and I shared with Cleese in particular the slightly paranoid sense that whenever we did anything, we could almost fill in all the negative reviews we could hear in our heads as we were doing it. And therefore there's this huge desire to get your retaliation in first, as the phrase has it. I mean, I do it to myself all the time, so when I'm in a film or something I'm actually muttering the *Time Out* review in my head while I'm waiting for the lighting to be done.'

One of Stephen's favourite parables tells of a professional critic at the gates of Heaven, being quizzed by St Peter about their qualifications for entry: 'You know, other people wrote things, performed things, painted things and I said stuff like, "thin and unconvincing", "turgid and uninspired", "competent and serviceable" . . .' Having recanted his own career in criticism, *ABOF&L*'s crumpled reviewers would provide a memorable pre-emptive strike against brickbats to come. He once told Michael Parkinson about his love of sport, saying, 'I just think there's something so glorious about it, it's so supreme and unquestionable, you know – if a wicket is knocked down it's knocked down . . . you don't get people going round saying, "Did it work for you?" You know, the sort of scum who appear on late night BBC2 – "It seems to me there's a sense in which . . ." – oh, bugger off! It's so irritating. It's just so clear and so absolute, sport, in that respect. And so theatrical!'

Returning to the hallowed halls of BBC TV Centre the next day, rehearsing bright and early from 10:30 a.m., by 7:30 p.m. Stephen & Hugh were in front of their programme's first live studio audience, beginning the evening with an introduction which would not make it to the screen:

HUGH & STEPHEN ENTER & ADDRESS THE CAMERAS.
HUGH: Good evening, ladies and gentlemen, thank you for bothering.
STEPHEN: Very kind of you to be here.
HUGH: For those of you new to this sort of thing, a particular welcome.
STEPHEN: That's right. It should all be fairly straightforward. Help yourself to anything that particularly takes your fancy.
HUGH: Though do remember to try and leave it pretty much as you left it, others may want to use it after you.
STEPHEN: We'll start over here, if that's all right. Try and remember not to move around too suddenly.

HUGH: And make sure any hot drinks or sharp implements are kept well away from direct sunlight.
STEPHEN: Otherwise, just enjoy yourself.
HUGH: Well, there's a fair amount to get through, so I suggest we just crack on really.

This early attempt to anchor the show was dropped in favour of an espionage-themed opener on film, with the stars as two not terribly mysterious figures being tailed at an airport – a sequence which allowed Stephen to crowbar in the code phrase 'Trouser trouser trouser!' at last. The original script, however, then led directly to a chess-based sketch in which Stephen's ignorance of the game was compounded by his white-hot anger at every move Hugh made. This, along with their 'Prompt' skit, 'Honour' and the psychiatrist sketch, were the only items which failed to make it into the pilot once it was edited together and broadcast on BBC2 on Boxing Day. Running to an unusual thirty-six minutes, there was one glaring incongruity – a short extract from American artist William Wegman's *Selected Video Works 1970–78*, in which the joys of underarm deodorant were extolled, as an armpit dripped with spray. Stephen explains, 'We had thought to ask art students in the very nascent branch of video to contribute little clips that might be worth inserting (rather in the way Python had Gilliam), but unfortunately this was the only one that was submitted! So we shoved it in the pilot but lost belief in the idea once we went to series.'

The makeshift credits, with details from works of art depicting 'bits' of the two colleagues in question, now seem alien, but the chosen theme tune does not. 'Hugh said, "You know Professor Longhair?" And I thought, "Is that a cartoon character?" I'd never heard of Professor Longhair. And he said, "I'll play you this, he played this live on the *Queen Mary*." And it was extraordinary. It's called "Mardi Gras", a New Orleans kind of name, with a kind of whistle in it. It was just the perfect introduction to a comedy show.' Laurie adds, 'The BBC said, "we can't afford to pay for that every week, so we'll record our own version of it", with Harry Stoneham – who did the fantastically hip *Parkinson* theme.'

There are few comedy pilots which do not seem rough and ready with hindsight, and *ABOF&L* was no exception, but the programme debuted to a modestly warm reception despite the critic-bashing, and the greenlight for a full series was no surprise to anyone – it was the end of a truly momentous year for Fry & Laurie. 'The pilot seemed to go well,' producer Ordish recalls, 'the BBC were very happy with it, and we were on a winning streak.'

1987 was, admittedly, momentous in another way for Stephen, as it was around this time that he first inserted a powdered derivation of the coca leaf up his celebrated nose. His hobby of collecting London club memberships did not stop at the ancient and crusty, and when media watering hole The Groucho Club opened its doors in 1985, Stephen's name was not far down the members list – he even penned the club's official rulebook. The Dean Street establishment would become a second home for Fry, who was often to be found discussing projects in the bar, or shooting pool or losing at poker in an upper room, and as the 1990s came round, Groucho's would become infamous as the playground of the Young British Artists including Damien Hirst and Tracey Emin, and others of their hedonistic group including original Alternative anarchist Keith Allen.

The nose-candy's effects suited Stephen with worrying precision, fuelling the kind of party-going hedonism which came with his chosen career, but which hitherto had never appealed to him. 'There was ever something darker, more dangerous and – let's be frank – more stupid about me than about my friends,' he wrote. 'By the end of the 1980s I would no more consider going out in the evening without three or four grams of cocaine safely tucked in my pocket than I would consider going out without my legs . . . the real reason I embraced it is that I found it could give me a second existence. Instead of performing and being in bed with a mug of Horlicks and a P. G. Wodehouse at 11 p.m., coke gave me a whole new lease on nightlife.'[6] Despite this boon, Fry has always claimed above all that the substance actually soothed rather than energised him, in those days before he was diagnosed with a bipolar disorder. It was never taken in any working environment, and fuelled neither performance nor composition – one sketch features an executive trying to market heroin and cocaine, but you could not call the Fry &

Laurie *oeuvre* 'drug-induced' because of how one half of the duo liked to power his spare time. Cocaine would complicate Stephen's life in the years to come, of course (two years later he would narrowly avoid a drink-driving sentence on his motorbike, coming dramatically close to having his personal 'stash' discovered by the officers in question, to whom he offered *Blackadder* recording tickets) but otherwise, the sad truth is that 'comedian takes cocaine' is the definition of a non-story. If anything, Hugh's lack of any such substance addiction marked *him* out as the weirdo, in most comedy circles, so all-encompassingly rife was, and is, coke-snorting in the comedy world. Besides, Laurie adds, 'I partook – nothing like the scale he did, and it was largely as a result of his generosity. Or his desire to co-opt me in his scheme so I could not then disapprove of him! One or the other, or both. That's how they get you, isn't it? They get you to kill someone and you're in. I suppose if it had been anything he was doing where you had to wonder about his health, if he ate nothing but cheeseburgers and weighed forty-five stone, you would say, "Well, hold on, old chap, dial it down a little!" But I don't feel like Jo and I ever tut-tutted . . . part of it is that he slightly enjoyed casting us in the role of parents, because we were the straight couple, and he quite enjoyed that dynamic of putting us in the position of going, "Well, now, Stephen, what's all this we hear . . .?" But I don't think we ever did, it just made him feel rebellious and mischievous. Although I must say we were never aware of the extent of it – he's quite a secretive bloke, he gets a buzz from the idea of living another life where he is burning the candle at both ends. I read parts of his memoir, going, "Shit, I had no idea about that . . ." – which he quite enjoyed.'

From here on in, then, it is just to be assumed that this level of Groucho abandon was one private affair which slightly separated Stephen & Hugh away from the cameras, as domestic joy awaited the latter, and new-found addiction only seemed to give the former more energy than ever. As Fry noted of their home life, 'I would awaken with a spring and a bounce and Tigger my way down to the kitchen in search of breakfast, much to the grumpy annoyance of Hugh . . . Never the larkiest bird in the morning sky, Hugh, after a day in the gym, bed at 11:30 and not so much as a gin and tonic in between, still managed to feel like hell until mid-afternoon and seven coffees the next day.'[7]

Stuffed Vine Leaves?

These years of cohabitation came to an end in the spring, with the momentous news that Jo was pregnant with Charles Archibald Laurie, who would enter the world in December, by which time Hugh and Jo had built a nest in their own corner of Camden, leaving Stephen to establish a confirmed bachelor existence in the very heart of the metropolis – a seemingly idyllic life, shuttling between Norfolk and London W1 in a newly bought black taxi cab which he had gone so far as to adorn with a carefully created plate reading 'Not licensed to carry any passengers. Neapolitan Police', lest anyone should confuse him for a real cabbie.

A life-shapingly crucial family arrival also came for him at this time, when his sister Jo arrived in town. 'I came to London in January to pursue my dreams of doing make-up for television,' she says, 'following the advice of one Sunetra soon-to-be Atkinson, I took a BBC-oriented course, but soon discovered that although I adored the world of make-up, I didn't actually like touching people I didn't know! I was slightly gagging . . . A lot of time had gone by, and Stephen and I only really saw each other on holidays, it was a more grown-up world. But we went to dinner, and I remember thinking as I was getting ready how much I loved the camaraderie of his world – but behind the scenes, and unbeknownst to me, Stephen was flapping about thinking, "I wonder if Jo will help me out?" Because he was going away filming and coming back to find his Barclaycard payments weren't made, and fan mail was coming in. And we immediately found a professional footing, I very quickly knew what my job was. When my son George was born, I was very proud that I came home from hospital and sent a fax. I just kept working.' To this day, Jo remains the kind but forceful guardian of the Fry diary, but the secrets of the Fry & Laurie chemistry remain a mystery to her: 'It was all such a whirl! When I lived with Stephen, Hugh would appear, crash helmet dumped wherever, and they'd repair off to Stephen's study at the top of the house, while my office was in the basement. Hugh would pace around, and what was great for me was he'd come down and hit the piano just above where I was, so I'd hear, most memorably, when he was mastering "Bat Out Of Hell". I was the sandwich girl, I'd take an order and beetle off, and then Hugh would get very angry for about twenty minutes about sandwich packaging, then eat the sandwiches, and they'd go back to work. I was never party to their writing, so at recording time – I'd go most Sundays – it was all new to me. I occasionally went through lines with Stephen, but very rarely.'

Although no longer in each other's pockets domestically, Stephen & Hugh's chief professional preoccupation in 1988 was of course to write and perform the rest of the first series of *ABOF&L*, but there were many duties to perform before those recordings came round at the end of the year. Firstly, Dan Patterson had talked Stephen into becoming a regular in the new Radio 4 game show devised with his friend Mark Leveson, after an eye-opening sample of the improv scene in America. *Whose Line Is It Anyway?* debuted at the start of January, teaming Stephen with a comic a few years his senior, *Spitting Image* voice, incurable extemporiser and Ken-'n'-Em cohort John Marshall, who took the stage name Sessions. Fry was of course game for any game, but it was a rare achievement for him to talk Laurie into playing along for the second episode, alongside *Spitting Image*'s Enn Reitel. The duo only ad-libbed together for one round, introduced by host Clive Anderson as a partnership that 'have worked together on many a comedy show and advertisement', and they played it safe by slipping into the roles of Gordon & Stuart, trying to sell self-raising flour to the audience. The six episodes rapidly led to a Channel 4 spin-off in the autumn, but despite excelling at the game (perhaps excepting any musical round, which he staunchly played in agonised *sprechgesang*), Stephen could not commit to more than a few appearances as the TV show took off, though they included a memorably inebriated episode alongside Peter Cook, plus bonus appearances in a *Whose Line?* special for the second Comic Relief Red Nose Day in 1989, and one-off return in 1997.

It had always been the plan for Curtis's benefit show to expand into a full-blown telethon, and when the very first Red Nose Day captured the imagination of the British people in February 1988, Fry & Laurie were naturally a key part of the evening's entertainment – as well as popping up on *Wogan*, to publicise the event alongside the cream of their comedic generation. Both Stephen & Hugh took on so many disparate roles for Comic Relief – from documentary strands about disability to fake news items – it would be exhausting to list them all, but their key duty in those early days, and another way in which they cemented their place in the national consciousness as a partnership, was being the hard-nosed keepers of the 'Gunge Tank'. Children who tuned in to CBBC voted each year on which of their least favourite presenters deserved to be dipped into a pool of unspeakable gunk, 'the biggest pot noodle in history'. On the night, the winning loser – Mike 'Smitty' Smith, Sarah Greene, Andy Crane – would have to face a barrage of abuse from Fry & Laurie before they pulled the lever which jettisoned them into the foul brew below, with palpable relish. Parallels with Cook & Moore always prove irresistible, and in this case it's worth pointing out that the very concept of TV gunge has its roots in *Not Only . . . But Also*, in which Peter & Dudley improvised poems with their guests until each was dunked in synthetic filth.

Besides more criticism from Simon Clituris, Fry's last duty for that Red Nose Night was to take his place as a *Blackadder* monarch at last, in the short special *The Cavalier Years*, in which he essayed a convincing impersonation of the beheaded monarch's great-to-the-power-of-eleven-grand-nephew, Prince Charles – although when he reprised the role for a Royal audience ten years later, he couldn't bring himself to mimic the current heir, and fell back on full Melchett bombast. The Civil War squib was not to be the last of the *Blackadder* duties for the year.

Given all this hectic comedy activity, it's little wonder that Paul Jackson's last live series, now moved back a day to become *Friday Night Live*, contained much less from Stephen & Hugh. Indeed, so busy was Fry with a number of jobs, including taking David Lander to TV in Hat Trick's *This Is David Lander,* that he only showed up once, to compete against the indie company's founder Jimmy Mulville in a game show called 'Stupid', presented by Ben. Hardly cut adrift, Hugh remained to perform a few monologues and a sketch or two with new regular Josie Lawrence, while Fry & Laurie's place as resident duo was taken by up-and-coming Scottish duo Jack Docherty & Moray Hunter, in a very embryonic form of their Don & George characters. The series was ultimately hijacked by 'Junior Boy' Harry's success as Loadsamoney, leering his way to zeitgeist icon status and on the way to launching his own TV comedy empire.

David Lander's move to Channel 4 was successful, a mockumentary of singular realism for all its ludicrousness – but even then, Stephen became so busy he could not commit to a second series in 1990, and at his suggestion to Hat Trick, a name change to *This Is David Harper* was necessitated, introducing the new investigator Tony Slattery, who had been busy making anarchic children's television but would soon break through as the most audacious *Whose Line?* player of all time. Even before Lander translated to TV, however, Stephen was out of circulation for an extended period, with a return to the theatre.

Hedonistic playwright Simon Gray was the junior member of a theatrical triumvirate with Harold Pinter and Alan Bates, and his world of Cambridge academe, of spies and pained privilege clearly made young Stephen an ideal new find for his stable of performers. *The Common Pursuit*, a semi-autobiographical story of a student literary magazine and the lives it mashed together, debuted to little notice in 1984, but four years later, Gray had a hit on his hands thanks to his reluctant acceptance of a cast full of comic names. Stephen filled the role of the mild-mannered donnish Humphry and was reunited with Sessions, and the real wildcard, Rik Mayall, in a new production which took up much of March to July 1988, with a highly successful run at the Phoenix Theatre in Camden – successful not just with critics and audiences, but behind the scenes as well, with director Gray finding a new lease of life amid the 'Alternative' stars he claimed never to have heard of before casting them. Two years later, Simon would make Stephen the hero of his *Screen Two* drama *Old Flames,* joining Simon Callow and Miriam Margolyes in career best performances at the heart of a tale of public school revenge – and two years after that, Fry was to be the only returning *Common Pursuit* cast member when the play was adapted for the same strand, making him almost part of the Gray furniture.

Stephen wasn't too busy to turn down one irresistible but ultimately quite embarrassing invitation, to be one of a number of comic turns filling in time between huge musical legends at a special show to mark Nelson Mandela's seventieth birthday, at Wembley Stadium on 11 June. This was by far the biggest live audience Fry & Laurie ever played to – a source of unimaginable terror to them both, trying to hold the attention of a worldwide audience of 600 million (or, as they called them, 'Colin') while Tracy Chapman prepared to come on – but what was the worst that could happen? Perhaps a microphone malfunction, which meant that Stephen's half of their specially written dialogue went largely unheard amidst a soundscape of squealing, until both tried to plough on by bellowing into the same mike. Still, at least Hugh managed to get a photo of Stephen with 'Colin', to prove to his mother that it all actually happened.

With all this going on, there were those five remaining episodes of *Saturday Night Fry* to be recorded, triggering Stephen's preternaturally rapid week of stream-of-consciousness composition. He could no longer rely on the solid line-up of Emma and Hugh, who each had to cry off some shows, but out of necessity came an enviable cast of replacements, including Julia Hills, Mike Leigh alumni Jim Broadbent and Alison Steadman, old friend Robert Bathurst, and Emma's mother Phyllida Law – Stephen & Hugh were naturally friends of the Thompson family and knew Phyllida well, allowing for a degree of in-joking, with Emma presented as a diva who uses her mother as an understudy. A whole host of TV and genre pastiches were included, and there was an extended examination of the beautiful language of Strom. The full run of *SNF* was broadcast in the late spring, and despite Stephen's quite ridiculous work schedule, it was a rich stew of sketches and oddities, regularly giving the host opportunities to send up a persona that was only growing in public consciousness:

ROBERT:	... Er, that's not tea, that's a magic potion which turns you into a parody of Stephen Fry.
JIM:	Oh, pox and seven pence! So it does. Well isn't that a turn-up...
STEPHEN:	... For the trousers. *En passant*, it is an important and worthy observation that the word 'trousers'...

FX: TAPE SPOOLS OFF.[8]

'I did used to say "fluffy" and "pink" rather a lot, but people started using them back and I got embarrassed,' he admitted. 'I use words like other people hum tunes. Any fool can detect the melodic possibilities of "gorgeous", "splendid" and "bliss crisis"!' The show aired from April to June, *Radio Times* wireless critic Gillian Reynolds recommending it as 'The most cheering new comedy programme to come along in a great while . . . it proves it is possible to love Radio 4 a lot and still see its ludicrous side. It really is very good indeed.' *SNF*'s overdue commercial release in 2009 belied its influence, not least on *On The Hour*, and Fry repaid the tribute shown to him by Armando Iannucci and Chris Morris when he played 'Comedy Controller' for Radio 4 Extra in 2014, including an episode of their media satire alongside his own (plus *The Men from the Ministry, Hitchhiker, Clue* and *Down the Line*). When Fry presented a Radio 4 programme with the exact same title in 1998, many fans were disappointed to find that this time it was a rather earnest discussion programme, albeit, of course, a terribly erudite one, with regular monologues from John Sessions.

While Stephen was busy with his theatre work, radio show and fake consumer investigations, Hugh took on a number of roles: an ITV sitcom cameo, a spot of screen time in the David Hare movie *Strapless* – and his career could have taken a very different path had he passed the audition to play Rimmer in new sci-fi sitcom *Red Dwarf*. But both were champing at the bit to get stuck into their primary project, the BBC2 sketch show which could put them up there with their greatest heroes. 'Cook & Moore were of course sort of gods to us, and Morecambe & Wise and The Two Ronnies', Hugh says, 'we just grew up loving sketches!' From start to end, the parallels between Peter & Dudley's act and Stephen & Hugh's often seem too glaring to ignore, but Laurie says, 'People can make a comparison, but I don't know that we come out of it favourably, probably not – but they were such towering heroes of our time, their influence was irresistible, as it was for so many people. They took the duologue to such heady heights, and we admired them so much that on some level it would have been impossible for us not to be striving for similarity – how far short we fell is for others to say, of course.'

'We did have this idea of going away,' Hugh continues, 'lots of writers try and do this, they persuade themselves that they're too easily distracted – so we went to Crete. I don't know why. Cheap tickets or something. Pin in the map, could have been Basingstoke. And we tried to live the good life – we would swim round the bay in the morning, and then write all day and then play backgammon all night. And I amassed a fairly healthy lead. In fact, I think I'm right in saying that Stephen owes me a million and a half pounds . . . I had a million and a half pounds' worth of satisfaction out of annoying him by beating him at backgammon.' This kind of concentrated comedy collaboration in exotic climes was a tradition established years earlier by the Python team, and the UV rays, retsina and dolmades undoubtedly worked wonders for our sun-tanned colleagues. Stephen certainly needed a holiday, albeit a working one: to cap a year of non-stop activity, in August he had nearly died of a beer-triggered asthma attack and was only saved by Ben Elton diverting their shared taxi to speed him to Barts hospital.

Greece was a fecund locale for the colleagues, and soon the sketches were beginning to mount up, with little or no collaborative discord. 'The honest truth is we've never had a row,' repeats Hugh once more. 'Partly because we're English and middle-class and we don't do that. I think we're so afraid of it that it doesn't happen . . . probably the finest bit of acting we ever do is to say "this is the finest and funniest thing I've ever read", but to be able to say it in such a way as to hint that it probably isn't.' Although Hugh was always more inclined towards pen and paper than tapping away at a keyboard, the Fry & Laurie writing days tended to be scrupulously intense for both comedians, each chain-smoking at separate opposing desks as they explored their muses together and apart, and tried not to get too distracted by the cricket. 'The typical sketch comes about by one or the other of us taking a line for a walk,' Stephen explained. 'M'colleague or I will continue with this on our own for a while, and then yell across the room, "This is arse-wash, see if you can improve it!"' 'There were days when it went well, writing with Stephen, when things would just sort of flop out onto the page in an incredibly pleasing way, just like landing a big gleaming salmon – which, by the way, I've never done, but I imagine would be a satisfying thing. We would make each other laugh, and the laughter would provoke the next idea and the next idea, and all of a sudden, sometimes in a matter of minutes, you would have something that you knew was a genuinely good and interesting and funny piece of work that you could actually present to the public without shame.'

The writing continued on their return to Blighty, but in November one hiccup which could have challenged Hugh's claims never to have fallen out with his colleague actually led to an even deeper level of understanding between the two. 'Hugh and I were writing, and we'd write every day, Monday to Friday and we'd give ourselves the weekend off. I was asked if I would present a documentary on the Chess Olympiad in Thessaloniki, in Greece. And it was great, because it was only four days, Friday to Monday, so I for some reason said to Hugh, "I can't make Friday or Monday because of . . ." something or other.' Hugh would only have been mildly put out by this rapid return to Greece, but of course, by his own admission, Stephen *lies* – not vindictively, but as a matter of course, white-ish lies to avoid unpleasantness, and a delayed flight led to unavoidable discovery. 'Anyway, the point is, he found out,' Stephen continues, 'It was not that big a deal, but it was, as parents say to their children, "It was the fact that you *lied* . . ." So he was furious.' Fury, between two such impeccably brought up gentlemen, emerges in the form of a carefully written letter, which awaited Stephen on his return. In the letter, Hugh explained his hurt at being pointlessly deceived, using a phrase which signified an extraordinary declaration for a straight, sporty Old Etonian: 'It's as if you don't realise how much I love you.' 'He used that word!' Fry remembers, 'And I thought, that's so un-Hugh to talk like that – men don't talk like that to each other. So it was actually a rather wonderful breakthrough in a way. It was sweet.' It's certainly an admission it would be hard to imagine Eric making to Ernie without a punchline, or vice versa, but of course one of Fry & Laurie's many unique points was their different sexualities. Fry jokes, 'We were very traditional – he was the straight man, I was the homosexual man, which is the way it always works', but then there is always that unworthy question, was their magnetic pull towards each other entirely platonic? Stephen gamefully insists, 'One of the most fortunate things really for me, as a gay man, is that I never fancied him. Although he's extremely good looking – which he is, and a lot of women could faint at the sight of him – fortunately, for some reason, that switch was never on with me and Hugh. And it would have been embarrassing if it had been, if you think about it.' In a way, if this protestation isn't entirely sincere, that makes this one of the greatest love stories in comedy history, but the frank admission of devotion from Hugh, as a particularly hot-blooded ladies' man, wonderfully silences any tiny inkling, perhaps born of homophobia, that their friendship was built on any unrequited passion.

Otherwise, Laurie adds, 'We had no conventional double act dynamic – because we were close to being the same height, we couldn't get that, you know, "short fat funny one and tall laconic one" thing, we just weren't naturally that kind of a double act.' 'It was a relationship untainted by any sort of schoolboy rivalry or any sexual overtones,' Stephen summarises. 'I wasn't in love with him or anything so there was no kind of complication in that sense but we had an absolute instinct. People would remark very quickly after we'd met that we said exactly the same thing at the same time in response to something. We started writing together and we just never stopped.'[9]

TV was not short of all kinds of double acts at this time – Smith & Jones were the mainstream bosses on the verge of promotion to BBC1, Hale & Pace were starting their ITV reigns, and French & Saunders were just finding their feet in their own BBC2 vehicle. Dawn & Jennifer were to equal Stephen & Hugh's feat of being the sole writers of their own show – but neither accomplishment could top that of Victoria Wood, who crafted two series of uniquely funny *As Seen on TV* entirely on her own.

An Extra Pint of Damn for the Weekend

In August, although touring was no longer needed to amass new material, Stephen & Hugh made their only appearance as a double act at Edinburgh, the scene of their first great success seven years earlier. For the last three days of the month, they presented an hour at the Assembly Rooms which utilised the best of their new sketches, with a fresh item at the halfway point – 'Troubleshooters', again inspired by the cheapest TV, a drama about yachting types which polluted Sunday nights on BBC1: '*Howards' Way* to me symbolised a certain kind of British drama which now, perhaps sadly but probably thankfully, doesn't exist any more,' Fry says, 'in which the idea of BUSINESS was a very hard, tough thing, and it was full of people shouting about "business!" – "*Those stock options are MINE!*" – and drinking a huge amount on screen, usually with Kate

O'Mara in the background somewhere . . . I find the business machismo very bizarre in programmes like that. It's all the deep manly voices that suggest they're carrying their testicles around in a wheelbarrow.' Putting themselves through this display one evening, it's not surprising the colleagues found themselves aping the testosterone-fuelled nonsense on screen. 'Hugh and I did – not exactly a parody, but a world a bit like it, with a couple of businessmen who shout at each other. Marjorie was always dogging their footsteps, and they were always splashing huge amounts of Scotch down themselves.' John Barraclough & Peter Sherman emerged quite fully formed, their first sketch remaining identical from stage to screen, but it wasn't until viewers and friends began to repeat their bombastic cries of *'DAMN!'* in diverse ways that they realised they had characters worth bending their rules on repeated sketch formats for, and the details of their business – the vicious high octane world of Uttoxeter's health and leisure services – began to be fleshed in.

Laurie says, 'I know the one thing we were determined to do was to keep doing new things. We had a few repeated things, but we tried to avoid doing that, so when we did something we tended to do it once, but then we just went on for too long. There were sketches that were nine minutes long, that's unforgivable! There wasn't anything too deliberate or calculated about it, we just wrote what came out. That's not good enough, is it? We thought about it long and hard and decided this was the way to go. We were wrong, *okay?*'

Exceptions to this rule of ever moving forward onto new scenarios (or as Fry had it, 'the sort of pride and mad, stubborn, stiff-necked insistence that every sketch was new and original') were few and far between, but the other celebrated running sketch came from Hugh's lifelong preoccupation with British spies – a fixation more than shared with Stephen. The cosy world of Control, head of the British Secret Service, and his employee Tony Murchison, was an ever-subtle undermining of the hard-bitten worlds of James Bond and George Smiley. Jon Canter had been Footlights President several years before Hugh, but only got to know him via his friendship with Jo, and he was to gain a singular insight into the Fry & Laurie method. With the Spies sketches, Canter observes, 'Hugh, being a consummate comedy actor, could write things that only he could perform – like with Control &

Tony, there was nothing on the page – if you'd sent it in to a comedy show, it wouldn't have meant anything. But you knew he was a master at extracting the maximum comic juice from it, which nobody else could have done. He has such a comic ear.' By taking the twee platitudinous dialogue shared between Tony & Control as the former prepared the latter's morning coffee, and performing every line with over-obvious deliberation, like reluctant school children in a nativity play, Hugh & Stephen found an almost inexhaustible source of silly laughs, and although the scenario did not debut until the second episode of the series, it was thought that their weekly familiarity could draw in viewers, making them a beloved part of the *ABOF&L* recipe.

'Writing is the most agonising thing in the world to do, writing sketch comedy is just awful,' Fry says. 'You just want to stab yourself, you meet every day, you try and cheer yourselves up, you end up watching some horse race, but then you start something, and Hugh would have a look at it and go, "I'll add to it, you can see what I've started, it's terrible . . ." But you have to keep at it. It sounds awful complaining, but it is really difficult. So the answer to that is to develop a series of characters you can repeat.' However, Hugh adds, 'We tended not to give them backstories; I've subsequently discovered that it's a very admirable American device, performers and writers put a lot of work into trying to establish the provenance of characters, to make them, in that dread word, "grounded". I don't think we ever *wanted* to be grounded, we were preoccupied with first impressions, and surfaces, and inasmuch as the surfaces are funny, or tell you something underneath, we would pursue it that far, but we never discussed backstories, unless we could use it as material. We would sometimes get excited about a Tony & Control thing – which were immensely enjoyable to think about and write and play – but we were only thinking "Oh and another thing they could do . . .", rather than "Here's a thing they might have done which we'll never see, but it's good to know that." I think you can go too far with what makes characters the way they are, it can be unrewarding – apart from anything else, human beings are so chaotic.'

Having forged six half-hour scripts' worth of sketches over months of diligent office hours, gallons of coffee and hundreds of cigarettes, the time for recording the first series of *ABOF&L* was drawing near, the even more pressing deadline of Charlie Laurie's birth being just one complication to factor in to another stressful Advent. Shortly after arrival, however, the little fellow proved an absolute boon to one particularly obtuse episode closer, 'Special Squad', in which Fry & Laurie played two insane (naturally) menaces demanding the whereabouts of one 'William Popey' – who turns out to be the babe-in-arms-in-question, and they grill him viciously. 'We assumed that he would be awake when he came onto the set,' recalled his father, 'but while waiting, he fell asleep, bless him, so when he was brought in, in the bright lights and the pair of us shouting at him, he started crying. As a result of that, I got a huge number of letters from people with very odd ideas: "It's quite plain that you were using needles to provoke this reaction!" . . . *What?* What's in your *head*? That you would think anybody could stick needles in a baby? So strange.'[10]

Mrs Popey was played by the colleagues' one regular co-performer in this first series, Deborah Norton, who had just completed her run as the closest thing to a fourth member of the hallowed *Yes, Prime Minister* trio, and would star in Andrew Marshall's 1993 medical sitcom *Health and Efficiency* as the Thatcherite administrator. Although from a generation above Stephen & Hugh, Roger Ordish knew Norton could fill their few spare roles admirably. In the final episode, she was even granted the licence to step out of character just as Stephen & Hugh had throughout the series, berating Hugh for his plan to murder a chicken on national TV. However, she now says, 'There were four of us in the marriage: Hugh, Stephen, me – and the inchoate spectre of Stephen's eventual breakdown. I don't think it was a happy period for him; he was charming, he was professional, we got the work done, and we went home, Stephen in one of his huge collection of vintage cars that he loved so much . . . Sometimes, looking back, I feel perhaps I was participating in some kind of elaborate therapy session. However, I met him at a charity show we did for Miriam Margolyes five or six years ago and was quite astonished at the change in him. A big generous warm bear of a man, making us all laugh, and surrounded by a peaceful contented aura. A National Treasure. I was so pleased for him.'

The utter destruction of the fourth wall was one of *ABOF&L*'s overriding characteristics from the start, with characters wandering off set and the pilot's 'Soup' sketch kicking the trend off by appealing to viewers for a workable punchline. Despite the wealth of material generated by them both, the thinness of some concepts was always a cue for Stephen or Hugh to step out of character and admit their shortcomings to the audience – akin to the Critics' pre-emptive rubbishing of the script. Within a few episodes, viewers could never be sure whether any given sketch would develop, or if one of the pair would suddenly chastise the other for having no idea where it was all going – the first full 'Dalliard' item, episode one's 'Barber' sketch, even closed the episode on such a tiff. This wasn't always a cheap get-out either – the one other notable supporting player in the series, Benjamin Whitrow, popped up in episode four as an incensed comedy writer accusing Stephen & Hugh of plagiarism, and one interrupted sketch, 'Inspector Venice', had been written in full, despite being curtailed by angry protests after the opening gag.

For all these references to individual episodes, of course the series was recorded in the most logical order possible, and largely shaped in the edit. Running jokes like Whitrow's disruptions helped give some weeks a special flavour, but with no real attempt to anchor the programme, the result was an ever-surprising stream-of-consciousness reminiscent of *Monty Python* or indeed *Alfresco* – in the first show, Hugh simply walks from one comic set-up to another. It was clear, however, that something else was needed to put some kind of Fry & Laurie stamp on the proceedings. Nobody has ever claimed credit for coming up with the idea of the 'Vox Pops', quick interstitial snippets of dialogue from the colleagues in an abundance of disguises, interviewed on the street, but it was a masterstroke, not least as it's one of the first things people bring to mind when the series is mentioned to this day. 'We realised that a lot of our stuff was wordy and tended to go on rather a lot, and we wanted to find ways of breaking things up,' Hugh says, 'That was one thought, the other is that when we were sitting there writing stuff, and it gets to the end of the day, you get half an idea and you write a line and then your pen just stops moving and you go, "I don't know what to do with that." And we'd go through them, and say, "Actually that's quite a funny line on its own, why don't we just do that?"' Stephen philosophised further to David Frost in 2013: 'One of the things that Python discovered is that when you have a flow of disconnected sketches, you need a desk, an anchor. In sketch comedy, there's something that goes wrong if you just have a stream of sketches without some regular place to return to. And the Pythons' first joke was that they would have a desk, but it would be on a beach, with Cleese saying, "And now for something completely different." They'd take the metaphor of the desk, and make it real, and put it somewhere surreal. And that's one of the things we missed, we didn't have a desk... But we had the Vox Pops instead, where Hugh and I would dress up as members of the public on the street, like the sort of people Esther Rantzen interviewed on *That's Life*.' Sketch shows had been desperately avoiding comparison to *Monty Python's Flying Circus* for decades, but the lack of paranoia about this was evident in *ABOF&L*, not least in the willingness to slip into opposite gender personas, Hugh often making a surprisingly glamorous woman while Stephen specialised in slightly more disturbing matriarchs. As the years went by, individual personas were found for these wittering strangers, Stephen's middle-aged brunette lady being 'Ivy', his lairy cabbie (in his own cab) was 'Frank', Hugh's young lady and moustachioed toff being 'Toyah' and 'Dominic' or 'Colonel Tweed' and so on. Further helpful guides were provided for the make-up and costume teams, such as 'Totteridge Woman is brunette, makes up quite carefully every day and is the wrong side of 42, but thinks 25. She wears a blouse, skirt, hat, necklace and a brooch too. She believes she looks soft and sensuous', or 'Sweet Old Lady is as the name implies. White hair, poppety hat and poppety cheeks and poppety everything.' Crossdressing for laughs was a thorny ploy, and Stephen observes, 'It is a sadly typical feature of male comedy I suppose, but I did like it – though never in a camp sense. I always liked what the great Stanley Baxter did when he played a woman, he *lowered* his voice and gave it a throbbing quality.'

Ordish's production did not suggest an opulent budget, some sketches taking place against a black backdrop, giving a theatrical feel to many studio items. 'I remember the sparseness,' Hugh says, 'think of that as our Dogme period! I always liked that, maybe it's my Presbyterian upbringing, but I liked the sort of severe black curtains, and as little fanfare as could be managed. Keeping things plain, it's the most satisfying setting for a joke, nothing to distract from the idea. I make it sound conceptual but it wasn't, they probably just said "You've got seventy-five quid, have at it!" But I think of it with pride, and it got more daunting as the series went on.' The Vox Pops constituted the only location filming for this first run, and were recorded well in advance. At this stage, the snippets were just that – complete non-sequiturs created in the edit, but in time the Vox Pops became an ideal repository for gags which had no other home. Each series would begin with filming sessions in London's shopping centres and street corners, armed with pages of ridiculous observations which could be used to structure the episodes – only a percentage actually finding their way to the screen, leaving a glut of overflow never to see the light of day until now:

STEPHEN: (IVY) I went to the garden centre and asked for some clematis. Jacksoniensis, I wanted, for my south wall. The nice young man said that they didn't have any Jacksoniensis, but they had some other varieties I might like to look at. And I said to him, 'blow it out your arse, you pig-eyed sack of shit'.

HUGH: (TOYAH) Well, we had this big argument. I wanted to send the children to private school, but Derek wanted to spend the money on building a conservatory. In the end we compromised and decided to go and see 'Les Miserables'.

STEPHEN: (FRANK) What about the good news, eh? The good news. Eh? They keep that from you, don't they? The good news. F'rinstance, I heard that that Martyn Lewis fell over and broke his leg the other day while mowing the garden. Did that make the 6.00 News? No. Bleeding disgrace. Could have cheered us all up.

HUGH: (DOMINIC) In our village there's a marvellous old game we play every Lammas Eve. Tradition has it that all those living in the village on state pensions have to dress up as bales of straw, and then the rest of us split up into packs of twelve, in four-wheel drive vehicles, and we have to hunt them down and beat them to death with fence posts. I'm not absolutely sure of its origins. Something to do with the Conservative Party, I believe.

And so on. Fry & Laurie tended to do without catchphrases of any water, if you'll pardon the pun (there isn't one), but these talking heads were an unmistakeable calling card for their humour, bringing a sense of familiarity without constant repetition (excepting the deliberately puzzling rounds of Stephen's old man laughing 'I wouldn't suck it!' in the first series finale).

After such a flurry of activity *ABOF&L* recordings hit a seasonal hiatus, with remaining sketches being recorded in January, and a relaxing festive period seemed in order – however, there were two joint sitcom bookings to see to in this non-stop period as well. Two years previously, Rik Mayall had approached sitcom stalwarts Laurence Marks & Maurice Gran to craft a whole new comedy persona for him – despicable Tory MP Alan B'Stard – and the second series episode of *The New Statesman*, 'The Haltemprice Bunker', required an uber-revolting (and, yes, cocaine-shovelling) City type to 'do lunch' with B'Stard in an achingly hip fascism-themed restaurant, inveigling the MP into a scheme profiting from General Pinochet's slavery programme – and Rik was delighted to learn that his mates were on board for the episode, Maurice Gran recalls: 'We wrote the roles especially for Stephen and Hugh. Stephen, I remember, did have quite a lot of input into his character, pontificating somewhat about his theory of comedy, despite which we got on very well and have remained friends.' The 1980s was of course packed with such greasy, greedy characters, and Fry would play a similar role in Malcolm Bradbury's *Anything More Would Be Greedy* the following year, alongside Robert Bathurst. Hugh's part, however, was not so plum, as a waiter reduced to homicidal destitution by the braying yuppies – more crucial 'being beaten up' experience.

The colleagues were on more equal footing when rejoining their chums for *Blackadder's Christmas Carol*, which had a troubled production in mid-December, recorded and then remounted only a week or so before broadcast on the day before Christmas Eve. Ebenezer Blackadder's travels through time allowed for the return of both Melchett and George, while the pair had the best fun dressing up outrageously for the sci-fi silliness of Christmas Future – a bronzed Hugh as Lord Pigmot, Majestic Prince of Frumpity complaining about missing '20,000 Years of the Two Ronnoids', and Stephen as Frondo, Mighty Birdlord of Thribble, festooned with horned helmet screeching for Blackadder to be sent to the 'sprouting chamber' – silliness 'plumpened' to bursting point in rehearsal. At the end of all this, it was a merry Christmas indeed for Stephen, Hugh, Jo and little Charlie.

Tally Ho, Pip Pip and Bernard's Your Uncle!

Friday 13 January 1989 was a very lucky day for BBC2, as it debuted the first episode of *A Bit of Fry & Laurie* at 9 p.m. It was traditional in those days for the comedians some programmes were 'By and With' to pen their own facetious entries for the *Radio Times*, and the show was sold as 'Three hours of interrupted viewing pleasure, handily divided into six stylish, convenient, bite-sized programmes, that say much more about you than the clothes you eat. With Deborah Norton as everyone else.' In fact, the stars had hoped to leave all salesmanship for their own vehicle at just that, Stephen telling the mag, 'Things get such a lot of hype these days, I think it would be splendid if we just appeared on the screen without any fanfares. If someone thinks we're good, they can tell their friends. If they don't like us, they can turn off . . . Just say it's a six-part series about concrete.' Hugh deflected attention further by claiming, 'Actually, we didn't write any of it. We farmed it out to a Puerto Rican collective in Whitechapel and paid them sixty pence an hour . . . There is a degree of procrastination when we sit down to write, and some panic too, because we have to come up with three hours of material. You can always write *something*, but with comedy it has to be something good. Some of the best sketches we finished in twenty minutes, but we spend an awful lot of time thinking of the right names for our characters.' On the subject of names, Peter Cuminmyear be blowed, some kerfuffle was caused in higher echelons by the namechecking of fictional author Ted Cunterblast. 'The name got us into a lot of trouble with the Controller of BBC2,' Hugh said. 'He called the producer the next day and said, "They used the word c-u-n-t!" and Roger said, "Well, actually, they used a name, Cunterblast." I wouldn't dream of asserting there was anything clever or witty about that, but for some reason it amused our childish selves as the time.'

The new year brought a rare comparative pause for breath after the stresses of 1988 – and they were stresses, Hugh suggesting his thirty-a-day habit went up to around 150-a-day in recording weeks. 1989 was to be of particular import to Laurie on a personal level. His mother Patricia had been suffering for some time with motor neurone disease, Ran lovingly caring for her to the end, and she passed away that year without any dramatic moment of emotional resolution with her famous youngest. Hugh's father remarried the following year and had another eight years of seeing his son's career go from strength to strength.

More happily, on 16 June, Hugh and Jo's nuptials were celebrated close to home in Camden, with their troops of friends, famous and non, all in attendance and of course, his colleague was best man, just as he was an obvious godfather to Charlie, and indeed all Hugh's children. Stephen has to date totted up at least thirteen godchildren, but asked by *The Times* about his chances for settling down, he admitted, 'It is quite obviously the sensible thing for Hugh, and it works terribly well for him. But for me . . . You can look at a marvellous shirt, but realise it wouldn't suit you. I might like to be that person, but you have to find out if you can be that person who is married. I'd like children, but that is the image of the father figure with lots of chickadees running around – a sentimental self-image. You are not really saying you want to have children, but rather to be a father figure, which you can easily be without having children yourself.' 'The thing that makes him happiest is company,' Laurie responded. 'He loves to sit at a table with a group of friends and a bottle of wine. And he adores games of any kind, too. At Christmas you can hardly get in the front door for the boxes of Waddington's games and he can't wait to tear off the cellophane, memorise the rules in four minutes and explain how a particular game is played. He has no children of course, but I've never seen a child who isn't thrilled to be with him, probably because in many ways he is very childlike himself.' Hugh was adamant that the tabloids should be kept at bay for his and Jo's happy event, but went so far as to say of his love life, 'Someone repressed like me, with a word like that, goes "steady on!" Crippled by fear of failure, I wouldn't approach unless I was fairly sure of success. I struck rarely but accurately . . . I've gone through a lot of my life thinking that people didn't like me. Jo is a great administrator, she has a very good logical brain. At home we are opposites – I don't answer the phone if I can possibly avoid it and I don't open letters, especially ones in brown envelopes.'

With a second series of *ABOF&L* confirmed, much of the year was to be spent once again stacking up fresh sketches together. Although Ordish's indulgent production had suited them well, this time they brought in Nick Symons – old friend and housemate, Stephen's co-godfather and budding comedy producer – to learn the ropes, with a view to eventually taking the reins of the show. The team was complemented further by bringing Jon Canter in as script editor, and he explains, 'It wasn't easy for outsiders to come in to their world . . . The great thing about Roger was that he adored them. He called them "the boys". But you could say that's not enough. And Kevin Bishop came in on the third series, he was great, but a shy person. You could say their role was just to let "the boys" do what they wanted to do, but it wasn't a show with a disciplined headmaster figure, like John Lloyd. I tried my best, but they had each other – an intensely private bond. But you had absolute faith because their hearts were so in it, and they were so talented. They could be quite *funny* sometimes, if you suggested a different way of doing a sketch, they would look at you as if to say, "this isn't quite cricket". They were quite resistant to that.' Ordish agrees: 'It was very much their stuff, and they'd both come from *Blackadder*, arguing over every line, so the fact was, this was written by them and wasn't open to the same dissection.' On the other hand, he adds, 'I think maybe Hugh missed the cut and thrust; we were all saying "This is brilliant stuff, don't touch a hair of it!"

Hugh always wanted more conflict, that was my feeling, he was a bit of a pugilist. I remember him once saying to me, "Why do you always agree with me?" I told him it was because I thought his ideas were brilliant, but that didn't seem to satisfy him.'

Symons adds, 'Hugh's contribution to the partnership was a bit like when a chef tempers chocolate. Stephen would provide this incredibly rich, verbal idea for a sketch, and Hugh would get it to shine, and bring a quality to it. If you actually read Stephen on his own, it can get a bit too rich. But when Hugh contributed, it got into more of a Pete & Dud type feel. Stephen would have liked every sketch to be set in some Jane Austen drawing room, but Hugh said, "No, we're going to do a sketch set in a mini-cab office, or a police station." That's where you get the wonderful balance between the two.' 'There are some things that may feel particular to one or the other of us, but very few,' Hugh insists. 'In most cases, we wouldn't even remember which one of us had started something, or finished, or changed the idea and turned it into something else.' Stephen suggests, 'Hugh is a genius at finding ways in which logic falls down. Or, the directions logic can take you to when extended and extended. He is a natural logician, which is very rare thing in the world. He also, of course, has a very funny face indeed. Like a disappointed horse. We both share a predilection for turning stock phrases inside out or suddenly subverting them, but I think I may have learned that at his feet perhaps. Over the years we unquestionably took threads, mannerisms and modalities from each other. I just used the phrase "threads, mannerisms and modalities". I am not sure what to do with myself now.'

New boys aside, differences for the second time around were to be subtle – there was a more concerted effort to anchor the show, the hosts generally bookending each half hour together on a sofa (originally intended to be desks, Two Ronnies-style) and occasionally popping up for some random business. Canter had urged them, 'What I would try and do with them is say, "These sketches are great, but we need some visual place to come from." It sounds wanky, but let's call it the album cover, you know, a fireplace for them to stand in front of. They didn't seem to think very visually, which is ironic with Hugh, because he always seemed made for movies. But at that stage they were curiously reluctant to engage with television as a medium.' Also, Tony & Control were to return, alongside now regular weekly appearances from Troubleshooters Peter & John, roaring their testosterone-heavy bilge at each other in increasingly unlikely working environments. 'Any regulars were partly dictated by the economics of the thing,' Hugh says. 'Once you move away from the black curtains and start building sets, then obviously you've got an anxious producer going, "Oh, can we use this more than once?" But we tended not to do that, we just loved the thrill of starting a sketch, the moment an audience fastens onto the idea and what we're getting at, is sort of the best bit. In fact, the first five minutes of anything is where you're salivating and anticipating at the highest level.'

As the work continued, Stephen & Hugh learned that their other main project for the year would see them finally synchronise on the regular *Blackadder* team for what, on the basis of historical logic if nothing else, was looking like the final series. The *ABOF&L* pilot had featured an item in which Hugh lambasted his partner for finding humour in The Great War, but as they reported for duty in August, it was clear that Elton & Curtis had struck just the right note for their trenches comedy, getting laughs out of the very real insanity of the situation, while never losing sight of the sacrifice made by a generation – many survivors, indeed, were still around in 1989, and still able to write outraged letters. Hugh says, 'It had as its backdrop the greatest tragedy of modern man, and that gave the thing a poignancy and a texture that few other things I've been involved in have had, or could have had. We had various histories of WWI lying about – I don't know who supplied them, where they came from, I suppose the designers wanted photographs – and in an idle moment I think we were all sort of gradually soaking up these absolutely heartbreaking details of life in the trenches, and the loss of that generation.' Nevertheless, their reporting for duty at the Colchester barracks that summer remains the one moment in his career Hugh nominates as the hardest he has ever laughed. The original idea for the show's opening credits would have seen Stephen mounted on an enormous steed called Thunderbolt, but when the band struck up, the horse bolted and reared, with Stephen barely managing to stay in the saddle, twelve feet off the gravel and screeching for his very life. Hugh, Rowan, Tim and Tony fell about at this extraordinary sight, and Laurie still says, 'If I ever laugh half as much as that again, I shall be a lucky man.'

With both colleagues as regulars, Lloyd had assembled his ultimate 'plumpening' crew, and so every episode was subject to more obsessive analysis and rewriting than any other comedy in history, particularly when it came to the trademark extended similes – causing more genuine wounded pride for writers Richard & Ben than has ever been acknowledged, but Laurie protests, 'People fought for their patch. Nobody just toed the line and stood where they were told to stand and did what they were told to do, everyone stood up for themselves and for their characters. Let's just say it was very free . . . "Just read it out!" Richard said.' Stephen will never forget how fraught things could become: 'I said, "What will happen in six months' time when a taxi driver says to you, 'Oh, those *Blackadder*s, I bet they're fun to make, aren't they?' Will you go, 'Yes, marvellous fun!'?" And they all said, "No! We'll be honest and say they're absolute hell!"' It's testament to the extent of the colleagues' input that an entire character, Captain Cartwright, was renamed 'Darling' by Stephen in memory of a continually embarrassed old school friend – to McInnerny's delight, and this one change led to some of the series' best-loved gags.

Playing descendants of their previous characters, Fry & Laurie sent themselves up, Melchett and Lt George being Cambridge men, but despite all the nepotism that suggested, their stations were different. Hugh remained the third member of the central trio, symbolising the cream of Britain's gullible nobility, cut down in their prime: 'George's sort of happy-go-lucky, "home in time for tea" attitude was especially tragic,' he observes. 'His ideas about war come from games. George could only see real warfare in those terms. He genuinely was a lamb to the slaughter . . . the kinship of stupidity between Baldrick and George was a very heart-warming one. They were companions on the great road of idiocy.' Stephen, on the other hand, became the figure of imbecilic authority, General Sir Anthony Cecil Hogmanay Melchett, turning his '*BEHHH!*' up to eleven, and bagging an undisputed career highlight as a result. Hugh says, 'His performance for me was really the triumph of the whole show in a way, because, of course it would have been possible to get an older actor to play that sort of Kitchener figure, but it wouldn't have been the same somehow. It was important to have a younger person mocking or satirising the officer class. I can't think of anyone else who could have done it in the way Stephen played Melchett, it was an extraordinary thing.' 'Young people playing old people are funny', Fry adds, 'somehow funnier than if I'd been the right age to be a general, which I am now. Slightly red cheeks I had, because he was always puffing . . . I had in my head that he had piles.'

As autumn arrived and the series progressed, each episode seemed more stressful than the last – the tragic finale was filmed on a cheap polystyrene No Man's Land which seemed certain to suck on screen, and then there was a stressful clash when the eve of the Sunday recording for the last recorded episode, 'General Hospital' also happened to be the evening of the second *Hysteria* show, filmed at the Sadler's Wells Theatre on 23 September.

For this 'Second Coming', Fry had amassed a greater variety of acts for the 2,000 punters, with some returning artists, a stonking new school sketch from French & Saunders, John Cleese snogging Tina Turner onstage, Chris Lynam shoving a firework up his arse, and the most memorable item of all – a Shakespeare sketch starring Rowan and Hugh which just about scraped its way into *Blackadder* lore, despite Atkinson's Jacobean theatre producer being an entirely different character, and Hugh's sulky bard also being a standalone creation. Richard Curtis had written the sketch, and despite the writers' treatment on *Blackadder* he gave it to Stephen, saying, 'That's yours. From me. But take it now so I'm not tempted to use it for Comic Relief', but on the night, it nearly failed to happen at all. The tabs went up, the audience quietened in expectation, and . . . nothing happened. Hugh comes clean, 'We were laced, cross-gartered and cod-pieced for such a long time waiting for our shot at glory that Rowan lost patience and said he was getting out of his clobber until closer to the moment. The person assigned to make sure we were ready was a young Jewish lady named Jo. (Reader, I had already married her.) It is true, though, that once we realised we were "off", as they say in the theatre, Rowan would not be rushed. He insisted on a full rinse, set and blow dry while M'Col extemporised so magnificently. A strange night.' Stephen was rapidly alerted, and took to the stage to provide emergency cover, can of lager in hand: 'It's so *fucking* embarrassing, isn't it? Have you ever worked your *bollocks* off trying to put on a small, light family entertainment, and then two artists that you thought were friends decided it would be amusing to get pissed instead of going on and doing a carefully rehearsed sketch? It's happening to me all the time . . . Meanwhile you can imagine there is a scene of serenity and peace backstage. Trickles of blood are about to appear down each side. Little thumping noises and so on . . . So, a little about the genesis of the sketch you're about to see. It's called simply "Who Killed Maureen?" and is set on one of the South Sea Islands in 1926 . . . dot dot dot . . . to the power of twenty-five . . . Well, we are now ready, I think, for some more action. Thank you for this frank talk; I've enjoyed it very much. And I have rather fallen in love with you and decided perhaps to give up my celibacy because there are one or two people here I'd rather like to go to bed with. So see you later in my dressing room.' Fry's passionate diatribes against the bigotry surrounding AIDS, the unacceptability of any god who would inflict such suffering, and the need to combat the endless tragedies arising from the disease, were a cornerstone of the *Hysteria* shows, but this fill-in spot of stand-up was so elegantly performed, it was tempting to wonder whether the whole thing had been deliberately set up. The moment was, however, as un-premeditated as the host's sudden desire to urinate mid-speech.

No matter how wild the celebration after this barnstorming benefit show may have been, all reported diligently to London W12 the following day to record their last spot of *Blackadder* at BBC TV Centre, and on the following Thursday, the first episode of *Blackadder Goes Forth*, 'Captain Cook' was broadcast on BBC2. The feared complaints came thick and fast at first – not least from Ben's own uncle, the historian Sir G. E. Elton. Like many veterans, however, even before the epochal 'Over the Top' ending (which had been famously saved in the edit and made into an eternal 'Top TV Moment'), Ben's Uncle Geoffrey withdrew his complaints, acknowledging how sincerely the series mourned the insanity of WWI's carnage.

The Purity of the Turf

At some point in 1989's months of sketch writing, Stephen & Hugh were alerted that they were very much in the frame as stars of a new Sunday evening ITV drama masterminded by producer Brian Eastman, who had scored hits with adaptations of Tom Sharpe books *Blott on the Landscape* and Cambridge romp *Porterhouse Blue*, and most recently with the David Suchet incarnation of Hercule Poirot – brought to the screen with style via the scripting of Clive Exton, a writer with a wealth of experience taking in adaptations as vastly varied as *Red Sonja* and *10 Rillington Place* – the planned series title was *Jeeves & Wooster*. Granada TV had agreed to a co-production and, five years after *Alfresco*, company executive Steve Morrison told Eastman and Exton he knew the perfect pair for the leads – no other actors were even considered.

'I do remember them being very nervous about it, out of respect for Wodehouse, uncertain whether they could do it justice,' Eastman says, and his separate dinners with the colleagues were not shining with success. Stephen & Hugh's devotion to The Master has already been explored, and, like any fan, their immediate reactions were of the most concerned scepticism. While radio stars Michael Hordern & Richard Briers had proven perfect in sound only, there had been only imperfect attempts to translate the world's most famous gentleman's personal gentleman and his daffy but honourable employer to screens: Arthur Treacher & David Niven in the cinema, and the more successful TV twinning of Dennis Price & Ian Carmichael in the 1960s, in *The World of Wooster*. This last adaptation was a broad monochrome sitcom with a live audience, and defined the roles for a generation, despite the reported distaste of the elderly Wodehouse.

Although as literary figures they were and are immortal, by 1990, fifteen years after their creator's death, sadly Plum's 'inimitable' duo were largely in the public consciousness only as advertising tools, a grotesque depiction of the pair flogging sherry. Few wordsmiths in the history of English literature could bring print to life quite like Wodehouse, and the *Jeeves* stories in particular were beloved for their first-person narration from the ever-bamboozled Bertie, so it's little wonder that any attempt to drag the characters off the page and onto TV was liable to be met with some degree of consternation. Some have pontificated on what might have been had the roles been reversed – as Stephen & Hugh first requested, in a bid to stretch their acting muscles – but it is no slur on the skills of either actor to say that Fry had none of the raffish air of youth required for Wooster, and that *gravitas* which Laurie always felt he lacked ruled him out of essaying Jeeves. As it is, despite the character never being physically described beyond being a 'darkish sort of respectful Johnnie' with a head that bulges at the back, the precedents suggested Fry was a little young to play the venerable valet. 'I went to a very nobby school and saw some pretty crusty figures,' Hugh said. 'Bertie Wooster is about a certain kind of gormlessness, which tends to overcome me when I'm nervous. I hope I don't spend my entire life pulling silly faces and saying "By Jove!" but perhaps I will . . . something tortured and profound would be a big challenge.' 'Both of us had the immediate reaction, "This can't be done, you can't do it and not only can't you do it you're playing with a delicate porcelain figure and we are going to break it",' Fry adds. 'And if you make it up, you really are in such trouble, because one knows what Wodehouse adorers are like. Lots of these people who like Wodehouse are a bit mad. It's a religion for them. They live it and if you don't come up to scratch they let you know. They all have an image of Jeeves & Wooster's world in their heads, and there is always a possibility that anybody who plays with them might ruin that image.'

With mutual reluctance, Eastman withdrew, and left his chosen stars to get on with their sketch construction. But then, Hugh actually read one of the scripts that had been sent their way, and realised Exton had pulled off the improbable. 'I just read it in one sitting and I laughed all the way through it. There was some really great stuff and so I rang up Stephen and said, "Wait, don't say no yet!"' Fry remembers, 'I said to them, "When we said no, we really meant yes", before adding, "Look, if anyone is going to bugger this up it's going to be us, thank you very much" . . . The scripts were like an antiseptic cream. It was so gracefully done, capturing all of Bertie's enchanting language. Theirs was a wonderful world that one just wants to dive into, like being able to dive into a soufflé.' For each episode Exton tended to extract the gist of two or three short stories, or maybe half a novel, shift around a few characters to suit, and of course, usually close with Jeeves triumphant. As with his past adaptations, he simply made it *work* on screen.

'And so it was that, a few months later, I found myself slipping into a double-breasted suit in a Prince of Wales check while my colleague made himself at home inside an enormous bowler hat, and the two of us embarked on our separate disciplines. Him for the noiseless opening of decanters, me for the twirling of the whangee,' Laurie wrote, for the *Telegraph*. 'I soon learnt that I still had much to learn. How to smoke plain cigarettes, how to drive a 1927 Aston Martin, how to mix a Martini with five parts water and one part water (for filming purposes only), how to attach a pair of spats in less than a day and a half, and so on.' Coming straight from the sitcom trenches, there was little need for haircuts to ease the stars into their roles, and they were soon on location in the stately homes of England, and feeling their way into this new, idyllic comic world. Despite Exton's scripting magic, Hugh continued, 'The thing that really worried us, that had us saying "crikey" for weeks on end, was this business of The Words. Let me give you an example. Bertie is leaving in a huff: "'Tinkerty tonk', I said, and I meant it to sting." I ask you: how is one to do justice of even the roughest sort to a line like that? How can any human actor, with his clumsily attached ears, and his irritating voice, and his completely misguided hair, hope to deliver a line as pure as that? It cannot be done . . . Wodehouse on the page can be taken in the reader's own time; on the screen, the beautiful sentence often seems to whip by, like an attractive member of the opposite sex glimpsed from the back of a cab. You, as the viewer, try desperately to fix the image in your mind – but it is too late, because suddenly you're into a commercial break and someone is telling you how your home may be at risk if you eat the wrong breakfast cereal.' 'The books are written by Bertie, as it were, in the first-person,' Stephen adds, 'and he describes Jeeves, for instance – his feet don't touch the floor, he shimmers into rooms, he oozes out of rooms. He seems to flicker and then he isn't there. He coughs and it's like a sheep clearing his throat of a blade of grass on a distant hillside or something. I tried practising that but sounded more like a goat clearing his throat of a piece of cheese on a nearby hillside. These things are difficult.'

It was, nonetheless, the realisation of an undreamt dream for them both, to be re-enacting some of their most beloved stories, in such beautiful – albeit autumnal – settings. Director of the original five episodes, Robert Young, complemented the art deco design of the credits and composer Anne Dudley's perfect soundtrack with stylishly composed shots of the two heroes looking every inch the part – Stephen may have been only thirty-two, but his subtly pained physiognomy when the young master expressed pride in his loud plus-sixes showed that they were on the right track from the start, whereas Hugh had never looked so blue-eyed and bushy-tailed, his matinee idol looks coming to the fore in the same way that his partner's lifetime of being accused of 'knowing everything' was finally paying off.

The cherry on the top came about purely by accident towards the end of production, Eastman recalls, 'When it came to the end of the schedule, filming all the stuff in Bertie's flat, with only two days to go, the editors came to me and said the episodes were going to be under-running, three or four minutes short, because Stephen & Hugh said the lines so fast! So there was a terrible scramble at the end of the first series to invent new scenes with the limited resources we had left. And they turned out to be really wonderful, Clive and I laughed about it afterwards, saying we should write all our scenes with incredible restrictions. They amplified the plot rather than just driving it along. And we said, "why don't we do a song?" But as always, Hugh was very reluctant about it – "oh no, Brian, I couldn't possibly do that . . ." I can't remember if I gave him the sheet music or a recording of "47 Ginger-Headed Sailors", but he came in and he'd learned it overnight, and it was great.' The invented dialogue, albeit potentially needling Wodehouse puritans, provided some of the series' most successful sequences, beginning with Bertie's attempts to get to grip with Cab Calloway's 1931 hit 'Minnie The Moocher':

BERTIE: You know, I can't help feeling, Jeeves, that I could do better justice to this song if I understood what the words meant.
JEEVES: Oh, I doubt that, sir.
BERTIE: All this 'ho de ho de ho' stuff is pretty clear, but what do you suppose a 'hoochie-coocher' is, exactly?
JEEVES: It's difficult to say, sir, unless it's in connection to one of the demotic American words for 'ardent spirits'. I'm thinking of 'hooch', a word of Eskimo origin, I'm informed.

BERTIE:	Tchah! You bally well are informed, Jeeves. Do you know everything?
JEEVES:	... I really don't know, sir.
BERTIE:	Hm. Erm... (PLAYS) 'She had a dream about the King of Sweden, He gave her things that she was needin''... No, you see, now that is clever, Jeeves... That line about the King of Sweden and things she was needin'.
JEEVES:	Yes, His Majesty King Carl Gustav does seem to have been exceedingly generous to the young lady, sir.
BERTIE:	No, no, I meant the fact that it rhymes, you see — 'Sweden', 'needin''.
JEEVES:	Almost, sir.[11]

The series was an instant hit for ITV, Patrick Stoddart observing in *The Sunday Times*: 'Clive Exton does seem to have kept a period feel without consigning them entirely to a long-gone age, and that suits the work of Hugh Laurie & Stephen Fry, who managed to keep the humour modern enough to laugh at. This is the job Fry & Laurie's partnership might have been born for.' Stephen relishes the memory, 'The Aston Martin that we drove – 1928, I think it was – the cocktail shakers, the glassware ... even though there's a camera in your eyeline, just handling these beautiful objects was something so marvellous, you feel for a second that you are actually in that world, and it's a beautiful world.' 'It was an immensely pleasurable experience,' Hugh agrees, 'sort of embarrassingly pleasurable. We should really have paid to do it, I think we probably would have done, actually. We had canvas chairs with our names on the back ... When shooting, the crew, who I wouldn't say are foul-mouthed, but had their own rich Anglo-Saxon way of putting things, often took on the Wodehouse language, so when a big tattooed scene-shifter dropped a spanner on their foot, they would say, "Oh heck!" or "Dash it!" Of course there are no swear words in Wodehouse, "Oh heck" is the strongest you get. And only a couple of hecks in each show; we don't want people to phone in and complain. In

Wodehouse's world, the bedroom is a place where Jeeves delivers tea, that's all. It is all innocence.'

The same, naturally, could not be said of their own comedy, but although production for *ABOF&L* series two was looming at the dawn of the new decade, it was an intense season of filming for *J&W* that closed the year, and all the while accolades were pouring in for *Blackadder*'s stunning finale. Letters to the *Radio Times* spoke of teachers using the series for fun in history lessons for the first time, audience approval was off the scale and a second BAFTA was in the bag. The tabloids began filling space with speculation about a fifth series, and three decades later, they haven't stopped. The announcement of *J&W* was less edifying – *The Sun* broke the news with the despicable headline 'I Say, Jeeves, You're a Right Bertie Woofter! – ITV nick gay comic Fry to star in cult series.' Amid the unsurprisingly error-riddled text that followed, an 'ITV boss' was quoted: 'You couldn't ask for a better combination of people to play the pair. Fry & Laurie are hot property. They bridge the gap between old and new perfectly – and they're both upper-class performers themselves.' It's hard to know where to start with this barrage of bilge about the 'self-confessed homosexual' and his colleague, but the last point was beginning to become a particular bugbear of Hugh's, and shortly after he requested the *Telegraph* not to mention his Eton background: 'It's not that I'm ashamed of it or anything like that, and it's probably ridiculously conceited of me to make a fuss, but one dreads a sub-editor picking this fact out in fourteen-point bold and then the tabloids would not be able to resist calling Stephen and myself "Upper-class Wits".' It's little wonder that a few years later Stephen was insisting to the *Guardian* that he was finished with paying any attention to any newspaper: 'I've always said that if you appear as much as I do in different things you're bound to have thousands, millions of people who absolutely detest the sight of you. You're bound to. It's just obvious. It's not that . . . I don't want to give the impression that it's special pleading, it's just that I'm sure all kinds of unpleasant things have been said about me in the past year, but the great thing is that I don't know about them.' When a journalist calling themselves Geoffrey Wheatcroft announced in the *Daily Mail* his desire to punch Fry, the periodical went so far as to offer Stephen Fry punchbags to readers.

On the other hand, protestations against poshness seem more futile in light of that festive period's cast-iron anecdote – a New Year visit from HRH Prince Charles and Princess Diana. On top of all his dizzying diary-filling, Stephen believed in doing Christmas right, and his country home, an old rectory deep in the Norfolk countryside, was always filled with friends at the festive period. Proud of his culinary prowess, the host attentively catered to every guest's whim, involving himself with all the cooking, with a roast Norfolk turkey from brother Roger, his signature home-made mayonnaise, and all abundance of rich goodies. This year, of course Hugh, Jo and Charlie were at the table, plus Nick Symons, Jon Canter, and Rowan Atkinson, with partners, and more. It was always Rowan who savoured the closest links to royalty, in an uncanny reflection of Edmund Blackadder's throne-hanging – his best friend Curtis even included a dig at the star's royal preoccupation in his first film, *The Tall Guy*. Some time halfway through the twelve days of Christmas at the turn of the last decade of the millennium, Rowan was seen taking an important call on his brick-sized mobile phone, Charles and Di being reasonably close Norfolk neighbours at Sandringham, but the import of this call didn't become clear until Stephen later answered the phone to the heir to the throne, and tea with the Windsors was organised, with all the feverish hoovering and secret-service-operative-tea-brewing that entailed.

Prince Charles always made good use of his elevated position to become a trailblazer among comedy geeks, since his days as a starry-eyed *Goons* fanboy trying to impress Peter Sellers with his Bluebottle impersonations, and this young generation of performers was no less catnip to HRH – on his visit, he monopolised Rowan, Stephen and Hugh, leaving the onerous task of entertaining Diana to Jon, Nick and the less famous contingent. Once the Princess had signalled it was home time and the blue bloods had disappeared into the frosty night to be home in time for *Spitting Image*, it was Canter who delivered the punchline to the evening, telling the stupefied gathering, 'Nice couple . . . I didn't get *her* name, though.'

Ampersands and Air Apostrophes

As the 1990s rolled around, filming began for *ABOF&L*'s return – once again, there was little location filming besides the upbeat new opening credits (in which Stephen & Hugh visited London's tourist hotspots on their way to the dear old BBC TVC, to the sound of comedy maestro Phil Pope's brassy new theme), plus one of Hugh's odd monologues where he reminisced about past girlfriends. These filmed inserts were streams of Laurie consciousness which allowed for much material to be edited out:

HUGH: ... And then there was Persephone. Now she really was strange. She had this wild red hair which she used to sell to the Libyans — made quite a good living out of it, as I remember, always seemed to have brand-new clothes anyway. She works at the Home Office now. And then not long after that I married Libby, who was a lovely girl — always reminded me of Rab Butler. Libby had two sons by a previous marriage — and although they were as different from each other as two children could possibly be, they both became travel agents. And then... let me see... then there was Amanda, who used to drive a bright orange TR7 and called men 'warthogs'. I think I was just a staging post for Amanda, because she went off and married a board-game designer who worked for the South African government. I'm pretty sure she'd been seeing him all along. Who was next? It must have been Dora...

The location shoot also included the first instance of inadequate eyewitness Hugh earning a punch from an exasperated off-camera Stephen and of course, the Vox Pops. These interstitials were more gag-based this time, as the colleagues took on a variety of personas in London's marketplaces – some characters even featured in a wine-tasting strand, and the more cogent use of Vox Pops was indicative of the stronger shape given to each of the six episodes. Deborah Norton was unavailable this time, and the chamber-piece feel of series one was gone, with a host of talented supporting actors joining 'the boys' in the studio, including ex-Footlighter and original Ford Prefect Geoffrey McGivern, comic actress Harriet Thorpe as presenter of TV feedback show 'Over To You', Anne Reid taking her turn to be a housewife bothered by two complete lunatics, and veteran performers Ralph Michael (Uncle Tom Travers in *J&W*) and Liz Smith, who was seventy, but still had over twenty glorious years ahead of her.

Canter recalls, 'There was something like 170 scripts on my desk, and let's say I thought ninety were great, forty were terrible, and another forty needed work – I'd really work hard on that forty, and almost without exception those sketches didn't make the final cut. It's rare in comedy that so much would turn up pretty much perfect, but if I'd just said, "This is great", I wouldn't have been doing my job! I remember Geoffrey Perkins had looked at one of their scripts, and said "This is just words!" Whereas I said, "Yeah, but what fantastic words!" Just to have the two of them on camera saying these words was worth it . . . Their work to me always seemed to come from a really deep place, and to always be about something. They didn't set out to make a minor show, but they didn't compromise either.' Canter is a modest man, but he does claim two credits for this series – encouraging his employers to go with the 'custody'/'custardy' gag in a John & Peter sketch (echoing their own 'Henrietta' pun), and the widely befuddling employment of one particular Vox Pop quickie. Stephen, dragged up as 'Ivy', came out with the line, 'Well I think . . . Oh, Christ, I've left the iron on!' and just in passing, during the editing process, the script editor had a brainwave: 'I said, "That's great, you should put that in every show." Because really comedy thrives on repetition. We needed a way, every week, of making it so it had its own look, and repetition.' What seemed at first to be an editing error when episode two aired, became a facetious comment on the lure of the familiar in sketch shows.

Bookending each half hour in a cosy mock lounge festooned with entirely random *mise en scène* clutter, a small upright piano completing the set, the pair introduced the proceedings with Stephen's flagrant air apostrophes and a bit of a chat. Fry & Laurie now prevented their lovingly stockpiled sketches from drifting off in a nebulous stream by introducing themes, such as the sponsorship of Tideyman's Carpets (a neat way of downplaying their advertising fame), Stephen's unstoppable dance moves (with more Phil Pope music, pastiching Michael Jackson) or indeed, the double act's bid to become such big stars they no longer have to perform their own sketches. This run boasted some of their finest standalone sketches – 'Major Donaldson' made the ultimate use of Hugh's clichéd Nazi; Stephen's wilfully weird shopkeeper frustrated Hugh's desire to buy an engagement ring; Hugh was committed to an asylum for writing letters to the *Daily Mail*; and then there were the two apparent cricket (actually darts) commentators who worked themselves up into orgasmic fits about a lost kind of England, with 'heaps of cream and lawnmowers' and in a returning reference, the '29 bus going up the Garboldisham Road' (a Norfolk transport service it's painful to admit is now defunct) – all random items played out at what was becoming a trademark leisurely pace. A real effort was made to craft a comfortable atmosphere, with studio audiences – more used to being treated as laugh fodder – feeling like guests in a strange living room, buoyed through long evenings by the best young warm-up act in the business, Tony Hawks, performing as 'The Fabulous Tony'.

A gifted comic song performer, Hawks also bagged a role in one of the oddest sketches Fry & Laurie ever created – the epic tale of Freddie Muldoon, 'The Cause', and the bomb in the restaurant. Nick Symons recalls the emphasis always tended to be on convenience for the show's stars: 'They were never lazy, but they would much rather do two Peter & John sketches back to back, and then none the following recording, rather than be four different characters in something. They needed to keep moving forward, shark-like.' The Muldoon character arose, Laurie recalls, because 'We were both particularly devoted to Peter Sellers in *Doctor Strangelove* doing Group Captain Lionel Mandrake. He's trapped in a room with the mad Colonel Jack Ripper, and his sort of discomfort and awkwardness, trying to play along with this lunatic, and we used to recite that to each other constantly: "Yes, Jack, of course, of course, yes . . ." and all that stuff which was such an exquisite part of that film.' This first such sketch, in which Hugh's original pathetic toff is forced into terrorism by Stephen's shady puppeteer, also marked the last appearance from trusted 1980s alter egos Gordon & Stuart, here given long-suffering partners who are almost gender-swapped versions of the other – the restaurant in which they're dining is even run by the same Greek waiter as in the first series, Dimitri Andreas. This one attempt to double-up in a scene had Hugh playing Stuart and Freddie, while Stephen played Gordon and the waiter responsible for one of *ABOF&L*'s most direct political diatribes. It was inevitable that the UK's four-channel TV system could not last forever, but the Conservative push for 'consumer choice' which would hand over even more power to Rupert Murdoch and his ilk was angrily mocked via the replacement of silver cutlery with plastic coffee-stirrers: 'The exchange ends with me trying to strangle him. Heavy-handed satire perhaps, but that was how it looked to me we were in danger of going: thirty or forty channels but all filled with dreck.' We certainly do now have endlessly more 'choice' of entertainment than we did in 1990, but whether any of it can match the quality of television crafted under the old system is moot – the very space of London W12 where this issue was played out for laughs, BBC TV Centre, birthplace of some of the greatest entertainment in history, has now been turned into apartments for ludicrously rich people.

Hawks had his work cut out making this complex sketch work for the audience, as well as playing the badly translated French lounge singer ('*Hold your legs up skyward, for you to smell just as I would . . .*'), and it's little surprise that this was Fry & Laurie's only experiment with multi-character sketches. These complex set-ups would become a regular feature of Harry Enfield's own *Television Programme* when it began later in the year, and his key collaborator got a taste of both comedy worlds – ex-plasterer Paul Whitehouse bagging a downbeat cameo in episode three as an audience member with a terminal need to have his bottom fondled. Whitehouse was not a famous face at the time, but there were cameos from celebrated performers – Paul Eddington himself ran into Gordon & Stuart in that doomed restaurant, and a pre-recorded segment in the finale featured Nigel Havers credited as the aforementioned master-joke-timer, with his own name passed on to Rowan Atkinson. This last outing for series two was also to have featured Rowan in a specially written boardroom sketch, but to his regret, Ordish had to drop the item. 'I wish I still had it on VHS,' he says. 'I don't know why it was abandoned now, but it was supposedly a high-powered business meeting, high-powered except for Rowan, who was this weedy person who couldn't cope with it all . . . I don't know why, but it didn't gel.'

Gordon, Stuart and girlfriends would survive the hapless Muldoon's terrorist atrocity, but they were never seen again – and similarly, this series sounded the knell for Tony & Control (some attempts were made to bring the spy characters back, but they never reached the screen) and indeed Peter & John, whose boardroom bollocks could have been strung out for as long as any of Whitehouse's *Fast Show* characters, but Fry & Laurie had a totally different approach, immediately doing away with the mystery of the unseen hard-nosed Marjorie character by having *A Fish Called Wanda* actress Maria Aitken stride into their office, effectively destroying the status quo for good. Even then, the roars of 'DAMN!' were hard to resist, and the characters returned in two more sketches, showing how their management style suited alternative jobs as toilet attendants and bishops, but that was as far as the creators could bear to take them. Having crafted six episodes of watertight, familiar, strong sketch material, by the end of the series Fry & Laurie had dispensed with much of the apparatus which sustained *ABOF&L* – Stephen even killed off his 'writer, comedian and light sketch actor' partner in the last episode, in another act of piano-based violence. The BBC had given their two sophisticated sketch stars no ultimatum, but by the time their second series was wrapped up and filling homes at the start of 1990, they were effectively right back to square one for any third series, which Hugh admits with typical self-flagellation: 'Again, that was rank stupidity, we should probably have marshalled our resources in a more intelligent way, and made more out of what we had! It made it very difficult. It was either an act of supreme arrogance, that we thought "Oh, we can just reinvent the whole thing", or just the complete opposite – cowardice, that we felt like no one would notice, so we could do what we wanted. I'm not sure that we were ever confident enough to feel that people were following the progress of these characters. I remember, I always used to get in trouble with my parents for not writing thank-you letters. But I never believed that anyone would notice! A pretty lame argument, I agree. It's pretty absurd to be going on national television assuming no one will notice. Why would we be doing it?' It had been a hugely accomplished run nonetheless, containing some of Laurie's favourite moments: 'I think Stephen would admit he's more of a verbal performer than a physical one, but the "Dancercises" sketch was one of the best things we ever did.'

Separate projects came next for the pair, with Stephen continuing to work on the novel which had been slowly growing over the last few years, and Hugh making his only professional foray into the theatre. *Gasping* was far from Ben Elton's first play – he had written at least a dozen as an undergraduate – but it was his first attempt to translate his huge TV success into theatrical respectability, years before the 'jukebox musicals' which either made or damned him in theatrical circles, depending on your view. It was a typically ecological story, making good use of Hugh's ability to mock corporate marketing by casting him as Philip, an anti-hero executive of Lockheart Industries, a company that has run out of products to repackage and sell to the population, and so they decide to market 'Suck & Blow' designer air – a move so popular, it eventually becomes impossible to breathe real oxygen for free. Although undeniably slight at only two acts, when it opened at the Theatre Royal Haymarket on 1 June, *Gasping* received generally approving reviews – Hugh's manic performance was picked out for praise even in the less impressed papers, who noted his 'formidable energy' and 'superb' mime skills. Ben had written the part specially for Hugh, despairing at his friend's modesty and potential for stardom, but Hugh was to joke, 'So he says, but it may be all lies. Perhaps he crossed out Rik Mayall and Rowan Atkinson, though my name did appear alone on the package containing the script – at least he had the decency to buy a new envelope.' In truth, the whole experience was a nightmare for Laurie, who never again accepted a theatrical role in front of those rows of imaginary males all silently willing him to fail. Years later, he complained to Jay Leno, 'I thought I was going out of my mind, I really did. The repetition, eight times a week, standing in the same place in the same clothes saying the same things, I actually started to go a little bit mad, and have out of body experiences. I could leave my body and sort of float around the theatre and watch myself.' Still, he admits it was no disaster: 'I don't know how the hell we managed to pull it off.

Ben had never written a West End play before, I'd never starred in one and the director had never directed one before either. As well as all the usual nerves, butterflies in the stomach, shaking a bit, inability to swallow, I was almost hallucinating and things were starting to spin. Most frightening of all was that once the play had started, there was no moment in the whole of the first half to get my breath. I shouted all through the first act, then was back on again. By the end I longed for a play where I could lie on the sofa in a dressing gown with a glass of cold tea and gently talk and stare at the ceiling.'

With this theatrical outing and the broadcast of *J&W* coming almost immediately after the second outing of *ABOF&L*, 1990 saw acres of newsprint analysing the Fry & Laurie appeal, and the Wodehouse adaptation in particular elevated the two colleagues to a new level of fame, ten years after their very first collaboration. The overwhelming praise was not enough to blind Hugh to brickbats, however, and as he sat in the Haymarket dressing room, he was moved to take issue with one letter-writer to the *Telegraph*, replying in person:

> SIR – I am humbled by Mr Hastings's remarks (letter, May 31) on my attempt at Bertie Wooster. On quite a few counts I am inclined to agree with him and promise to do better if I am given another chance. But where does he get the idea that Wodehouse 'limits Bertie to a severely brief range of expressions'? Have I gone mad, or are the books written in the first-person? How would you expect a narrator to describe his own facial expressions, and if he did, how could you be sure he was accurate? (I asked with a huge, sneering frown? Or did I?)
>
> HUGH LAURIE London WC2.

The Literature of Lies

More Jeeves & Bertie was of course already in the offing by this point – the Granada series had provided perhaps the biggest shot in the arm the Wodehouse estate had ever known, and *Jeeves* reprints bearing the images of Stephen & Hugh, both photographically and in caricature, were beginning to show up in bookshops to capitalise on the boon –

© Nicola Jennings

The terribly sophisticated 'Piano Masterclass' caricature created by Nicola Jennings for the 1991 Terrence Higgins Trust charity book *Amassed Hysteria*.

the Footlights revue at the ADC
MEMOIRS OF A FOX
Wed 4th – Sat 7th Feb at 11.00 pm
Advance booking – Arts Cinema

FOOTLIGHTS ADC PRESENT
THE SNOW QUEEN
THE FOOTLIGHTS/ADC PANTOMIME at the ADC THEATRE
Tues 25th Nov to Sat 6th Dec at 8.00 pm (not Sun 30th Nov)
Matinees Nov 29th & Dec 6th at 2.30: Dec 4th & 5th at 4.30
Advance Booking: Arts Cinema 352001

DEATH IN THE AISLES
FOOTLIGHTS · LATE NIGHT
REVUE
ADC THEATRE · 6 TO 10 FEB
11.00 PM

FOOTLIGHTS
REVUE
NIGHTCAP
1979
CAMBRIDGE ARTS THEATRE
Founded by Lord Keynes in 1936
Manager & Licensee:
ANDREW R. BLACKWOOD
Box Office:
Opening Hours (Telephone 52000)
Monday to Saturday - 11.00 a.m. to 8.00 p.m.
Saturday - 10.30 a.m. to 8.00 p.m.
Tuesday 5th to Saturday 16th June, 1979
Times of Performances:
Monday to Friday 8.00 p.m.
Saturday 4.30 and 8.15 p.m.
Prices: £3.50, £3.00 and £2.25
(all prices include V.A.T.)
SEATS AT ALL PRICES ARE BOOKABLE IN ADVANCE

Above: The greatest Footlights show since 1963, 1981's seminal *The Cellar Tapes*, advertised with espionage-swamped edginess.

Opposite: A gallery of nostalgia for seasoned Footlighters – the smoking concerts and shows where Stephen and Hugh learned their trade. From top left, clockwise: Hugh's early smoker *Memoirs of a Fox*; the 1980 pantomime *The Snow Queen*, which first united Fry & Laurie; the 1979 Footlights May Week revue *Nightcap* – Stephen's first sight of his colleague in action; and sundry, forgotten smoker *Death in the Aisles*.

The CAMBRIDGE FOOTLIGHTS, the Cambridge University Revue Club, was founded in June 1883 and has produced annual 'entertainments' ever since. Its past members include Jack Hulbert, Richard Murdoch, Jimmy Edwards, Peter Cook, Eleanor Bron, Jonathan Miller, David Frost, Tim Brooke-Taylor, Bill Oddie, Graeme Garden, Graham Chapman, Eric Idle, John Cleese, German Greer, Clive James and Julie Covington. Thus, four of the major comic forces of the past twenty years – Beyond The Fringe, The Frost Report, The Goodies and Monty Python's Flying Circus – all have their roots in the Cambridge University Footlights.

Robert Bathurst does not juggle, has never been stuck in an imaginary glass cage and cannot tuck his legs behind his head, a result of going to Cambridge and not R.A.D.A. As a writer/performer he is working on the third series of Injury Time for BBC Radio 4 with Griff Rhys Jones and joins Emma Thompson, Stephen Fry, Hugh Laurie and Paul Shearer in a new radio series starting shortly. He soon starts work on a new BBC Television series both writing and performing topical sketches.

Stephen Fry is an extremely shy and sensitive young man who shrinks from personal publicity of any kind.

Hugh Laurie Apart from the odd two and a quarter hour lapses, Hugh is without question the funniest person in the world. He spent most of his time at Cambridge rowing, gaining his Blue in the 1980 Boat Race, when Cambridge lost to Oxford by 6 feet; which was enormously funny. He read Social Anthropology, and his performance tonight is a gesture of gratitude to the British taxpayer. If you can't pick him out from the photograph, he is the funny one.

Paul Shearer As you can see from the photograph, Paul does not have a body. The one he will be using in tonight's performance is borrowed from a contemporary of his at St. John's College, Cambridge. Paul read Computing Science, is bi-lingual in English and ALGOL 68, and has persistent nightmares about coming to terms with the 1980's.

Emma Thompson Emma's greatest success has always been her ability to do everything brilliantly. She read English at Cambridge brilliantly. She sings brilliantly. She's appeared on stage, radio and TV, brilliantly. She's a light bulb.

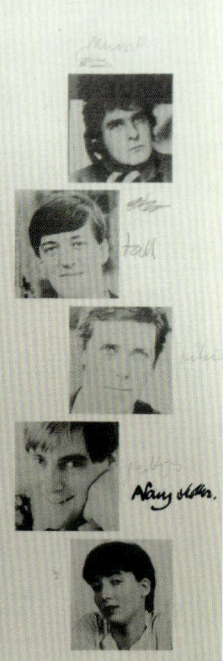

The cast of *Cellar Tapes* spin-off *Beyond the Footlights* pen their own biographies for the programme, 1982.

Cambridge's ADC Theatre: the arena which played host to some of the earliest first funny bits, not just of Fry & Laurie but hosts of comics from Cleese to Ayoade.

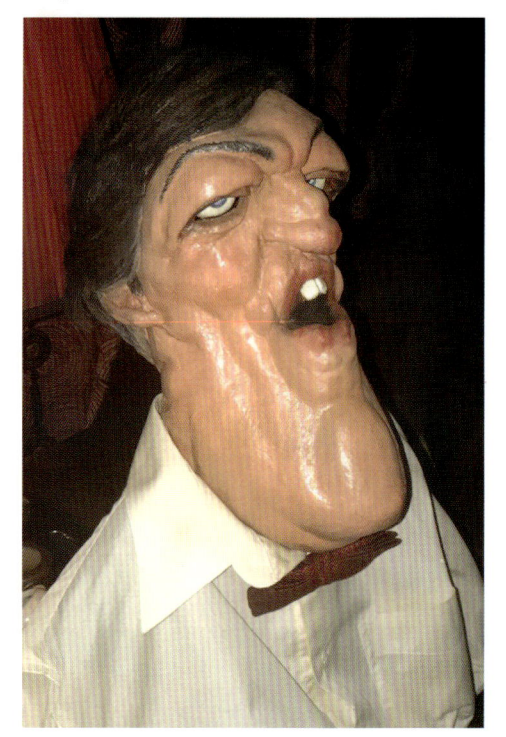

This photo is taken from Stephen's own collection: his mouldering *Spitting Image* puppet was recently rediscovered, and the priceless latex head carefully renovated, to the horror of all who behold it.

© Lincoln, Rutland & Stamford Mercury

Members of the Cambridge Footlights Revue before their Civic Hall Show.
Lichfield Festival.
Robert Bathurst: Hugh Laurie: Emma Thompson: Stephen Fry: Paul Shearer

Stephen not at all perturbed by the way the *Lincoln, Rutland & Stamford Mercury* picked out Emma as the talent to watch in *A Sense of Nonsense*. From left: Robert Bathurst, Hugh, Emma, Stephen, Paul Sparkes.

© Daily Mirror

tv mirror
Double act on the fringe of a great future

by JAMES SEDDON

DON'T say Cleese—say Hugh Laurie and Stephen Fry.

The names mean nothing now, but just wait.

These two young student comics look sure of graduating to stardom.

They're treading the same path to success taken by Monty Python funnyman John Cleese and a host of others.

The pair are among the cast of THE CAMBRIDGE FOOTLIGHTS REVUE (BBC-2, 9.30).

In the past, the university revue has produced such talents as Peter Cook, David Frost, Graham Chapman, Eric Idle, Tim Brooke-Taylor, Graeme Garden, Bill Oddie and, of course, Cleese.

This year's show is likely to produce names just as big.

STEPHEN FRY
Peter Cook style

Revue

Producer Dennis Main Wilson says it's the best revue since Beyond the Fringe in the Sixties.

And he describes Hugh Laurie as a brilliant extrovert comedy actor in the Cleese mould.

He writes his own scripts and music, plays the piano and guitar.

Stephen Fry, who also writes his own material is another brilliant comic—but in the style of Peter Cook.

Watch out, too, for character actress Emma Thompson and singer Tony Slattery.

Penny Dwyer and Paul Shearer complete the glittering cast. Usually the revues are full of topical quick-fire gags and short, snappy sketches.

"This year it's different," says producer Wilson. "The sketches last anything from eight to ten minutes—and that's long for a revue.

"But it works."

HUGH LAURIE
In Cleese mould

The *Daily Mirror* make an almost uniquely accurate prediction back in 1982 – no doubt assisted by a nudge from Stephen & Hugh's veritable agent, Richard Armitage.

The *A Bit of Fry & Laurie* script books added extra value to their plate sections by including completely spurious captions such as, 'This shows the gender difference even more clearly. Not the distended folds (or flaps).' However, we do not have that licence, and so this is a picture of Hugh Laurie (left) and Stephen Fry (equally left).

Above: Laurie & Fry explore odes less travelled. Below: A crucial dialogue on the perversion of the lovely word 'gay', both from the *ABOF&L* pilot.

© BBC / Everett Collection Inc / Alamy Stock Photo

© Trinity Mirror / Mirrorpix / Alamy Stock Photo

Above and opposite: Various publicity shots for the early incarnations of *ABOF&L*.

BBC LIGHT ENTERTAINMENT presents

"A BIT OF FRY AND LAURIE"

by and with

STEPHEN FRY and HUGH LAURIE

TELEVISION CENTRE

Sunday
8th January, 1989

Doors open 7.00 p.m.
Doors close 7.15 p.m.

Children under 14
Not Admitted

Complimentary Ticket
Not for Sale

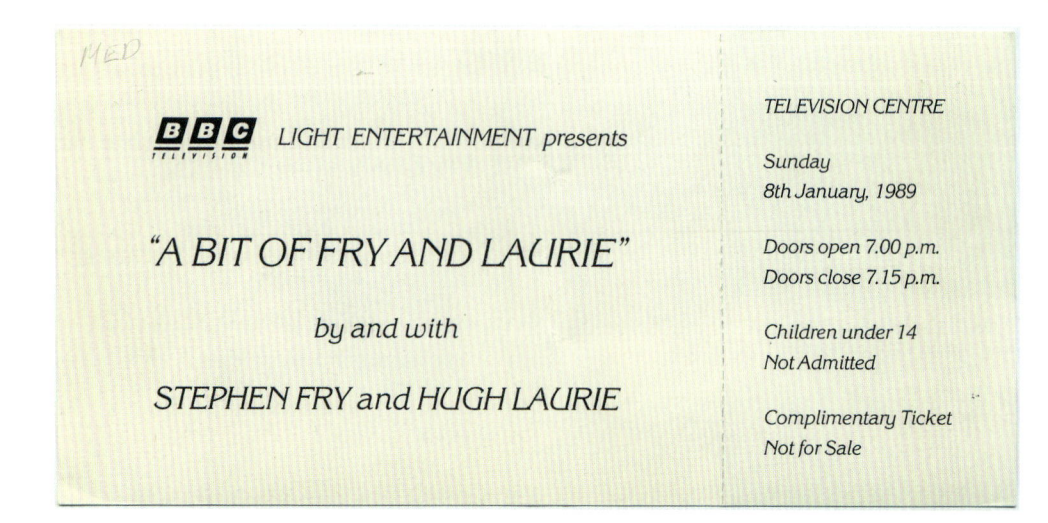

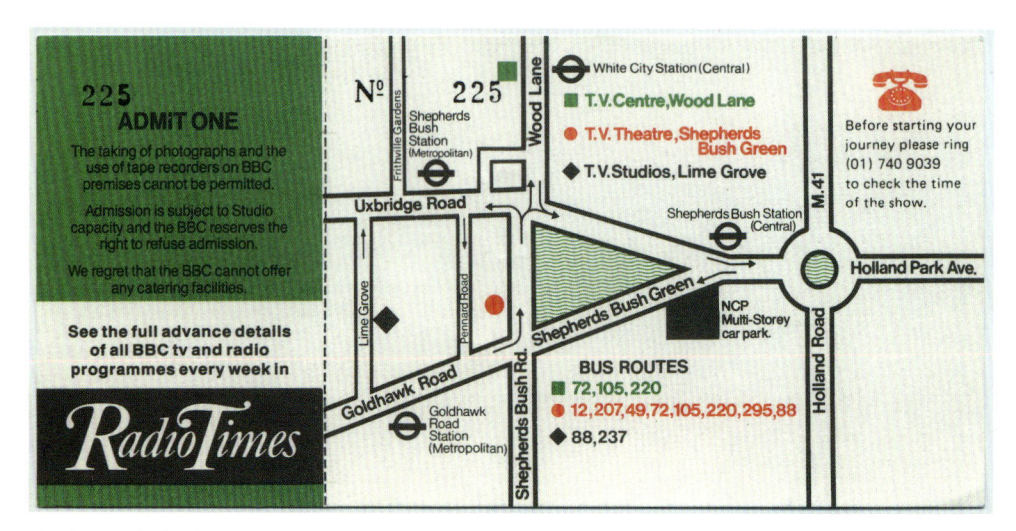

225
ADMIT ONE

The taking of photographs and the use of tape recorders on BBC premises cannot be permitted.

Admission is subject to Studio capacity and the BBC reserves the right to refuse admission.

We regret that the BBC cannot offer any catering facilities.

See the full advance details of all BBC tv and radio programmes every week in

RadioTimes

Nº 225

Shepherds Bush Station (Metropolitan)

Uxbridge Road

Goldhawk Road Station (Metropolitan)

■ White City Station (Central)
■ T.V. Centre, Wood Lane
● T.V. Theatre, Shepherds Bush Green
◆ T.V. Studios, Lime Grove

Shepherds Bush Station (Central)

NCP Multi-Storey car park.

Holland Park Ave.

BUS ROUTES
■ 72, 105, 220
● 12, 207, 49, 72, 105, 220, 295, 88
◆ 88, 237

Before starting your journey please ring (01) 740 9039 to check the time of the show.

The fore and aft of an actual vintage ticket for a recording of *ABOF&L* series two, with grateful thanks to Steve Medcraft, who was there.

Brown trousers time at Wembley Stadium, preparing to face half a billion uncomprehending faces around the globe, with a broken microphone, as a strange way to mark Nelson Mandela's 70th birthday, 11 June 1988.

Queen Aspixia, Supreme Mistress of the Universe, with two of her triple husbandoid, Lord Pigmot, Majestic Prince of Frumpity, and Frondo, Mighty Birdlord of Thribble. A Christmas Yet to Come from *Blackadder's Christmas Carol*, 1988.

All (bar one walrus) destined to go goose over stump in No-Man's-Land. A BAFTA-laden career high for everyone present – Tim McInnerny, Sir Tony Robinson, Rowan Aktinson, and Stephen & Hugh – *Blackadder Goes Forth*, 1989.

The ultimate gentleman and the ultimate gentleman's personal gentleman – Brian Eastman and Clive Exton provided the chance for Hugh & Stephen to embody their literary heroes Bertram Wilberforce Wooster and Reginald Jeeves for all generations, in twenty-three episodes of Granada's *Jeeves & Wooster*.

'And so it was I found myself slipping into a double-breasted suit in a Prince of Wales check while m'colleague made himself at home inside an enormous bowler hat, and the two of us embarked on our separate disciplines. Him for the noiseless opening of decanters, me for the twirling of the whangee.'

Publicity images for 1992's flirtation with cinema, *Peter's Friends*. Stephen & Hugh pose with director Kenneth Branagh, co-writer Rita Rudner, Emma Thompson, Imelda 'Snutty' Staunton, Alex Lowe, Alphonsia Emmanuel, Tony Slattery and Phyllida Law. 'I can think of no finer, fluffier, shinier people to see in the new year with, than your good selves.'

Above, below, and overleaf: The two colleagues reunite on the streets of California to unveil Hugh 'Excellent Sermon, Vicar' Laurie's star on the Hollywood Walk of Fame, 25 October 2016. 'I can say, like Dr Watson of his Holmes – "the kindest and wisest friend I ever knew" ... Right at the beginning, wherever that meeting took place, we made each other laugh. And we continue to do so to this day.'

© WENN Ltd / Alamy Stock Photo

inspiring many lifelong Wodehouse fans to set off on their own journeys through the Master's enormous *oeuvre*.

The recording of the second series was the colleagues' main remaining task in 1990, once again doing their best to recreate Wodehouse's eternal summer in the grey seasons, but their punishing work schedules brought about one odd characteristic of the series that only became apparent second time around – the roulette-style casting of the many Drones and supporting characters who drove Wooster's numerous scrapes. Brian Eastman says, 'The thing that determined when we shot the series was when Stephen & Hugh were available! Each year it was always quite a juggling match, and everybody else just had to fit in with that.' So although the first series cast perfectly embodied the characters of Gussie Fink-Nottle or Aunt Dahlia, if those actors had landed other jobs during the period Fry & Laurie had cleared to film the show, Eastman would just have to re-cast accordingly – only a few lasted the course, with Robert Daws as Tuppy Glossop perhaps the first among equals of the familiar cast. Towards the end of production in January, the shoot was even denied its hero, when word came through to Hugh halfway through a scene that Jo had gone into labour with their second son William, and he had to dash to the hospital leaving Stephen to finish off his side of the dialogue, and follow on later just in time to be present for Bill's birth, both in costume.

The new editions of the *Jeeves* books were not the only publications to feature Fry & Laurie on the covers, and in 1990 Heinemann released the first tie-in *A Bit of Fry & Laurie* book. The Eric Idle-led Monty Python books had set the standard for comedy cash-ins, packed with features and material inspired by the TV shows, but Stephen & Hugh did not go down that route, preferring instead to have their sketches released in script form, albeit with a very silly fresh introduction from the pair. Their writing sessions had produced an abundance of sketches, some of which were either recorded and cut, or had not even got that far, and the books allowed this unused material to be shared, with titles like 'Jeremiah Beadle' or 'The Old Folks' teased in monochrome studio photographs (replete with entirely inaccurate captions, such as 'This shows the gender difference even more clearly. Note the distended folds, or flaps.') and finally available to fans in text form; while the second book, *A Bit More* . . . featured on the cover the duo in remarkable paisley shirts mounted on Hugh's motorbike, and included an unseen 'Spies' episode featuring Control's twin brother, which has otherwise never seen the light of day. With Red Nose Day inspiring charity revues up and down the country, thanks to these books (which were guaranteed 'Actual size', and contained 'No satire at the expense of dolphins'), Fry & Laurie sketches were not uncommon additions to amateur productions, with express publisher permission.

A more professional production was staged on 30 June 1991 at the home of variety, the London Palladium, when Fry presented the third *Hysteria* show – by far the most polished of all, and sadly the last benefit he staged. Much crucial new blood was introduced for this evening, the presenter's place as generous member of the comedy old guard not undermined one bit by his introducing the proceedings with a glitzy high-kicking dance alongside the Tiller Girls, complete with surprisingly complementary tights. Fry & Laurie involvement mainly stretched to another outing for 'The Hedge Sketch', but in came new acts including American improv star Mike McShane alongside short-lived double-act partner Tony Slattery, protest icon Billy Bragg, and on his own, Vic Reeves, singing 'I Remember Punk Rock'. With his own comedy partner Bob Mortimer, Vic (real name Jim Moir – no relation to the Falstaffian TV exec) had exploded onto the comedy scene at the turn of the decade, and in a way the pair filled the same post-modern slot for Morecambe & Wise that Fry & Laurie did for Cook & Moore.

At this stage, Reeves & Mortimer's absurd humour drew as many quizzical looks as laughs, and their debut on the recent spring's Comic Relief, 'The Stonker', was a larky disaster. Stephen & Hugh's own short skit for the evening generated louder howls of hilarity – or perhaps, horror – as they took to the stage with unusual solemnity:

STEPHEN: Ladies and gentlemen, you're looking at two people whose metaphorical bottoms are extremely sore, because I have to tell you that Hugh and I are sitting on the horns of a dilemma.

HUGH: We asked for stools, they gave us horns.
STEPHEN: And pretty sharp horns at that. So sharp, in fact, that I don't even know that we can explain this dilemma to you.
HUGH: Well, I'll do it if you like... We have received a written offer from an engineering firm in the Midlands, who have asked to remain anonymous, of half a million pounds to Comic Relief.
STEPHEN: That's one horn of the dilemma.
HUGH: That's right, that's horn number one. They will give half a million pounds, if — IF! — Stephen Fry will masturbate live on this programme.
STEPHEN: Now, that is horn number two. You see, the dilemma is this — half a million pounds is a great deal of money, a very great deal of money.
HUGH: Close on to half a million pounds.
STEPHEN: It's not far from it, yeah.
HUGH: You can do an awful lot with half a million smackers.
STEPHEN: That's right. But you can do even more with half a million pounds. Now, most people, I'm sure, would like to see another half a million pounds floating into the coffers of Comic Relief... Very few people, however — and I may be wrong — very few people would like to see me thrashing wildly around the studio holding a framed photograph of Bob Holness... Apart from anything else, it's perfectly possible I would cause half a million pound's worth of damage here, and we'd be right back to square one.

HUGH: Back to square one, but with a memory to live with us forever.
STEPHEN: A memory, I venture to suggest, that we could well do without...
HUGH: We also wrote to Bob Holness, asking if he wouldn't mind being featured in this important piece of fundraising. He said yes, and sent us a photograph of himself in the uniform of a bus conductor.
STEPHEN: Perfect. Perfect...[12]

'It was always very chaotic,' Curtis recalls, 'and they arrived very happy with this sketch. I greeted them with smiles, and they told me what they had planned, and my heart just sank. I said, "I beg you, just as friends, please, on a charity show, don't tell me that public masturbation is the only option", and they just said, "Too late, mate, that's all we've got!" But they did it and it appeared harmless, because of their sweet nature.' Besides, the harmless solution was that Stephen was prepared to *kiss* himself on live TV, for £1.

Returning to *Hysteria 3*, Vic Reeves, billed as the country's 'top light entertainer and singer' was on his way up, and a similar trajectory lay ahead of the last noted newbie on the bill – while Stephen & Hugh had been building up their career since 1981, Eddie Izzard had only slowly been transforming himself into the must-watch surreal stand-up of his generation, and his ten-minute spot about being raised by wolves was a success which helped twang him to the very top of the comedy tree. When Stephen announced his arrival to the audience, hardly anyone knew the name, but by the end, Fry recalls, 'I stood in the wings and watched as Eddie left the stage to a gigantic round of applause. How much better to go on to polite clapping and off to roars.'

Another highlight of the evening did involve Fry & Laurie, as the former introduced a number of erotic literary readings performed by Laurie, Atkinson, Craig Ferguson and Emma Freud, promoting protection. Each reader received their own sexy introduction, apparently provided by their partners (Jo, Sunetra, Helen Atkinson-Wood and Richard Curtis, respectively), which required Hugh to keep a straight face as Fry read out: 'The sight of Hugh Laurie's body when burnished, oiled and sprawled on a rug in front of the fire, is enough to tempt the most jaded of appetites. Notable features are the rosy, "come kiss me" cheeks, and the big round blue "come hump me savagely" nipples, which are kept scrupulously clean at all times.'

It wasn't until the year after this final *Hysteria* that Fry was most personally touched by the tragedy the shows were designed to help combat. Kim Harris says, 'In 1992 I and my partner, Alastair, were both diagnosed with HIV. At that time there were no drugs. Not really. We were a few years shy of seeing the treatments that would eventually help manage and to some extent domesticate the condition into a chronic and manageable one. It was a time of monthly funerals and memorial services, of desertion and loneliness and tabloid uselessness, of grim, attritional death. It was a time when hospital orderlies in Hazchem outfits were flinging food trays under sickbay doors before legging it down the corridor. Sadly, Alastair didn't make it. But what he and I both received from Em and Stephen, Hugh and Jo was a sustained and committed campaign of support, care and tenderness the likes of which I had not thought possible beyond dreams or fiction. They could easily have found excuses to remain at arm's length, as did several of our friends. They had families of their own after all and were, you know, busy. But they didn't. It is a debt I cannot ever hope to repay and one which even now, as I reflect upon it in the stilly watches of the night, floors me utterly.'

Almost concurrent with Heinemann releasing the second *ABOF&L* script book, they published Stephen Fry's *The Liar*, which debuted in autumn 1991. The blatant semi-autobiographical nature of at least half the tale of a bisexual Cambridge wag apparently getting caught up in international espionage (pertaining to a lie-inhibiting machine dubbed 'Mendax') was never denied, and in oceans of newsprint publicity, the author admitted, 'I used to go for poses a lot and did invent new languages. I've always been interested in the way people speak and that was one of the pleasures of writing the novel – the simple linguistic pleasure . . . I was taught by people who worked at Bletchley and I used to pump them for information the whole time. The whole world of subterfuge – adolescent subterfuge and what's now called gay subterfuge, and spying subterfuge – is bound together in a fascinating kind of way.' While allying himself with the hero Adrian Healey, Fry told the *Shropshire Star,* 'Liars lie because they find the truth uninteresting and they feel out of place. It's solipsism, an adolescent thing where you believe you are the only person in the world and everybody else is like an extra in a film. All adolescents are like that, which is what most people think Englishmen are.'

The Liar rattled along entertainingly as Adrian proceeded from public school love affairs (Healey's passion for school friend Cartwright being drawn directly from real life) to undergraduate scandal (forging a lost and highly pornographic Dickens novel concerning the Victorian child sex trade), and Fry's masterstroke was to revive Professor Donald Trefusis, Regius Professor of St Matthew's College, Cambridge – making the character no longer a disposable radio voice but a fully formed academic eccentric with a heart of gold and a mind of even higher value. Nonetheless, in years to come, Fry admitted that the plot switch from the personal to the thrilling was not a wise move: 'One of the problems with *The Liar* was my lack of confidence that people would be interested enough in Healey and Cartwright and so I shoved in all the spying crap, which, in fact, most people found less interesting than Adrian in love.'[13] The cricketing sequence, based on a real match while teaching in Yorkshire, was included in a cricket anthology the following year, *Bloody Lucky,* with Stephen's name emblazoned on the front – *The Liar* had after all become a best seller by then, almost universally approved by reviewers, with no less a comedy hero than Frank Muir concluding in *The Times* that 'This is a quite brilliant first novel – the sort of book which we all hoped and, dangerously for the author, *expected* Stephen Fry to come up with . . . Trying to understand the plot is like trying to unravel wire wool. But the wit sparkles, the comic set pieces work a treat. An enjoyably penetrating intelligence pervades throughout.' The book received a further unique tribute when the University of Dundee's 'Liar' bar was established to mark Fry taking his place as Rector in 1992.

Laurie was also toying with his own novel at this point, but he was to admit to being somewhat hamstrung by his colleague's success: 'I think I probably would have written a novel much earlier if it hadn't been for him; I just dreaded the possibility of comparison, because he uses very long words, and he knows what a lot of them mean.' As if that weren't enough, that very year a collection of Fry's collected journalistic musings, radio blessays and early play – dubbed *Paperweight* – simply flew off the shelves when Heinemann published it, plastered with quotes from periodicals such as the *Literary Review* describing the anthology as 'Huge, crammed, wise, hilarious and utterly captivating' and from no less hallowed wit than Alan Coren: 'Fry is by turns observer, humourist, reviewer, philosopher, parodist, autobiographer, academic, scourge, clown and, as often as not, an antic amalgam of all these and more, and his variant style conforms flawlessly with each selected role.' Who would wish to take on such a standard?

Enter Pewnack the Destroyer

Fry's career as an author had not held back the regular growth of Fry & Laurie sketches on his Macintosh hard-drive, and by the time the last *Hysteria* was over, series three was ready to roll – in writing terms, that is, though a new regime was required to produce the show, with Roger Ordish retiring from the business. 'I was pleased to notice that the highest audience appreciation index was for the first series,' he says, 'but that may have been because it was the boys' best stuff. With each series, more money was asked for and it became more elaborate, but I'm not sure it actually made them better. I know the desperate feeling they had, "Good God, we've got to be funny for half an hour *again* this week." I wouldn't want it to sound like sour grapes, but I felt that later on it became too complicated, what was lovely was just them standing in front of an audience being delectably silly.' Three decades on, Ordish says, '*ABOF&L* was a wonderful experience, but at the time I was too occupied with another series which is now unmentionable; I don't think the boys liked that very much, because I was always having to keep an eye on that. Nowadays you look at TV credits and there are four or five producers and executives, it's amazing that I was *the* producer and *the* director, and that was it.' 'Because his experience in entertainment was so different to ours,' begins Laurie, 'well, we didn't have *any*, but our aspirations had nothing to do with anything Roger had done, so with the arrogance of youth, we felt like we knew what we wanted it to be, and he was happy to make that happen, he was not a man to try and steer us in any particular direction. His role was to provide a safe, happy, supportive place where we could explore these things, and he did so with such good humour and, my God, patience – there must have been times when he drove home at the end of the day thinking, "I could cheerfully shoot both these blokes." But he never betrayed it to us, he was always so kind, and a very funny man.' For this third series, Kevin Bishop joined the team – as a director, he was a seasoned booking despite his relative youth, helming series for Kenny Everett, French & Saunders and Victoria Wood, but this was to be only his third show as producer, fresh from Rita Rudner's eponymous new BBC2 sketch show, which boasted a Fry guest spot.

With a young production team and a bare canvas, Stephen & Hugh's third outing began to rack up a new set of targets. Fry & Laurie's reputation for wordy whimsy may make 'targets' sound a trifle extreme, but Canter remembers the pair regularly being fired up by real life – even when it was petty things that set them off. One day, Hugh arrived 'puce with rage' about the smarmy treatment he had received in a car showroom, but the one phrase which stuck in both his head and craw was the oily salesman's assurance: 'M'colleague will be along in a moment'. This sparked off a sketch set in a petrol station with two ex-estate agents who were almost the new Gordon & Stuart, but once the punchline had been reached, the show's two stars still could not stop themselves falling into this drawling yuppie idiom, and from that day on, they became 'm'colleague' to each other.

The new series did away with the cosy clutter of the previous outing, and there was to be more location filming than ever before, not just for the Vox Pops (of which there was a fresh batch, including Stephen's trendy ginger vicar and an elderly gent who went so far as to provide a direct link into this series' 'weird shopkeeper' sketch, plus Hugh as a bespectacled uber-nerd who turned up in a later sketch as Nigel Carter – the muse of louche artist Simbold Cleobury). The shoe shop sketch was the first to introduce the mysterious unseen (and very probably imaginary) figure of Mr Dalliard, and was also a sketch the two colleagues struggled hysterically to complete in front of the audience – Fry's unfettered lunacy in the vein of this deceptively obsequious shopkeeper maniac being a particularly dangerous trigger for the two friends' ability to make each other corpse time and again, against the clock. The final Dalliard offering, set in a model maker's shop, formed a whole chunk of the BBC's blooper strand *Auntie's Bloomers*, with neither performer able to make it past the line 'Fly to Dover?' without one or the other's faces forming a rictus grin, requiring another retake. Even in *Blackadder*, often the pair had to be separated to get through a full take without the slightest glint during eye contact setting the other off. 'It's pathetic in some ways,' Laurie admitted to the *Mirror*, 'and it gets very tricky when we're filming. The director can say, "Look chaps, we've only got five minutes to shoot this last scene, otherwise the crew's into triple overtime . . ." You see, unfortunately, the more serious a situation becomes, the more it makes us want to laugh. All rather silly, isn't it?'

The Dalliard shop sketch was one of the few strands linked to previous series, though Hugh returned under the moniker of Tony Inchpractice to present more unlikely TV shows (including the climactic 'Flying a Light Aeroplane Without Having Had Any Formal Instruction With . . .', for which Fry's stand-in as pilot was his own brother-in-law, flying the biplane Stephen had bought for him). The Bishop & The Warlord returned to debut their hit single 'Grease My Gristle, Blow My Whistle', and the language of Strom popped up for the first and last time in *ABOF&L*, in a translation sketch which also turned the cameras on the audience to pick on an apparently innocent 'rather shy looking man in glasses' – one Nick Symons.

Then there was more from The Department – Major Alan Tarrant, the hard man Hugh was born to play, had been challenged to watch a whole episode of *The Krypton Factor* in the second series, and returned in two thrilling vignettes which almost seem like clips from a spoof feature film that never existed, a testament to Bishop's cinematic approach to putting Fry & Laurie's scripts on screen, although Symons insists Hugh was essentially calling the shots. Hugh himself of course rejects such an idea passionately: 'That strange macho world, somewhere between *The Ipcress File* and Lewis Collins wearing sideburns . . . Stephen and I both enjoyed that genre both comically, but also seriously – we loved it for what it was, but we were greatly entertained by the absurdity of it. Men showing how tough they are is just an endlessly amusing thing. I don't remember influencing Kevin at all, but I do know *The Ipcress File* better than anyone else you'll ever meet in your life. That's a sad confession, but the Len Deighton world is one I know very well, and I felt like I knew Sidney Furie's direction, I could draw every frame of it, every shot that he did. But the idea of "calling the shots", that sounds appalling! Kevin's very talented, I mean, he's a proper director. He had an idea of how shots and images can enrich and add to something rather than simply record it, so I hope he would say that is his instinct, to offer that service to any piece of material. I remember it being a healthy collaboration of picture and word.' Both comics were of course obsessed with spies and espionage, but it's still tempting to see Laurie as the primary drive behind these very silly takes on le Carré and Co. – and the first sketch provided a chance for Footlights inheritor Morwenna Banks to join the colleagues:

```
WOMAN:     Excuse me, Admiral... Major Tarrant seems
           to doubt my abilities.
HUGH:      You're damn right.
WOMAN:     Would it make any difference if I said
           that I was the case officer on Operation
           Richard Whiteley?
STEPHEN:   Since your time, Alan. Ugly business.
           Russians tried to flood Europe with
           counterfeit Richard Whiteleys. The
           Department was on a Code 1 for
           three months.
HUGH:      All I'm saying is, I don't carry passengers.
WOMAN:     Neither do I, Major.
STEPHEN:   Ho ho ho. Looks like you've met your
           match at last, Alan.
```

Mention of the late Richard Whiteley also brings to mind perhaps *ABOF&L*'s most successful TV lampoon of all, the *Countdown* sketch in which Steve Steen's Gyles Brandreth cipher suggests the eight-letter word 'sloblock', meaning 'bollocks'. Fry & Laurie's media parodies often seemed to settle on targets with regrettably brief shelf-lives, requiring extensive explanation for those too young or too foreign to instantly get the reference – particularly in the second series, where figures like Robert Robinson and Rhodes Boyson, or the Yellow Pages ads featuring fictional author J. R. Hartley, so quickly lost all the instant recognisability they had when the sketches were first recorded. Further lampoons of *Question of Sport* and *Going for Gold* seem similarly dated now; but somehow, even years after the death of Whiteley, the *Countdown* sketch remains popular – veteran co-presenter Carol Vorderman even called her home 'Sloblock Hall', and Fry visited the real Dictionary Corner more than once, without any physical reprisal.

The last solid link to previous series came with the arrival of the late Freddie's brother Neddy Muldoon, another fall guy for Stephen's mysterious and murderous believer in 'The Cause', who this time coerced his victim into ousting John Major as PM, before being stabbed on prime-time TV. This episode was originally to end with Hugh singing a sad song, 'The Ballad of Neddy Muldoon':

He was an average lad, if a little bit sad, with a heart as big as a van,
If trouble was brewing and a job needed doing, Neddy was always your man . . .
Yes they're digging a hole up on Haverstock Hill,
For the corpse of Neddy Muldoon . . .

However, the option to end an episode on such a note was soon taken away with the establishment of a brand-new Fry & Laurie trademark which would stay with them to the end, and for many people sum up the double act to this day – the closing cocktail recipe, with smooth jazz provided by Laurie on piano and virtuoso mouth trumpet, as Fry did his business with the shaker. Although this was the one concession made in the new series to any kind of anchor for each episode, interestingly, both Symons and Canter volunteer this regular climax as their least favourite bit of Fry & Laurie's output, and rue the decision to use it every week, the latter complaining, 'I used to hate that, I was worried the audience would miss the irony and think, "There's those two Oxbridge toffs." I said,

"You are so much more than this."' From Flanders & Swann to Kit & The Widow, the Oxbridge cliché of two men in dicky-bows being witty at the piano was certainly unworthy of Stephen & Hugh, who could never fit into that simplistic mould, but the latter colleague protests the lashings of irony that made the set-up work: 'I hoped that we were making it perfectly clear we didn't see ourselves in that way, it was a joke! We were dressing up and playing that part, making fun of it – the fact that Stephen could make the word "Well" last about thirty-five seconds, that sort of Robert Robinson urbanity in front of the camera we found amusing, and I hope to God no one thought we saw ourselves as genuinely urbane, sophisticated entertainers, because we never were that.'

The ludicrous cocktails certainly stuck in the public imagination and even provided perhaps the closest thing Fry & Laurie ever had to a catchphrase – the parting, inane cry of 'Soupy twist!' – and the closing tradition was never dropped, despite the misgivings of their production team. This display of stubbornness was atypical, Canter adds, as 'Hugh was such a worrier. He used to call me "Rock" for some reason, and on studio recording days his catchphrase was "Rock, we're DEAD". It was like crying wolf, I thought, "Well, you can't mean it, because you've done several series and you're loved", but he always did mean it. Whereas Stephen would say to him, "Don't be a silly billy . . ."' 'Generally speaking, Stephen is a more commonly optimistic person than I am, he has a sort of "Well, what's the worst that can happen?" approach to life, which I wish I could have, because if someone ever asks me that question, I can then speak for a couple of hours – you're not leaving the room, because I've got a lot to tell you.' Hugh explains, 'I called Jon "Rock" because I felt he was the rock on which we were built. I don't know whether he would say he took that role, or if I just so desperately wanted him to take the role, I thought that if I gave him the name, he would live up to it. Sometimes that can work.' Asked for any clue to the derivation of the phrase 'Soupy Twists', Laurie can only respond, 'No idea. I think it was probably Stephen, my guess. I never had such a facility for nonsense words, that's something he can do, and does, with such fluency, he's almost got a Stanley Unwin-type facility for that kind of thing. I do remember being on holiday somewhere and there was a piano in the house we were staying in, and we just started sort of messing about. It was our own cap-doffing to Cook & Moore doing "Goodbye" with Dud at the piano. A sort of joke formal vaudeville ending, we quite enjoyed – but I remember Jon absolutely hating it, seething with disapproval at the cuteness and silliness of it, I think. But that was exactly why we loved it! And Stephen's mixing the cocktails still makes me laugh just to think of it, never mind watching him do it. So we overrode Jon.' Stephen fills in grey areas: 'We were in Vence, south of France, it would have been shortly before Bill was born, Christmas-ish, 1990, and it snowed. There was a piano in the villa we hired, and we got into this silly habit, to entertain Jo, of Hugh doing voice trumpet and playing the piano, and me doing preposterous dances with a cocktail shaker. I think somehow we came up with this ridiculous phrase which made ourselves laugh.'

The tuxedo closers also began to cement the double act personas after their hitherto quite liquid on-screen relationship. Fry insists, 'We have no sense of senior partner in our working relationship – or indeed our wider one. It's really all unspoken', which was true behind the scenes, but in 'soupy twist' terms, Stephen's predilection for punching his colleague off the piano stool was now joined by an insistence that Hugh 'shut his neck' any time a valedictory thought came to mind, and this jocular balance of power held to the end. Hitherto, Fry continues, 'We never had a specific sense, unlike some other pairings, that one of us was the dummy and the other the smart arse. It was often Stephen the smart arse and Hugh the dummy, but as with Alliance & Leicester it could easily be the other way around too.'

Once again, the six episodes which eventually went out on Thursday nights from 9 January 1992 contained too many standalone classics to list completely – from young Timothy Forrest's quest with Berwhale the Avenger to the two mad monks damning UHT milk to Hell, the combative Yorkshireman, the ballsy bookshop complainer, the aged toff discussing his favourite pants – some items, such as the 'Marmalade' two-hander, or the simple, wordless quickie with Hugh as a manic balloon-animal maker who creates a perfect dachshund – certainly present Fry & Laurie at their very best. All of this was wrapped up in a bright, exciting new package quite unlike the woody modesty of the first two series – the new opening credits marrying salsa rhythms with

Latin American fiesta fireworks and flashy, colourful graphics. 'I have a horrible feeling that I talked Stephen into that,' Hugh says, 'and, gentle soul that he is, he agreed to go along with it. I'm not sure if he liked it, before or afterwards – or me either, actually, I'm not sure that it really worked.' The third outing still performed well, triggering a third script book, this time combining the previous two releases into the 'odourless' *3 Bits Of Fry & Laurie,* running perversely from back to front and offering '18 hours of television trapped in a prose net and bludgeoned to death in direct contravention of EC regulations'.

The two sophisticates were becoming quite comfy on the plush beige seats of Terry Wogan's thrice-weekly BBC chat-a-thon, together and apart, so much so that while publicising the third *J&W* series, they decided to hurry along the publicity part and use most of their slot for a special magic trick taken from a children's activity book, in which the lady-stroke-gentleman avuncular Irish host's playing card turned up in the core of an apple, thanks to the intonation of the relevant magic words, 'The Relevant Magic Words!' As an avowed Wodehouse devotee, Terry was not inclined to give the young tykes an easy ride, praising the Price/Carmichael incarnation and getting the name of their sketch series wrong – 'A Little Fry & Laurie' – putting Stephen on the back foot as he admitted of the new *ABOF&L*, 'I don't think there was any demand. There was just a gap on Thursdays, and we leapt to fill it. We'd done two previously, which is why we decided to call this one the third series . . . BBC2 is a nice little sweaty underside to inhabit, you can swim about there and do things without being too noticed. I mean, heavens above, millions watch, obviously, I didn't mean to imply nobody watches . . .' Hugh next admitted in reference to the Vox Pops that 'Cross-dressing is very pleasurable indeed, and to do it professionally, and be paid for it, is obviously a heck of a bonus . . . Some of those characters I did in a police uniform, which was very fun. When they're setting up the camera, you can't resist walking down the street and checking people's tax discs, just great. I have to admit, I would love to be a policeman.' And if any *Wogan* viewers were afraid of being offended by any of the comedy purveyed by these seemingly harmless young men, Stephen closed by asserting one of his favourite aphorisms: 'Better sexy and racy than sexist and racist!'

Another time on Tel's sofa, Hugh had complained, 'I sometimes think comedy feels to me rather like the situation with house prices about ten years ago, you know, that all these double acts are sitting around rather like estate agents – in fact, they sound rather like estate agents, "Fry & Laurie" could be an estate agents' – and we're twanging our braces and going, "Yah, the market's pretty strong at the moment, actually". But pretty soon it's all gonna crash, and quite rightly so, I think we've all had enough, haven't we?' Nevertheless, more *ABOF&L* was politely requested by Auntie Beeb, though the annual frequency inevitably had to slacken – and of course, the books were all doing great business, both their own and Wodehouse classics with their faces on them.

It was a real oddity of the Fry & Laurie partnership that they never capitalised on their TV popularity with another live tour, quitting touring before they had a TV vehicle, unlike their contemporaries who were raking it in all around the country. 'It was partly our inferiority complex,' admits Laurie, 'we looked at Rik & Ade with such admiration, their confidence and energy with which they could attack a live audience was really something to behold. They were stunning, and Vic & Bob, and I remember seeing Mel Smith & Griff Rhys Jones, and their assurance and charm and control was just astounding. I think we both just felt that we weren't cut from that sort of cloth. I even remember seeing Cannon & Ball in Manchester – perhaps one of the funniest twenty-five minutes of my life! No, the funniest ever was Rik at the Dominion, absolutely unforgettable.'

We have also barely touched upon half the work which kept Stephen & Hugh busy behind the microphone, with animation making as good use of their voices as adverts, Hugh in particular becoming a familiar voice in many cartoons – perhaps due to having small children of his own – from the bird-like Squire Trelawney in *Legends of Treasure Island* to Mr Toad in a 1995 *Wind in the Willows*. Both colleagues also had an abundance of audiobooks under their belts, Stephen narrating not just his own work, *Jennings* school stories and the bawdy novels of Tom Sharpe, but also voicing a brace of famous bears, Paddington and the perfect Pooh to Jane Horrocks' Piglet – while Hugh gave perhaps the most apposite delivery of Jerome K. Jerome's humour on record, and both grabbed their own spot of Roald Dahl fun, reading *The Enormous Crocodile* and *The Giraffe and the Pelly and Me*.

With these media covered, there was one glaring medium remaining with no Fry & Laurie flag stuck into it – cinema. Since the *Gossip* debacle both colleagues had suffered further scrapes with the movie business, Stephen getting close to production with period offering *Bachelors Anonymous* (not the Wodehouse novel, but an original film based on the book *Foxprints* by Patrick McGinley, to be helmed by *The Wicker Man* director Robin Hardy), plus adaptations of *The Liar* were mooted, and a musical with Elton John; while Hugh was developing a film called *Galahad* with *J&W* producer Brian Eastman – a crime caper in which the hero is hypnotised into arranging a grand heist, but this too sadly foundered. There was no real attempt to translate Fry & Laurie's popularity into film, but Hugh says, 'When we were young fellows-me-lad, film did not really seem to be an option. It wasn't in the vocabulary. We'd have been laughed out of the office.' 'Like everyone we toyed with this idea and that from time to time,' his colleague adds, 'but were too lacking in confidence or starting power to get on with it.'

Two people who did have the confidence to get on with it were ex-Footlights President Martin Bergman and his Miamian stand-up wife Rita Rudner, fresh from performing with Stephen in her own show, in which he popped up as a trashy US executive pulling every trick to try to make soccer palatable to American sport(s) fans. Straddling the Atlantic, Rudner's quickfire gag-slinging was well supported by her husband, and their first screenplay, despite being intentionally small in its setting and scope, bristled from end to end with waspish killer lines. It was saddled with comparisons to 1983 movie *The Big Chill*, but *Peter's Friends* was directly inspired by Bergman's own time in Footlights, and more particularly his keen avuncular observation of *The Cellar Tapes* generation he led to Australia, and when the finished screenplay arrived on the colleagues' doormats, the inspiration was obvious, and a trifle embarrassing. Taking place at New Year 1992 at the kind of stately home which had become familiar to Fry & Laurie during two series of *J&W*, *Peter's Friends* focused on the lives of a group of Footlights friends ten years after graduation, and parts were marked off for Slattery, Thompson, Phyllida Law and young comedian Alex Lowe, while Branagh had confirmed the comedy to be his third feature as director. Stephen & Hugh's inverted snobbery complexes were piqued by the blatant 'golden team' snipes that would come their way; but Ken Branagh had not earned his place as 'the new Olivier' by letting such gloom hold him back, and he lambasted them for their lack of confidence in the film. He himself said, 'I was interested in making a film about how relationships endure through the passage of time and against the background of great events taking place in the wider world. I'd like the audience to feel as if they were eavesdropping on somebody else's party, glimpsing a particular moment in these characters' lives which we all at one time experience. Here is a group of affluent people in their thirties, materially comfortable, but they're getting to feel the sands of time are running fast and sensing intimations of mortality.' Filmed at a breakneck pace in only eleven days, *Peter's Friends* was a snapshot of the emotional messes of thirty-something graduates who did not get snapped up by Noel Gay – and if it had one glaring flaw, it was the deliberate avoidance of any real rapport between Stephen & Hugh, with Ken taking the part of Peter's Woody Allen-ish ex-comedy partner Andrew – in many ways a Bergman stand-in, making it anything but a Fry & Laurie movie. 'The reason that it didn't actually express any relationship between me and Stephen was because it was based more on Martin Bergman's rose-tinted memory of earlier times, before we had begun to work together – Martin left Footlights before Stephen joined, so they didn't have many dealings. We were anxious that it would look self-satisfied or cliquey, that's always been a thing that's made us shudder, the idea of people revelling in, or even having the nerve to talk about, their privileged background, their little coterie of friends, we felt uncomfortable with that. That's why I took it a step further and actually chose not to have friends.' Hugh's character Roger wrote commercial jingles with his wife, played by Emma's close friend Imelda Staunton, and their mourning for the death of one of their twin sons, and obsessive care of the surviving twin, was one of the film's emotional cores.

PETER:	Hello, you two, got everything you need? Towels? Spoons?
ROGER:	Heaps of spoons... No, it's good to get away, actually.
PETER:	Yes, I'm sorry I haven't seen either of you since...

ROGER:	No, don't be silly. Actually, this is the first time we've been out since it happened.
PETER:	Ben's all right though, isn't he?
ROGER:	Oh yes, Ben is very bonny, very bonny.
PETER:	So, all you've got to worry about now are murderers and perverts.
ROGER:	Quite.[14]

'I tend only to take on work that I know I can do,' Hugh told *Flicks* magazine, 'But with this film I got into something, emotionally, that was out of my depth and, er, well, it turned out better than I'd hoped. I was really lucky to be doing it with Imelda. It was like I'd got my coat trapped in a car door and was dragged along because she was so good.' Fry of course had the titular role, inheritor of the grand house and host of the party, and he clearly saw Peter as indicative of his own fears: 'It is not facile to describe him as having been cursed by the twin disadvantages of riches and intelligence, and so he has never known the hunger which causes other people to rise from the table to hunt. He has moved around in a dilettante kind of way without being seized by the kind of greed which is necessary for achievement.' Peter was to deliver the film's tragic bombshell that he is HIV positive, and although the colleagues were to laugh together years later about the melodrama of the big reveal, Laurie was kind enough to admit of his old partner, 'As a straight dramatic actor, it's as if there is some sort of profound sadness underneath all his gregariousness, his desire to entertain and make people feel good . . . I suppose I'm as well qualified as anyone else to say whether or not that's true, so is it true? Is there a deep sadness? Well, yes, there may be. That has a lot to do with his power and appeal as an actor, it's very engaging. I feel for him when I watch him.'

Peter's Friends was released in November 1992, to a not loudly applauding audience who nonetheless helped to make back the £4 million budget between the UK and US box office – while critics were slightly warmer, the *Guardian* calling the film 'well written, beautifully performed and highly entertaining . . . Fry's puzzled gentleman persona is perfect for this part and he does extremely well.' Viewed today, there's something unintentionally amusing about 1980s nostalgia from an early 1990s perspective, as if these early-thirty-somethings were somehow past it twenty-five years ago, but the film did capture a halcyon moment for a golden generation who were on the brink of all manner of fall-outs, not least the end of the 'Ken 'n' Em' coupling shortly after.

Lending weight to Fry & Laurie's joint paranoia, despite having many friends within the *Spitting Image* team, and the puppets being regulars at Fry's *Hysteria* shows, the show did merrily pillory the 'upper class wits' on a number of occasions, with a weirdly unconvincing Hugh Laurie puppet, voiced by Alistair McGowan, joining the line-up in the sixteenth series, with Enfield's Fry voice being taken over by young turk Steve Coogan. Stephen, Hugh, Emma and Ken were shown having dinner with Sir Anthony Hopkins, and then ordering him to clear away the dishes after he admits to not attending Oxford or Cambridge (despite Branagh not being university educated at all), and there was one sketch featuring the two colleagues reminiscing in a dressing room:

'HUGH': What ho, Blackadder! What ho, Alliance & Leicester!
'STEPHEN': Nyehhh! Such trouser-filling versatility, Hughikins! What an erudite double act we are!
'HUGH': I'll say. Isn't it amazing good luck that we were in the same university? Foh!

CUT TO: FLASHBACK. ANOTHER DRESSING ROOM, WITH A SIGN READING 'LUVVIES COLLEGE CAMBRIDGE'. HUGH ENTERS.

'EMMA': Next snivelling undergraduate, please!
'HUGH': What ho, chaps!
'STEPHEN': Nyeh! Welcome to our audition, my moist and fluffy friend. And what is your name, pray?
'HUGH': Er, Hugh Laurie.
'CLIVE': Well, come along, come along, witty remark, we haven't got all day, smug one-liner, barbed comment. Er, what can you do?

'HUGH':   Erm, well, all sorts really, Clive, I mean, I can do rich and stupid, or I can do rich and stupid. Or another favourite is a stupid person who happens to be rich...
CUT BACK TO DRESSING ROOM.
'STEPHEN':   You know, Hughikins, I've never understood why TV people have paid you so much to play that one character.
'HUGH':   Hmm, perhaps it's because they're all rich and stupid![15]

This, of course, was an inaccurate as it was unfunny, but at least it showed in its own painful way that Fry & Laurie were at the top of their game, on a podium which made them fair game for satirists to have a pop at their perceived privilege. *Viz* comic popped up in *ABOF&L* via a 'Fat Slags' T-shirt worn by one particularly dumb Vox Pop, and always had more licence for savagery than the ITV puppet show, but was less vociferous when it first featured Stephen in a strip called 'Fry's Turkish Delight', in which the loquacious undergraduate was lumbered with a mountain of banned sweetmeat and had to eat it before his colleague could come to his aid with 'Hugh's lorry'.

The Bally Balliness of It All

The satirical barbs aimed at Fry & Laurie were of course the lightest of paper darts, but it could be argued that the most sophisticated comedy double act in Britain had turned a corner by this point, and there was discernible gilt flaking off the gingerbread in places. *Peter's Friends* not only gave ammo to their critics, the film in some ways foreshadowed their separate future paths, with Hugh being pushed to a new level of serious thespian effort by his tragic turn, pointing him towards escaping the kind of typecasting *Spitting Image* was getting at, while Stephen was up front in a title role attuned to the persona he had been selling to the populace since the Perrier triumph, a positively eerie piece of character observation from Rudner & Bergman which pinned Fry down quite firmly.

Once the film's cinema run was all over, Stephen & Hugh's projects were taking them further apart, while the final series of *J&W*, which aired in the late spring of 1993, seemed almost designed to send the eyebrows of the Wodehouse faithful shooting up into the stratosphere. Even in the third series, as the action became split between New York and Blighty, the plots had diverged greatly from Wodehouse's original writing – usually in the interests of giving more screen time to Robert Daws' amusing turn as Tuppy Glossop, tweaking stories to feature the minor Drone while shifting the action to the USA, and doing everything possible to maximise Laurie's undeniable physical clowning skills.

If there was a notable saving grace for these wanderings from the truly Wodehousian, it was the release of the LP *The World of Jeeves & Wooster*. Thirty years earlier, Ian Carmichael had recorded his own Wooster single, 'What Would I Do Without You, Jeeves?' – so there was a precedent to the CD and cassette release which brought together Anne Dudley's ripping incidental music with new recordings of memorable dialogue, and shining syncopated performances from Hugh in character with the Dover Street Jazzomaniacs, including forgotten hits like 'If I Had a Talking Picture of You' and of course, 'Minnie the Moocher'. Twenty years later, the publicity surrounding Hugh's album *Let Them Talk* fixated on it being his 'debut', but these memorable Wooster recordings belied such talk, and the album remains a highly cherishable collector's item.

Clive Exton is sadly no longer around to explain the extraordinary departures he took from the hallowed 'Plum' source, and the protestations we are left with for the latter liberties in *J&W* always seem rum. When Sir Pelham slipped away on Valentine's Day 1975, he left us a huge wealth of material, and although Exton's approach to adapting his work made voracious use of the *Jeeves* adventures, by 1993 there were still a number of short stories yet to be adapted, and two late period novels, *Jeeves in the Offing* and *Aunts Aren't Gentlemen*, barely touched, skipping unique characters peopling plots which took in horse racing and cat abduction and noted brain specialist Sir Roderick Glossop disguised as a butler. There was much to work with here, and yet the final series of *J&W* introduced a barrage of wild invention as Exton frequently painted himself into a corner by heaping peril upon peril for poor Bertie, concluding with the absolute zenith of being betrothed to Lady Florence Craye and Madeleine Bassett at the same time. And so, unimagined extremes were deemed necessary – the young master and his unflappable servant jumped ship and sailed adrift in an open boat, returning home to Berkeley Mansions like a pair of Robinson Crusoes, and both had to pass as women to solve another impossible tangle. The very last episode in June 1993 took the bare bones of *Much Obliged, Jeeves* before veering off as an entirely new confection with Tuppy disguised as a cockney plumber offering his 'Plumbo Jumbo' service to Sir Watkyn Bassett, leading to Totleigh Towers positively exploding, while the latter's soppy daughter was only ultimately joined at the altar by fascist Roderick Spode by the introduction of a blackmailing kangaroo. Before this weight of bizarre invention could cause the programme to entirely crumble, the whole saga concluded with a farcical Benny-Hill-style chase. Viewed without prejudice, it was funny to see the two heroes caught on the hoof in the finale, and perhaps that should be the entire point. But while it was one thing to show Jeeves raising his eyebrow more than a quarter-inch, these liberties were manifestly off the scale. 'We got through so many short stories and longer novels,' Fry protests. 'I held my tongue as far as new non-canonical material was concerned, but I think Clive wrote some good stories that got the best out of the characters. Most would agree *Aunts Aren't Gentlemen* wasn't mid-season form from the Master and something of a retread really.' 'I think the estate were not so happy about that,' Eastman admits, 'but in terms of the television series, it was a successful way to bring those characters to a conclusion – we were never going to do any more, because we'd run out of material.' Laurie adds that one indication that the series had to end came when a perfectly good take was stopped because 'I started to go bald; that was pretty galling. I'm quite tall and get away with it most of the time, but somebody had to swoop in before takes and dust my pate, which we felt was sort of inappropriate for Bertie somehow.' Nonetheless, his insistence that they had 'filleted the *oeuvre*' seems fishy, and from a Wodehousian perspective, it was an unexpected conclusion to what had always been a truly perfect adaptation.

Be that as it may, to this day, P. G. Wodehouse's two greatest characters have remained defined by Fry & Laurie for a generation or more, with all subsequent attempts to fill the roles both on radio and in the theatre overshadowed by the colleagues' performances. Andrew Sachs & Marcus Brigstocke tried on Radio 4, Andrew Lloyd Webber & Alan Ayckbourn's musical *By Jeeves* could not shake memories of Stephen & Hugh, and 2013's conceptually identical award-winning hit play *Perfect Nonsense* seemed overtly inspired by the Granada series. The admired, frenetic performances of successive pairs of actors Matthew Macfadyen & Stephen Mangan, Mark Heap & Robert Webb and John Gordon Sinclair & James Lance could never quite compare with Fry & Laurie's four years in the roles of Jeeves & Wooster, however – and any comparison could only be taken as the deepest compliment by their successors.

Between Fact and Breakfast, Madness Lies

By February 1994 it was time to head back onto the street to shout non-sequiturs at cameras in a variety of guises. However, for this fourth outing, a great many changes had been forced upon the *ABOF&L* powerhouse. Nick Symons, trained from the start to be the perfect facilitator for Stephen & Hugh's ideas, now worked for Carlton, and couldn't be involved, and even Jon Canter was unavailable. They all remain friends, and Jon recalls that the wealth of comic material being produced may have been symptomatic of Fry's growing mania: 'I wasn't married or anything then, so I did my fair share of cocaine nights with Stephen, and he was sad a lot of the time. Writing this stuff was a way of fending something off. In my memory, Stephen was producing more individual stuff, but he was writing with his best mate in his head. It felt like an intensely private, loving thing. It wasn't gay, they just both absolutely adored each other, like Reeves & Mortimer.' If ever Fry's reputation for an exuberant profligacy of output created a suspicion that *ABOF&L* on paper contained more 'Fry' than 'Laurie', then Symons insists strongly that 'If Stephen *was* writing more than fifty per cent, it wasn't much more.' But at this time, Hugh had so much more in his life, particularly since the arrival of daughter Rebecca Augusta in September. The Lauries' youngest had been dangerously overdue, and Jo, who had been busy designing a new kitchen for Stephen's Norfolk home, was soon in clear danger unless a caesarean could be performed. University College Hospital, where Charlie and Bill had been born, could not arrange the surgery for a fortnight and so the agonising decision was made to go private on that occasion, and with Rebecca's birth, their family was complete.

Stephen & Hugh's solo TV projects continued to diverge, the latter dipping his toe further into drama after the fillip of *Peter's Friends*, exploring the central role of a gambling addict in ITV's *All or Nothing at All*, a mini-serial which made much of its comedic cast playing it straight – Hugh, Steve Steen, Caroline Quentin and even Bob Monkhouse. Laurie was well reviewed in the role, although his established loveable persona was a large part of the charm: 'Leo is flawed, my God he's flawed,' Hugh said at the time. 'He brings untold misery to those who love him. But unless he was loveable it would be like watching someone breaking car aerials all the way down the street. You wouldn't care what happened to him.' He was quick to add, to any journalist dismayed at the idea of binary career paths, as if one can only be serious or comic: 'Making people laugh is what I've always wanted to do. Besides, I don't think I'll ever see myself as a proper actor, or escape the feeling that so many people can do it better than I can.' In that spirit, Stephen joined up with sitcom stalwarts Nicholas Lyndhurst and Geoffrey Palmer for a return to historical comedy, in David Nobbs' *Stalag Luft*, which used the very old joke of Nazi prison guards being as keen to escape as the British POWs, but Nobbs' genius for creating comic characters with whom you want to spend time made it into the ultimate POW comedy, a TV movie which gifted Fry the opportunity to embody both the suave RAF officer and snarling German Kommandant. He also popped over to America to film a dream cameo for US historical drama series *Ned Blessing*, which featured Oscar Wilde on his 1882 American tour. It was not a memorable show or an in-depth depiction, but how could Fry resist what may have been his only chance to step into the shoes of his true hero, in the Old West?

Soon after Rebecca's birth, Hugh fell ill, and Fry's diary entry for 3 November 1993 reads, 'Hugh called in early this morning to report sick: or rather Jo did on his behalf. Flu, sinus, that kind of nonsense. This has left me with the day to myself. A chance to "clear my desk" of plenty of correspondence and other dribble. A sketch didn't come though, so I biked off a mock sketch to Hugh detailing how difficult it is to write a sketch.' Luckily, this survives in the archive:

STEPHEN: (BANGING HEAD ON KEYBOARD) Come on! You useless, crappy bastard. You shining, spinning ball of Welshman's gob. Oh yes, you can get 3 Down straight away can't you? Bloody clever and helpful, that is, I must say. You can take thirty-five minutes to write a thank-you letter and another ten to go and post it. You can do that all right. Bloody world class at that. Doubt there are four men of your age and weight in the world who could do a tricky thing like write a letter and stick it down a slit with such remarkable flair. But a sketch? Oh no.

HUGH: (FROM HIS BED OF PAIN: CROAKING) We're dead. Only two and a half months to go and we're dead. Oh Jesus. Oh Godding Jesusing God. Write a sketch about... um...

STEPHEN: I'm waiting.

HUGH: About sinus headaches.

STEPHEN: Thanks. Great. Mm. 'Doctor, I'm worried about my synovial fluids.' 'Take a seat, Mr Prettycock, take a seat...' I mean it's not really going anywhere, is it?

HUGH: Well, write a sketch about a couple of men with reasonably promising careers in medium-weight, dependable comedy, but who throw it all away because THEY CAN'T BE RINSING ARSED TO WRITE ANY FRIGGING SKETCHES! (HUGH LEANS BACK, COUGHING, EXHAUSTED BY THIS LAST SUPREME EFFORT.)

STEPHEN: Well! Someone got into bed on the wrong side this morning, didn't they?

HUGH: I'm sorry. It's just that I had this sweet

	idea in my head that I wasn't going to have to pay the BBC a snillion pounds for breach of contract and then move into the street with my wife and nine children, earning money by giving blow-jobs to passing terrorists. It was a dream I had. It's shattered now. I see that.
STEPHEN:	Look, things aren't that bad... Let's not get hasty. There's still a good few hours left in the day. Perhaps a sketch idea will come.
HUGH:	It had better. It had bloody better, that's all.
STEPHEN:	Talking of better, you'd better be better tomorrow, because 'Chris' from the Labour Party is coming round at 10:00 a.m. to talk about the Broadcast.
HUGH:	Ten?
STEPHEN:	He's got a meeting at 11:30 and so ten it is.
HUGH:	Fucking hell.
STEPHEN:	Exactly what I said when his grandmother rang to confirm the date.
HUGH:	How did she react?
STEPHEN:	Accused me of date rape and told me to name my lawyers.
HUGH:	And you said?
STEPHEN:	I said my lawyers had already been named, at a very early age, by a priest at a christening service.
HUGH:	That shut her up.
STEPHEN:	Not a bit of it. Accused me of undermining the peace process.
HUGH:	And had you?
STEPHEN:	Only a tiny bit.
HUGH:	You do live, don't you?

The Labour meeting was apropos of a Party Political Broadcast sketch aired later that month, featuring Fry & Laurie as Weaver & Dodge, tax consultants who pointed out all the duplicitous ways in which the Tory party allowed businesses to avoid paying tax – a sketch which would be no less topical and necessary if broadcast a quarter of a century later.

The BBC boss this fictional Hugh was afraid to disappoint, on the other hand, was one of the top comedy producers in the business – Jon Plowman had come a long way since directing *Beyond the Footlights*, and he was now taking the reins of *ABOF&L*, with his right-hand man Bob Spiers as director. 'In my memory, it was Stephen who came to me and said, "Is there any chance you and Bob would do our next series . . .?" He didn't quite say, "Because we need rescuing", but there was a sense that they wanted what Bob and I had done with French & Saunders, which was sort of allow them to be silly! And also they had this thought about the shape of the show, they wanted it to be much more of a piece, and Bob and I agreed. I remember a meeting between the four of us, and I don't think we put down too many demands. But they were so much the opposite of what Bob and I had been working with, I think we were rather grateful. What Dawn & Jen do is quite loose, and we'd slot their sketches into shows, but Stephen & Hugh wrote very precisely, the structure was much more built by them from the writing stage, it worked well.' Spiers, who died in 2008 leaving a TV CV any director would envy, told the BBC's *Comedy Connections* in 2005, 'I think up to that stage it was more or less a kind of conventional eighties sketch show, very much out of the Oxbridge Monty-Python-Goodie-Peter-Cook kind of tradition, which is hugely funny and I'm a huge fan, and very clever, but I think there was just a general feeling that maybe it just needed a little bit of a change.' 'Plowman was a star producer by that point,' Nick Symons adds, 'because of *Absolutely Fabulous*, so he was more inclined to be dictatorial, whereas my job, whether with Stephen & Hugh or Harry Hill or whoever, has always been to "get it", and to realise what they need, to be funny. You do need to have that understanding of where they're coming from, and everybody going in the same direction, at the same speed.'

As the sketches began to thud out of Fry's printer, some familiar items went through numerous permutations before their placement in the eventual series, such as the hospital-set 'Operational Criteria':

STEPHEN: Mmm. Not good, I'm afraid.
JANE: It's his heart, is it?
STEPHEN: Probably. Now, Mr Spiers, hearts are slippery customers at the best of times. We can wait for a couple of days, nothing, then wallop, three come in at once.
JOHN: Like buses.
STEPHEN: A bit like buses, yes. But with certain important differences, obviously. We do, at the moment, have one heart hanging around. Not a bad little chap... Trouble is...
JOHN: Yes?
STEPHEN: We're a little bit worried about the way you eat soup... it's resources, you see. Limited resources. I have to decide who's going to make the most of the one heart we've got. Now, Mr Thurloe eats soup in a perfectly acceptable fashion, but his clothes...
JOHN: What about them?
STEPHEN: Hideous. Not a clue. Brown shoes with a grey suit. A horror to behold. Not nice at all. Then Mr Fistfuck...
JOHN: Fistfuck?
STEPHEN: Exactly. Nice enough chap, but do I want to put a heart inside a man called Fistfuck?

The third series of *ABOF&L* had been so warmly received that a big budget increase was announced, plus a further promotion – a slot on BBC1 was theirs for the taking. 'I think that would have been down to Alan Yentob moving from BBC2 to BBC1 as controller,' Plowman suggests, 'because they wanted bigger audiences, and we got a bigger pot of money. I'm not *sure*, but I think that in itself is indicative of the fact that we never let the move worry us. Once they'd decided to do this notionally friendly format, much more down the camera, and with guests the audience have heard of, then they'd done what was needed to make it a BBC1 show.' Plowman had produced *Wogan* for years and ferried Smith & Jones and French & Saunders from BBC2 cults to mainstream BBC1 success, and it was felt that Stephen & Hugh, with their cocktail-shaking sophistication, could outdo all of the above. Comedy had moved on once again, with BBC2 series *The Smell of Reeves & Mortimer* a defining hit for the channel, while two different pairs of Cambridge graduates had been altering comedy their own way in *The Mary Whitehouse Experience* – one pair were even called Steven & Hugh. Punt & Dennis and their loosely associated co-performers Rob Newman & David Baddiel had been snapping at their predecessors' heels since they had graduated from the university – Newman the only non-Footlighter – and the latter duo's arena-filling success inspired the decade-defining hack observation 'comedy is the new rock & roll'. Perhaps it was the right time for Fry & Laurie to graduate, as it were, to the nation's first television channel.

The BBC1 move was nonetheless a surprise, as they already planned to top each show with a spot of televisual horseplay involving the famous BBC2 logo. For years, one source of pained sphincter-tightening for them both had been people's regular inability to get the name '*A Bit of Fry & Laurie*' right, and they wanted to deal with this every week:

A BBC2 LOGO HANGS ON THE SCREEN, AS AN ANNOUNCER ANNOUNCES:
ALAN: But now, it's time for 'A Little Bit of Fry & Laurie'.
A PAUSE. THEN STEPHEN AND HUGH, ALSO IN VOICE-OVER:
HUGH: 'A Bit of Fry & Laurie.'
ALAN: What?
HUGH: It's 'A Bit of Fry & Laurie'. There's no 'Little'. It's not 'A Little Bit of Fry & Laurie.' It's just 'A Bit of Fry & Laurie'.
ALAN: Oh.

STEPHEN: I know it seems trivial, but we've come this far, we may as well get it right.
ALAN: It says 'Little' here.
STEPHEN: Well that's a mistake. It should just be 'A Bit of Fry & Laurie'.
HUGH: If I introduced you to someone at a party as 'Little Alan Sharp', you'd get a bit annoyed, wouldn't you?
ALAN: Well I suppose...
HUGH: Because it's not your name, is it? Your name is Alan Sharp. There's no 'Little'.
STEPHEN: The same applies here, you see. It's the same principle.
HUGH: 'A Bit of Fry & Laurie.'
ALAN: Alright.
STEPHEN: Off you go...

Each week, Stephen & Hugh would be forced to become more and more threatening to 'Alan', pulling a gun, kidnapping his family, cutting off his legs and pushing the soggy bit up his nose, and so on, while he cruised further for bruises by making mistakes such as introducing the programme as 'A Bit of French & Mortimer'. Ultimately, and despite shows like Alexei Sayle's *Stuff* playing with the format of TV in extreme ways, with such a towering stack of sketches to choose from, this rather complex opener was dropped – there wasn't even much of an opening theme this time, just a bit of guitar twiddling over a short and ridiculous piss-take of Kate Moss's adverts for 'Obsession', by Calvin Klein, breathily invoking 'Pretension, by Fry & Laurie', as the colleagues wandered along the wintry beach in scratchy handheld monochrome accompanied by young Charlie Laurie, making his last appearance in the series and answering his godfather back this time, rather than bursting into tears. Particularly given Hugh's sobbing voiceover, it wasn't the most prepossessing opener to a mainstream BBC comedy show imaginable. But they had planned alternatives:

WE HEAR THE GREENWICH PIPS. A DRUM ROLLS. AN ANNOUNCER'S VOICE INTONES. SPOTLIGHTS PLAY ON THE STAGE.

VOICE: Ladies and Gentlemen: The British Broadcasting Corporation Entertainment Group, in association with the Department of Lightweight Comedy, present, by kind permission of Mr David Liddiment and Mr Jon Plowman, under the terms of the Broadcasting and Rediffusion Act of 1934, revised 1986, in accordance with EC Comedy Directive 95738, for your private use, thirty golden minutes in the company of Mr Stephen Fry and Mr Huuuuuuuuugh Laurie!

APPLAUSE. THE LIGHTS GO UP. THERE IS A SOFA. MR STEPHEN FRY AND MR HUGH LAURIE ARE SLUMPED ON IT. HUGH HAS A KNIFE STICKING IN HIS CHEST AND BLOOD OOZING FROM HIS MOUTH: EYES OPEN AND GLAZED. STEPHEN HAS A BULLET-HOLE IN HIS FOREHEAD. THEY ARE BOTH DEAD. PAUSE. CUT TO STEVE RIDER IN GRANDSTAND STUDIO.

STEVE: Well, we're sorry about that. Seem to be having problems there. We'll return you to live comedy action, just as soon as we can. Meanwhile we can I believe show you a recording of an old Fry & Laurie. I think we've got for you one of their 1974 shows from the series 'Fry & Laurie's Comedy Box'. Once again, apologies and we will return you to the action as soon as possible.

CUT TO VERY OLD-FASHIONED BBC2 LOGO. AN OLD STYLE BBC2 CONTINUITY VOICE ANNOUNCES.

VOICE: A choice of viewing on BBC television, over on BBC1 the news read by Mr Gareth Glitter, on Two...

Stephen & Hugh and Jon & Bob agreed on further changes to the *ABOF&L* recipe, extending the series by one episode, and making a feature of guest performers every week. 'I think the idea of having other guest actors in it probably wasn't our idea,' Laurie says. 'I get the feeling that somebody in the BBC had said, "You know you *can* do this, you are *allowed* to do this? You've got a budget, we can have other people, you don't have to do all the voices!" And we went, "Oh, we've never thought of that, you mean, have other human beings? Well okay, we'll give it a try . . ." It was quite an exercise, writing for other people, because you know, they would make things work that we couldn't imagine working, and they could also fuck things up that we couldn't have imagined them fucking up. But that's the way of it, that's bound to happen.' To welcome the guest performers each week, the fake front parlour was reinstated, this time all beige exposed brickwork with sofas, cocktail bar and grand piano adjacent, or as Hugh had it, 'We've got a sort of Des O'Connor set and two guests a week, but we've deliberately given them very unfunny lines and as little rehearsal time as possible.'

The Fry & Laurie archive contains remnants of correspondence, from those days when few people other than Stephen and Douglas Adams were firing off emails at each other, and Hugh was very much on top of the approach for the fourth series. First, Plowman was presented with the earliest sketches:

> The Fry & Laurie Office (Room 7008),
> The Corridors of Power, BBC TVC,
> Wood Lane, LONDON
> 9th December 1993
>
> Dearest of dear, dear Jons,
> Here are two putative and shy Fry & Laurie scripts for you to look at and (ultimately, perhaps, if things work out) to read. They should be self-explanatory. As you will see, we have imagined a male and a female guest (different each week) whom we have named John and Jane. Confusingly, Jane refers to the male guest and John to the female . . . If you hate anything then do please shout out loud. It will make no difference, but you may feel better.

Meanwhile may beauty bound you and serenity twist your nipples,

The Desk of Pain,
A Small Room, LONDON
A Bit of Fry & Laurie
'Where comedy comes first . . . naturally'
Rome • Paris • Amsterdam • London • Welwyn Garden City
Est. 1981 • Directors: Stephen Fry & Hugh Laurie
• Registered Vaduz Lichtenstein • A Member of Findus
• F&L 'serving the community with a smile'

At roughly the same time they contacted the set designers: 'Thanks very much for your faxes. It looks great – more substantial than we'd imagined, but definitely a place to be relaxed and funny in. If they can find the right people . . . Only two thoughtlets were that the screens for projections etc. shouldn't stray too much into hip Jonathan Ross skylines, i.e. that the whole place doesn't look too penthouse cool . . . That's to say, it can look cool, as long as it doesn't look as if, by being in it, we think that we're cool. Because we aren't, let's face it. Then again, we must avoid looking as if we're doing a direct chat show pastiche. Damn tricky, but there it is.'

Each series left hangover sketches that never made it into the programmes or books, and by this stage the backlog was heaving with a hideous embarrassment of riches. An ambitious movie spoof that never reached the budgeting stage was a mash-up of period drama and *The Terminator* which would have required extensive make-up for Stephen to play Schwarzenegger against Hugh's Van Damme, in an explosive adaptation of *The Important of Being Earnest.* That remains a sight we shall never behold, but the basic idea was so blatant it surfaced later that year in the first series of *Harry Enfield and Chums*, with Martin Clunes playing a Merchant-Ivory T-800. Then there was gadget-crazy Stephen's thrillingly prescient feature on videophones, in which the latest technology meant that a call to Nigel Havers could not disguise his hastily hidden rent boy. Another extensive abandoned sequence was entitled 'The Two of Us Again', a sickened demolition of domestic sitcom beginning with the script directions 'We are in sitcom land. A horrible place to be . . .' Stephen & Hugh were to play actors 'Tom Acton-Badleigh & Robert Overhill', regurgitating a script by 'Richard Cosy & Andrew Formula' which was just a series of obvious painful sitcom tropes – a desperate farce in which the two starring couples have swapped partners, but live identical lives. As each predictable scene and treacly exchange becomes more cloying and inane, the swell of off-screen retching grows in intensity, until a news reporter steps in to describe the hideous dangers of being exposed to such sugary tweeness that you puke up your kidneys. It was not as concise an attack on cosy sitcoms as Vyvyan's *Good Life* tirade in *The Young Ones* a decade earlier – but although such a swipe may have had more clout going out on BBC1 than anywhere else, the script feels like the two colleagues exorcising a few demons and taking an idea for a walk, and with enough material kicking around for maybe a dozen half-hours of sketch antics, this complex item was dropped – with guests to introduce and cocktails to be shaken, there was less time for a huge variety of sketches anyway, although vomiting with disgust was to remain a feature of the series.

Gelliant Gutfright's final tale of terror 'Flowers For Wendy' was one of a diminishing number of recognisable regulars for this series. Besides just a smattering (or 'snatch') of Strom in one episode's introduction, a triple helping of Dalliard was offered up for consideration, but only the model shop sketch was aired – with typically obtuse sales disasters in which Hugh tried to buy cigars or a piano sadly failing to make it into the nation's front rooms. Once all was arranged, the very last *ABOF&L* sketch broadcast would arguably be a callback to one of the very first – the father urging his lazy spotty son to get off the games console, and 'bugger up the arse of Level 9 with an anglepoise lamp' has Hugh as an obstreperous youth called Terry, just as in 'Prize Poem' seven years earlier.

With all preliminary concerns taken care of, early 1994 saw the final location shoots for *ABOF&L*, a last cache of demented Vox Pops to get in the can, and looser segments allowed these quickie characters to interact at last, Hugh's *Daily Mail* Lady memorably ruining a Vox Pop from Fry's 'Ivy'. A school provided a handy swimming pool, classrooms for a sketch on pantheistic religion, and a football item dangerous for Hugh – 'The football coach, coaching children on how to con a penalty out of the referee and how to fall over, I remember one of those falls, I actually thought I'd broken my neck. I hit the ground, and there's a moment when I go "Oh, that's it, I'm never going to walk again."' Finally, a beautiful day at Knebworth shooting a mockumentary on the lives of the Duke & Duchess of Northamptonshire felt like *J&W* all over again. None of the guest stars were present for these location shoots, but a few last-minute external scenes were filmed close to TV Centre on recording days.

The chosen pairs of guest performers were largely actors Stephen & Hugh had worked with before, with a few exceptions. The first brace of bookings did have the actual names Fry & Laurie had assigned to the theoretical guests while writing the sketches, but although Jane Booker was an experienced comic actor, playing a memorable yuppie nightmare in under-valued Mel Smith sitcom *Colin's Sandwich*, her CV had little overlap with either colleague. The same was true of her companion, satirical pioneer and Footlighter John Bird, but this was to change dramatically in the coming years, thanks to a 1989 novel by Mark Tavener, *In the Red*. The sketchy roles of two bitchy BBC Radio controllers in this comic murder mystery were given to Fry and Bird for the Radio 4 adaptation in 1995, and the pairing of the former's mercurial Charles Prentiss and latter's louche Martin McCabe became a lynchpin for three sequels which followed on radio, 1998's *In the Chair* adding Laurie as obvious Tony Blair cipher, guitar-twanging megalomaniac PM Kenny Ball (who sadly never interacts with Prentiss). That same year, Stephen and John reprised their roles for a TV adaptation of the original novel, and when Tavener felt he had completed the story of shabby hero, BBC reporter George Cragge, he built a new sitcom around Prentiss & McCabe, masters of their own PR empire and masterminds of a series of shadowy backdoor 'wheezes' for the New Labour government, and others. *Absolute Power* ran for four radio series with a live audience and two TV series without, and only halted in 2005, Tavener's untimely death in 2007 ruling out any return. Regrettably, the explosive arrival of Malcolm Tucker in *The Thick of It* around this time rather overshadowed Fry's depiction of a despicably brilliant spin wizard.

Of the second couple to join the hosts, Kevin McNally had acted with many Alternative comedy stars in his long career, but never

Stephen nor Hugh, while Fiona Gillies – although known at the time for playing Robert Bathurst's ex in Steven Moffat sitcom *Joking Apart* – had originated the role of Lady Florence Craye, that intellectual scourge of Bertie, in *J&W*. Only in the third episode did two old colleagues of the colleagues join the fray, with Clive Mantle (made famous by *Casualty* since joining Hugh in *The Party Party*) paired up with 'Snutty' – a completely made-up nickname for Hugh's great emoting coach in *Peter's Friends*, Imelda Staunton. Two comedy luminaries followed next – National Theatre of Brent mastermind Patrick Barlow and Caroline Quentin, a freshly minted star due to *Men Behaving Badly* who had only recently appeared with Hugh in *All or Nothing at All*. Similarly, Stephen Moore had claim to comedy greatness as the original Marvin the depressed robot in *Hitchhiker's Guide*, while his partner Phyllida Law was of course as good as part of the Fry & Laurie family. Finally, Janine Duvitski, whose reputation as a fine and distinct funny performer predated even her role in *Abigail's Party*, took the last female guest spot. She had worked with Stephen as David Lander, but her companion had appeared with the hosts more than most – Robert Daws proved perhaps the most natural conduit for the *ABOF&L* brand of silliness, being clearly in his element ('I can remember my mother used to drive me absolutely to school every morning in an old Wolseley – you know, the kind with wheels?'), and he even got to show off his jazz trumpeting skills. As an odd aside, both Moore and Daws had played Tuppy Glossop in the past.

With one extra episode making a feature of the lack of guests, these seven half-hours packed in as much material as they could, numerous items clearly switching Fry or Laurie roles to accommodate the talented guests: Imelda making tea (from seed), Kevin extolling the hot new craze of Fascism, and so on. While the format was malleable, in general Fry & Laurie would introduce their 'hospitality customers' onto the sofa in either egregiously flattering or blisteringly unnecessary ways, indulge in a bit of 'verbal frotting', then send them plunging into the audience to hand round plates of condoms and twiglets as the show delved into the 'valley of sketches'. On the other side, they would be present in their finery to select that evening's cocktail, be it the 'Long Confident Suck' or perhaps the 'Swinging Ballsack', which Fry prepared in his usual dancercising way (only occasionally smashing glasses) before sharing the drinks on a silver salver for the concluding cries of 'Soupy twist!'

There was some kind of arc to the studio sections this time: the concept of The Comedy Charter. For a decade or more, Fry & Laurie had been mining the repellent world of commerce for material, sniping at the yuppies and corporate executives, but by the 1990s there was a feeling that their targets had won, and were ruling the country and the BBC, in the anaemic exemplar forms of Johns Major and Birt. And so, sober suited on the sofa, Stephen & Hugh joined them, pledging the 'viewing several' guarantees of amusing sketches, and of course, 'the ruthless subversion of family values'.

Two sketches have often been held up as the standouts for series four: firstly the double entendres zenith of 'Barman', with Stephen offering a tipsy Hugh increasingly unlikely goods for filthy effect. 'Quite proud of it now,' Fry has commented. 'I think we thought it was a satire on Ronnie Barker-style innuendo, but of course such innuendo is funny.' Then there is the famed moment when the years of one-way theatrical pugilism between the two overstepped the mark, in the punchy punchline of the 'Race Driver' sketch. Sport reporter Stephen's frustration with Hugh's Schumacher-style whinger spilled over into a sock on the jaw that undeniably connected, sending him crashing to the floor, and character-breaking concern for his best friend flashed over Stephen's face before it seemed safe to cut. The next day, Hugh came in early and asked Make-up to give him the most hideous facial bruising, which he kept on, with accompanying groaning, just long enough to turn his partner into a puddle of horrified apology.

Besides the closing theme, Laurie upped the musical content, with a regular song for every show. He self-effacingly took on different personas for each genre, a wet balladeer for love song 'Steffi Graf', a Coward-ish wit for Page 3 satire 'Little Girl' – 'I was very proud of that song! A lot of people found it creepy and didn't like it at all. Including my wife, I think, although it is attacking creepiness.' The masterstroke here was the drafting in of Plowman & Spiers' regular maestro for *French & Saunders*, Simon Brint, to orchestrate Laurie's compositions. His Raw Sex partner and fictional son Rowland Rivron joined in on drums, and a solid band was formed to back Hugh up throughout the tunes. Brint, who died in 2011, was of course an old friend from *Saturday Live* days, and one of the finest TV and comedy composers around – equal to contemporaries Howard Goodall, Philip Pope and Peters Brewis and Baikie – and brought a new level of polish to the *ABOF&L* songbook: effectively producing an entire album of Laurie originals, twenty years before Hugh announced his solo music career. 'He was wonderful,' Hugh says, 'the gentlest, funniest, and without a doubt, most eccentric guy. He had a very peculiar manner, but that manner was so brilliant onstage, with Rowland in Raw Sex. They reminded me a little bit of one of the first shows I ever saw, when I was sixteen – Sparks. They had some of that oddity about them. But he was such a lovely guy, much missed.' This last series was a musical showcase for Hugh, but the blues star now muses: 'With comedy music, you have to find the balance . . . I don't mean to disrespect them in any way, but The Two Ronnies finishing their show with, oh, you think they're going to say "fuck" and then they say "truck" – that kind of thing never had any particular interest for me. It's finding a place where you're able to love the musical side of it, not because it's beautiful music, but because the idiom of it and the character of it is important, you're not just putting on a silly voice to do a country song with silly rhymes. Although when I do listen to Flanders & Swann, I do think "Bloody hell!" *"'Twas on a Monday morning when the gas man came to call . . ."* That's an absolutely brilliant song. But you've got to have a particular persona to be able to make witty rhymes work, because otherwise witty rhymes can become annoying if they're too pleased with themselves. And once you start having too many internal rhymes, I think the whole thing goes up its own arse. One of my favourites was the one Stephen did, "You You You" – I don't know where that came from, he only did that once, never before or since, but it was absolutely inspired – Phil Pope did the arrangement for that. When Stephen throws himself into a thing, it's quite a sight!'

When not on screen, Hugh was also to be found playing keyboard for Poor White Trash & The Little Big Horns, a comedy combo led by Lenny Henry, with Ben Elton's wife Sophie on sax and Ade Edmondson on guitar – for many years, available for weddings and parties thrown by the more discerning celebrities. In 1993, he even joined Clive Anderson and Peter Cook as posh backing singers on that year's Comic Relief single from Right Said Fred, 'Stick It Out' – admittedly a rum way to have a hit single. 'I do remember being there with Right Said Fred,' Hugh just about recalls, 'because they had another single, "Deeply Dippy", which was based on one of my lines from *Jeeves & Wooster,* it had just stuck in their heads.' Hugh also featured in the song's video, but this was not a first – he had already popped up in pop promos for two of music's greatest female icons, Kate Bush and Annie Lennox. Fry would also collaborate with Bush (lending his tones to 2011 track '50 Words For Snow'), but otherwise his dabbling with pop plateaued in the form of a Gelliant Gutfright-ish cameo on 1995 EMF track 'Glass Smash Jack'. Despite having a comic songbook second to few, Hugh's explosive music career has never delved back into his funny past – although he did perform a blistering full-band reprise of 'America' on a rare 2003 appearance on Radio 2 comedy music show *Jammin'* – presented by the aforementioned drumming legend Rowland Rivron.

Grey and Hopeless

Series four was all on tape by the end of April 1994, and our colleagues took their leave and headed in different cinematic directions – Hugh to the Czech Republic for communist drama *A Pin for the Butterfly*, and Stephen to Hollywood to play the bumbling Brit in period rom-com *I.Q.* with Meg Ryan, Tim Robbins and, as Einstein, Walter Matthau. 'I'm the unromantic lead,' he assured the *Radio Times* on the film's release. 'I think my voice can go in the romantic direction, but my features and body are not subjects that would inspire people to believe in me as a romantic hero. And that's fine. As Harry Callaghan says in the film *Magnum Force*, "A man's got to know his limitations".' Fry hadn't been having much luck as a screenwriter, with two unproduced screenplays to his name: an adaptation of *A Confederacy of Dunces,* and something called *Long Island Iced Tea* 'about a divorced couple who meet again at someone else's wedding, Long Island, Hamptons kind of a deal – it was deliberately designed to be a throwback to the Nick & Nora *Thin Man* films, with a nod to the style and pace of the Howard Hawks screwball comedies, which I and producer Scott Rudin, love.' But as an actor, BBC Films knew his value, and he landed the part of pompous pest Mr

Mybug in a new feature based on *Cold Comfort Farm*, which aired on New Year's Day. 'One feels guilty about participating in this myth of the emotionally constipated and cold-fish Englishmen but I suppose those are the parts I often get to play in England, let alone anywhere else. The Americans especially seem to think all British actors carry around the complete works of Shakespeare in their heads.'

Hugh had a smaller but lighter role in Emma Thompson's *Sense and Sensibility*, wed once again to 'Snutty' Staunton as the scene-stealing Palmers, but although there may not have been a role for Stephen to rejoin his old friends in the cast, the film owed its very existence to him in a way. One day, while he and Hugh were puzzling over a chunk of series four, Emma came to Stephen's door in tatters, explaining that her screenplay had apparently been entirely wiped from her Mac. It took Fry several hours to retrieve the data and piece the script back together, before printing off a copy for Laurie, who was at first intended for Alan Rickman's role of Colonel Brandon. Stephen noted in his diary, 'It could make Hugh a star, which he thoroughly deserves, but yours truly is going to be a bit of stay-at-home naffness, while Hugh jets off to Hollywood as Mr Big. I have always known that this will happen, but what will come hard will be everyone's sympathy for me.' Hugh still had a few years to wait on that score, but Emma Talent was to scoop her second Oscar for Best Adapted Screenplay. 'I spent years trying to prove myself, particularly to Stephen & Hugh, wanting to write and wanting to be a comedian,' she says. 'One of the great pleasures of having finished *Sense and Sensibility* was they liked it so much. I suddenly realised I'd wanted that for a long time – their approval.' As an added bonus, Poor White Trash had their wildest ever gig at the premiere party.

While Rebecca Laurie was beginning to crawl, Stephen took delivery of his own third child – *The Hippopotamus* being published in the spring. It was the largely epistolary story of scabrous poet Ted Wallace uncovering a scandalous mystery in a grand country house, sifting between notions of belief and rationality, on the reluctant hunt for a miracle. The combating of superstition and general weak-mindedness was of course crucial to both Stephen and Hugh – they made a rare non-promotional joint TV appearance on James Randi's TV show in 1991, pooh-poohing an astrologer's reading for Hugh, plus a sketch cut from their last series would have had Stephen as an obvious mockery of TV 'astrologist' Russell Grant, warning viewers that their stars said they would be faced with 'a fat little irritating git' who would make them want to throw a brick at the television.

The Hippopotamus has often been cited as Fry's most successful novel – it was certainly a hit commercially, and became the subject of an episode of Radio 4's *Bookclub* in 2005 before finally getting the movie treatment in 2017 with the perfectly dour Roger Allam in the title role, directed by John Jencks. 'I deliberately stayed out of it,' the author says, 'because a novel uses a different limb, and I was very happy for them to do something with *The Hippopotamus*. But I visited the set, and I thought Roger Allam was fantastic, beyond my wildest dreams, and Tim McInnerny was unbelievably good. It was charmingly done, and obviously when you write a novel, a film can only capture part of it, but I was pleasantly surprised.' Before Allam's snug casting, the beguilingly bitter anti-hero had called to mind late-season Peter Cook, a grizzled, vice-embracing and reluctant investigator who must qualify for one of the most successfully realised characters Fry has ever created. And what was most extraordinary, from the writer and performer who still loudly proclaimed his intense disgust at the newsprint media, was that this protagonist was a *theatre critic*, albeit fired on the first page. Ted's tale was still crammed with autobiographical themes, being largely set in Norfolk, with Martin Neumann's background inspiring the heart of the book, while the denouement – revealing the true nature of the brothers David and Simon – closely reflected the author's view of his brother Roger: honest and real where he was egotistical and deluded. Nonetheless, the further stride from *The Liar*'s glaring self-reference made for a more satisfying narrative, and *The Hippopotamus* was quickly and hotly feted, with cardboard cut-outs of Fry crouching in a bathtub filling bookshops everywhere.

The year otherwise passed with the usual chockablock-Filofax engagements, and not all commercial voiceovers – though around this time the joint espousal of Alliance & Leicester came to an end. Stephen had opted to return to the West End, accepting one of the lead roles in

Simon Gray's new play *Cell Mates* – a long-gestated project examining the relationship between double agent George Blake and Irish lag Sean Bourke, who sprang Blake from prison in 1966. Fry has admitted that the chain-smoking Gray was another crucial model for Ted Wallace, and once the playwright and director had complimented Stephen on the new novel (without any suspicion of its protagonist's inspiration) and tempted him into taking the central role, Stephen in turn easily persuaded Rik Mayall to join the *Common Pursuit* reunion as Bourke, and preliminary meetings and rehearsals at the Old Vic were shaping up well for opening at the start of the new year. Gray remembered the early development of the play as a hilarious blossoming of affection between the three, but noted the vast difference in Rik and Stephen's approaches to performing – the former a sensitive soul far removed from his swaggering comic persona, onstage a neurotic craftsman concerned about getting every tic just right. The latter actor, however, was word perfect in no time, knew his every mark blindfold, and barely seemed to break a sweat, making it look all too easy onstage and off. This suited the characters, perhaps, but signalled an unevenness in the performances, and the writer/director was appalled at the ease with which young Fry hopped in and out of character to improvise when technical hitches cropped up, while Mayall remained desperately rooted in Bourke, grasping for imaginative support from his co-performer. Nonetheless, Gray observed, Rik passionately adored 'His Stevey', and they played together comedically with a reportedly infantile abandon.

Simon was to gnash his teeth even more vociferously when Stephen had to pause rehearsals of *Cell Mates* for a crucial project airing on BBC2 two days after Christmas, which was, accidentally, to sound the knell for the comedy partnership of Stephen Fry & Hugh Laurie. Michael Jackson, the young Controller of BBC2, knew that Fry & Laurie were due to abscond to BBC1, but when they were suggested as the hosts of the planned reboot of classic festive TV tradition *Christmas Night with the Stars*, it seemed no duo could be more perfect – the broadcast was even officially given the prefix *Fry & Laurie Host* . . .

Resplendent in dinner-jacketed 'soupy twist' mode, the pair were largely called upon to present a dozen or so links between pre-recorded items, in the spirit of the original variety shows which ran from 1958 to 1972 – and although producer Claudia Lloyd was quite fresh from her debut, *The Real McCoy* (whose stars peppered the show), Geoff Posner was a very safe pair of hands as director. Like the veritable spirits of Light Entertainment, Stephen & Hugh eschewed the despairing tone of their last series by going overboard with the Christmas charity, bitterly ticking off the modern developments since *CNWTS* was axed, but then making amends:

STEPHEN: ... North against south, rich against poor, man against woman, straight against slightly curved, we came to define ourselves as a nation not so much b'what we loved, but b'what we hated.

HUGH: And we're not going to take it any more, because you know what I hate, m'colleague?

STEPHEN: What's that, m'colleague?

HUGH: I hate hate.

STEPHEN: Poetic... Let's use this opportunity to start an age of loving. For the next seventy minutes or so, why not just try, try to love each other. We can't, as a nation, all hold hand... but what we're asking you to do tonight is hold the television...

HUGH: And we'll put our hands on the camera like so...

STEPHEN: And I want our minds now to turn to all those we thought we hated, and to imagine now that we love them. Would you like to begin, m'colleague?

HUGH: I love you, Virginia Bottomley...

STEPHEN: Jeff! Jeffrey Archer! Love your arse...[16]

During the evening they introduced seasonal items from Govan and Norfolk icons Rab C. Nesbitt and Alan Partridge, Alexei Sayle (the closest Fry and Sayle ever came comedically), Felix Dexter, Reeves & Mortimer, and sketches from the *Fast Show* cast including, of course, ex-plasterers Paul Whitehouse & Charlie Higson, lavishly introduced by Laurie: 'M'colleague and I have watched as these young fellow-me-snappers cut their teeth on the edge of the bath, we've sent them a £5 record token every birthday and Christmas, we've darned their socks, we've wiped their runny bottoms. It's a great privilege now to watch their coming of age. So without wishing to condescend or patronise in any way at all, will you please give a big loving welcome . . .' Veterans Ronnie Corbett and Sandie Shaw also bolstered the line-up, but in general, and despite being no older than most of the performers involved (Fry impersonator Steve Coogan aside), Stephen & Hugh were there to play the senior boys of British Comedy. They were both some years away from forty, and not much more than a decade into their partnership, but Fry & Laurie signified the Establishment.

However, the curse of Fry & Laurie, as ever, was just how convincing their smart, presentable outward appearances were – and how their incorrigible taste for the distasteful could unseat hidebound viewers who 'expected better' from such well-spoken chaps. Apparently, accompanying Shaw's soulful rendition of 'Little Drummer Boy' by shaking cereal packets in rhythm was seen as somehow disrespectful, as was Fry smashing a champagne bottle over his colleague's head at the conclusion of his rendition of 'Show Me the Way to Go Home', and Laurie calling their attempts to bring joy to the nation 'so much cock'. Before New Year rolled around, letters began to thud into the *Radio Times* office protesting at what this pair had done to a veritable old Christmas tradition. Valerie Robey of Essex huffed: 'I regret that the BBC should spoil its reputation by showing such lavatorial rubbish, and if Fry & Laurie found this programme funny, I am very sorry for them. We have always enjoyed Fry & Laurie, so sat down to enjoy the programme, thinking it would be one of the few things which could be considered "family entertainment". Instead we had to watch and listen to utter filth and sexual innuendo. How sad that two sophisticated humourists have sunk to such a low level.' The great temptation to echo the views of the producer in *ABOF&L* who reassured his critic, 'perhaps it would help if I explained that I couldn't give a flying toss' must have been almost painful, but Laurie braved the Basildon Bond to respond for the magazine: 'As a parent, I quite understand people feeling excluded from something because they think it's trying to offend them. I don't think either of us would set out to do that.' Over twenty years on, Hugh says of the special, 'I don't remember it being anything but an awkward mess', but the two evenings at TV Centre which went into the making of *CNWTS* turned out to be the last times Stephen & Hugh appeared in front of a live BBC audience, and this feedback wasn't the warm reaction anyone would have hoped for – there was no attempt to reboot that festive tradition until a decade or so later, this time with Michael Parkinson safely in charge.

And still, the seven half-hours of *ABOF&L* Stephen & Hugh had recorded at the start of 1994 had not been broadcast, in contrast to the quite rapid turnaround of the previous series. 'That's just how it was,' Plowman insists, 'sometimes scheduling pans out like that, although it's deeply annoying. It's because of other programmes – what else was in that slot, how it matches up, etc. There's nothing sinister there, it's not that somebody watched the show and thought, "Bloody hell, we're not letting that out!" It's the machinations of scheduling. Stephen & Hugh may have rung Alan Yentob, or asked me to – I don't remember wild fury, but I'm sure they were a touch annoyed.' Hugh, however, counters, 'I don't remember any impatience – "We've got to get this out and get onto the next thing!" We were never that canny about the mechanics, which channel et cetera, in the same way that when you write a novel you don't really care whether it's Penguin or whomever. In our naive way, we thought, "What's the difference? It's all just television." I think we both assumed it would sort itself out, and if we did it right, it would be okay. We could have done with some calm words of advice, but I never felt we had much in the way of pastoral care, you know, people strategising how you play this field – perhaps we were cocky and felt we didn't need it. I feel like we were both just falling downstairs together for ten years – just two blokes with no idea of where we were going to land. We had comic heroes we wanted to emulate, but we didn't have any careers planned – "We'll do this, then you'll host the Royal Variety Show for ten years, and I'll go and be Richard Stilgoe for ten years . . ." We were just so random, going where the wind took us. Looking back on it, if it looks designed at all, it probably looks poorly designed.'

Besides, anyone suffering from *ABOF&L* withdrawal symptoms had some respite in 1994, when the show made its audio debut, repackaged into two 'best of' shows for Radio 4. The same compilations were released on BBC Audio in their 'Laughing Stock' range, but the cassette lacked the colleagues' special introductions:

HUGH: Good evening, oblique stroke morning, oblique stroke luck, whichever is the sooner. Welcome to *ABOF&L*, the increasingly unpopular television series that has gripped the nation like a wisp of grey cotton trouser fluff... As for the title, well we think it speaks for itself, if not for a generation... m'colleague was unhappy about the suggestion of 'A Bit of Fry & a Phenomenal Amount of Laurie', neither of us being entirely confident about the spelling of 'phenomenal'. Still, there you are. If you have ears, prepare to shed them now...

STEPHEN: Hello. What you're about to listen to is the second part of an audio collection culled from the television series *ABOF&L*. Last week, as has been widely reported, m'colleague Hugh Laurie introduced the first part. If you didn't listen to that first part, you must now switch off your wireless. It is actually illegal under the terms of the new charter agreement negotiated by the Birt-ish Broadcasting Corporation to listen to a series a) in the wrong order, c) incompletely, or 2) in fragments... Now, those who were lucky enough to tune in last week will know that Marie's punishment for shoplifting was a month's community service, and a forced appearance as a witness on *The Moral Maze*...[17]

A similar video compilation was assembled bristling with the pair's chosen favourites, from 'Sound Name' to 'Get Well Card', necessitating a special BBC advert with the duo in full commercial mode, selling not just themselves but their comedy competitors:

```
STEPHEN IS IN A WHITE LAB COAT, HUGH HOLDING BBC
VIDEO TAPES.
STEPHEN:   Susan. How satisfied are you with the
           comic power of your leading non-bio?
HUGH:      Well, my husband's a cabinet minister, so
           obviously, stains are a problem.
STEPHEN:   Susan, I'm going to surprise you now
           — BEHHH! — supposing we took away your
           original madcap formula...
HUGH:      Oh no, please don't do that! (HANDS OVER
           RUSS ABBOT)
STEPHEN:   And your concentrated rib-tickling
           formula...
HUGH:      Not that as well! (HANDS OVER SMITH &
           JONES)
STEPHEN:   But offered you instead our new
           double action formula? (PRODUCES FRY &
           LAURIE TAPE)
HUGH:      Double action? But will it be tough on
           stains even without boil-washing?
STEPHEN:   Nnno, it's a video — you put it in a
           cassette machine and watch it.
HUGH:      Oh. Any stale odours?
STEPHEN:   Some.
HUGH:      But how can I believe you right through
           the cycle?
STEPHEN:   Because eight out of ten cats who
           expressed a preference said they would
           band together in small groups and whisper
           about you if you didn't buy it.
HUGH:      (SUDDENLY SURROUNDED BY CATS) Fair enough.[18]
```

Eventually the all-new series debuted on BBC1 on Sunday 12 February 1995, at 10 p.m. – a total departure for *ABOF&L*, but what a promotion for the colleagues, to be let into millions of the nation's homes on the cosiest night in the schedules! However, as with the confounded reactions to *CNWTS*, this was not the jolly slice of Light Entertainment many viewers expected. It's easy to overdramatise, and Plowman is right to warn, 'Don't read too much into the darkness of the material, they were bright, but they were comics, and they wanted to make an audience laugh as well as think.' But the fact remains that from the very first item, in which Stephen & Hugh rattled off a long list of reasons everything was 'grey and hopeless', through the maudlin, sob-soundtracked titles, counting up all the sketches steeped in impotent rage, depression and vomitous despair, right up to the grand finale, in which Stephen hysterically bewailed the state of 'Modern Britain', mixing a poisonous cocktail while Daws played the Last Post and Duvitski lowered the Union Flag, the final series is sodden with a unique kind of comedic despair: 'Another packed half-hour of misery and abject desperation, a catalogue of cynicism and emptiness, and a whole ottoman full of vapid excuses.'

ABOF&L of course always concerned itself to some extent with the state of the nation, and in a way the final finale echoed Fry's oration which closed series two, predicting a Britain stained with 'family fun and amenity', and urine, and vomit. But the concentration of sheer misanthropy and hopelessness was so high it couldn't be ignored. Even a memorably silly sketch like 'Pet Shop' confronts Stephen's revoltingly twee animal lover with Hugh's flat announcement that he's having his cat destroyed, due to 'cancy-wancy'. 'I don't remember being conscious of that tone as we did it,' Hugh says, astonished: 'but as a strange comparison, I do remember some very dark days working on *House*, when I became quite severely depressed – not to the degree of self-harm, but it was not far from my thoughts. And David Shore pointed out the obvious thing, that had never occurred to me, that to play a self-destructive, self-loathing addictive man in immense physical and psychic pain for fifteen hours a day, it would be pretty remarkable if that didn't take a toll. I suppose I thought I was impervious, and what was getting me down was the mechanics of doing it, not the tone. But maybe unconsciously there was some sort of existential anxiety going on.' 'Maybe part of it was, if we knew we were going to BBC1, we deliberately wanted not to go down the path of being all showbizzy and bright', Fry offers. 'I mean, we *were* showbizzy, but in vast "Fry & Laurie" inverted commas.'

Perhaps most disconcerting of all, with over two decades' reflection, in the second episode, there was a special Vox Pop package on the subject of 'Depression', in which Stephen's red-faced Tory delivered a Vox Pop that originated as a quickie for Hugh:

HUGH: Do you ever wonder, what's the point? Do you ever think to yourself, there are but a few brief spasms of experience between now and the grave? Do you ever think to yourself, I'm going to cheat death, by killing myself? Resign before I'm sacked? Well, it's not easy. I sat in a car with a hosepipe attached to the exhaust coming in through the window, sat there for two and a half hours, and got a slight headache. Couldn't believe it. The bloody car had a catalytic converter. Pointless.

This nihilistic gag went out on Sunday evening, 19 February. By sheer dumbfounding coincidence, that very night, Stephen was sitting in his own car, a shattered man, attempting the exact same thing for real. Only the thought of what his success would do to Alan and Marianne Fry, twenty years on from his adolescent attempts at self-destruction, blessedly stayed his hand upon the ignition key.

The story of how Stephen 'found himself' in that position seems all too well known by now, and his subsequent identification as a sufferer of cyclothymia, and his campaigning for increased understanding of mental health issues, do leach much of the drama from the events of February 1995. But at the time, the lack of any suspicion, certainly no diagnosis, of bipolarity in his mental make-up prevented the clear signs of building pressure, of a manic phase headed over the cliff into a calamitous depression, from being picked up by even those closest to him. His days had always been packed with a punishing level of activity, but this was not straightforward workaholism, and after fourteen years of incessant eagerness to please, something had to give.

The year had hardly got off to an auspicious start with the thundering tragedy of Peter Cook's death, on 9 January. Peter and Stephen had been particularly close, buddying up on holidays including a famous jolly up the Nile arranged by Cleese in 1992, where Cook with some irony ventured to suggest the founding of a comedian's support group called 'Melancholics Anonymous', to which Fry responded, 'I really didn't know what he was talking about! It is very common, there's no question, a lot of people who are in the business of amusement do seem to get very low all the time; I don't . . .' All media paid tribute to Cook, one of comedy's all-time heroes, and yet there was a pervading air of disapproval, that Peter had wasted his talents by boozing around Hampstead rather than becoming a Hollywood idol like Dudley, and on the evening following his passing, Fry visited the *Late Show* studios to fight back:

> Tributes have been flooding in these past thirty-six hours, for Peter Cook. Tributes that rightly talk of the unimaginable influence of this extraordinary man on the development of British cultural life. I loved him. For the first part of my life I loved him as I listened to record after record of his voice and wriggled with bliss at his comic genius, and for the second part of my life I loved him as a friend, too. Not having him about is dreadful. Being British in this part of the century meant living in the country that had Peter Cook in it . . . he had Funniness, in the same way that beautiful people have Beauty . . . He was not an ambitious man, not concerned with being a star . . . I suppose if one thing upset him more than anything else, it was the idea that people somewhere might in some way feel sorry for him. Why should they? . . . I watched in distress the silly remarks last night on the news: 'flawed genius', 'undeveloped potential'. What silly, ignorant nonsense! Flawed? I'd be very happy to hear of

a list of unflawed human beings. Unrealised potential? What does that mean? That his potential would have been realised by appearing in more Hollywood films or having a regular prime-time TV show? Why commentators have to write and talk about extraordinary people as if they are composing school reports is beyond me . . . Whatever you may have heard to the contrary, Peter was a man absolutely untainted by bitterness, or remorse. He didn't want . . . a knighthood, nor a pool in Beverly Hills, complete with a string of therapists and pseudo-religions. His achievements in worldly terms are well-known . . . Life was good to him, and he was good to life . . . he never lost a scintilla of his wit, or fun, or kindness. The only regret to be uttered is on behalf of a Britain that now has no Peter Cook in it. So let's hear no more sententious hogwash about 'disappointment', 'frustration' or 'regret'; such talk may deepen or lengthen the obituaries, but it's a lie.

'It made me shudder with rage,' he adds, 'this kind of "Yes, could have done better, slight disappointment, didn't live up to . . ." I thought, "You fuckers, you didn't know him, what's it to you? How dare you behave like a sort of common room prep school creep talking about someone like that?"' It could be suggested that Stephen's own work rate was a way of heading off similar accusations, and the morning after this impassioned address, he was back in the rehearsal room, prepping for *Cell Mates* previews in Richmond on 30 January, which would be followed by a spell in Guildford, and finally, the West End opening on 17 February. Stephen could still send Simon into apoplectic fits with his offhand improvisations, but a night or two facing an understudy (Rik had burst an eardrum blowing his nose) seemed to compel him to fully engage with the central relationship, just in time for the previews. This was an odd time for Fry to agree to a newspaper interview in which he lambasted the press and swore never to glance at the papers again, but when Gray mentioned the lacerations he was receiving in the usual rags as a result, Stephen hooted with delighted derision, 'I *knew* they'd do that!'

This was the situation as the final series of *ABOF&L* finally reached UK TV screens on Sunday nights, with Stephen & Hugh briefly uniting to face the press as a final push for the replanted programme, where they confirmed that series five had been commissioned, and mused further on the problem of comedic offence. To *Deadpan* magazine, Hugh ventured, 'I'd love to believe, just as a pure theory, that there aren't any taboos, but I actually don't think it's true . . . I think you can or should be able to take any subject seriously AND comically but actually, when it comes down to it, you have to be aware that people do get upset by what they see on television.' 'The fact is,' his colleague concluded, 'there is absolutely nothing you can do to protect people's upset on any particular day. You can have the most bland sitcom in which someone says, "Oh God, you nearly gave me a heart attack," and if someone's father happened to have died that day from a heart attack, then that remark wouldn't be funny to them. But no one, not even the most widely fanatical censor could suggest that a line like that was bad taste even though to certain people, in certain situations, it will be about as funny as a car crash. So, in a sense, there's nothing you can do that isn't offensive.' The assembled critics were kind about the series four opener, and despite the downbeat intro, Plowman says, the audience reaction was no problem: 'You always expect to have a bit of a bumpy ride when you transfer channels, because it's a different audience, but I don't remember any bad feedback, and I think I would. We certainly weren't knocked back.'

With only one episode aired, the press night at the Albery Theatre arrived, and Gray's play debuted to the first London audience that mattered, gloomy monochrome posters of Stephen and Rik separated by iron bars towering over the exterior of the theatre. Plowman continues, 'I was present at that performance, and went round afterwards, and they weren't in too bad a state. Nobody was more surprised than me to hear that Stephen had gone to Belgium – it was unclear whether that was a euphemism.'

Indeed, the opening night had been nothing short of a triumph for pretty much everyone present. A few months later, Simon Gray would bring out his record of events, *Fat Chance*, probably his most highly regarded publication and perhaps the one consolation he was to scrape out of the whole debacle. The book earned a reputation as an extended poison pen letter, but despite lashings of Gray's trademark invective, it actually seems a relatively even-handed story of heartbreak, all these years later, with Stephen the only living member of the theatrical tragedy's central trio. Simon recorded the bonhomie of the first night party, Stephen's parents telling him, 'They'd never cared as much for anything Stephen had done before, but now, here he was, showing the world he was a real actor.' Gray glanced across the room at Fry and Mayall: 'They were obviously into one of their double acts, spiralling together down – or is it up? – into the nursery . . . On the one hand this volatile, emotional and nakedly expressive man, and on the other, a man slightly cloaked, in a constant public personality – no, no, it's a *semi-public* personality, that sense he gives of sharing with great generosity half of himself, without giving you the slightest idea of what the other half is . . .' The warm reception of the play that night was borne out across the reviews when they appeared, with appreciative coverage in nearly all the papers that mattered, providing the playwright with his pick of quotes to proudly display on the theatre hoarding, and the prospect of a respectable run of lucrative bums on seats.

On Sunday, the first inkling of there being any cause for concern occurred to Gray when a routine ring of Stephen's number reached the answerphone message – *'I'm sorry. I'm so very sorry . . .'* It was a day off for most of the *Cell Mates* company, and Simon put this disconcerting apparent joke out of his mind. Stephen of course gave himself no day off, and despite feeling the effects of a late night after a party thrown by Griff Rhys Jones, he honoured his own inevitable booking for the day, narrating a lunchtime charity performance of *Peter and the Wolf*, before returning to his home, and to his car, and his lowest ebb, having arranged the delivery of letters to all who would be most directly affected by his disappearance – his family, Simon, Rik and of course, Hugh. Less than fifteen years into his 'accidental' career, Stephen was a national star with international promise, a BBC1 personality and a highly respected artist in pretty much every field into which he stepped a size-thirteen foot. But in the eye of the storm of depression, all of that was, in Hugh's words, 'so much cock'.

'We are distressed. But we have an unshakeable faith in Stephen, and his relish for being alive' was how the media reported Alan Fry in the coming days, and we can all be grateful that this simple faith proved to be well-founded. Stephen decided that if he could not leave the planet, he nonetheless still desperately needed to escape, and so he headed for the continent, almost blind with acute, alienating distress. It wasn't until Monday, when Gray received his letter and sat down with compadre Harold Pinter to decode its meaning that the phrase Stephen had used while apologising profusely for what he saw as his total failure as an actor – 'the lumpen, superior "act" which I inflict on a bored audience every time I open my mouth' – revealed to them that he had somehow allowed a stinker in the *Financial Times* – one of the least important theatre reviews amongst a host of approving articles – to sow the seeds of despair which had triggered . . . well, neither Gray nor Pinter knew at that stage what it had triggered. The deep concern that grew that week as news stands across the country blazed 'FEARS FOR FRY' had yet to turn into anger for the company, when word finally trickled through that their absent star had been spotted, despite attempted disguise, in Bruges, en route to numerous locations in the Low Countries.

And what was his best friend doing during this painful period? 'Whatever I was doing, I wasn't so furiously busy that I wasn't able to get on a motorcycle and go and find m'colleague. Which I did, but by that time he was in France – it wasn't a great piece of detective work, but eventually I tracked him down there. I got on my motorcycle and I rode to France, and spent about a week with him, he'd borrowed someone's flat. Obviously I was extremely concerned – who wasn't? It was an absolutely calamitous thing, and nobody won, nobody got anything good from it. I remember just looking at all the broken pieces – Stephen being the principal one, but also Rik, who was so magnificent in that play, and arguably he was never quite the same again after that, it was a tremendous blow for him, and Simon Gray of course, who never forgave Stephen. He obviously got himself into a really terrible frame of mind, and depending on the sympathy you instinctively feel for Stephen . . . well, the sympathy I felt was considerable, but I know that others felt less, and they would say he got himself into that frame of mind and it was up to him to get himself out of it, but a lot of it is to do with how you regard mental health. There are people who don't want to believe in such a thing, they dare not allow it too much credibility, otherwise you enter into murky waters.' Stephen adds, 'That is the final soupy twist to the story, you might say . . . Hugh was so kind, and totally understanding, all the qualities a true friend has. There was none of that "Let's sit down and discuss it", it was just easy, we spoke about things when we needed to, and otherwise just went for walks and laughed, and it was just the most helpful and wonderful thing. And it got him online for the first time – I had accounts with AOL and CompuServe, and somehow he got hold of someone's computer and got in touch. He was the first person to get in touch with me, and then my father.'

Once it had been only the Fry family's immediate circle who had to be faced after one of Stephen's inexplicable episodes, but this time, it was the whole country whose minds had to be put at rest, and before the week was through, Lorraine Hamilton released Stephen's apology to the press: 'I have been horrified and embarrassed to see from the papers how much attention my departure has provoked. I do want to apologise for all the distress and concern I have caused . . . I can only offer cowardice, embarrassment and distress as excuses for such absurd behaviour . . . I would also like to say that I hold no grudge against the theatre critics. I left not out of pique, because I had been wounded or hurt, but because I was afraid that they were terribly right and that I was letting down Rik Mayall's brilliant performance in Simon Gray's remarkable play. They both deserved better . . . I have been selfish. I cannot deny that. But I only have one life to lead and no dependents. I desperately needed to go away and rethink my life. I may live for another thirty-seven years and it would be foolish to carry on doing things for which I haven't either the aptitude or perhaps the desire . . . perhaps I am not cut out for the business I have been engaged in for the last fifteen years . . . I am offering this to the press in the hope that they will accept that I am not a Lord Lucan or Reggie Perrin . . . In time, I will have to return and no doubt face the music, but for the moment I need a little quietness, and if you could find it in yourselves to allow it me, I should be very grateful . . . I'm a silly old fool and I don't deserve the attention. Thank you and sorry.'

Gray's play would never recover despite the urgent drafting in of Simon Ward, and Rik was inconsolable – before *Cell Mates* limped to its close on 25 March he would be arrested for wildly threatening

American tourists with a toy gun, just outside the theatre. Worse lay ahead for him, of course, as a life-threatening quad bike crash three years later would do more damage than anything else he experienced, permanently affecting his remaining sixteen years. Still, Rik would never let Stephen off the hook if there was a gag to be wrung out of it, writing in his anti-memoir *Bigger Than Hitler, Better Than Christ* that Fry fled because he was heavy with Rik's child, and as *Bottom* went back on tour, he told the press, 'When I walked into our office, Ade said, "I told you not to muck about with those Cambridge bastards. Come back here, be a good boy and shut up" . . . I was enjoying the play an awful lot, so it was a shame Stephen buggered off. But we're still friends, oh God, yeah. I don't think he was running away from me – just because I was a lot better than him in the play . . . This time, Mr Fry, I'm going to make sure Ade's handcuffed to me for the whole tour. We had this idea of getting the *Spitting Image* puppet of Stephen and having him pop his head through the door occasionally. We'd go, "Who's that? Lord Lucan? Shergar . . .?"'

With cold water thrown on the story by Stephen's press release, the following Sunday's third episode of *ABOF&L* went out as usual on Sunday night, and the final run continued as if nothing had ever happened. But to anybody watching, the real world events could hardly be entirely put out of mind, and Stephen's obvious distress pooped the party of Fry & Laurie's celebrated sophisticated comedy sketch show, in its eighth year, going out on the nation's first channel. 'They said they didn't know it was going to be the last one, but I thought it might', Robert Daws says. 'They'd worked together solidly for fifteen years and I knew, talking to them both, that they were looking to pursue things in a solo capacity. So maybe subconsciously they knew it too. I was just nervously trying to get the "Soupy Twists" trumpet solo right. Hugh said, "we'll jam along", but he's such a brilliant musician, and I'm such a particularly average one, I was immediately intimidated; they were so meticulous. But they are the most spectacularly generous, kind people to work with.' That said, when Robert played 'The Last Post' on Sunday 26 March 1995, nobody watching guessed that it would presage the last ever cries of 'soupy twist!'

THE LAST BIT

'Time, like a thief in the night, has smashed our near-side window, and stolen thence the stereo from our dashboard therein. For the last time, I turn, wiping a sad, soft, salt tear from my crimsoning cheek, to entreat this entreaty of my colleague . . . please, Mr Music, will you play . . .?'

'I'd just like to say a big "Hi!" to historians of the future, who may be looking at this show as part of a higher education course in the year 2010 entitled, "Britain: Just What the Bloody Hell Went Wrong?"'

Happy endings are an enormously useful thing to have in the bag. Nobody can claim that Stephen Fry & Hugh Laurie have suffered or starved, cast adrift from that binding ampersand, no matter how many people miss the comedy that came expressly from the two colleagues' combined desires to make people laugh. Their work ethic has never flagged, and so to examine their solo careers in comparable detail would take this entire book again, but thirty years after the first broadcast of *A Bit of Fry & Laurie*, fans can at least content themselves that Stephen & Hugh remain at the top of their respective games, and the less than spectacular end of their on-screen double act is ancient history. 'I don't look back on it as a dark period,' Hugh insists, 'one of the reasons that had never struck me is that socially that was never the position!' No matter where their separate paths have taken them since 1995, Stephen remains the godfather to Hugh's three children, and above all, his best friend. 'There are opposite versions of that you can find, probably more in music than comedy – the music business is littered with people who went on performing together even though they couldn't stand each other. The Eagles went on and did three massive albums after they couldn't bear to look each other in the eye. And we were the other way around, we couldn't bear not to be able to look each other in the eye, and we never wanted to stop enjoying each other's company, but we did stop working together. For that reason, the end of our partnership feels like an innocuous event, because we didn't walk away from each other.'

The comparisons with Cook & Moore's partnership which have dogged this narrative remain glaring – the pianist unexpectedly became a major sex symbol in LA, while the tone-deaf dominant wit followed to experiment with US sitcom, but otherwise became a beloved elder statesman of comedy at home. However, Laurie cites a crucial difference: 'In *Derek & Clive*, that's the end of Pete & Dud's partnership on screen, there's an abrasiveness there and it makes me unhappy to look at it. We never had that, and never wavered in the pleasure we took in each other's company. It just fell out that way, and if we'd been more strategic, and cleverer, frankly, we might have found a way of navigating past 1995, we might have said, "We can't leave it here, let's go away and write something, start again, do a show at the Edinburgh Festival and start from scratch, or take a sabbatical and climb the Alps or something." But we didn't, there was no Svengali guiding us through these waters, so we wound up, as I say, just falling downstairs together – at the bottom of the stairs, I suppose Stephen hit the ground first, and harder. And I suppose I fell on top of him, if I'm going to flog this analogy further . . .'

There was some talk of the promised fifth series – when Hugh appeared on Clive Anderson's chat show, he insisted, 'I don't know, to be honest, I watched Stephen on this show because I was keen to find out . . . I now think there is far too much comedy about, far too much. I think there's going to be a big slump, the bottom will drop out of the comedy market and we'll all be stuck in a negative comedy trap.' But when asked the same question on the BBC's *Comedy Connections* a decade later, he said, 'I don't remember why we stopped. Did they have enough of us or did we have enough of them, or did the two things happen at once? Not absolutely sure, maybe I'm so traumatised by the circumstances that I've actually blanked it out, I've got some false memory syndrome. And I'm going to imagine that they sent us a big cake, you know, "Any time you want to come back!" That probably didn't happen though. I think maybe they'd just had enough of us.' 'We never decided *not* to do another Fry & Laurie, did we?' his colleague argues, 'Whenever we talk about these things, we say we still want to work together . . . I almost don't dare think what life would have been like if I'd never met Hugh. I can't imagine how I could have had anything like the pleasure and fulfilment that I've had in life because of him.' Decades on, the memories of *ABOF&L*'s twenty-six half-hours is slight: 'Looking at *ABOF&L* is a strange experience. It's impossible ever, I think, to overcome the natural human vanity that makes one despair at the corpulence one is now prey to, and the slimness that was once one's own. I see Hugh, and I see myself, and I remember the frenetic energy, and the pleasure we had from making them. There is an element of it which harks back to the classroom, when you are doing imitations for the benefit of people sitting around you, of the school teachers. It's that that gives it a sort of – I hate to say "dangerous edge", it's preposterous, we're not talking about ghetto art here – but it gives it that frisson. I suppose if there was an identity, it was a love of language. We wanted it to be a bit like when we were at university, that real pleasure you get just from being funny, or creative. The weirdest thing is I've forgotten the sketches. I look at them, and I do not remember one second of that sketch, where I was, what I was thinking, what the next line is, how it ends – it might just as well be someone else you're looking at. And that's something I never imagined would be true . . . I think there is a sense of "Goodness, I'd forgotten that, and it's rather good and wasn't so shameful after all!" But I suppose the ones that get flagged on YouTube are the ones that are more memorable, and some have seemed to be quite prophetic, like privatising the Police and the parody of *It's A Wonderful Life* in which Murdoch suddenly realised how much harm he'd done to the world . . . I'm deeply proud of what Hugh and I were together, which is so different from what we are as individuals, and we kind of miss it,' Fry continues, 'I love him dearly, he's my best friend. It's a great shame, we talk about working together again, and we will I'm sure, because we're lucky to have found each other.' 'We did these shows that some people liked, some people didn't like,' his colleague concludes. 'The truth is that actually, compared to the huge thing which is my relationship with Stephen, the actual finished shows themselves I think of as being quite a small thing. But what they have allowed me to have in my life is a long and wonderful relationship with him. He's given me a huge amount, and I wouldn't be who I am, doing what I am doing, if it weren't for him.'

The Importance of Being Earnest

As Fry gradually eased himself back into society, slimmer and blonder, he owed his rehabilitation to two very different witty playwrights – Oscar Wilde and Ben Elton. Before the year was out, Stephen was back at the BBC in front of a live audience providing the kind of Melchettian guest appearance only he could deliver for Ben and Rowan's police sitcom *The Thin Blue Line*, the horrifyingly mad Outward Bound expert Brigadier Blaster-Sump bringing the first series to a hysterical, and very loud, close.

Alan Bennett had been the first person to suggest the Wilde resemblance years earlier, and the passion for playing his greatest hero had been growing within Fry ever since – so keen was he to bag the lead in a new biopic directed by *Tom & Viv*'s Brian Gilbert, he even personally underwrote his insurance, knowing that backers would prefer a bigger name for Oscar. Stephen was certainly never to regret his passion for the role, and when *Wilde* was released in 1997, it may not have been a blockbuster but there was nary a dissenting voice among the critics, who applauded his central role in the warmest tones. Fry was to land numerous roles in hit movies in his career, from the almost tailor-made role of a brilliant gay TV host in *V for Vendetta* to voicing Tim Burton's Cheshire Cat in the Disney CG iteration of *Alice,* one of the highest grossing movies of all time – but it seems no role will ever compare with that chance to take on the mantle of his greatest inspiration, and *Wilde* unequivocally washed away the taste of *Cell Mates*. The real Oscar was said to have had a high, reedy voice, and Stephen was wise to play the part with more of his innate gravity, but if the perennial criticism of his acting is that the Fry persona always shows through, never was it of more benefit to a performance than in *Wilde*. The onerous task of filming sex scenes with Michael Sheen, Ioan Gruffudd and Jude Law also reflected another crucial development for the star – the end of celibacy: 'One of the things I realised after the crisis of *Cell Mates* was that I was lonely. It was like a blinding flash. Of course! I'm terribly lonely . . .' Stephen had always found funny ways of beating himself up in public, from maligning his bent nose to describing the battles with weight that came from being such a gourmand – likening his torso to 'a bin bag full of yoghurt' was a familiar gripe, and his frame's girth has palpably fluctuated over the years. This has never dented his fans' love for him, but to have someone in his life to quieten those cruel self-criticisms was a great step forward.

In those first years of professional estrangement, Hugh had no starring role comparable to Stephen's in *Wilde*, but was far from slacking on the Hollywood front. Not that he eschewed TV comedy – he popped up supporting three of our greatest funny women: Tracey Ullman, Dawn French and Victoria Wood – but it was his support of Glenn Close as Cruella De Vil in 1996's *101 Dalmatians* (forming a surrogate duo with *The Fast Show*'s Mark Williams, just as Stephen partnered up with John Bird) that triggered a bound forward in Hugh's career – leading to a standout role in *The Borrowers*; a memorable cameo abusing Jennifer Aniston in *Friends* and becoming the star of *Stuart Little*, playing the all-American father to Michael J. Fox's mischievous mouse (his casting admittedly not entirely unconnected to on-screen wife Geena Davis being well over six feet tall). The film spawned a sequel and a cartoon, and introduced Laurie to a vast US audience, who never suspected his Britishness.

For all this measured advancement, Hugh discovered he was no more protected from depression than his erstwhile partner, the realisation coming when he was in the middle of a dramatic crash at a stock-car race, and found himself, in the moment, actually *bored*. 'I diagnosed myself as being depressed and decided I would try and sort it out,' he says. 'I don't know enough about the illness to say whether it was clinical, but it was certainly more than feeling a bit sad. It went on for long periods and had all the other symptoms, lethargy and not wanting to get out of bed in the morning. It's actually selfish to be depressed and not to try and do anything about it . . . I know a lot of people think therapy is about sitting around staring at your own navel, but it's staring at your own navel with a goal. And the goal is to one day see the world in a better way and treat your loved ones with more kindness and have more to give.' Ben Elton once said of his old friend, 'Hugh's problem is that he is afflicted with serious self-doubt. It's debilitating for him and for his friends as well. He knows it. And he knows his friends won't put up with it any more', and at the turn of the millennium he tried to do something about it by giving Laurie his first stab at a romantic lead, with his own sex scenes to worry about. But although *Maybe Baby* reunited him with old friends French, Atkinson and Thompson and stretched his dramatic capabilities, with his first ever on-screen nudity thrown in for good measure, the film was no smash hit, bolstering Hugh's lifelong self-doubt. Stephen was one of many who fought this banana oil: 'He's absolutely brilliant, but also painfully self-critical. He has athletic prowess, command of several musical instruments and laser-like attention to logic and detail. I don't think I've ever heard him say he's pleased with anything he's done, except things to him that really matter, like friendships, parenthood, love. He's just a remarkable man to have as a friend.' Hugh seemed to find the nub of the problem when he said, 'I don't have a single complete show or movie or anything else that I could look at and say, "Nailed that one". But endless dissatisfaction is, I suppose, what gets us out of bed in the morning.'

Hugh and Stephen are obviously not the only comics to have dealt with depression – Ruby Wax is a voluble mental health campaigner and Tony Slattery's stratospheric rise to fame in the 1990s led to a crippling breakdown which all-but ended his career. Having been diagnosed as a cyclothymic manic depressive (a label subject to change, currently altered to 'bipolar 1'), Fry went so far as to front not one but two TV documentaries, *The Secret Life of the Manic Depressive* and its follow-up, which detailed a further attempt on his own life in 2012, after facing down a frothing Ugandan anti-gay spokesman for his film on homophobia around the world, *Out There*. As before, and as ever, Stephen's work rate pushed him beyond endurance, his indomitable exterior making it easy to forget the fragility inside. He explained on Sky

Arts' *In Confidence* in 2011, 'You can do the whole Janet Street-Porter thing, "Oh, why don't they walk it off? It's only celebrities talking about their moods!" – and then they kill themselves. It's a morbid condition. Any doctor will tell you, it's one of the most serious morbid conditions in Britain. The fact that I'm lucky enough not to have it so seriously doesn't mean that I won't one day kill myself. I may well . . . It is always worth remembering that mostly what one's talking about is not celebrities talking about how occasionally their life is slightly unhappy or sometimes slightly bouncy . . . it is worth saying for the sake of those millions out there whose lives are utterly blighted and whose prospects are more or less hopeless.' That fragility could also be physical, as Fry learned when taking on the mantle of his late friend Douglas Adams by travelling the world visiting endangered species for *Last Chance to See*, during which he fell between two boats and shattered his forearm.

These are just a few of the subjects Stephen has tackled in his career as documentarian. Ever since Michael Palin first followed in Phileas Fogg's footsteps, comedians have fought to claim their own factual territory, and those comics over forty who haven't made documentaries of some kind are few and far between – but with the possible exception of Sir Tony Robinson, all must bow to Fry, whose investigations include Wagner, Gutenberg, HIV, spectacled bears, America, Central America, a whole series as *Gadget Man* and of course, above all, his continuing love letters to language, *Planet Word* on TV and *Fry's English Delight* on Radio 4. Some of the above were produced by Sprout Pictures, the production company he co-founded in 2004, despite his aversion to office life – 'I'm a totally silent partner, I let them run it. The odd documentary has been a Sprout production, but I don't do production meetings and offices, I'm hopeless, it's just not what I was put on this earth to do, and I know Hugh feels the same.'

This diversity of topics is all part of the national institution Fry has become – a kind of millennial Betjeman, trudging around the country, and dozens of times around the world, tackling crucial issues and sharing his passions. Like his original role model Bennett, this is one of the things that has put Stephen in the highest echelons of that category that was once a great compliment, but in time has become a tiresome term – National Treasure. 'He *is* a national treasure,' Hugh laughs. 'He's also a personal treasure. I share him with the country.' Stephen blushes, 'It's very embarrassing, you have to put it to the back of your mind, because if you allow yourself to believe it, of course, you become monstrously vain . . . I think it means you are a kind of regimental goat mascot. A genuine National Treasure, Alan Bennett, once said in Britain if you live long enough to be able to open a boiled egg unaided, then you eventually acquire status.' It's telling that when Viz devoted a second comic strip to 'banana-nosed bonk-ban polymath' Fry, he was presented as a young lad's peculiar but lovable pet with a tweeting addiction.

The problem with being the nation's teddy bear, however, is that it cuts both ways – cuddly toys can be kicked as well as cuddled, and occasions on which Stephen has let his honesty override diplomacy on chat shows and online have generated frothing headlines in the usual places. For the best part of four decades, Stephen Fry's presence in our culture has never flagged, his original lust for fame long since sated, but ubiquity has been the price paid for the great communicator to do what he loves best – broadcasting. The unstoppable expansion of the internet into every area of our lives has stoked this, of course, with Fry the ultimate early adopter (he even launched his own app, a 'Virtual Fry', which was only briefly updated) and his place on numerous social media has complicated his unquenchable desire to present an honest face to his public, for all his horror of glancing 'below the line' at trolling comments.

Stephen's place on the list of Britain's Most Adorably Ubiquitous Public Figures has actually been more defined in this century by another writer's work than his own. When J. K. Rowling threw a dizzying host of fantastical influences into a cauldron and magicked up the greatest phenomenon in the history of children's publishing, she was in no small way inspired by Fry's own tales of public school life, as well as British comedy including *Blackadder*. Fry & Laurie may be two of the few British comedy actors never to pop up in the *Harry Potter* movie franchise, but Stephen's 128 hours of performing the saga have ingrained that golden voice in the hearts of millions of younger fans, becoming a Christmas treat for many, despite the US audiobooks being read by Jim Dale.

His own career as a novelist has been sidelined with the publication of memoirs, and many permutations of online publishing via his own website, with 'blessays' aplenty. However, wood-pulp-based releases bearing his name include works on classical music, specially presented editions of Wilde's children's stories, and a comprehensive exploration of his love of poetry, *The Ode Less Travelled*. As a novelist, Fry followed *The Hippopotamus* with the sci-fi time-altering philosophy of *Making History* (in which Hitler's birth is averted, resulting in a world far worse than the one we know) and *The Stars' Tennis Balls*, published in the USA as *Revenge,* which began as an original rumination on revenge, but morphed into an updated take on *The Count of Monte Cristo* once the similarities had been pointed out to him. This remains the last fiction release from Fry, although his *oeuvre* nearly extended to a fifth entry of sorts in 2009 when the audio series *The Dongle of Donald Trefusis* resurrected Fry's beloved academic, only to kill him off to trigger what was intended as a clue-packed quest for the downloading audience via a USB stick bequeathed by the unpredictable professor to the narrator (i.e. Stephen himself, who proved to be, like Adrian Healey, one of Trefusis's most difficult students). Regretfully, only three instalments were released, which Fry admits is down to 'Sheer incompetence and laziness!' Or rather, 'This is a feeble excuse, but it's true so I'll use it – it was actually at a time when my bipolar disorder was least under control and I had a period of intense creative activity, a burst of new projects, and that was one of them. I wrote at incredible speed, but then I had this big downswing, and I just couldn't get back to it! But I should look at it again, and make it the slowest sequel of all time.'

Hugh knows this feeling well – his own novel *The Gun Seller* enjoyed an enthusiastic reception when it was released in 1996, but ever since, not only has the story been kept in eternal development hell as a movie, but the planned follow-up, *The Paper Soldier,* has never seen the light of day. This is a shame as Hugh's one existing novel, a suitably espionage-centred action narrative not far removed from the doings of Major Tarrant, was far more comedic than any of Fry's novels – in typical Hugh fashion, he demanded that it proved its worth first by being accepted under the pseudonym of 'James Calum', utilising his unused names.

The other cliché perennially attached to Stephen is of course 'polymath', and his every over-extended chat show introduction underlines the fact that he is perhaps our most celebrated and qualified example of the cliché, with the result that his infamous work ethic has ensured that there is simply too much Fry to squeeze into these remaining pages. He added 'Director' to the list in 2003 by writing and helming the Evelyn Waugh adaptation *Bright Young Things,* featuring an incredible who-will-soon-be-who of British acting talent. Critics were generally approving of Fry's skill in creating a world of *Jeeves & Wooster*-esque sumptuousness for his debut, but the attempt to depict the twentieth-century youths of *Vile Bodies* as more debauched than their modern counterparts didn't quite inspire the latter demographic to visit cinemas in droves. His standing in the movie world remains good, however, and twelve years of helming the BAFTAs at the end of every winter erased any doubt that his appeal is solely a British thing, like lay-by picnics and tea-cosies – over the years he's flirted with DiCaprio and snogged Streep. But of course, nothing has defined Fry's public persona in the twenty-first century quite as much as *QI*.

The 'Quite Interesting' panel game where rigorous intellectual enquiry meets whacking great knob gags was created by Johns Mitchinson and Lloyd, when the latter experienced a post-*Blackadder* awards-fuelled crisis which inspired him to rethink the way people are educated. The pair's original grand designs for a *QI* empire were eventually downscaled, but the central TV show has endured, a BBC institution and a heavy presence on repeat channels, thanks in no small way to Fry's crucial place as the schoolmaster figure in charge of the unruly panellists. The casting was famously accidental, with Stephen stepping up from team captain when Michael Palin cried off presenting the pilot, but from 2003 to 2016, Fry was the mascot for *QI*'s particular brand of benevolent academic pedantry, presenting every episode with naughty dunce Alan Davies by his side and generations of comedians old and new basking in his avuncular glow, fronting board games and DVD games, featuring in books and annuals, and generally cementing his place as everyone's favourite know-it-all – a role for which he was positively engineered from infancy. His thirteen years in charge of the show will be repeated for years to come, but sadly the demands of squeezing in multiple episodes every day to save costs compelled him to call it a day after series M, his place taken with absolute naturality by Sandi Toksvig, who for over thirty years has been a kind of balancing yin to Stephen's yang.

More than anything, *QI*'s extraordinary success defined the British Cult of Stephen Fry – which went so far as to inspire a series of books entirely unconnected to the man, created by the Twitter handle 'Mrs Stephen Fry', sharing her secrets about the great man's macho, hetero private life, while the equally unofficial *Tish & Pish* was a 'Talk like Fry' stocking-filler of such unspeakable point-missing tweeness, no Fry fan could digest it vomit-free. 'I always think it best to hold my peace,' he says. 'The Mrs Fry seemed benign enough (and often witty, judging by the tweets), I didn't mind that sort of thing, so long as they at no point pretended that they were official or written by or in collaboration with me. The second one I try very hard not to think about and haven't read a syllable of. I don't want to be the first human to show that it is actually physically, medically possible to die of embarrassment.' Nigel Planer was also once paid to work on a screenplay based on Fry's early years, while in 2008 a Radio 4 play, *I Love Stephen Fry,* centred on a typical Stephen groupie, a frustrated housewife captivated by brains, and featured a passionate cameo from the idol himself – a crucial part of the plot, made possible largely because it was written by Jon Canter.

You Can't Always Get What You Want . . .

While his colleague was working flat out recording hours of *QI* and becoming Britain's all-time reigning brainbox *polymath*, Hugh was of course not idling, but stoking an already monstrous complex by playing the part of a medic, for considerably more remuneration than his beloved doctor father could ever have imagined. Doctor Gregory House was not the first physician Laurie had played – just a year before, in 2003, he took the central role in Nigel Williams' ITV comedy drama *Fortysomething,* playing the awkwardly named frustrated Wimbledon GP Paul Slippery, unhappily attached to wife Anna Chancellor and colleague Peter Capaldi, and father to a trio of sex-mad boys including Benedict Cumberbatch (who, incidentally, had once been presented with second prize in a Harrow reading competition by Stephen Fry). Hugh went to great lengths to save a troubled production (including directing some external sequences naked, thanks to a predictable plot point) but *Fortysomething* was weakly received and frightened schedulers quickly buried it in a graveyard slot. If ITV had known the star power they had with House, The Doctor and Sherlock Holmes in the same cast, they may have shown more guts.

Fortysomething also has the distinction of being the very last time Fry & Laurie ever performed together, after twenty-four years of partnership. For all that *ABOF&L* screeched to a halt in 1995, the colleagues didn't immediately abandon all joint offers, and in 1998 Stephen presented an offspring of *Hysteria* called *Live From the Lighthouse* on Channel 4, a comedy show involving the latest offerings from the Cambridge Footlights, Ali G, played by Sacha Baron Cohen, and double act Mel Giedroyc & Sue Perkins. Perhaps it was fitting, given their presence, that Hugh was on hand to join in with one last run-through of 'The Hedge Sketch', the final Fry & Laurie sketch performed to date. They did, however, regroup with Robert Bathurst and Patrick Barlow shortly after, joined by James Dreyfus for a historical sketch about European diplomats carving the world up in the Treaty of Westphalia in 1648. Broadcast on the BBC to mark the turn of the millennium, *The Nearly Complete and Utter History of Everything* was a star-packed two-parter which also allowed Fry to step into Cleese's shoes in a historical reworking of the classic *Frost Report* 'Class sketch' with the Two Ronnies, but the treaty sketch is largely remembered as the source of too many embarrassing bloopers, Stephen & Hugh making each other corpse right to the end.

Around the same time they reprised the roles of Melchett & George in *Blackadder Back & Forth* for the Millennium Dome, with modern descendants of their most famous sitcom personas, plus Stephen wearing a shockingly short skirt and spouting Latin as a senior Roman general – and even giving his Wellington one more time, opposite old friend Simon Russell-Beale's camp Napoleon (oddly, in the same year he played the General yet again for European comedy *Sabotage!*, Bonaparte in that case played by David Suchet). Sadly, although everyone put their bravest faces on for the occasion, this last helping of *Blackadder* was unsatisfying for all involved, with John Lloyd's crucial perfectionism kept at bay by Elton & Curtis.

It was a few years later that Lloyd emerged from his years of self-exploration and re-education to launch *QI*, and for Episode 1, Hugh made his one and only panel game appearance, lending his old colleague support at the beginning of his thirteen-year sojourn as Chairman. Stephen himself, of course, has remained a panel game fiend, appearing on everything from *Celebrity Mastermind* to *Never Mind the Buzzcocks*, and remaining a stalwart for *Clue* on Radio 4 – even spending an evening in the Chairman's chair when the great Humphrey Lyttelton passed on.

QI's debut was almost simultaneous with *Fortysomething*, which featured in its second episode a very familiar fishmonger fated to foil Slippery's plans for an erotic fish supper:

PAUL:	Hello, I'm wondering…
DEREK:	Just a moment, sir, I'm adjusting a crab. (TO ASSISTANT) There, you see? Pincers overlapping, it's not rocket science. Off you go. Sorry for the hold-up, sir, how can I help you?
PAUL:	I was wondering if you had any oysters?
DEREK:	Well if I don't you're out of luck, sir, it's all internet cafés round here at the moment. Don't know how they pay their rent.
PAUL:	Right. Because I'm trying to make something called 'Bivalve Burst', and apparently you need two dozen oysters and a pint of sherry.
DEREK:	Aha. Are we talking about 'The Big Book of Erotic Food', by any chance?
PAUL:	Do you know it?
DEREK:	Inside out, if you take my meaning. (WINKS) No, my brother-in-law submitted a recipe for the publishers: 'Prawnographic', which we all enjoyed. But they said it had too much garlic for the average

	reader. So, you have a special lady in mind, sir?
PAUL:	My wife.
DEREK:	... As you wish, sir.[1]

This final and really rather random duologue, nine years on from the last *ABOF&L* recording, may not have had the ring of classic Fry & Laurie to it, but the episode did at least credit Jon Canter as 'Script Consultant'.

Interviewed at this time about his numerous film roles, the star of the show happened to say, 'Hollywood is a fantastic place to visit on safari, and take pictures of the wild animals there – film stars, Sunset Boulevard, all of that. But that's enough.' And yet he persevered with the American side of his career, co-writing witty crime pilot *Dragans of New York* for CBS, which allowed him to remain English while playing the long-desired role of a crime-fighting hero; and taking roles in films like the remake *Flight of the Phoenix*. Famously, it was during production of the latter that he sat in a bathroom in Namibia, tired, sweaty and dishevelled, as a cast-mate filmed him reading a few pages of a pilot script sent by his agent – and shortly after, on reviewing the audition tapes back in LA, that pilot's producer Bryan Singer pointed at the drawling, pained figure of Hugh and allegedly shouted, 'Now *this* is the kinda strong American actor I'm looking for!' American accents traditionally attract great criticism when coming out of the mouths of non-American actors – nowhere more so than in Britain, where critics tend to have zero idea of the vast spectrum of accents in the USA – but from the moment Dr House began popping painkillers, limping around on his stick and dispensing miraculous diagnoses and deadpan killer lines, the American audience never questioned his nationality once. Hugh Laurie *became*, in the eyes of the world, American.

The creation of *L.A. Law* veteran David Shore, *House* would run on Fox for eight seasons, becoming one of the most successful TV shows of all time, and there in the centre of it was Laurie, the stubbly, lugubrious, smart-assed – but never less than brilliant – malady detective key to solving each week's teasing medical problem. At first, Hugh assumed his role would be the wise guy sidekick to hero Dr Wilson, played by Robert Sean Leonard, and would never have signed a contract had he known what lay ahead – but by the time the series' popularity became manifest, he was already locked in. And so began several years of straddling the Atlantic, dealing with a sudden and unimagined level of international fame – Laurie-mania! – which made strolling down the street in most countries a near-impossibility (although bizarrely not the UK, where botched scheduling meant that *House* never quite grabbed the nation in the same way).

Jo, Charlie, Bill and Rebecca had no interest in uprooting their lives to LA, but as the titular star Hugh could hardly walk away from what by 2008 had become literally the biggest TV show in the world, and Laurie himself for a time the highest paid actor on the box. He took an Executive Producer role, and Gregory House took on numerous Laurie traits, including, of course, a varied musical talent. Hugh was also finally acclaimed as the sex symbol so many always insisted he was, despite his years of egregiously English pop-eyed gawd-help-us-ness back home in Blighty – his natural accent shocked millions of his new fans, but never seemed to put them off. 'It's totally absurd,' he of course responded. 'Weird. Deranged. Very amusing. I can't explain it. Even my wife doesn't think I'm sexy, it's a miracle we have children.' However, and despite numerous attempts by tabloids over the years to do all they could to splash fruity exposés of the newly hot star and undermine their marriage, Hugh and Jo came out of the other end of the *House* experience as strong as ever, and for all his back-breaking hard work in LA (rising at dawn to ride his motorbike to the studios for a fourteen-plus hour day only broken by bouts of boxing to stay hench) Hugh never rescinded his loyalty to home and family, coming out of the punishing period an A-list star, able to hold his own with the likes of George Clooney in Disney's *Tomorrowland* (which was poorly received, but did no harm to anyone involved). He was even famous enough to make a speech at the Hollywood Star ceremony for double Oscar winner, Emma Thompson.

A couple of decades after mocking perfume ads in *ABOF&L*, Laurie surprised the world by taking on a job as the male face of L'Oréal, but thankfully, his reasons for doing so were certainly 'worth it': 'If you're going to ask me questions about skincare, there's not much I can tell you. Don't rub a cheese grater up and down your cheeks. That would be my advice. Don't dunk your face in engine oil or other caustic substances. I don't know anything about it. They sort of ask you to do this thing and you go: "You're out of your fucking mind, not in a billion years would I consider such a thing." Then, as they tell you it's a great deal of money, the thought crosses your mind: "With that money I could build a school in Senegal." And then you *can't* say no. Because if you do say no, what you're saying is that your public pose is more important than people getting a school in Senegal or polio vaccinations in Uganda or whatever. You can't do that. You just can't . . . So I went ahead with it, and in return, good works were done. L'Oréal also chipped in a large amount, so it worked out well for everyone . . . and I look pretty.'

'In England there's an element of treachery in going abroad to ply one's trade, it's rather frowned upon,' he told *Playboy* in 2009. 'There were two beacons on that front: Peter Cook & Dudley Moore. Both were fantastically talented, but Peter stayed in London and Dudley left. Because he left and lived in glorious California, Moore was widely assumed to have made a deal with the devil that involved beautiful blonde women and beaches and sunshine and Ferraris. Peter maintained the slightly drizzly temperament we revere in England. Moore was perceived as a traitor.' In fact, Cook had attempted to follow his partner to LA, but playing a butler in sitcom *The Two of Us* only exacerbated his homesickness – Fry almost played a butler in sitcom *Super Clyde*, but it never made it past pilot. 'I suppose I have too much of a Presbyterian streak from my parents ever to rejoice in the fruits of my labours and give over completely to whatever it was Dudley succumbed to,' Hugh confided in *Playboy*. 'I've actually always rather enjoyed Los Angeles. It's partly to do with what people tell you to expect. People said, "Los Angeles is the most terrible place of all. You'll go crazy. You won't last a month. You'll be going out of your mind, it's so superficial." Well, I am superficial, so it suits me down to the ground. For instance, I like fast cars and motorcycles, and there's no better place to be for that.' He went further when talking to the *Guardian* after *House*'s conclusion: 'I've got very little sympathy with actors who come back and go: "I'm just a real bloke, you know, all that Hollywood bullshit." Oh, fuck off. It's such wank. It's a lie that the British press wants to be told that LA is very shallow, glitzy, venal, superficial, all that stuff. British readers find it very comforting: "Yes, that's why my ancestors didn't cross the Atlantic with the Pilgrim Fathers. They knew that it would end up as Sodom and Gomorrah and life in Chipping Norton is actually much realer." I'm damned if I'm going to use the conventional cliché about Los Angeles. There's good and bad. The trees are fantastic: some of the best trees you'll see anywhere. The architecture: miserable, looks like a petrol station.'

During these years of American awards and indeed rewards, Stephen was sometimes seen by his colleague's side, applauding with sincere relish as another Golden Globe was picked up, and he bagged a regular role on TV series *Bones*, which was filmed 'literally a cricket ball's toss' from the set of *House*: 'My agent in America said, "Would you do an episode of this series *Bones*?" which I have to confess I hadn't heard of . . . and I said to Hugh, who *is* American television, "What do you know of this *Bones*?" and he said, "Oh, they're awfully nice, they're just round the corner on the Fox lot." So I thought it would be sweet to do an episode and say hello to m'colleague. So we had lunch together, which greatly annoyed him in some ways, because, for very good reasons, playing an American, he keeps his accent all day – be rather stupid to dive in and out of it – so of course he finds it embarrassing when an English person comes and he goes, "Hi, great to see ya, Steve, how ya doing?" "Hugh, snap out of it, man, what are you doing?" On the other hand, if he lopes forward and goes "Hello, what ho!" The Americans go, "What is Hugh Laurie *doing*?" So he's kind of trapped between two accents.'[2] At the time, Hugh told Jonathan Ross on his own BBC chat show, 'When he's over he stays in my house, and we go to work together, and sit and eat cheese sandwiches together – we don't do that, it's all lobster over there – but it's a lovely thing, we sit there in the gorgeous Californian sunshine and reflect on our amazing good fortune, and don't think that we take it for granted for one second, because we don't.' 'He's my best friend,' Fry told journalists, 'and I've always known how brilliant an actor he is in every sense. Because he's so often played blue-eyed rather idiotic upper-class Englishmen, people are astonished to see him play this unshaven, fierce, haunted, drug-addled vicious doctor. But to me, it's just so thrilling to see when other people recognise his brilliance. He's been garlanded with recognition and rewards, and I think it's absolutely right . . . it's staggering hard work, what he does.'

One side effect of Hugh's new-found international following was, of course, that more people than ever were retroactively discovering the pleasures of *ABOF&L* both online and via the DVD box set released at the height of *House*'s popularity – certainly, once fans had got over Laurie's vocal gymnastics. 'It's nice that that's happening, because a lot of it is of course to do with the fact that so many Americans have just discovered Hugh and they want to know what he's been up to for the last twenty-odd years.' *ABOF&L* has an ever-growing reputation as the connoisseur's choice of sketch comedy – not as ubiquitous as Python, a minor cult for sure, but its fan base continues to swell. During publicity for *Mad Men*, the show's star Jon Hamm confused the press by announcing that as a student he loved performing sketches from the Fry & Laurie *oeuvre*. On page or on screen, most sketches still work, internationally.

Fry's own dramatic vehicle in the 2000s could barely have been more different from his colleague's, he having been approached in 2006 by TV writer and producer Simon Wheeler, who had co-devised with Alan Whiting a typically pastoral Sunday night confection for ITV to be called *Kingdom* (coincidentally also the name of a 1985 Radio 4 pilot featuring Stephen, produced by Nick Symons). Fry starred as another Peter, the cuddly but lightly tortured family solicitor of the title – and, yes, it was another role no great leap from his well-loved persona, but the real star of the show was to be the wide-skied beauty of his adored home county of Norfolk. '*Kingdom* was a delight to make,' he says. 'A wonderful group of actors coming up to Norfolk to be part of our little world over three series. We set out to make, yes, absolutely unapologetic cosy Sunday evening television, but also there are a lot of juxtapositions between cosiness and real terror, weirdness.' As Kingdom travelled around the county in a classic car, solving the problems of the folk of fictional town Market Shipborough, scores of fine comedy actors joined the show, with Phyllida Law as Peter's aunt and Tony Slattery as smelly local menace Sidney Snell, plus guest appearances from Bathurst, Margolyes and more – while Fry's new sidekick was trainee solicitor Lyle Anderson, played with some degree of blue-eyed Laurie-ish haplessness by Karl Davies. ITV were pleased with the drama's progress, and it returned for two more series until the channel's cost-cutting in 2009 forced an end to Kingdom's practice.

There have simply been so many, many notable projects over the two decades since the final 'soupy twist' – *Gormenghast, The Oranges, Pocoyo, Monsters vs Aliens* – and both colleagues have, joyfully, experienced great personal fulfilment in their own ways – Stephen making peace with his theatrical past with a feted run as Malvolio at Shakespeare's Globe and on Broadway, as well as touring his autobiographical one-man show around the world. He's still often criticised for having the inescapable stamp of his own personality on every role, but besides that being the case for many legendary movie stars, he does have the pluck to respond: 'It's true people say I play myself, but then I think there are facets to oneself. Two television characters that I might be well known for would be General Melchett and Jeeves. They both lived in the same time, roughly, given that Melchett would have survived the war, he might have bumped into Jeeves at some point, but they're incredibly different really. And yet both incredibly me. But the trouble is I have no gift of being mysterious and held back – I wish I could be like Hugh, who just says no to interview requests and no one hates him for it, in fact they respect him, for saying no.'

Hugh has meanwhile channelled his *House*-fuelled power into an Indian summer as one of the world's most successful blues artists. Naturally, he is lambasted for this in certain quarters, as a wealthy white Englishman, but a lifetime of pitiless self-laceration seems to have finally been downgraded to 'affable modesty' for Hugh, who now simply *cares less*, finally getting the message and no longer able to shrug off the proof of his talent after the world-beating success of *House*. 'Americans don't quite understand the English fetish for self-deprecation,' he says, 'and quite rightly. They're a little bit baffled by it, and you have to sort of keep it in check, because you can see them very rapidly lose interest, if you don't think you're worth talking to then they don't either. They don't find it charming, nor should they. Look at that, I'm being self-deprecating about self-deprecation, that's crazy.' Nonetheless, when music companies started approaching Laurie, he of course batted them back: 'A man with a fat cigar came to me, and said "Do you wanna give this a try?" And my first reaction was to say "No, I'm a white Englishman, what business have I got trespassing on this holy ground?" And then I thought, "Well, if I say no to this, I may never get another chance, and ten years from now, I don't want to be looking back saying "I could have done that, and I didn't." So I thought, "I'm gonna jump in." Having formed the Copper Bottom Band from some of the finest blues musicians on the scene, Hugh went on to release the resiliently titled *Let Them Talk* in 2011, and its success as the best-selling blues release of the year inspired an ongoing series of live gigs around the world, the follow-up album *Didn't It Rain?* and even an unusual dip into presenting, with *Hugh Laurie's Blues Changes* on Radio 2, and documentaries including ITV *Perspectives* specials *Down by the River* and *Copper Bottom Blues*, which showed Stephen rendezvousing with his old colleague on the Queen Mary pre-gig to herald him as 'Professor Shiny Scalp!' As a musician, Hugh seems more content and at ease than many of his friends would have dreamt was possible: 'I care much less than I did about what people think, this is something I love and am very proud of, and I stand by it . . . What I've realised about this experience is that whereas acting is about disguise, to put it crudely, I think music is about removing that. I feel as if I am exposing myself to an audience, it's a very naked, and therefore liberating, experience.' He adds, 'To be free of the whole self-effacement dance is very liberating.'

This rare sight of the two best friends at play – as with the two documentaries made about their joint career, the BBC's *Comedy Connections* in 2005 and GOLD's charming celebration *Fry & Laurie Reunited* in 2010 – does not alter the fact that Stephen & Hugh have not performed together since that scene in the fishmonger's. There have been rumours over the years, of course – in 2004 the papers were filled with certainty that they would become the new millennium's incarnations of Holmes & Watson for a series of ITV movies, notwithstanding that channel's broadcasting of Jeremy Brett's definitive turn as Sherlock, and Stephen semi-confirmed, telling the *Independent*, 'I've given myself six months to lose forty stone. I think I ought to. It's very noticeable that words like "lean" and "cadaverous" are used for Holmes, but words like "lard arse" are not. Not once does Conan Doyle say, "Holmes wobbled over to his chair and sat down and stuck a pipe into one of his chins."' There was a time that Fry & Laurie would have fitted the parts admirably, but even then, it would surely have been a waste of their chemistry, and *House*'s numerous allusions to Holmes aside, both have subsequently found roles in other permutations of Conan Doyle's work, Stephen playing Holmes' smarter brother Mycroft in Guy Ritchie's high-octane movie series, and Hugh playing the exact same role in yet another spoof adaptation, this time starring Will Ferrell and John C Reilly.

Then there would have been *The Canterville Ghost*, a CG animation of Wilde's famous supernatural romp executive-produced by Fry. Despite reuniting their voices with 'Snutty' in the cast, the colleagues' names were twinned above the title on every teaser poster throughout the film's long, complex production period – it was originally intended for release in 2014. Another virtual reunion came with that year's PlayStation 4 sequel *LittleBigPlanet 3*. Stephen has a long history of videogame performing, playing the amoral Reaver throughout Lionhead Studios' seminal *Fable* series, and was Narrator for the adventures of *LBP*'s hero Sackboy from the start – but when Hugh signed up separately to play the third game's villain, he had no idea of this. He simply said, 'I'm attracted to anything I can do for the first time, and I was very taken with this. Storytelling is storytelling, whatever form it takes . . . The strange thing is, I did not know until I got there that he was Narrator! But it was actually completely delightful to think that he's on the other end of this, well, beginning and end of the game, as the all-wise, all-seeing, all-knowing Narrator . . . Oh my GOD how he would love to be described as all those things. Which he is, of course.'

But as the thirtieth anniversary of *ABOF&L* comes round to knock them both in the solar plexus, whither any further bits of Fry & Laurie?

Thicken and Engorge with Mounting Excitement

'Never go back, ladies and gentlemen, never go back', a wise guy once said, and Stephen & Hugh have always stuck to their guns when questioned – as any *Blackadder* alumnus often is – about a return to their comedy roots. Unquestionably, the truth is that both men needed to spread their wings and take on new challenges as they matured as performers, and nothing could be more understandable. And yet, they both put forward the additional hypothesis that it's funnier to see two twenty-somethings dressing up as figures of authority than an actor who could actually *be* a headmaster, or general, Hugh griping, 'We are now not only the age of cabinet ministers, we are actually probably older than half the cabinet!' The riposte to that would be, why was the gifted aged actor Ralph Michael hired to play a doddery old judge in the 'Pimhole' sketch, when Paul Whitehouse, for instance, could have doddered apparently more amusingly in the same role? 'It's a very good point,' Fry concedes with customary politeness, 'our theory, as such, is an assertion that is not "necessary and efficient", as a logician would say, that you have to be young in order to be funny in a sketch. It's clearly not true, and Harry & Paul and others are doing their best to prove it's not true!'

In truth, comedians of the 1980s Alternative generation have long been a diminishing breed, those not presenting documentaries or playing detectives nonetheless a rare sight in the TV schedules – the aforementioned Enfield & Whitehouse bucking the trend, Reeves & Mortimer still at it, Elton returning to form with *Upstart Crow* and above all, Jennifer Saunders trumping all with the international success of *Absolutely Fabulous*. Neither Stephen nor Hugh have ever set their faces against comedy entirely, and Fry has retained a presence in most Red Nose Days, even becoming a crisp flavour – 'Stephen Fry Up' – in 2011, though *House* dictated that Hugh's Comic Relief input had to become solely (but significantly) financial for many years. He flexed his sketch muscles a few times for presenting stints on *Saturday Night Live,* playing a borderline libellous Derek Acorah and matching his sexy TV doctor chops with Clooney, but these skits were for a very different audience to that of *ABOF&L*. Stephen has had his fair share of comic torch-passing over the years, not just becoming The Book for the *Hitchhiker's Guide* movie but popping up in very silly TV roles including Cuddly Dick in *Yonderland*, Dr Bevelspepp in *This Is Jinsy*, and perhaps best of all, taking on the mantle of Colonel K in the rebooted *Danger Mouse*.

There was also a *Blackadder*-ish tinge to Fry's turn as Skulkingworm in 2011's very silly Dickensian spoof *The Bleak Old Shop of Stuff*, where he played senior boy to a pair of Footlights inheritors, David Mitchell & Robert Webb. Inevitably, throughout the decades since Stephen, Hugh, Emma & Co. groaned with nerves in the Footlights clubroom, gazing up at their forebears' photographs and damning their hopes of achieving comparable fame, Cambridge graduates from David Baddiel to John Oliver to Lucy Montgomery have continued to percolate into the comedy industry (and, despite Fry & Laurie's years of savaging the corporate mindset, it certainly is an industry). While Oxford was producing Lee & Herring, Cambridge's *Mary Whitehouse* crowd was giving way to a new bunch, including Mel & Sue – a duo not entirely dissimilar to Fry & Laurie, with one a tall, dark, gay panel game wit and BAFTA presenter. Hot on their heels came another contender for Stephen & Hugh's mantle, Alexander Armstrong & Ben Miller being some years separate while at Cambridge, but combining for numerous series of character-based sketch shows, occasionally playing on their Footlights heritage with X-rated Flanders & Swann pastiches. But perhaps the greatest echo of the success of the 1981 generation came with the synchronicity of the award-winning actress Olivia Colman with Mitchell & Webb, who for a flurry of reasons bear the most material similarities to Fry & Laurie, as much as the two colleagues have inescapably drawn comparisons to Cook & Moore. This pair's sketch shows have always seemed to have a high percentage of *ABOF&L* in their DNA, with few repeated characters and Mitchell's pedantic preoccupation with correct language usage. Of course, when they were staging their own Cambridge revue in the late 1990s, David, Rob, Olivia and Co. had groaned with nerves in the Footlights clubroom as they gazed up at an old, torn poster that dominated the room, for *The Cellar Tapes*, and damned their hopes of achieving comparable fame.

Patriarchal privilege is a reality, and only one colleague's sexual bent keeps Fry & Laurie from the full package of rich, white, male and straight, but as this narrative has surely shown, neither star could be accused of not having worked to get where they are. 'People don't want to know that,' Stephen told Clive James in 2007, 'And now never more so in our culture, if you tell someone, "Yes, I can tell you where the golden palace is, and I can tell you how to get there – it's a very long, hard climb though, and you'll blister your knees and hurt yourself and fall down and have to start climbing again", they'll go "Oh, in that case I don't want it, but you're so lucky to get there." I'm not saying I've got to the golden palace, but what attributes I have are ones that I've worked at and run towards with enthusiasm, and people now seem to think not only that it's unfair, but that it's their right to be given it without making the same journey, and that'll never happen on this Earth.' It's been a while since Footlights produced anyone of note, but the Oxbridge system still in many ways acts as scaffold for the British entertainment industry. However, Stephen continues, 'I know it must be sickening to hear it, for people who want to make a career in comedy and think, "It's just because you went to private schools and Cambridge" – and maybe it is, I don't know. I can't think that's the only reason, it seems odd if it is. And I apologise, I did my very best not ever to go to a public school by being expelled from three of them, so I think I can in some way let myself off.'

The TV landscape in which Fry & Laurie's successors ply their trade is of course vastly different to the one in which *ABOF&L* was forged – this story has been one of a lost world. Already begrudgingly acknowledged is the sale of BBC TV Centre, and the fact that *ABOF&L*'s Room 7008 could be your bathroom, if you have the requisite million pounds loose upon your person, and with the North Acton rehearsal rooms also long demolished, the system that gave us *ABOF&L* has disappeared. 'Hugh and I were both immensely aware from the very first, when we recorded the Footlights' show in 1982, we couldn't believe we were there at TV Centre, with the *Top of the Pops* audiences queuing outside and the sitcoms being recorded – and it was an absolutely *alive* place, buzzing everywhere! It absolutely was the centre of broadcasting.' 'We were incredibly lucky to arrive on the scene – and it is a scene – when we did, so much was about timing, we'd never have a chance like that now, it would be a completely different story. The audience has so fragmented. When we were doing *Jeeves & Wooster*, for example, 10 million people would watch, and that wasn't even considered an especially gigantic hit – now if you can get 2 million people to watch a show you're enormous!' Of all TV formats, sketch comedy is the most glaringly absent from today's TV schedules, and Jon Plowman says, 'Sketch comedy has got lost, because TV has become more competitive, more channels against each other. Comedy is risky, and sketch comedy the most risky bit, so channels are loath to go there. Most channel controllers say, "We just want hits", and you think, "Oh damn, and I was going to offer you a copper-bottomed disaster!" It's a while since we had a controller who realises that in order to get hits you have to have some flops, and see what sticks.' In 2013's *David Frost on Sketch Shows*, Fry told the late interviewer, 'Sketch comedy has come to a sort of end . . . a turning perhaps, a bend in the river. It's a young person's game, comedy, and I think young people are more and more drawn to stand up than they are to revue, but even as I speak, there will be a group of people who met at a university or college somewhere who will be planning to go up to Edinburgh this year, who will be noticed and get an award, like the League of Gentlemen or so many others, Mitchell & Webb, you know, a lot of them double acts more specifically, but that's still sketch comedy.'

Plowman keenly volunteers to offer his services for any Fry & Laurie reunion, but what form would such a lap of honour take? Hugh has spoken of 'A sort of Flanders & Swann-type stage revue with a couple of wing chairs and a rug and a decanter of Madeira; m'colleague will recount amusing stories and I will sit at the piano and play ditties. I know no more than that – we have not advanced with this idea but that would be my pick of the way to go.' 'I think a run in a theatre would probably be most fun,' Fry agrees. 'It's more direct than recording sketches in a studio. Just to go on the road and play theatres and things, not necessarily stadiums exactly but nice places. Never say never! Now that I'm not an entirely unstable drug fiend flake and Hugh is an even better musician, we could have great fun if we could be bothered to get off our arses. We keep talking about it, but we'll be dead soon – or seventy, before we know where we are. I see him as often as possible . . . and we just fit right back into our old modes of speech and silliness and it's divine.' 'We will probably go to our graves talking about it like two old duffers,' Hugh continues. 'I certainly hope we do something. We're not very good at planning, to be honest, we don't have a Sasco year planner, which is something we keep meaning to get, with the months written on it so we can say, "Invade Poland in February!" We just bumble along without ever really planning what we're going to do.'

Career-wise, then, they may still be the same two friends falling down stairs together, but the thirtieth anniversary of the first broadcast of *ABOF&L* finds Fry & Laurie in a very good place. It's often in

America, but that is always the direction in which their careers have been pointed. Hugh has of course for many years based himself at home and in LA with success, but Stephen has become a figure it's impossible to imagine not being part of the weave of British culture and public life – be it offering top value for money on any chat show couch, or showing up to the odd Royal Wedding. Not only has he had TV documentaries made to celebrate his career, with his half-century celebrated in *50 Not Out!*, there was even *Fry Night*, a whole evening on BBC Four devoted to his doings, and chief among the talking heads paying tribute was HRH Prince Charles, still a close friend. The Prince described his Norfolk neighbour as 'A jolly good egg. I can never get over the range of his knowledge and understanding, whenever talking to him it's absolutely fascinating, because he knows about everything. I always worry about him, I keep saying "You're doing too much". The country's incredibly lucky to have someone like Stephen. Fortunately we still produce people like that.' And yet, the tawdry voice of the people rises, with most of the cast of the Prince's favourite sitcom, *Blackadder*, all having gongs of some kind – including Hugh Laurie, CBE – how has his colleague somehow not become Lord Fry of St James's Park? 'If I had been offered an award and turned it down, to say so would be the height of impropriety – which is not to say that I have been! It may be that I have been snubbed all my life, and sit crying in the corner wondering why. It's the equivalent of never being asked to do *Desert Island Discs* – "Here I am without so much as an MBE to my name!" It's not something that concerns me. Of course, honours are nothing to do with the Royal Family. I've been partially responsible for ensuring that at least ten people have been given honours, which is why I know the system, and it's a preposterous one. I would say two things, firstly there's the story of the German philosopher whose students asked, "Sir, you are said to be one of the greatest philosophers in Germany, why do you have no statue?" And he said, "You know, in life, it's very wonderful to be asked why there is no statue of you. It is very terrible to be asked why there *is* . . ." So, I would rather people ask why there isn't. And the other point is, look at the great American icons – awful word, but we'll use it. Imagine if they had our system, would Frank Sinatra be in any way more Frank Sinatra if he was a Sir? He would be diminished!

Dame Katharine Hepburn? Sir Bruce Springsteen? You know? Keep your name – we all have titles, mine is "Mister", and I want that to be used only rarely, otherwise call me Stephen. That's my name.'

Unquestionably, the greatest change in Stephen's life came when he married comedian Elliott Spencer in January 2015 – there was all the gossip about the couple's thirty-year age difference, as there would have been were they a heterosexual couple (and indeed, as there has been, for some of Fry's hetero contemporaries), but this is all so much fluff, and no newly-weds could be more demonstrably delirious in their happiness – Stephen proudly displaying his wedding ring on Jonathan Ross's chat show. 'It's genuine happiness too,' sister Jo says. 'The Fry family are a funny lot, when we get together it's all rather formal, but we absolutely adore each other, and our parents are formidable – eighty-four, eighty-seven, and still on good form, driving, emailing. They're generous and optimistic people who value happiness above all else, and I overheard my mother saying to Elliott one Christmas just before the marriage was announced, how happy they were that Stephen had someone like him in his life.' Stephen is embarking on a new chapter, having collected up credits expanding his stateside reputation in Hugh's wake, from a grotesque turn in *The Hobbit* (his long friendship with Peter Jackson has also led to scripting a long-gestated remake of *The Dam Busters*) to playing PM Alastair Davies in *24: Live Another Day*, and he has moved his base to California for now. The CBS sitcom *The Great Indoors* only lasted one season, but his regular role as ex-adventurer and dipsomaniac magazine proprietor Roland, father figure to *Community*'s Joel McHale, did let him share his unquenchable love of language with a fresh crowd – with online videos, *Words with Stephen Fry*, exploring etymological oddities for a millennial audience. In 2017 he hit sixty, but despite his warmer environs, retirement is of course unthinkable: 'To me, work is the nice life. The idea of spending six months a year in Barbados mixing with rich trash is horrible. I'm terrified of being overcome by lassitude and not having energy to do new things. As you walk through life you see an oasis on the horizon and think, "That will do me!" The moment you reach it, you see another. I thrive on that pressure, but most of what I do isn't terribly hard. I don't have to "disappear" into a character in some terrible way.' Besides acting, he's been busy recording the entire

Holmes *oeuvre* and writing his own retellings of Greek myths, *Mythos*, so there's no flagging just yet. In early 2018 Stephen announced that he had undergone surgery to defeat prostate cancer, so let's hope there's a few aeons left for some form of Fry & Laurie comedy comeback.

Hugh also stars in an American sitcom, but a different kind to *The Great Indoors*' live studio audience affair – Armando Iannucci's *Veep* was a brilliantly realised instant satirical classic before and after Laurie joined as Senator Tom James, it's just a shame that the reality of the US Presidency has now entirely outstripped all possible satire – and also that Laurie did not appear in the sixth season episode 'Georgia', in which Fry cameoed as a poisoned Russian oligarch. Of late, Hugh has been in the UK with probably misguided whispers abroad of a second series for his long-gestated and eventually award-laden le Carré adaptation *The Night Manager*, which he produced and starred in alongside Olivia Colman and Tom Hiddleston, playing Richard Roper – by far the most despicable character in his CV to date, the Laurie charm taking him to new places as an actor. His latest sojourn on the US West Coast was for the second season of *Chance*, for Hulu – another doctor role, but this time Eldon Chance, a San Francisco forensic neuropsychiatrist with dark secrets.

This makes Stephen & Hugh LA neighbours, a few valleys apart, as *ABOF&L*'s thirtieth hoves into view, but of course neither has gone the full Dudley – besides, Stephen adds, as actors they spend most of their year on film sets all round the world, so where their socks are stored becomes less of an issue. Many have asked Fry why he would choose now to make the USA his primary base, but Trump's America is hardly any more beyond the pale than Brexit Britain. And so, as the Californian sun goes down, the colleagues find time to get together, sit under the lemon trees, and laugh. 'I get terribly upset when I hear people spreading malicious rumours about Laurel not getting on with Hardy and everything, and I'm sure that's a lie, I can't bear the thought of it,' says Fry, and Laurie adds, 'Right at the beginning, wherever that meeting took place, we made each other laugh. And we continue to do so to this day.'

When they were but young, broad-shouldered, long-fingered comedians, Fry & Laurie were asked by the tabloids what they would put on each other's tombstones. 'I'll probably put "A very Interesting

Man", Hugh responded. 'Anything more elaborate would embarrass him. But to my own grave I'll take the memory of the hours and hours and hours we've spent laughing together.' Stephen spared no blushes: 'When Hugh dies I know exactly what I'll put on his tombstone: "Thank you, God, for letting me know him."' But we all of course hope such talk is premature by many a decade – and that this *Soupy Twists!* story will need updating, once their hectic separate schedules somehow finally allow us an autumnal offering from Britain's most sophisticated comedy double act – never has this maddening country more deserved their particular brand of loving hatred.

As yet, of course, a further 'Bit of Fry & Laurie' is but a vision – a vision of smooth cocktail blues, greasy corporate horror men, dragged-up *Daily Mail* readers, perverse authority figures, awkward spies, pig-eyed sacks of shit, outrageously obstreperous shopkeepers, loony toffs, heartless doctors, references to bottoms and Cocteau, good old Berent's cocoa, sloblocks, pink fluffiness, *Daily Mail*-baiting, inked ravens of despair, vulvas, Opal Fruits, Bath Olivers, cream, heaps of cream and lawnmowers, light metal, ruthless subversion of family values, Tideyman's carpets, tsunamis of dizzying English verbiage, family heritage urine, and fun amenity vomit. But soon, soon, with luck, sincerity, and steadfast voting, it may become a reality.

A BIT OF A FRY & LAURIE GUIDE

TV & RADIO
CAMBRIDGE FOOTLIGHTS REVUE
TX 20/05/1982 BBC2 (*The Cellar Tapes*) Written and performed by Penny Dwyer, Stephen Fry, Hugh Laurie, Paul Shearer, Tony Slattery and Emma Thompson. Directed by John Kilby. Produced by Dennis Main Wilson.
THE CRYSTAL CUBE
TX 07/07/1983 BBC2 Written and performed by Stephen Fry & Hugh Laurie, with Emma Thompson. Directed and produced by John Kilby.
SATURDAY NIGHT FRY
TX 19/12/1987, 30/04/1988–04/06/1988 BBC Radio 4 Written and performed by Stephen Fry, with additional material from Ian Brown & James Hendrie. Featuring Hugh Laurie, Emma Thompson, Jim Broadbent, Julia Hills, Phyllida Law, Robert Bathurst and Barry Cryer. Produced by Dan Patterson.
ABOF&L PILOT
Rec 8–9 Dec 1987, TX 26/12/1987 BBC2 Written and performed by Stephen Fry & Hugh Laurie. Directed and produced by Roger Ordish.
ABOF&L SERIES 1
Rec Dec 1988–Jan 1989, TX 13/01/1989–17/02/1989 BBC2 Written and performed by Stephen Fry & Hugh Laurie, with Deborah Norton. Featuring Dimitri Andreas and Benjamin Whitrow. Directed and produced by Roger Ordish.
ABOF&L SERIES 2
Rec Jan–Feb 1990, TX 09/03/1990–13/04/1990 BBC2 Written and performed by Stephen Fry & Hugh Laurie. Featuring Rowan Atkinson, Julia Binstead, Camille Coduri, Nigel Havers, Tony Hawks, Geoffrey McGivern, Ralph Michael, Anne Reid, Liz Smith, Harriet Thorpe and Paul Whitehouse. Directed and produced by Roger Ordish and Nick Symons.
ABOF&L SERIES 3
Rec July–Aug 1991, TX 09/01/1992–13/02/1992 BBC2 Written and performed by Stephen Fry & Hugh Laurie. Featuring Kay Adshead, Morwenna Banks, John Grillo, Geoffrey McGivern, Nicholas Parsons, Rebecca Saire, Steve Steen, Jo Unwin. COCKTAILS: 1) Whisky Thunder 2) A Slow Snog with a Distant Relative 3) Everything in the Till & No Sudden Moves 4) A Mug of Horlicks 5) Beef Goulash

6) Berliner Credit Sequence. Directed by Kevin Bishop. Produced by Kevin Bishop & Nick Symons.
ABOF&L SERIES 4
Rec Feb–April 1994, TX 12/02/1995–26/03/1995 BBC1 Written and performed by Stephen Fry & Hugh Laurie. Featuring: 1) John Bird & Jane Booker (Golden Meteorite) 2) Kevin McNally & Fiona Gillies (Long Confident Suck) 3) Clive Mantle & Imelda 'Snutty' Staunton (South Seas Vulvic Wart) 4) Patrick Barlow & Caroline Quentin (A Quick One with You, Stephen) 5) Stephen Moore & Phyllida Law (Swinging Ballsack) 6) Nobody (The Silver Prostate) 7) Robert Daws & Janine Duvitski (A Modern Britain). Directed by Bob Spiers. Produced by Jon Plowman.
FRY & LAURIE HOST A CHRISTMAS NIGHT WITH THE STARS
TX 27/12/1994 BBC2 Presented by Stephen Fry & Hugh Laurie. Directed by Geoff Posner. Produced by Claudia Lloyd.
HYSTERIA!
Stage directed by Stephen Fry. *Hysteria! Hysteria! Hysteria!* recorded at the Victoria Palace Theatre, 07/06/1987; *Hysteria II; The Second Coming* at Sadler's Wells Theatre, 23/09/1989; *Hysteria 3* at the London Palladium, 30/06/1991.
JEEVES & WOOSTER – 1990–1993 ITV
Series 1 TX 22/04/1990–20/05/1990; Series 2 TX 14/04/1991–19/05/1991; Series 3 TX 29/03/1992–03/05/1992; Series 4 TX 16/05/1993–20/06/1993 All series adapted from the P. G. Wodehouse stories by Clive Exton. Directed by Robert Young (series 1), Simon Langton (series 2) & Ferdinand Fairfax (series 3 and 4). Produced by Brian Eastman for Granada.
LIVE FROM THE LIGHTHOUSE
TX 28/11/1998 CHANNEL 4 Presented by Stephen Fry. Directed by Geoff Posner. Produced by Geoff Posner, Jeremy Salsby and David Tyler.
COMEDY CONNECTIONS – FRY & LAURIE
TX 04/04/2005 BBC1 Produced by Gregor Sharp for BBC Scotland.
INSIDE THE ACTOR'S STUDIO: HUGH LAURIE
TX 31/07/2006 Bravo Written and presented by James Lipton. Directed by Joe Wurtz. Produced by Joe Wurtz and Sabrina Fodor.
STEPHEN FRY WEEKEND
TX 17–18/08/2007 BBC4 Two evenings of programming celebrating Fry's fiftieth birthday, including documentaries *50 Not Out* and *Guilty Pleasures*. Produced by Sophie Deveson for BBC.
FRY & LAURIE REUNITED
TX 24/11/2010 UK Gold Directed and produced by Mike Riley for Tiger Aspect.
A LIFE ON SCREEN: STEPHEN FRY
TX 29/12/2015 BBC2 Directed and produced by Samantha Peters for BAFTA and BBC.

BOOKS
A Bit of Fry & Laurie (Mandarin 1990); *A Bit More Fry & Laurie* (Heinemann, 1991); *3 Bits of Fry & Laurie* (Heinemann, 1992); *A Bit of Fry & Laurie 4* (Methuen, 1995) **STEPHEN FRY** *Me and My Girl* (with Noel Gay, Douglas Furber, L. Arthur Rose, Mike Ockrent) (Samuel French 1990); *The Liar* (Heinemann, 1991); *Paperweight* (Heinemann, 1992); *The Hippopotamus* (Random House, 1994); *Making History* (Random House, 1996); *Moab Is My Washpot* (Random House, 1997); *The Stars'*

Soupy Twists!

Tennis Balls (Hutchinson, 2000); *Stephen Fry's Incomplete and Utter History of Classical Music* (with Tim Lihoreau) (Boxtree, 2004); *The Ode Less Travelled* (Hutchinson, 2005); *Stephen Fry in America* (HarperCollins, 2008); *Last Chance to See* (with Mark Carwardine) (HarperCollins, 2009); *The Fry Chronicles* (Michael Joseph, 2010); *More Fool Me* (Michael Joseph, 2014); *Mythos* (Michael Joseph, 2017)
HUGH LAURIE *The Gun Seller* (Heinemann, 1996)

TV DOCUMENTARIES (Selected)
STEPHEN FRY *The Secret Life of the Manic Depressive* (2006); *HIV and Me* (2007); *Stephen Fry and the Gutenberg Press* (2008); *Stephen Fry in America* (2008); *Last Chance to See* (2009); *Stephen Fry on Wagner* (2010); *Stephen Fry's 100 Greatest Gadgets* (2011); *Fry's Planet Word* (2011); *Gadget Man* (2012); *Stephen Fry's Key to the City* (2013); *Stephen Fry: Out There* (2013); *Stephen Fry Live: More Fool Me* (2014); *Stephen Fry in Central America* (2015); *The Not So Secret Life of the Manic Depressive* (2016)
HUGH LAURIE *Perspectives: Down by the River* (2011); *Copper Bottom Blues* (2013)

VHS/DVD/BLU-RAY (Selected) *Hysteria!* (Palace Video, 1988); *Hysteria 2* (Palace Video, 1990); *A Bit of Fry & Laurie* (BBC Video, 1994); *Peter's Friends* (Eiv DVD 2001); *Bright Young Things,* (Warner Bros, 2004); *Jeeves & Wooster* (ITV Studios, 2005); *The Secret Life of the Manic Depressive* (Digital Classics, 2005); *A Bit of Fry & Laurie: The Complete Collection* (2 Entertain, 2006); *Hysteria 3* (Laughing Stock, 2007); *Stephen Fry in America* (Digital Classics, 2008); *Blackadder Rides Again* (BBC1, 2008); *Blackadder Remastered* (BBC DVD 2009); *Alfresco: The Complete Series* (Network, 2009); *Last Chance to See* (Digital Classics, 2009); *Wagner & Me* (Digital Classics, 2010); *Stephen Fry and the Gutenberg Press* (Digital Classics, 2011); *Hugh Laurie Live on the Queen Mary* (Eagle Rock, 2013); *Stephen Fry Live: More Fool Me* (Amazon download, 2014)

AUDIO (Selected) *The World of Jeeves & Wooster* (EMI, 1993); *A Bit of Fry & Laurie* (BBC Laughing Stock, 1994); *Fry's English Delight* (BBC Radio 4, 2008–17); *Saturday Night Fry* (2 Entertain, 2009); Hugh Laurie *Let Them Talk* (Warner Bros, 2011); Hugh Laurie *Didn't It Rain?* (Warner Bros, 2013); *Stephen Fry in His Own Words* (BBC Audio, 2013); *Hugh Laurie's Blues Changes* (BBC Radio 2, 2015)

GAMES (Selected) *Fable* series, Big Blue Box, Lionhead Studios 2004–10; *LittleBigPlanet 3* (Sumo Digital, 2014)

FURTHER BIBLIOGRAPHY (Selected) Adams, Douglas (ed.) and Fincham, Peter (ed.), *The Utterly Utterly Merry Comic Relief Christmas Book* (Fontana, 1986); Bradbury, David & McGrath, Joe, *Now That's Funny!* (Methuen, 1998); Elton, Ben, *Gasping* (Sphere, 1990); Ferris, Stewart, *Tish & Pish* (Somersdale, 2005); Fielding, Helen, *Cause Celeb* (Picador, 1994); Fry, Edna, *Mrs Fry's Diary* (Hodder & Stoughton, 2011), *How to Have an Almost Perfect Marriage* (Unbound, 2014); Gray, Simon, *Fat Chance* (Faber & Faber, 1995); Hewison, Robert, *Footlights!* (Methuen, 1984); Hind, John, *The Comic Inquisition* (Virgin Books, 1991); Marks, Laurence & Gran, Maurice, *The B'Stard Files* (David & Charles, 1988); Mayer, Lise (ed.) and Swann, Rachell (ed.), *Amassed Hysteria* (Penguin, 1991); Tavener, Mark, *In the Red* (Hutchinson, 1989); Various, *The Utterly,*

Utterly Amusing and Pretty Damn Definitive Comic Relief Revue Book (Penguin, 1989); Various, *Peter Cook Remembered* (Mandarin, 1997); Wilde, Oscar, *Stephen Fry Presents Oscar Wilde's Stories for All Ages* (HarperCollins, 2009)

FURTHER VIDEOGRAPHY/AUDIOGRAPHY (Selected) *Blackadder: The Whole Rotten Dynasty* (GOLD, 2008); *Britain's Best Sitcom: Blackadder* (BBC2, 2004); *Briefings* (BBC Parliament, 2008); *Robert Llewellyn's Carpool* (Online, 2010); *Charlie Rose* (CBS, 2013); *Clive Anderson All Talk* (BBC1, 1996); *Clive Anderson All Talk* (Channel 4, 1993); *Clive James Talking in the Library* (Sky Arts, 2007); *Comedy from Merton to Enfield: Stephen Fry* (ITV, 2003); *The Culture Show: The Sounds of Hugh Laurie* (BBC1, 2011); *Danny Baker Radio Show* (BBC Radio 5 Live, 2013); *Desert Island Discs* (BBC Radio 4, 1996, 2015); *First on Four: Saturday Live* (Channel 4, 1998); *Friday Night with Jonathan Ross* (BBC1, 2009); *Frost on Sketch Shows* (BBC4, 2013); *TV AM* (ITV, 1991); *In Confidence* (Sky Arts, 2011); *Jay Leno* (NBC, 2006); *Living the Life* (Sky Arts, 2011); *Larry King Now* (Online, 2013, 2016); *The Late Late Show with Craig Ferguson* (CBS, 2010, 2011, 2014); *The Late Show* (BBC2, 1995); *Loose Ends* (BBC Radio 4); *News on ABC* (ABC, 2011); *Open to Question* (Channel 4, 1989); *Parkinson* (BBC1, 1999, 2000, 2003, 2007); *Saturday Night Clive* (BBC1, 1992); *The South Bank Show: Beyond the Footlights* (ITV, 2008); *Wogan* (BBC1, 1990, 1991)

PERIODICALS (Selected) *Cambridge Evening News; East Anglian Daily Times; Deadpan magazine; Flicks; GQ; The Guardian; The Independent; The Listener; Loaded; Daily Mail; Daily Mirror; Morning Star; The New York Times; Oxford Mail; Playboy; Radio Times; Shropshire Star; Smash Hits; The Sun; Tatler; Daily Telegraph; The Times; The Times Literary Supplement; Today; TV Guide; TV Times; Woman's Own*

WEBLINKS (Selected) BFI: bfi.org.uk; Comic Relief: comicrelief.com; The Footlights: footlights.org; Hugh Laurie official: hughlaurieblues.com; QI official: qi.com; Stephen Fry official: stephenfry.com

UNSEEN EXTRACTS FROM THE FRY & LAURIE ARCHIVE

TWO UNDERGRADUATES

STEPHEN AND HUGH ARE PART OF A DOCUMENTARY ABOUT THEMSELVES.

STEPHEN: I remember when I met Hugh, I thought, "Wow! Like, this guy is seriously deranged. This is psychopathy taken to – what? – the nth like degree." He was really into this punting on the river and wearing blazers.

CUT TO:

HUGH: See, like the thing about Stephen at Cambridge, was like, he was this animal, you know? I met him when he was writing an essay on George Eliot's 'Middlemarch' and I thought, this is weird, like weird-weird, you see what I'm saying?

STEPHEN: I mean the way he like spread butter on crumpets and poured a glass of Pimm's. It just said 'freak'. Who is this guy? I don't want him near me. This is like angst in your pangst. Like look out Brother Karamazov and

	look out Kafka, this guy -- just in the way he pays for a May Ball ticket -- it's dangerous. Too dangerous. Is he for real?
HUGH:	There was this whole existential anti-karma about his anger, his like TOTAL rage when he was busted for stepping out of line. I remember the senior tutor fined him for leaving a champagne bottle on the steps outside his rooms and he like literally he turned, on a sixpence, into this screwed-up ball of like street fury.
STEPHEN:	So much frigging pain, you know?
VOICE:	(OFF) Do you like him?
STEPHEN:	Like him? He's an event. He's a system, a force, a pathological state. I hate the bastard.
HUGH:	I love him. Love him like you love a pizza. Hate. I hate him.

17/2/91 SPIES TAXI

STEPHEN HAILS A CAB, SOMEWHERE IN LONDON. HE IS IN BOWLER HAT AND GREATCOAT. HUGH, AS TONY, IS DRIVING THE CAB STEPHEN GETS IN.

STEPHEN:	Grosvenor Square, please, and drive quite quickly if you wouldn't mind.
HUGH:	Grosvenor Square. Right you are guvnor. (LOOKS IN THE MIRROR) Wait a minute. This is an extraordinary event.
STEPHEN:	What is, driver?
HUGH:	If it isn't my old friend and former boss Control, head of Britain's Secret Service.
STEPHEN:	Well well. Tony Murchison, who once worked for me and whom I had the unfortunate job of having to sack only a few years ago.
HUGH:	Yes.
STEPHEN:	Mmm. Grosvenor Square please.

HUGH: Oh yes of course. I nearly forgot that that was where you wanted to go in no uncertain terms.

HUGH DRIVES ON

STEPHEN: So Tony, how has life been treating you since last we met? You appear from all appearances to have landed on your feet, at any rate.

HUGH: Well my bottom, really, Control.

STEPHEN: I beg your pardon?

HUGH: You see, driving a taxi is a sedentary occupation, which calls for more sitting down than an old cold warrior espiocrat like myself is used to.

STEPHEN: Ah. So you're a taxi driver, then?

HUGH: Yes, Control. The employment situation in this country dictated that I become a taxi driver in order to earn enough money to live on.

STEPHEN: I see.

HUGH: And how are things at Fripton House, the headquarters of the Secret Service, and my old stamping ground?

STEPHEN: Well of course I shouldn't really be telling a common taxi driver details of my work as Britain's top spymaster, but seeing as it's you, Tony, I think I can say that it's pretty much a case of business as usual.

HUGH: Oh good. You haven't been too snowed under with recent unhappy events in the East European former Yugoslavia as was region?

STEPHEN: What unhappy events would those be, Tony?

HUGH: Well I suppose I was referring to the full-scale war between Serbs, Croats and Muslims, Control.

STEPHEN: Mm. I'd not actually heard that about this, Tony. I've been so busy organising the Departmental squash ladder, that I have allowed my in-tray to become a little fuller than I'd like.

HUGH: Control, I don't want to alarm you, but I think we may be being followed.

CONTROL LOOKS OUT OF THE WINDOW.

HUGH: Probably best if you don't turn round and look out of the window, Control.

STEPHEN: Ha. I can see you've not lost your touch, Tony. What does he look like, perhaps you can tell me?

HUGH: Age about sixty, brown hair, blue raincoat.

STEPHEN: Mmm. What sort of car is he driving?

HUGH: (CHECKING IN THE MIRROR) He's not actually driving a car, Control. He's a pedestrian.

STEPHEN: Ah. Worrying all the same. Whatever shall we do?

HUGH: I could put my foot down and try and lose him Control?

STEPHEN: That would be very kind, Tony. There's an extra five pounds in it for you if you succeed.

HUGH: (HANDING THERMOS OVER HIS SHOULDER) Help yourself to some coffee from my thermos flask, Control, and sit back and enjoy the ride.

TONY SETS HIS MOUTH IN A GRIM LINE AND THE SCENERY MOVES PAST A LITTLE QUICKER.

STEPHEN: Excellent coffee, Tony. It really takes me back. Any luck, meanwhile, with shaking off our pursuer?

HUGH: He is standing on the pavement with an expression of baffled rage, Control,

	shaking his fist in frustration at having been so expertly outsmarted. I think we may have shaken him off.
STEPHEN:	Well done, Tony. I wonder if he was someone known to us.
HUGH:	I'm not sure Control. I know I've seen him before.
STEPHEN:	You have?
HUGH:	Yes. He was my last passenger.
STEPHEN:	Interesting. He has a ride in your taxi and then immediately starts a dogged pursuit on foot. Some old ghost from your professional past who has risen up to haunt you perhaps.
HUGH:	Perhaps. (THEY HAVE ARRIVED) Grosvenor Square, Control. The American Embassy. I expect you've got some liaising to do.
STEPHEN:	Hush-mum is the word, Tony. Here's that extra five pounds for dodging our tail.
HUGH:	No, no, Control. This one is on me. For old times' sake.
STEPHEN:	Well that's exceptionally quite kind of you, Tony, thanks.
HUGH:	Don't forget your briefcase, Control.
STEPHEN:	Briefcase?
HUGH:	(INDICATING THE BACK SEAT) That one.
STEPHEN:	That's not my briefcase, Tony.
HUGH:	Oh. (PAUSE) I wonder if...
STEPHEN:	Voh!

2/1/90 ETIQUETTE

STEPHEN AND HUGH ARE IN THEIR AREA. HUGH IS READING A MOTORBIKE MAGAZINE, BURPING CONSTANTLY. STEPHEN IS WRITING LETTERS AT A DESK. EVERY NOW AND AGAIN HE LOOKS UP TO THE POSTER OF DEREK RANDALL FOR INSPIRATION. HUGH BURPS. STEPHEN TUTS. HUGH BURPS TWICE.

STEPHEN: Arnold, old love?
HUGH: (BURP) Yes?
STEPHEN: Must you belch so?
HUGH: Belch?
STEPHEN: Belch, keck, retch, repeat, burp.
HUGH: What's wrong with burping?
STEPHEN: Scarcely etiquette, is it old dear?
HUGH: (BURPING) Bugger etiquette.
STEPHEN: Mm. (HUGH BURPS) Have you ever wondered, Arnold my lovelet, why it is that you earn forty pounds a month as a short hand cook while I am regarded as one of the most promising psalmists of my generation?
HUGH: (BURP) No. Why is it?
STEPHEN: Etiquette, manners, style.
HUGH: Oh yeah?
STEPHEN: What do etiquette, élan, brio and panache all have in common?
HUGH: They are all available in eau de toilette or original perfume spray?
STEPHEN: They are all passports to success, Arnold. Look, try this. Say after me. "The rain in Spain falls mainly on the plain."
HUGH: (SLOWLY) In Dagoland it mostly pisses down on the flat bits.
STEPHEN: Oh dear oh deary.
HUGH: Are you saying I'll never make something of myself unless I speak better?
STEPHEN: It's not just that, Arnold my pleasant. Do you remember yesterday when you and I stopped off at the Castle Hotel to relieve ourselves? (HUGH BURPS ASSENT) As we entered, someone came out of a cubicle. Do you remember how you greeted him?
HUGH: Poo! Fwor! Did you make that horrible stink?

STEPHEN: Exactly. Was that polite, Arnold? Did it put the unfortunate gentleman at his ease? Do you feel you made a friend of him?
HUGH: But it was a horrible guff.
STEPHEN: Horrible or otherwise as the guff may or may not have been, Arnold, you showed a distressing lack of etiquette. You should have passed it off with a light remark. 'Good morning, sir. Fine traffic we are having for the time of year.' Something like that.
HUGH: Right.

THEY RESUME THEIR WORKING AND READING ATTITUDES. THERE IS A DISTINCT FARTING NOISE. STEPHEN APPEARS OBLIVIOUS. HUGH LOOKS UP. AFTER A WHILE HUGH WRINKLES HIS NOSTRILS.

HUGH: Oi.
STEPHEN: Yes?
HUGH: Good morning, sir. Fine traffic we are having for the time of year.
STEPHEN: Doh.

4/1/90 COFFEE

BUSINESS MEETING. STEPHEN ENGLISH. HUGH AMERICAN.

STEPHEN: (HANDING HUGH A COFFEE) There you go. White no sugar, I think you said.
HUGH: Thanks, Greg. I'm sorry, but I really can't get on top of the case without coffee.
STEPHEN: No, right. Now then.
HUGH: I wish you'd have let me buy you a cup of coffee.
STEPHEN: No well that's alright.
HUGH: Maybe I can buy you a cup of coffee tomorrow?
STEPHEN: That'd be great. Now I think what we should be looking at is how we're going

	to present this option to the various people who've expressed an interest...
HUGH:	Mm. Great coffee.
STEPHEN:	Oh good.
HUGH:	I oughta come here more often.
STEPHEN:	Right! Now, when I showed the plans to Sarah, she felt that...
HUGH:	How d'you make this?
STEPHEN:	The coffee?
HUGH:	Yeah.
STEPHEN:	Well, a spoonful of coffee with some hot water.
HUGH:	You make it sound so simple.
STEPHEN:	Well it is fairly simple.
HUGH:	Greg, I like you.
STEPHEN:	Good. Now Sarah felt that when we travel to Paris, we should try to fix up a meeting with...
HUGH:	Beautiful city, Paris.
STEPHEN:	Yes, it is lovely.
HUGH:	You ever been to a restaurant called the Seven Moons?
STEPHEN:	In Paris?
HUGH:	No, Philadelphia.
STEPHEN:	No, I haven't.
HUGH:	My God, the coffee there is unbelievable.
STEPHEN:	Is it?
HUGH:	I don't mean to put your coffee down, Greg, cos this is great coffee, but if you're ever out Philadelphia way, be sure and do yourself a favour and try some of their coffee.
STEPHEN:	I'll do that. If the Board approves our idea, then Sarah feels...
HUGH:	I gotta tell you, my wife makes terrible coffee. Just terrible. I don't know what

	she puts in it. But this... this is good coffee, Greg. Fine coffee.
STEPHEN:	Thank you very much indeed.
HUGH:	You're welcome.
STEPHEN:	Now. (WAITS TO SEE IF HE'S GOING TO BE INTERRUPTED) I think...
HUGH:	Best cup of coffee I ever tasted was Buffalo City Train Station. You ever been there?
STEPHEN:	No.
HUGH:	No, kinda hard to get to. You can take a train, obviously.
STEPHEN:	Obviously.
HUGH:	It's a five-hour journey from Detroit, but by God it's worth it. That coffee is out of this world.
STEPHEN:	You go there just for the coffee?
HUGH:	Hell, yes. I'd go anywhere for a good cup of coffee. A good cup of coffee is something that you can't put a price on. I sometimes think...
STEPHEN:	CHRIST!!!!!
HUGH:	Pardon me?
STEPHEN:	Will you shut up about your bastarding coffee!!!
HUGH:	Is there something wrong?
STEPHEN:	It's a drink! It's a hot drink! It's not a religious experience, it's hot water with some ground up coffee beans in it!
HUGH:	I'm gonna have to disagree with you there, Greg.
STEPHEN:	Oh God!
HUGH:	(SINGS)

4/1/90 CLIVE & CLYVE

A ROOM, SOMEWHERE IN ENGLAND: HUGH AND STEPHEN, THE STARS OF THIS PARTICULAR TELEVISION SHOW THAT WE ARE

ALL IN THE BUSINESS OF MAKING, ARE STANDING RIGHT IN IT. YES INDEED.

STEPHEN: Would you like to sit down?

HUGH: Thank you very much indeed.

STEPHEN: Perhaps it would be best for all concerned if you sat down on that chair there, right there.

HUGH: I'm going to sit down on this chair right here, as per your suggestion.

STEPHEN: Good. I think, just to add a bit of variety, I'll sit down over here.

HUGH: That's a very nice shirt you're wearing today.

STEPHEN: Thank you. I bought it.

HUGH: So. How do you fancy England's chances in the World Cup football competition that's contested by various nations every four years?

STEPHEN: I think that, barring accidents and other unforeseen accidents, the English football team who represent England have a very good chance of doing quite well.

HUGH: Would you put money on that in the form of some sort of wager or bet with another party who would have to pay you a return on your investment if England did indeed do quite well?

STEPHEN: No.

HUGH: So. You're not one of those people who gambles money on the unpredictable outcomes of sporting competitions?

STEPHEN: No. If my relationship with my mother has taught me one thing, it's that you're better off not.

HUGH: Mm.

STEPHEN: Mmm.

HUGH: That really is a very nice shirt you're wearing today.
STEPHEN: Thank you. I have only one shirt that is nicer than this, and at the moment I'm afraid to say it's being repaired.
HUGH: That's the trouble with really nice shirts. They're great when they work, but when they go wrong they can be absolutely maddening.
STEPHEN: Exactly. Sometimes you wonder whether it's worth it.
HUGH: That could have been me talking, it could really.
STEPHEN: It would have been surprising if it were, though, would it not?
HUGH: Surprising, alarming and not a little impossible.
STEPHEN: Clive?
HUGH: That's my name.
STEPHEN: Yes. I hope you don't mind me using it as a means of attracting your attention.
HUGH: Not in the least.
STEPHEN: Clive?
HUGH: Hello, you've attracted my attention there. How may I be of service or help to you?
STEPHEN: I have been drinking a number of warm liquids this morning.
HUGH: In the shape of tea?
STEPHEN: In the shape of tea, coffee and instant whisky. As a consequence of this large-scale intake of liquid, a quantity of excess fluid has been building up in the small membranous sac or fleshy bladder I keep inside me for the purpose.
HUGH: I have just such a receptacle about my person.

STEPHEN: It is now beginning to exert pressure to the point of minor discomfort. I feel it would helpful to me if I were to discharge this fluid through the urethra I handily keep in the centre of my penis.

HUGH: Good idea. Better certainly than bottling it up with all the attendant danger or urinous retention in the blood stream that that implies and entails.

STEPHEN: And I was wondering Clive if you had any kind of vessel into which this waste liquid would best be expelled?

HUGH: In that room through there I have a large porcelain bowl I keep especially against just such a contingency as this. It is connected to a cistern which will flush all your discharged fluids into a series of channels, drains and sewers, safely carrying it into the national water supply.

STEPHEN: I might try that out now if you'd be so kind.

HUGH: Please make free. I should advise against attempting the feat from here, however. I would stand up on your legs and make the journey over there.

23/2/91 GASLIGHT

STEPHEN, HUGH AND JANET ARE IN VICTORIAN GARB. STEPHEN IS A DOCTOR, JUST FINISHING AN EXAMINATION OF THE ANXIOUS JANET. HUGH IS JANET'S FAINTLY GERMAN HUSBAND.

STEPHEN: Hmm. Interesting. Damned interesting. You say you feel well enough, apart from these lapses of memory?

JANET: Oh, a little tired perhaps, but otherwise...

HUGH: My wife is tired, Doctor. She tires very easily. All the time I beg her to rest. To sleep.

STEPHEN: Yes, well, probably a good idea.

HUGH: So Doctor, what is your opinion? What is your professional diagnosis?

JANET: Please don't hide anything from me, Doctor. I don't think I could bear it.

HUGH: Yes, Doctor. Please be perfectly candid. Is my wife insane? Is she dangerously barking mad, or what is it?

STEPHEN: Well now Mr Trevellyan, I have examined your wife as thoroughly as I can under the circumstances, and can find no evidence of what you might call physical illness.

JANET: Physical illness?

HUGH: Yes Doctor, my wife and I noticed that you said physical illness. Physical. You have said nothing so far about her mental condition. Is my wife starking up a tree like a mad parrot, or isn't it?

STEPHEN: You will understand of course that I am a physician, not a psychiatrist. However...

HUGH: Yes, Doctor, however, you feel that she is out of her loopy tree? Hm?

JANET: Yes, Doctor. Am I mad? Am I losing my mind?

STEPHEN: Well, I wouldn't like to go quite as far as that.

HUGH: Oh? But of course, Doctor, that is your opinion.

STEPHEN: Yes. Hm. I am a little worried about your feet, though.

HUGH: I beg your pardon?

STEPHEN: You have.

HUGH: Her feet have lost all capacity for human reasoning? They are behaving wildly, irrationally. They are off their onions, or how much?

19/3/91 PLAY FOR TODAY
A COMFORTABLE SITTING ROOM. JANE IS ON THE SOFA WITH A GIN AND TONIC, SITTING NEXT TO JOHN, WHEN HUGH, AS RICHARD ENTERS WITH SIDEBURNS AND A BRIEFCASE.

JANE: Richard, you're back.
HUGH: No I'm not.
JANE: Richard...
HUGH: I'm still on the motorway. Traffic's terrible, and I won't be here for another half an hour.
JANE: Richard, please, we have to talk you and I...
HUGH: Yes I had a marvellous day at the office, thank you my darling wife.
JANE: I'm sorry, Richard, but I'm leaving you.
HUGH: I beg your pardon?
JANE: I'm leaving you. I can't take it any longer.
HUGH: Can't take it any longer? Can't take what any longer?
JANE: Us. What's become of us.
HUGH: I see. And what has become of us, my little prairie oyster?
JANE: We've grown apart, Richard. Maybe, I don't know, maybe we've grown up. We've changed. Or maybe the world's changed, and we've stayed the same.

HUGH CLAPS IRONICALLY.

HUGH: Bravo. A beautifully executed speech. Now perhaps you'd care to drop this charade and tell me what's for supper?

JANE: There isn't any supper, Richard. There never will be any supper again. I'm leaving you.

HUGH: No supper ever again, I see. Does that include frozen pizzas?

JANE: Damn it Richard, will you stop this bloody torture! Listen to me. It's over, finished, our marriage is a farce. It's been a farce ever since you went to Stockholm.

HUGH: Stockton, my darling. I went to Stockton.

JANE: Whatever...

HUGH: Well there we have it, don't we? That little 'whatever' as you call it, happens to have paid for our new garage. From which you derive, let's face it, enjoyment and enhanced standing within the local community.

JANE: I don't mean to run you down, Richard. I know how much your work means to you, but there are other things...

HUGH: Apart from garages, you mean...

JANE: Yes.

HUGH: Name them.

JANE: Such as... love, such as friendship, such as thought and expression, such as... oh I don't know...

HUGH: Well let me suggest one. Such as getting soaked while you're trying to unload the car, d'you mean? Such as not having anywhere to keep the stepladder? Well you takes your money and you pays your... you pays your... you're twisting my words now...

JANE: I'm not twisting anything, Richard. It's you, can't you see?

HUGH:	I'll tell you what I see. I see a bloody hard day's work, I see getting home to have to face a lot of hysterical slappery-flappery-flip-hell about you leaving me, and I also see another bloody takeaway, which, I might add, will be the twenty-third Chinese meal I've eaten this week...
JANE:	Have you finished?
HUGH:	No I haven't bloody finished... (PAUSE)
JANE:	Well?
HUGH:	Alright I have.
JANE:	This is Vernon.
HUGH:	What is?
JOHN:	(GRINS) Hi.
HUGH:	Where the bloody hell did you spring from?
JANE:	Vernon teaches abuse counselling at the Technical College. He's also my lover.
HUGH:	Oh that's beautiful. That's just beautiful.
JANE:	You're upset, aren't you?
HUGH:	Upset? Upset? Upset? Of course I'm upset. There are only two spring rolls. Who's going to have to go without? Only the man who buys you garages, I suppose. Great.

19/4/91 THE SEVEN FUNCTIONING ARSES OF MAXWELL FURNITT

I don't really know a great deal about this sketch, except that it is to be called The Seven Functioning Arses of Maxwell Furnitt.

16/5/91 GENITAL NONSENSE

HUGH IS ONSTAGE.

HUGH:	Hello. In a minute, I'm going to show you my genitals. Well I'm not really, I just wanted to get your attention, because I

know how it is. You settle down to watch a bit of telly and your mind sort of drifts, doesn't it? At least mine does. There I am, plonked down in front of the regional finals of 'One Man And His Dog', and however much I want to concentrate, I find myself just drifting. And then suddenly Phil Drabble says, 'Well that's all for this week,' and I suddenly realise that I haven't the least idea who won or by how much.

6/6/91 INSURANCE

STEPHEN SITS AT THE PIANO: HE PLAYS A COMPLETELY RANDOM SERIES OF NOTES, HAMMERING AWAY AND MAKING A FRIGHTFUL RACKET. EVENTUALLY HE STOPS.

STEPHEN: Ladies and gentlemen, it may surprise you to learn that that piece was entirely improvised.

MILD TITTER FROM AUDIENCE: HUGH ENTERS.

HUGH: Bad luck.

STEPHEN: Bad luck? What do you mean, bad luck?

HUGH: Well, you know, that not being very funny.

STEPHEN: What?

HUGH: That. It didn't get much of a laugh.

STEPHEN LOOKS AT THE CAMERA

STEPHEN: I don't do 'laugh' humour as you well know. Mine is a sort of internal 'smile' humour.

HUGH: It didn't get much of a smile either.

STEPHEN: Yes, alright, but it so happens that I take risks. I do things that perhaps other people wouldn't dare do, and sometimes, you know...

HUGH: It's completely unfunny.

STEPHEN: Yes.

HUGH: Well I think you're very brave. I just couldn't take those sort of risks. I have to protect myself.
STEPHEN: I hope you're going to explain to the ladies and gentlemen what the frig it is that you're talking about?
HUGH: I protect myself. I am insured.
STEPHEN: Insured?
HUGH: Yes. I took out a policy, with the Scottish Prudential Mutual Providential Mutual Widows Assurance Union, that covers me against the risk of doing a sketch that isn't funny.
STEPHEN: Like this one?
HUGH: Well... yes. If, when I say this funny name, it turns out not to be funny, I just write off for a claim form, and in three weeks' time a nice fat cheque comes through the post.
STEPHEN: What funny name?
HUGH: Gyles Brandreth.
STEPHEN: So you're now going to get a cheque from the Scottish whatever?
HUGH: Yup.

17/6/91 LAVATORY MONOLOGUE
STEPHEN IS IN THE LAVATORY.
STEPHEN: Since the dawn of time, man has found solace in the lavatory. It is a place of repose, of solitude, of calm thought, rational reflection and inner peace. A place above all in which to be alone. So would you please get out.
CAMERA MOVES AWAY. DOOR SLAMS IN ITS FACE.
STEPHEN: (OFF) Thank you.
STARTS TO GROAN AND HUM AND MAKE STRANGE NOISES. CUT TO LAVATORY-RELATED VOX POP.

5/11/93 DEED POLL

HUGH SITS IN A WAITING AREA NOT UNLIKE A DOLE OFFICE. WE SEE A SIGN ON THE WALL. WHICH SAYS "DEED POLL: NAME-CHANGING DEPARTMENT". WHILE HUGH WAITS, VARIOUS NAMES ARE CALLED OUT AND SLIGHTLY EMBARRASSED PEOPLE GO IN.

ANNOUNCER: Janet Smell. Miss Janet Smell, Room 3 please. (HUGH CAN'T HELP LOOKING AT HER AS SHE GOES OFF FOR INTERVIEW.) Gerald Fatcurtain, Room 6. Mr Fatcurtain, Room 6. (AGAIN HUGH LOOKS.) Wendy Arse, Room 7. (POOR WOMAN, HUGH THINKS.) Michael Prettycock, Room 2. Michael Prettycock, Room 2.

AT LAST, HUGH'S TURN. HE GETS UP EMBARRASSEDLY, IGNORING ANY SNIGGERS OR SIDEWAYS LOOKS. WE FOLLOW HIM TO ROOM 2 WHERE STEPHEN IS SAYING GOODBYE TO HIS PREVIOUS CLIENT.

STEPHEN: Goodbye then, Mr Fraser.
FRASER: Fraser... Fraser. Thank you so much. Fraser, it's wonderful. Wonderful.
STEPHEN: Right then... it's Mr Prettycock, is it?
HUGH: Michael Prettycock, yes.
STEPHEN: Hm. And you'd like to change that?
HUGH: Well... yes.
STEPHEN: Yes... not sure what we've got left. You catch us at rather a busy time. Did you have any particular kind of name in mind?
HUGH: I've always fancied something good and plain like Sergeant or Davies or Sterling.
STEPHEN: Hoo... they very rarely come up I'm afraid.
HUGH: That last gentleman was Fraser was it?
STEPHEN: Mr Turdlap as was, yes he got the last of our Frasers, there. (RIFFLING THROUGH FILES) If it's Scottish you want, I do have a Macnaulty.

HUGH: Not really.
STEPHEN: No? I really am awfully afraid that you've caught us absolutely at our busiest time. Stocks running appallingly low. Only seven names available, I'm sorry to say.
HUGH: Seven? What are they?
STEPHEN: Well, Macnaulty you've already turned down. I've a Price, if that's any use to you...
HUGH: (INTERRUPTING) Oh, that's perfect...
STEPHEN: Yes, unfortunately it comes with a Christian name attached, can't separate them. Must be sold as one.
HUGH: Oh... hadn't really reckoned on changing my first name. Still... what is it?
STEPHEN: (CONSULTING) Bottie.
HUGH: Ah. Bottie Price. No, I don't think so.
STEPHEN: No. So, moving on, what have we? Did you just fart?
HUGH: I'm sorry?
STEPHEN: That's the next name. Did you just fart.
HUGH: Don't think the wife would go for that.
STEPHEN: No... probably not. Pretty much a specialist name. What's next? Major.
HUGH: Major? Are you out of your mind?
STEPHEN: No. Never going to shift that one are we? (RIPS IT UP) Now, how about sex?
HUGH: Sex? Lord no... terrible name.
STEPHEN: That was just an honest enquiry... my flat's only two minutes walk away... No? Alright, then. Moving on. Butler.
HUGH: Butler. Butler. Yes, I like that.
STEPHEN: You do? Excellent.
HUGH: Michael Butler. Mm.
STEPHEN: There is one drawback, however.
HUGH: Oh?
STEPHEN: Mm. A rather unusual spelling.

HUGH: Ah.
STEPHEN: Yes. It's B-U-T...
HUGH: Mm...?
STEPHEN: ... T-O-C-K.
HUGH: Buttock.
STEPHEN: But pronounced "Butler", so the vendor assures me.
HUGH: Oh dear, how many left?
STEPHEN: Just two more. Sure I can't tempt you to a quick blow-job under my desk?
HUGH: I've told you... I really don't go in for that sort of thing.
STEPHEN: No. That's a name again.
HUGH: Sure I can't tempt you to a quick blow-job under your desk is a name?
STEPHEN: Sure I can't tempt you to a quick blow-job under my desk.
HUGH: Hm. It's tempting.
STEPHEN: Unusual, but rare.
HUGH: Again, it's a question of the wife and children. The teasing's bad enough as it is. No. Best not. What's the last on your list?
STEPHEN: (LOOKING) Hitler.
HUGH: Oh great.
STEPHEN: So sorry, Mr Prettycock. Looks like we can't help.
HUGH: Those really are the only names you've got left?
STEPHEN: Sorry.
HUGH: I was prepared to pay anything. Not my lucky day.
STEPHEN: Pay anything?
HUGH: I've been saving up for a new name for the past fifteen years. Twelve thousand I was going to lash out on a good one.

STEPHEN: Well... there's always my name. You're welcome to that.
HUGH LOOKS AT THE NAME PLATE ON STEPHEN'S DESK.
HUGH: (READING) Jefferson. Jefferson. It's ideal.
STEPHEN: You like it?
HUGH: Like it? It's absolutely wonderful. Jefferson.
STEPHEN: Cash, please. Here's the deed. Just sign here and here. I sign here.
HUGH HANDS OVER THE MONEY AND SIGNS THE DEED.
HUGH: I'm so happy.
STEPHEN: Mm. Me too. Excuse me just a moment, won't you? I have to... you know.
STEPHEN LEAVES. JOHN COMES IN.
JOHN: Oh hello... sorry to keep you waiting. Peter Jefferson.
HUGH: He's just popped out.
JOHN: I'm sorry?
HUGH: Peter Jefferson has just popped out.
MAN: No, I'm Peter Jefferson.
HUGH: Then who... (HUGH FRANTICALLY LOOKS THROUGH THE DEED PAPERS)... oh no. (HE IS CRESTFALLEN.)
JEFFERSON: So, how can I help you Mr... I'm sorry, I don't know your name.
HUGH: (WANLY CONSULTING THE DEED) Uglycock. Michael Uglycock.

5/11/93 NOVELS

HUGH: I don't know, I just can't read novels any more. I open a novel, and it says something like, 'Simon Thurkston straightened his tie, ran a distracted hand through his unruly mop of blond hair and pushed open the door marked

"Private".' And all I can think is, 'No he didn't. It's made up. Simon Thurkston doesn't exist. He doesn't wear ties, and his hair is dark brown and very neat.' Or if it says, 'The rain lashed against the window, blurring and refracting Laura's view of the stern, forbidding Welsh mountains,' I just think, 'No it didn't do that. It just didn't do that. There is no such person as Laura. Don't get sucked into this. It's a lot of made-up nonsense.' Now, it's my failing, I know. A lot of people get a huge amount of pleasure reading made-up stories, they don't seem to mind the fact that Laura is only called Laura because the author walked past a branch of Laura Ashley that morning, or that the rain 'lashed against the window' because rain has to lash against things in novels, it can't just fall out of the sky onto things that are underneath it, occasionally moving diagonally if there's some wind about. People don't mind. They buy it. And read it. And like it. But not me. Now, if someone wrote a novel that began, 'I sat down at my typewriter and typed the words: "I sat down at my typewriter and typed the words: 'I sat down at my typewriter and typed the words...'"' I'd go for that. I'd believe it. That's real.

5/11/93 RIVAL PARENTS
A SIX-YEAR-OLD GIRL, LOUISE, IS SITTING ON A BENCH IN A CORRIDOR SOMEWHERE, DRESSED IN A PARTY FROCK:

IN THE DISTANCE, WE CAN HEAR APPLAUSE AND WOBBLY PIANO MUSIC: HUGH COMES IN WITH A BOTTLE OF MINERAL WATER AND A BANANA: HE IS TRACK-SUITED.

HUGH: Louise...

LOUISE TAKES THE BANANA: HUGH HANDS OVER THE MINERAL WATER.

LOUISE: No thanks.

HUGH: Come on, sweetheart, you've got to keep your fluids up. You can't go out there and do the business on low body fluids.

LOUISE TAKES THE WATER AND SIPS AT IT: HUGH LOOKS AT HIS WATCH AND TUTS: STEPHEN ENTERS, HOLDING THE HAND OF ANOTHER SIX-YEAR-OLD, RACHEL, WHO SITS NEXT TO LOUISE: STEPHEN DUMPS A HUGE 'HEAD' SHOULDER BAG ON THE FLOOR AND HE AND HUGH EYE EACH OTHER WARILY.

STEPHEN: Hi.

HUGH: Hi.

HUGH LOOKS AT HIS WATCH AND TUTS AGAIN.

STEPHEN: Running late.

HUGH: Yeah.

STEPHEN: Not fair on the competitors.

HUGH: Not at all fair.

RACHEL TURNS TO LOUISE.

RACHEL: I'm Rachel.

LOUISE: Louise.

HUGH: Yeah, alright sweetheart, time enough for chit-chat afterwards. Just keep focused right at the minute.

STEPHEN: Tunnel, my princess, think tunnel. There's nothing ahead of you except winning, it's a long dark tunnel.

STEPHEN AND HUGH PACE NERVOUSLY WHILE THE GIRLS SIT LOOKING BORED.

HUGH: What is going on?

STEPHEN: Twenty past, they told me.

HUGH: Who?

STEPHEN: I don't know... someone...
HUGH: They said five past to me.
STEPHEN: We're probably both wrong...
PAUSE.
HUGH: Come far?
STEPHEN: Hitchin.
HUGH: Right.
STEPHEN: You?
HUGH: Got a caravan, out by the ring road.
STEPHEN: Right.
HUGH: We sold the house, so that we could get around more easily...
STEPHEN: Yeah. I was thinking of doing that, but my wife... you know...
HUGH: Yeah, well... they don't really understand, do they?
STEPHEN: Not really.
HUGH NOTICES LOUISE YAWNING.
HUGH: What's the matter, sweetheart? Are you stiffening up? Here... (HE SQUATS IN FRONT OF LOUISE AND PROCEEDS TO MASSAGE HER CALFS AND STRETCH HER FEET.) Loose, all the time loose...
STEPHEN STARTS FLAPPING RACHEL'S ARMS ABOUT THE PLACE.
STEPHEN: What are you, princess?
RACHEL: The best.
STEPHEN: Opposition?
RACHEL: Chopped liver.
STEPHEN: That's my angel.
HUGH LOOKS AT HIS WATCH AGAIN.
HUGH: This is getting ridiculous.
STEPHEN: Well they're not going to start without us...
HUGH: S'pose not.
THEY BOTH LAUGH AT HOW NERVOUS THEY ARE.
HUGH: Oh well, it's just a bit of fun.

STEPHEN: That's right. And the kids love it.
HUGH: Exactly, it's for the kids. We do it for the kids.
STEPHEN: Course we do.
HUGH: Yeah.
LOUISE: Dad?
HUGH: Yes, honey?
LOUISE: I think I've broken a shoe lace.

HUGH FALLS TO HER FEET AND EXAMINES THE SHOE.

HUGH: Jesus... what did I tell you?
LOUISE: I thought...
HUGH: Always check the equipment. You cannot afford equipment failure at this level. Hold on, I'm going out to the caravan...

HUGH RUNS OUT.

LOUISE: Have you got a spare one?
RACHEL: Loads. Dad? Can Louise have one of our spare laces?
STEPHEN: I'm afraid not, my princess.
RACHEL: Dad...
STEPHEN: Princess, listen to me. We're there. We're so nearly there. We're so close, I can taste it. Don't start throwing away chances like this. If the other guy has equipment failure, well, then... those are the breaks. It's dog eat dog. Chopped liver, remember?

HUGH RUNS IN, TEARING AT A PACKET OF LACES.

HUGH: Give me the shoe...

LOUISE STARTS TO TAKE IT OFF.

HUGH: They're a slightly different weight, OK? Don't let that throw you out...

STEPHEN WHISPERS INTO RACHEL'S EAR.

STEPHEN: She'll be off-balance, a little uncertain, use that... use it.

SOMEWHERE IN THE DISTANCE WE HEAR THE PIANO PLAY AN OPENING CHORD.

HUGH: (YELLING AND SLAPPING LOUISE'S CHEEKS) Okay! Okay! This is it! No break-downs like last time. Failure isn't a word we know.

STEPHEN: (SLAPPING RACHEL) Say it, say it!

RACHEL: I'm a winner. I'm a winner.

STEPHEN: Okay, princess. Got your salt tablets?

RACHEL NODS.

STEPHEN: GOT YOUR SALT TABLETS?

RACHEL: Yes, Dad.

STEPHEN: Go out there and tear their lungs out.

EXIT A DISCONSOLATE RACHEL.

HUGH: Your mother and I have spent every last penny on this. Go out and kick butt till it bleeds, Tiger. And remember. There's no pressure.

LOUISE TROOPS OFF: THE PIANO STARTS TO PLAY MUSIC OFF. STEPHEN AND HUGH PACE FOR A WHILE, UNABLE TO LOOK. SUDDENLY THE MUSIC STOPS.

HUGH: (YELLING) It's with you. It's with you, Louise... Jesus, girl.

STEPHEN: Hold onto it, Rachel. Hold the frig onto it! That's it.

HUGH: Stab her... stab her... do something.

STEPHEN: You've got it! Hold onto that bloody parcel and unwrap it. Unwrap it...

HUGH: JESUS! That's it. No pocket money for a week...

STEPHEN: Good girl. Good girl.

HUGH: What have you been giving your child, hm?

STEPHEN: I beg your pardon?

HUGH: (SHOUTING OFF) I demand a drug test. Now.

THE MUSIC STARTS AGAIN. STEPHEN AND HUGH START TO CONCENTRATE AGAIN. NO ENDING AS YET...

5/11/93 HELLO JULIAN WHAT ARE YOU UP TO?
STEPHEN IS IN THE STOCK OFFICE, SITTING AT THE STOCK DESK, TAPPING INTO A STOCK COMPUTER. HUGH ENTERS, STOCKLY. THEY TALK TO EACH OTHER RATHER PUBLICLY, FOR NO REASON.

HUGH: Hello, Julian, what are you up to?
STEPHEN: Mark, I'm drawing up a list of the differences between men, on the one hand, and women on another one.
HUGH: What have you come up with thus so far, Julian?
STEPHEN: Well. I've put here that generally, as a general rule mind, generally women are fonder of chocolate than men are.
HUGH: I like chocolate, Julian, so I do.
STEPHEN: Yes, men do like chocolate as well. I've factored that in. But with women chocolate is somewhere between... what was it? I wrote it down somewhere on a square piece of paper... here we are... research has shown that chocolate for women is somewhere between a religious experience and a secret demonic fear.
HUGH: I see you've written here something about pork pies.
STEPHEN: Yes, it's actually quite interesting. Pork pies are just a few items that men prefer to women. Oh no, that's not right. Men don't prefer pork pies to women, they prefer pork pies more than women do.
HUGH: That's what you meant to say.
STEPHEN: Pork pies. Red wine. Stilton cheese. Whisky. Red meat.
HUGH: That's not, you must emphasise this, that's not to say that women don't like pork pies, red wine, stilton cheese,

whisky and red meat... it's just that men like them more.

STEPHEN: TEND TO LIKE THEM MORE.

HUGH: Tend. Tend. Tend. Women also TEND to prefer brandy, I see you've noted down, brandy, soap operas, sorbet and fine sherry wines.

STEPHEN: A surprise that kept cropping up was that men also favour eggs more than women do. Generally. Generally.

HUGH: You could have told me that a thousand times without me ever knowing it. But I've noticed something you've left out that men prefer.

STEPHEN: Tell me it, Mark, and I'll remedy the defect almost simultaneously.

HUGH: Split beaver pornography.

STEPHEN: I thought that was in there... no, you're right. Split beaver pornography slipped through the net.

HUGH: Not to say that women don't like it...

STEPHEN: But men TEND to like it just that teensy bit more...

HUGH: In very general, broad swathes of terms...

STEPHEN: In the widest most generalisingly general sense, men TEND...

HUGH: TEND...

STEPHEN: To like it more.

HUGH: Right, so where are your researches leading you, Julian? Have you formulated a plan of action?

STEPHEN: My first, tentative, ballpark notion is that all men should be moved north of Birmingham and all women should move south.

HUGH: You're talking about drawing a line on a map, Julian.

STEPHEN: A line on the map is what I have in mind, Mark. North of Birmingham will be car dealerships and linseed oil manufacturers...
HUGH: And south of Birmingham..?
STEPHEN: Wine bars and chocolate distilleries.
HUGH: It's certainly a rational plan.
STEPHEN: I hope it has reason on its side, dozing fitfully in a string hammock.
HUGH: You could have separate television channels. Oop north, they could show films with people kicking down doors and saying, 'Freeze, you son of a bitch,' while down south they could run moving cinematic study 'The Piano' six times a night.
STEPHEN: I think medical happiness is almost bound to ensue, Mark.
HUGH: Right.

5/11/93 BRITISH NATIONAL
STEPHEN IS INTERVIEWING HUGH, WHO HAS A SWASTIKA TATTOO, A SKINHEAD CUT, AND ALL THE TRIMMINGS. STEPHEN IS A SYMPATHETIC INTERVIEWER WITH A LARGE OLD-FASHIONED MICROPHONE.
STEPHEN: I'm with Terry Carter here who is one of the shop-troops of the British Nationa...
HUGH: Shock troops.
STEPHEN: I'm sorry?
HUGH: You said 'shop-troops'... that's shock troops.
STEPHEN: Oh, I do beg your pardon, Terry. One of the shock-troops of the British National party. Terry, I understand you were behind the recent spraying of swastikas and destruction of grave stones in the local Jewish cemetery.

HUGH: S'right.
STEPHEN: And, again please do correct me if I go awry, Terry, you like to ring up rabbis and Jewish people in the area threatening them and reminding them of Hitler and so on.
HUGH: Yeah, I do that?
STEPHEN: Now, forgive me if I go off the track here, Terry, but I understand you don't like Jews, is that right?
HUGH: Hate 'em.
STEPHEN: Well, that's even stronger than dislike, isn't it? You hate them. What are your feelings about black people? Do you ring them up and threaten them?

HUGH LOOKS A BIT WORRIED.

HUGH: Well... if they're small or old.
STEPHEN: You hate them if they're small or old?
HUGH: Yeah.
STEPHEN: Mm. You see, let me put this to you, Terry. Quite a few black people are rather large and know how to look after themselves don't they. They say thing like 'bad-assed mother-sucker' and they frighten you, a bit don't they?
HUGH: (AGGRIEVED) Yeah, that's right: if you call them names and that they get nasty and beat the crap out of you.
STEPHEN: But rabbis, don't do that, do they?
HUGH: (CHEERING UP) No, they're great. They're mostly pretty old and that. You know, so you can really knife them up without them turning nasty.
STEPHEN: So if I was to call you rather a sad puny little stupid coward, how would you react?
HUGH: Are you a Jew?

STEPHEN: As it happens, I am, yes.
HUGH: Well, you're dead, you are.
HUGH GETS OUT A KNIFE. STEPHEN HITS HIM ON THE HEAD WITH THE MICROPHONE.
HUGH: Ow! Bloody hell.
STEPHEN: So sorry, I'm afraid I had to do that.
HUGH: Have you got a grandmother?
STEPHEN: Yes.
HUGH: I think I'll go and beat her up then.
STEPHEN: I should warn you she's got some cutlery in the drawer in her kitchen.
HUGH: I could write her a nasty letter though, couldn't I?
STEPHEN: Mm, I suppose you could, if you would enjoy that.
HUGH: Signed 'We've got our eye on you, old Jew-woman. Remember Auschwitz, signed the Shock Troops.'
STEPHEN: Yes, that would be clever and brave and amusing. I'm getting to be rather fond of you, Terry.
HUGH: Ere, you're not a queer as well, are you?
STEPHEN: Certainly am.
HUGH: Right you are dead meat...
STEPHEN HITS HIM ON THE HEAD AGAIN.
HUGH: Ow! Look, stop doing that, will you?
STEPHEN: I'm sorry, Terry, I don't know what got into me. Oh look there's a fly on the window-pane there. Flies don't fight back, try that.
HUGH BRIGHTENS CONSIDERABLY.
HUGH: Yeah. Right. You've had it fly-boy, faggot-fly, Jew-fly queer kike.
HUGH SLAPS AT THE WINDOW-PANE AND THEN HOWLS IN PAIN, BURSTING INTO TEARS.
STEPHEN: Oh dear, it was a wasp. Well, it's goodbye

from the shock troop of the new order and back to the studio.

5/11/93 **ATTACK DOG**

A HOUSE. LENNY IS A REVOLTING SLOB. HE IS SITTING ON A SOFA EATING A BIG MAC, READING 'GUNS AND AMMO' AND SCRATCHING HIS GENITALS. DOORBELL RINGS. LENNY ANSWERS IT AND STEPHEN ENTERS AS A PLAIN CLOTHES POLICEMAN.

LENNY: Yeah?
STEPHEN: Mr Alan Munt?
LENNY: Yeah?
STEPHEN: Detective Sergeant Colin Lewis. You are the owner of an American Pit Bull Terrier?
LENNY: Yeah?
STEPHEN: May we come in, sir?

LONG PAUSE

LENNY: Yeah.

THEY COME IN.

STEPHEN: Does your dog have a name, Mr Munt?
LENNY: Yeah.
STEPHEN: What is it?
LENNY: Yeah.
STEPHEN: The dog's name is 'Yeah'?
LENNY: Yeah.
STEPHEN: Well Mr Munt, it seems that twenty minutes ago, your dog Yeah attacked a number of people on the Silverdale estate.
LENNY: Yeah?
STEPHEN: The dog has caused a number of serious injuries. Three people are receiving treatment in hospital at this moment.

LONG PAUSE.

LENNY: Fantastic.
STEPHEN: We had no choice but to destroy your dog, Mr Munt.

LENNY: Yeah?
STEPHEN: Yeah. We had to destroy Yeah.
LENNY: Where is he then?
STEPHEN: His body is at the police station at this moment.
LENNY: Are you feedin' him?
STEPHEN: No. He's dead, Mr Munt.
LENNY: Don't want to feed him. He's useless if he isn't hungry.
STEPHEN: Well of course he's pretty useless now he's dead, Mr Munt.
LENNY: You killed him then?
STEPHEN: We had no choice, Mr Munt. He was attacking...
LENNY: What, you blow him away with a Magnum .357?
STEPHEN: I'm sorry?
LENNY: You should have told me. I'd a come down to watch that. Blow his brains out. Stupid bastard.
STEPHEN: Did you know the dog was violent, Mr Munt?
LENNY: What?
STEPHEN: Did you know he was violent?
LENNY: He's great with kids.
STEPHEN: Was he?
LENNY: Fantastic with kids, yeah. He grabs 'em by the throat and shakes 'em - it's great.
STEPHEN: Mr Munt, I have to ask you a rather difficult question now.
LENNY: Yeah?
STEPHEN: It concerns your motive for actually keeping a dog like this.
LENNY: Yeah?
STEPHEN: Like Yeah, exactly. Are you ready for the question, Mr Munt?
LENNY: Yeah.

STEPHEN READS FROM A PIECE OF PAPER.

STEPHEN: Is your penis quite incredibly small?
LENNY: You what?
STEPHEN: Your penis. Is it really quite so extraordinarily minuscule that you feel it necessary to own a dog like Yeah?
LENNY: You what?
STEPHEN: We need to know, you see, for statistical purposes. Research has already shown that people who own these dogs have penises of less than two inches long - but we need to know whether yours is considerably smaller than that. D'you mind opening your flies, Mr Munt?
LENNY: Get off.
STEPHEN: We have a warrant here, Mr Munt. Signed by a magistrate, and giving us the right to search your trousers.

LONG PAUSE. LENNY UNDOES HIS FLIES, BACK TO CAMERA I HARDLY NEED MENTION.

STEPHEN: (PEERING) Good Lord. Pretty much as we expected. (WRITES IN HIS NOTEBOOK THEN WHISPERS AT TO AUDIENCE) Negligible.

12/93 CURRICULUM COMPLAINT

STEPHEN IS IN A HEADMASTER'S OFFICE. HUGH ENTERS NOT WEARING A MACINTOSH.

HUGH: Are you the headmaster?
STEPHEN: Yes I am. Good morning.
HUGH: Is it?
STEPHEN: Sorry?
HUGH: Perhaps it is a good morning from where you're sitting, but from my end of the room it's a living hell of a morning.
STEPHEN: Oh.
HUGH: So I hope you won't mind if I reply 'living hell of a morning'.

STEPHEN: No, well I'm sorry about that. Can I help you at all?

HUGH: I hope so. I profoundly and earnestly hope so. I have come here to complain about the way you educate children here.

STEPHEN: I see. And what exactly is wrong...

HUGH: Just about everything is wrong with it, Mr Headmaster sir, with your eighteen weeks paid holiday a year so why should you care?

STEPHEN: All right. Could I have your name, first?

HUGH: Not likely.

STEPHEN: I beg your pardon?

HUGH: I'm not going to fall for that one. Do you want to know my date of birth?

STEPHEN: Not really.

HUGH: Well it wasn't yesterday, I'll tell you that much.

STEPHEN: I just asked you your name...

HUGH: Oh no thank you very much, Mr Headmaster with a secretary to cater to your every whim and your own parking space with Headmaster written over it.

STEPHEN: Well now, Mr...

HUGH: Frayne. Damn.

STEPHEN: Did you say Frayne?

HUGH: No I didn't. Actually. I sneezed, and when I sneeze it often sounds like Frayne...

STEPHEN: Mister Frayne.

HUGH: Bless you.

STEPHEN: If you have a complaint about how your child is being taught...

HUGH: Oh pardon me, hold on one second, a trap for the unwary or what is it?

STEPHEN: What?

HUGH: Did I say I had a child? Did I give you that piece of information, Mr Headmaster

	with a nice semi-detached house within easy reach of shopping facilities?
STEPHEN:	Well no, but I assumed...
HUGH:	You assumed? Oh, a man of science, I'm not inclined to think.
STEPHEN:	Well if you haven't got a child at this school, what are you complaining about?
HUGH:	I'm complaining about the things that I was taught at this school.
STEPHEN:	You?
HUGH:	Indeed. I was a pupil at this school from the age of 11 to 15, and basically...
STEPHEN:	Yes?
HUGH:	I'm not satisfied with the way I've turned out.
STEPHEN:	Hold on a minute.
HUGH:	Ah yes, I thought that might cause a bit of a ripple in your er... er... in your... er...
STEPHEN:	You're not happy with the way you've turned out?
HUGH:	Pond.
STEPHEN:	Sorry?
HUGH:	That is correct. I am not happy.
STEPHEN:	In what way?

HUGH REMOVES A SHEAF OF PAPERS FROM HIS INSIDE POCKET.

HUGH:	These are my school reports from the summer term of my last year here.

STEPHEN TAKES THEM AND STARTS TO READ

STEPHEN:	'William Frayne appears to be a happy and well-balanced young man, and I have no doubt that he will find success in any sphere he might choose.' 'William Frayne has a lively mind, and will do well for himself.'
HUGH:	And so on, and so on. Extravagant claims, I think you'll agree.

STEPHEN: Well, yes, they seem to be fairly good reports, yes.
HUGH: Mm. Fairly good reports, yes. But here is the nub of my complaint.
STEPHEN: Yes?
HUGH: They fail to tally with the subsequent course of events.
STEPHEN: In what way?
HUGH: D'you know I'd be fascinated to know how much you earn.
STEPHEN: I beg your pardon?
HUGH: Fifteen thousand? Twenty thousand?
STEPHEN: I hardly think...
HUGH: I only ask, because if all you have to do for it is sit there saying, 'In what way?' then I think you've got yourself quite a cushy little job.
STEPHEN: Now look...
HUGH: Since leaving school, I have not made a success of any sphere, let alone a sphere of my choosing. I have stumbled from one sphere to another without encountering success in the smallest degree. There is, so far as I am aware, no sphere that I could convincingly call my own. I am, to all intents and purposes, sphereless.
STEPHEN: I am distressed to hear this.
HUGH: Are you? Are you? You'll forgive me for saying so but I look across this lavish and extravagant desk (IT IS NEITHER) and I don't see a man in distress, I see a man who almost certainly owns his own lawnmower and has more cufflinks than he knows what to do with, that's what I see.

STEPHEN: I really don't see how I can be held responsible for the prognostic inadequacies of my predecessors.
HUGH: Do you do that sentence in English, by any chance, Mr Brand New Ford Orion with central locking and anti-lock brakes?
STEPHEN: I meant I really don't see what I can do?
HUGH: Well there I have the advantage of you, in spite of all the fancy letters after your name.
STEPHEN: I haven't got any letters after my name.
HUGH: Oh dear. Got them in your name though, haven't you?
STEPHEN: Well, yes...
HUGH: It seems to me that your obligations are clear. You will have to take me back, and do the job all over again.
STEPHEN: I beg your pardon?
HUGH: You have failed to discharge your duties adequately, and I therefore demand satisfaction. I wish to be taught all over again.
STEPHEN: What, everything?
HUGH: Everything except French.
STEPHEN: French?
HUGH: Français.
STEPHEN: You were satisfied with the way you were taught French?
HUGH: Comme ci comme ça.
STEPHEN: Very well, Mr Frayne. You will begin on October 13th.
HUGH: October the 13th.
STEPHEN: Sir.
HUGH: October the 13th, sir.
STEPHEN: That's more like it.
HUGH: Tssch. Fantastic. It's true you know.

STEPHEN: What is?
HUGH: The happiest days of one's life.

STAGE DIRECTIONS

STEPHEN: Good evening ladies and gentlemen, and welcome to the third in this series of 'A Bit of Fry & Laurie'.
HUGH: Third out of six, that is. If there are some kids watching, an easy way to remember it is, there are the same number of 'A Bit of Frys & Lauries' in a series as there balls in an over of cricket.
STEPHEN: So welcome to the third ball of the over hahahahahaha.
HUGH: Hahahahahahaha.
STEPHEN: Of course it's a funny thing about numbers isn't it, how some numbers keep on cropping up time and time again.
HUGH: You can't keep a good number down hahahaha.
STEPHEN: Hahahahaha. My telephone number, for example, the number 7 appears in it twice. Twice.
HUGH: That's extraordinary. How many digits are there in your telephone number?
STEPHEN: Seven.
HUGH: That is almost eerie.
STEPHEN: Isn't it? And of course it does mean that quite a lot of digits just don't figure in my telephone number at all...
HUGH: For example..?
STEPHEN: Well, for example, 4. There isn't even one 4 in my telephone number.
HUGH: That is sad, isn't it?
STEPHEN: Hugh, it is sad, but I perk myself up with the thought that I've got more than my fair share of 8s.

HUGH: And an 8, isn't it, is worth twice as much as a silly old 4?

STEPHEN: Yes and four times as much as a dafty old 2.

HUGH: Ng... and eight times as much as mincey-pincey 1.

STEPHEN: Yes and an 8 is of course worth an amazing seven times as much as a horridy-worridy old... an 8 is worth seven times as much as a... as a... 1.142857.

HUGH: That's right. And everyone has, haven't they, a number that's particular to them, whether it be their birth-date...

STEPHEN: Whether it be their height in inches OR centimetres... whether it be their bank PIN numbers... whether it be their car registration plates...

HUGH: The number of pencils they own...

STEPHEN: ... or are thinking of owning at some time in the future...

HUGH: Or whether it be the maximum number of people they've slept with during one twenty-four hour period.

STEPHEN: And so on.

HUGH: But the exciting number we'd like you to keep in your head this evening is the number 3.

STEPHEN: You'll find it cropping up again and again and again.

FAN CLUB

STEPHEN AND HUGH ADDRESS THE NATION.

HUGH: You know we've had a whole armpitful of letters from viewers recently, asking whether they can join the Fry & Laurie

STEPHEN: Fan Club, and I'm afraid the answer is no, because there isn't one.
STEPHEN: Wasn't one.
HUGH: That's right. There also wasn't one, as well as there being an isn't one.
STEPHEN: What a weaver of words you are, Hugh.
HUGH: Cheers.
STEPHEN: What I mean is, there wasn't one, but there is one now. Or rather there are two.
HUGH: We've got one each?
STEPHEN: No, our legs have got one each.
HUGH: Sorry?
STEPHEN: One club is called the Fry & Laurie Left Leg Club, and the other is called...
HUGH: Don't tell me... no, actually you'd better tell me.
STEPHEN: The Fry & Laurie Right Leg Club. For the frighteningly reasonable sum of four hundred and fifty pounds a month, you will be entitled to a yearly newsletter, containing articles, profiles, photographs, competitions, crosswords, and in-depth interviews with our right legs. Guaranteed to bring peace of mind in a troubled world.
HUGH: What extraordinarily good value this offer seems to represent. And does membership of the Right Leg Club give you automatic membership of the Left Leg Club?
STEPHEN: Sadly no, Hugh. We may be generous, but we're not nice.
HUGH: Gotcha.
STEPHEN: Membership of the Left Leg Club, however, is slightly cheaper, at three hundred and ninety pounds a month.
HUGH: Now why would that be, I wonder.

STEPHEN: I don't know. Marketing boys came up with it.
HUGH: Interesting. Couldn't we get any grown-ups to do our marketing?
STEPHEN: But if you join both clubs at once, you will be entitled to this T-shirt... (STEPHEN HOLDS UP A PLAIN WHITE T-SHIRT)... with our famous catchphrase on it. We will also send you a fully automatic Frank Windsor as part of this once-in-a-lifetime introductory offer.

SHOW PICTURE OF FRANK WINDSOR.

STEPHEN: Anyway, that's enough merchandising news. Now, on with the pitiless exploitation of gullible fifteen-year-old girls.

CRITICAL REVIEW

ROBERT AND JANINE ARE LYING IN BED.
JOHN: What do you think?
JANE: I thought it was enjoyable enough at times, but overall a little leaden.
JOHN: Leaden?
JANE: Leaden. I thought the themes were familiar, that I'd been there before... I thought your performance was rather wooden.
JOHN: So did I. I thought I was wooden, whereas you reminded me of a young Lesley-Anne Down.
JANE: Interesting.

THE DOOR OPENS AND HUGH COMES IN.

HUGH: Aha!
JANE: Godfrey!
JOHN: Oh lor...
HUGH: Well now, I appear to have discovered my wife in bed with another man...
JANE: Godfrey, can I ask you first of all, what is your reaction?

HUGH:	I suppose my first reaction is one of horror, shock, betrayal...?
JOHN:	A powerful experience then?
HUGH:	I wouldn't say powerful, no. I have experienced this before in the seventies, when my wife...

THE PROFESSIONALS

JOHN IS TIED TO A CHAIR IN THE MIDDLE OF A BOOK-LINED STUDY. VERY LEWIS COLLINS. STEPHEN PROWLS THE ROOM THE WAY DANGEROUS ANARCHISTS DO. SOME BAY CITY ROLLERS BOOMS FROM A STEREO. STEPHEN APPROACHES AND LIFTS THE NEEDLE.

STEPHEN:	So. The famous Peter Sherman. I am indeed honoured to face so worthy an adversary.
JOHN:	Go to hell.
STEPHEN:	No. You go to hell, Mr Peter Sherman. I am going to High Wycombe. They tell me there will be fresh lobster on the flight.
JOHN:	Look, spare me the victory speeches. You've won, alright? Just get it over with...
STEPHEN:	Get it over with? My dear Mr Peter Sherman, where is your sense of theatre?

THE DOOR OPENS AND JANE COMES IN

JANE:	What's happened to the music? I thought that... (SHE SEES THEM BOTH) What's going on? Peter?
STEPHEN:	Come in, my dear.
JOHN:	Look. Leave her out of this, will you? She's just...
STEPHEN:	Nonsense. The more the merrier. Join the party, my dear. Perhaps you could begin by pouring two glasses of that most excellent malt whisky. We have a little time before the submarine arrives.

JANE LOOKS TO JOHN.
JOHN: Look, Muller, I'm telling you, she's just a stupid, ignorant, hysterical, hormonally unbalanced bitch cow, who couldn't even spell her own name out of a paper bag. Let her go.
STEPHEN: I wonder if you are in a position to demand anything, my dear Sherman. Aren't you... (VERY ARCH) overlooking something?
JANE: Look, haven't you and your sort done enough harm?
STEPHEN: Dear lady, we have barely begun. What you have witnessed here tonight is just the hors d'oeuvre in a banquet of destruction.
JOHN: What's for dessert?
STEPHEN: The end of European democracy, Mr Sherman. Then with the cheese, I thought we might have the overthrow of Western Civilization.
JOHN: You bastard...
STEPHEN: Too rich for your blood, perhaps? No matter...
JANE: And what about the innocent people? Have you thought about them?
STEPHEN: Innocent. Which of us is innocent in this wicked world?
JANE: That's a very good point, actually.
JOHN: It is, actually, when you think about it.
THE DOOR OPENS AND HUGH COMES IN, AS A POLICEMAN

9/4/91 INTERVAL
STEPHEN AND HUGH APPROACH THE AUDIENCE HALFWAY THROUGH THE SHOW.
HUGH: Ladies and gentlemen there will now be an interval of three minutes.

STEPHEN: The show will recommence in three minutes' time. Thank you.
HUGH: If you could be back in your seats and...
CUT TO A SITTING-ROOM SET. WE ARE LOOKING AT A FAMILY WATCHING TELEVISION. WE ARE SEEING THEM FROM THE TV'S POV, SO THEY ARE STARING WITH SOME INCOMPREHENSION AT US. HUGH'S VOICE IS CARRYING OVER.
HUGH: (OFF AIR)...ready to begin watching again in three minutes, we would be very grateful.
STEPHEN: (OFF AIR) Thank you.
THE FAMILY CONTINUES TO WATCH.
MOTHER: Screen's gone black.
FATHER: What's going on, then?
SON #1:   Interval, stupid.
SON #2:   What, you mean adverts?
SON #1:   You don't get adverts on BBC2, derr-brain.
MOTHER: So it's just an interval then?
FATHER: I don't like it. I'm sorry, but I don't like it.
SON #2:   I mean, what are we supposed to do?
SON #1:   You can do what you like div-head. Get a coke out the fridge, have a slash, whatever you like.
FATHER: This never used to happen.
MOTHER: I think it makes a nice change. Gives you time to reflect on what you've just seen. Mull it over, have a think about it.
FATHER: Yeah, well, that's alright and I dare say, but these people are being paid aren't they? They can't just slope off like that without asking.
SON #1:   Why not? You do.
FATHER SWIPES AT SON AND CLIPS HIM ON THE HEAD. THE BOY'S HEAD COMES OFF AND ROLLS ALONG THE FLOOR.

MOTHER: There. You've knocked his head off now. I hope you're satisfied.
FATHER: Well he started it.

ODD

HUGH AND STEPHEN ARE BOTH READING PAPERS IN AN AREA HIGHLY SUITED TO THE READING OF PAPERS.
STEPHEN: Hugh...
HUGH: Mm...
STEPHEN: Notice anything unusual about me?
HUGH: Mm?
STEPHEN: Notice anything unusual about me?
HUGH: (LOOKING UP BRIEFLY) You're not picking your nose.
STEPHEN: No. Not that.
HUGH: Er... (NOT REALLY INTERESTED IN THIS GAME)... You're wearing odd trousers.
STEPHEN: No.
HUGH: Your ears are a different colour, you've had you're nipples enlarged, I don't know.
STEPHEN: Take a closer look.
HUGH PUTS DOWN HIS PAPER AND EXAMINES STEPHEN. HE SUDDENLY GETS IT.
HUGH: Good lord!
STEPHEN: Exactly.
HUGH: That's incredible.
STEPHEN: Tis, isn't it?
HUGH: How did you... ?
STEPHEN: David Bowie put me onto it.
HUGH: Well, I think it's brilliant. Absolutely brilliant.
STEPHEN: The amazing thing is, it'll never come off.
HUGH: What, never?
STEPHEN: Never. And it doesn't sting.
HUGH: It doesn't sting.

STEPHEN:	Except at first.
HUGH:	How many are there?
STEPHEN:	Nine all told.
HUGH:	And they all make the same noise?
STEPHEN:	They all make the same noise.
HUGH:	Fiff... tsoo. Brilliant.
STEPHEN:	But... if you don't clean them out fairly regularly they will start to... you know.
HUGH:	Smell.
STEPHEN:	Yeah. Smell.
HUGH:	Price?
STEPHEN:	Two of them, yes. The other seven haven't yet.
HUGH:	Amazing. If you light them, do you have to do it together, or can you...
STEPHEN:	Oh no, you can light them apart.
HUGH:	But then, presumably, they won't grow back.
STEPHEN:	Exactly.
HUGH:	And when do they fall over?
STEPHEN:	Tomorrow at eleven, with any luck.
HUGH:	Right! Same taste?
STEPHEN:	Same taste, oh for sure.
HUGH:	Just incredible. And if you widen them out? Any dribbling or overheating?
STEPHEN:	Depends on whose basket you're using.
HUGH:	Right, right. Cor!
STEPHEN:	Hmm.
FADE OUT	

PASSPORT

HUGH ADDRESSES THE CAMERA.

HUGH: "Her Britannic Majesty's Principal Secretary of State for Foreign and Commonwealth Affairs requests and requires in the name of Her Majesty all those whom it may concern to allow the bearer to pass freely without let or hindrance, and to afford the bearer such assistance and protection as may be necessary." A couple of weeks ago, I read that out to a customs official at Malaga airport. Can you guess what he did? Did he drop to his knees perhaps, and clutch at the hem of my coat, pleading with me in halting English not to send a couple of gunboats to his village? Perhaps he stiffened, you may be thinking. Perhaps he stiffened to attention and barked out instructions to the effect that the longest car in Malaga should immediately be put at the disposal of the English señor, and a basket of fresh fruit placed in his hotel room with the compliments of the Minister of the Interior? Funnily enough, he did neither of those things. Funnily enough, he snapped on a pair of rubber Marigolds and conducted an on-the-spot intimate body search. Of my body. Not his. Although it's not impossible that at some point he may have practised on his own body. He was very thorough. Very thorough indeed. He didn't skimp over the difficult bits, as you or I might have done in his position. No, if anything, he dwelt over the difficult bits.

SMOKING

STEPHEN AND HUGH COME ON WEARING TAP SHOES AND DJs. WE HEAR THE TAP SHOES QUITE CLEARLY. A BIT OF WARMING UP.

HUGH: Ladies and gentlemen, m'colleague and I

	have been literally snowed under with requests --
STEPHEN:	No, not literally. We've been figuratively snowed under. Literally snowed under is the one thing we haven't been.
HUGH:	Oh right -- take your point. Ladies and gentlemen, we've been literally sent many letters asking if m'colleague and I would reproduce our internationally acclaimed 'Broadway Medley'. (STEPHEN IS LIGHTING A CIGARETTE.) Well, rehearsal and practice don't... Stephen, what are you doing?
STEPHEN:	Appearing on a television show.
HUGH:	No. What are you doing with that cigarette?
STEPHEN:	What am I doing with this cigarette?
HUGH:	I think that was my question.
STEPHEN:	I'm trying to instal it as a client regime in the Republic of Panama.
HUGH:	You're going to smoke it.
STEPHEN:	That is the other thing I might do, yes.
HUGH:	You are seriously proposing to smoke on national television? The irresponsibility of that action virtually defies belief. There may be children watching this.
STEPHEN:	Yes.
HUGH:	Young, impressionable, plasticine children.
STEPHEN:	Exactly. So I'd watch how you chuck around that sort of sanctimonious bilge-tripe about smoking.
HUGH:	Sanctimonious bilge-tripe?
STEPHEN:	I think that's what I wish I hadn't said.
HUGH:	Better to talk sanctimonious bilge-tripe, than...
STEPHEN:	Than what? Come on, let's face it, smoking is cool.

HUGH: Cool?
STEPHEN: Cool, fashionable, hip, hep, fresh and groovy. You can attract sexual partners and cock a snook at the repressive adult world all in one simple sucking action.
HUGH: Cock a snook? Smoking lets you cock a snook?
STEPHEN: If you want to cock a snook.
HUGH: That is pathetic. It is pathetic, irresponsible and childish.
STEPHEN: It's also a lightly toasted blend of finest Virginia tobaccos.

HUGH COUGHS LOUDLY.

HUGH: I would appreciate it very much if you didn't blow that poison into my personal space.
STEPHEN: Your what?
HUGH: You're absolutely welcome to kill yourself, in fact it's rather a good idea, but I would be very grateful if you didn't include me in your suicide pact.
STEPHEN: (SMILING) Hugh!
HUGH: (CRABBILY) What?
STEPHEN: This isn't a real cigarette at all.
HUGH: It isn't?
STEPHEN: No!
HUGH: Tchersh!
STEPHEN: The prop department made it up.
HUGH: Oh lord.
STEPHEN: They took some tobacco and paper and a filter and made it up themselves.
HUGH: Well, that's all right then. Honestly, m'colleague, you are a one.
STEPHEN: I know. Have a try.

OFFERS HUGH ONE OF THE CIGARETTES.

HUGH: (LIGHTING IT) Mm — that's better.

STEPHEN: And no danger of influencing the kids.
HUGH: A perfect compromise.

STRANGE STUDIO LINK

STEPHEN AND HUGH ARE THERE. QUITE SIMPLY THERE.

STEPHEN: Well, love me or loathe me, I'm certainly not going to go away.
HUGH: That's a pity.

VIEWING CLOTHES

THEY'RE THERE.

STEPHEN: I've had sacks full of letters recently, saying that I'm great.

HUGH WAITS FOR STEPHEN TO CONTINUE, BUT THAT SEEMS TO BE IT.

HUGH: Good. I recently had an envelope full of a letter from a viewer in Thrad, in Nottinghamshire, wanting to know if we recommend that any special clothing be worn while watching 'A Bit Of Fry And Laurie'.
STEPHEN: Interesting. M'colleague, do we have any advice in that regard, bearing in mind our twin watchwords of cost and convenience?
HUGH: Well, yes, actually we have. For those of you watching 'A Bit Of Fry And Laurie' on a budget, we suggest an ordinary loose T-shirt and loose-fitting hat, a pair of ordinary loose shoes, a loosely fastened pair of pants, a loose set of knee and elbow pads, a loosely fitted aluminium tongue brace and a cup of hot freshly made loose at your elbow.
STEPHEN: But for those of you who want to splash out and do the thing properly...?
HUGH: Well, we've designed this...

JOHN COMES ON, WEARING A STRANGE COSTUME AND GOGGLES.
HUGH: The outfit comes in a variety of colours...
STEPHEN: Mmmm. Does it allow you to sit, smile, yawn, stretch and masturbate without discomfort?
HUGH: That's the idea. The goggles, by the way, allow you to watch while on the back of a fast motorcycle.
STEPHEN: Quite a package, Hugh. Cost?
HUGH: The cost is nine-nine pounds and ninety-nine pence, plus a ninth of a penny post and packing. State your size, allowing two extra sizings to make sure the outfit is properly loose.
STEPHEN: So call now...
HUGH: But do call...
STEPHEN: Do call. Our polite, multilingual receptionists, selected for their human and interpersonal skills, are waiting for your call...
HUGH: So call now...
STEPHEN: But do call...
HUGH: Do call now...

WHAT DO YOU THINK?

HUGH TURNS TO THE CAMERA RATHER VIOLENTLY.
HUGH: Well, that's one point of view. But we'd like to know what you think, so drop us a line, using both sides of the paper only, telling us, in not more than ten countries, what you think about the issues raised here tonight on the show tonight here tonight on the show. We desperately want to know your opinions, your thoughts, ideas, views, suggestions and anything else you've got lying around in your head.

If you haven't got a view, doesn't matter, drop us a line anyway, saying you have no view at all, because we need to know this, and we want to hear from you. The address is on page 296 of this week's 'Radio Times' if you live outside London, if not, drop us a line. So drop us a line - the address is anything you want, doesn't have to be right, just jot it down and stick it in your ear. But do it today.

(END)

CLIMB EVERY MOUNTAIN
HUGH IS IN CIRCLE MIMING AS SHIRLEY BASSEY... BASICALLY, YOU'VE GOT TO HEAR IT TO BELIEVE IT. THE IDEA IS THAT WE SHOW LOTS OF FOOTAGE OF JOHN MAJOR: AS MUCH AS WE CAN FIND. WE'LL TALK ABOUT IT WHEN YOU'VE HEARD THE TRACK. IT LASTS THREE QUALITY MINUTES. I PICTURE IT ENDING WITH JOHN MAJOR AT LAST ARRIVING AT TEN DOWNING STREET. AND — AT THE FINAL MOMENT — CLOSING THE DOOR ON US. THE '10' FALLS OFF. SOMETHING LIKE THAT ANYWAY. DOESN'T SOUND MUCH ON PAPER, BUT COULD BE BRILLIANT I THINK.

PENISES
HUGH ADDRESSES THE CAMERA.

HUGH: Big ones, small ones, thin ones, fat ones, stiff ones, floppy ones, ones that hang to the left, ones that hang to the right. I'm talking of course, about penises. What are they for? They expel waste fluids from the male bladder, they serve as a conduit in the process of insemination, but what else? You can't drive them. You can't live in them. You can't wear them. You can't borrow money from them at any rates, never mind favourable ones, so all in all, what good are they? I wrote to the Duchess of Kent to find out. I haven't received an answer yet.

SERGEANT DAVIES

JANE IS A BEARDED PRIMARY SCHOOL TEACHER IN A SWEET CLASSROOM, HUNG WITH GAILY PAINTED PAINTINGS BY CHILDREN. HUGH IS IN THE BACKGROUND, ARMS FOLDED LOOKING BENEVOLENT IN A POLICE UNIFORM.

JANE: (CLAPPING HANDS) All right children, let's gather on the mat now, shall we? That's right. Make room Josh, or Minna won't have anywhere to sit. Good boy. Now, we've got a special treat this afternoon. Who can tell me what a treat is?

A CHILD PUTS UP HER HAND.

JANE: Moira. What's a treat?

MOIRA: Chocolate.

JANE: Mm. Well, that's nice. A treat is a lovely thing that happens. A surprise. Our treat this afternoon is that a very nice man called Sergeant Davies is coming to talk to us. Sergeant Davies is a policeman.

CHILDREN CLAP AND GRIN AND SHOUT HURRAY.

JANE: Yes. So let's all sit very quietly and listen while Sergeant Davies talks to us.

HUGH COMES FORWARD. HE LAYS ON THE TABLE A SYRINGE, A SACHET OF POWDER, A SPOON AND SOME PILLS.

HUGH: (AFTER A PAUSE: HIGHLY AGGRESSIVE) Junk. H. Smack. Shit. Grass. Dope. Pot. Charlie. Coke. Crack. C. E. Ecky. MDMA. GHB. Speed. Ludes. Bennies. Mandies. Barbies. Works. Gear. Snadge. Stash. Toke. Fix. Hit. Arse. Celery. You know what I'm talking about. I want names.

	I want dates. You start talking and you start talking now.

BEWILDERED REACTION FROM CLASS.

JANE: Um... I wonder if...

HUGH: You stay out of this. (TO CLASS) I know at least one of you has been dealing and it makes me sick. Have you seen what it does, this shit? Have you? Now, come on. You!

HE POINTS AGGRESSIVELY TO A TINY CHILD.

HUGH: What's your name?

CHILD: Jeremy Timothy Alastair Potter.

HUGH: Oh, yeah? Been selling badly cut shit around the place have you Jeremy?

JEREMY SHAKES HIS HEAD.

HUGH: Don't give me that crap! Come up here!

JANE: Jeremy is a very good boy, but a little inclined to...

HUGH: I don't need help from civilians, stay out of it.

JEREMY COMES UP.

HUGH: Empty your pockets.

JEREMY LOOKS A LITTLE BEWILDERED AND FRIGHTENED.

HUGH: Now.

JEREMY EMPTIES HIS POCKETS.

HUGH: Oh dear oh dear, what have we got here?

A CONKER, A HANDKERCHIEF, A TUBE OF SMARTIES, A SHERBERT FOUNTAIN. HUGH POURS OUT THE SMARTIES AND OPENS THE SHERBET FOUNTAIN. HE TASTES THE POWDER AND WINCES.

JANE: Sherbet and Smarties.

HUGH: Wise up school teach. (TO JEREMY) Where d'you get this?

JEREMY CLAMS UP. HUGH TAKES HIS ARM ROUGHLY AND PULLS BACK THE SLEEVE. WE SEE THERE ARE TRACK MARKS.

HUGH: You sorry son of a bitch.

JANE:	Oh my lord...
HUGH:	Right. So. Talk.
JEREMY:	I don't talk to no pigs.
HUGH:	Oh, so you don't talk to no pigs. Well...

JEREMY WHIPS OUT A GUN AND SHOOTS HUGH DEAD. THE CHILDREN CLAP AND CHEER AND HURRAY. STEPHEN LOOKS IN ALARM.

JANE:	Back on the mat with you please, Jeremy. (TO CAMERA) They grow up so quickly these days, don't they?

THE FARKLING

HUGH BURSTS IN ON STEPHEN, WHO IS SITTING IN HIS CLUB. HE IS SUCKING UP A BRANDY THROUGH A VERY LONG STRAW. BOTH STEPHEN AND HE HAVE TOO-LARGE PIPES CLAMPED IN THEIR TEETH.

HUGH:	Randolph?
STEPHEN:	Tanner, my dear friend.
HUGH:	They said I could find you here...
STEPHEN:	And who are they?
HUGH:	The 'who' is not important. Neither is the 'they'. All that matters is.. the Farkling.
STEPHEN:	The Farkling, my dear Tanner?
HUGH:	Oh come on, man. We have but a matter of hours before the Farkling is out of the country. Where is it?
STEPHEN:	Steady yourself, Tanner. You are gabbling like a small, tired earwig...
HUGH:	If you'd seen what my eyes have seen these last weeks, you'd gabble yourself. But if you will give me the Farkling, then, and only then, will I sleep the sleep of the quite tired, knowing that this country is safe at last.
STEPHEN:	Suppose... suppose I were to tell you that the Farkling has already left...

HUGH: Left..?
STEPHEN: And that as we speak, it is far across the Austrian border, in the hands of men who know and appreciate its true worth.
HUGH: Randolph, I would have to call you a damned liar.
STEPHEN: Be careful, Tanner. I'm not sure I like your clothes.
HUGH: I saw the Farkling with my own eyes, not twenty minutes ago. It was dirty, covered in straw and vomit, but it was the Farkling all right. I'd stake my life on it.
STEPHEN: Where was this? Speak man, or I won't hear you.
HUGH: Trafalgar Square.
STEPHEN: Headed in which direction?
HUGH: Towards Brighton.
STEPHEN: If the Farkling gets to Brighton...
HUGH: Exactly. Brighton is only three hours from London.
STEPHEN: But the Prime Minister...
HUGH: ...is due to speak in London this very evening.
STEPHEN: He must be stopped.
HUGH: Don't you think I've tried?
STEPHEN: Tanner, I'm telling you. If the Farkling is within ten miles of Westminster when the Prime Minister rises to his feet we'll be the laughing stock of England.
HUGH: Europe.
STEPHEN: The world.
HUGH: Wales.
STEPHEN: Here's what we do. Procure a bicycle...
HUGH: At this time of day?
STEPHEN HANDS HUGH A PIECE OF PAPER.

STEPHEN: You'll find that this will open a few doors. Drive in the fastest car you can to Billingsgate, you should be able to find a bicycle there. Show them this chit. Procure your bicycle and pedal like a mad person with domestic problems towards Brighton.
HUGH: You mean..?
STEPHEN: I mean you must try and overtake the Farkling somewhere along the Brighton Road.
HUGH: The Farkling is fast, Randolph. It's travelling light. I don't know if I can do it.
STEPHEN: Then wear a mask, but for God's sake, Tanner! The free world is depending upon you.
HUGH: And you? What will you do in the meanwhiletime?
STEPHEN: I shall address the nation.
HUGH: And if the nation refuses to listen?
STEPHEN: Then we're all damned.
HUGH: But Randolph?
STEPHEN: Tanner?
HUGH: Suppose the Farkling does get to Brighton without me overtaking it and suppose, yes just suppose, it makes it to London in time for the Prime Minister's speech?
STEPHEN: You're painting an ugly picture, a horrible, incompetent daub.
HUGH: I know, I know, but hear me right out. What can the Farkling do? Actually do? It's tired, we know that. It's lost weight and it's friendless and unfashionable. Suppose we just ride out the threat?
STEPHEN: You're asking me to turn my back on everything I've ever believed in. You're

	asking me to gather up everything I value, place it in a large wicker basket, throw it over the side and watch it dash itself on the rocks below, while I look on, laughing and smoking and eating, with a young goat at my elbow.

HUGH: N-no... I'm saying sit tight and ride it out.

STEPHEN: (LOOKING AT CLOCK ON WALL) Well, it's too late now anyway. The Prime Minister will already be on his feet. He'll be speaking... now...

HUGH: If the Farkling is going to strike it'll be now. Listen.

THEY LISTEN, STRAINED. NOTHING.

STEPHEN: My God, Tanner, but you're a cool hand. I've never seen anyone play a wilder hunch.

HUGH: (RELIEVED) We've done it, Randolph. The Farkling's beaten. Spent. Exhausted. We won't hear from it again. We've won.

CLOSE-UP AND INCREDIBLE DRAMATIC MUSIC.

STEPHEN: Have we? I wonder? I wonder. I've a feeling, Tanner, that we haven't heard the last... of the Farkling.

WRESTLING

HUGH IS AN AMERICAN WRESTLING PRESENTER, BLAZERED AND HEADPHONED, SCREAMING INTO A MICROPHONE. NEXT TO HIM STANDS A MASKED FIGURE WITH HEAPS OF MUSCULATURE.

HUGH: But now, on W.W.W.W.W.W.F.W.W., it's the main event of the evening, Michael 'Chain Saw' Gonzales, W.W.F.F.F.W. champion of the world, goes mano a mano with Victor 'Sarcastic' Henderson. Chain Saw, you got something to say?

CHAINSAW: You're a dead man, Sarcastic. You so dead I already sent flowers to your house.

HUGH: Chain Saw, we were talking earlier, and you mentioned something about ripping out Sarcastic's heart. Did I get that right? You're gonna rip out his heart?

CHAINSAW: S'right, Tony. I gonna rip him out, and cook him with a little garlic and peppers, and then feed him to my dog.

HUGH: Well, the Chain Saw's strategy seems pretty clear. A ripping out of the heart, and then a feeding to the dog. Sarcastic, how do you feel about that?

PAN ACROSS TO FIND STEPHEN IN JACKET AND TIE.

STEPHEN: I'm terrified. I don't think I've ever been so scared.

HUGH: Wo, how about that? Not even in the ring, and already Sarcastic is throwing punches. Let's go ringside now, with Dave Wild and Skip Thompson.

THE BOUT IS IN PROGRESS. STEPHEN AND CHAIN SAW BOUNCE ROUND THE RING, SEARCHING FOR AN OPENING. SUDDENLY, CHAIN SAW LEAPS IN AND HURLS STEPHEN TO THE CANVAS, WHILE DAVE AND SKIP COMMENTATE.

DAVE: Well, Skip, a grudge match if ever there was one right here on W.W. etc. You have the Chain Saw going all the way?

SKIP: You got that right, Dave. Chain Saw is a seventh son of a seventh son of a bitch, and I just don't think Sarcastic has the hunger any more.

AS STEPHEN GETS TO HIS FEET.

STEPHEN: Oh I see. You're trying to hurt me, is that the idea? You're trying to throw me round the ring. How extraordinarily original.

CHAIN SAW STOPS, AND LOOKS A BIT HURT.

DAVE:	Take five, Skip, I think the Chain Saw's in trouble...
SKIP:	I don't believe what I'm seeing. Sarcastic has really hurt the Chain Saw. He's in trouble all right...

THE CHAIN SAW STARTS TO ADVANCE AGAIN.

STEPHEN:	That's it. You come towards me in that incredibly original way you have, and try and break my spine. Brilliant. I really am fabulously impressed.
DAVE:	He's hit him again, Skip, Sarcastic is gonna try and finish this right here...
SKIP:	Chain Saw's hurtin' real bad right now, Dave, I don't know...
STEPHEN:	No really, don't stop. I'm sure we'd all be fascinated to see what you're going to do next. Something howlingly interesting, I don't doubt.

CHAIN SAW LEAPS IN AGAIN AND GETS HIS ARM ROUND STEPHEN'S NECK.

DAVE:	Oh here we go, Skip...
SKIP:	I think what we're seeing right here, Dave, is a real mad Chain Saw...
DAVE:	And boy, they're the worst kind, aren't they..?
STEPHEN:	Oh that's great. You've got your arm round my neck. Incredible. If you don't get a Nobel prize for that, then there's simply no justice in the world...

CHAIN SAW BREAKS OFF AND STANDS BACK.

DAVE:	I don't believe this...
SKIP:	We're lookin' at a war out there today, Dave. It ain't pretty...
STEPHEN:	No, don't stop. Really. I simply can't wait to see what's going to happen next. You put one hand round my neck, and write

	an achingly beautiful violin concerto with your other hand, is that it?
DAVE:	Skip, I can't watch this...
SKIP:	This is a truly horrible display... they gotta finish this now.

THE BELL GOES: AND TAKE US INTO...

I'D LIKE TO BUY

STEPHEN IS BEHIND A SHOP COUNTER. HUGH ENTERS.

HUGH:	Hello. Are you open?
STEPHEN:	Yes, indeed, sir.
HUGH:	Oh good. I saw the lights were on, and the door was open, and the sign saying open, but I wasn't absolutely sure.
STEPHEN:	No, well, we are open.
HUGH:	Good. Thought I'd check.
STEPHEN:	Very wise.
HUGH:	I didn't want to buy something, walk out of the shop with it, get home, unwrap it, try it on, and then discover you were closed.
STEPHEN:	We are open, sir.
HUGH:	Oh excellent. Good.
STEPHEN:	So..?
HUGH:	So.
STEPHEN:	Can I help you at all, sir?
HUGH:	No, it's alright, I'll wait for one of the assistants.
STEPHEN:	I am an assistant.
HUGH:	Are you?
STEPHEN:	Yes, sir.
HUGH:	Oh lawks. I saw you standing there, behind the counter, advising people on their purchases and then taking money from them and then putting it in the till, but I thought you might have been a tourist or something.

STEPHEN: No, I am an assistant.
HUGH: Oh good.
STEPHEN: Can I help you at all?
HUGH: Do you sell socks?
STEPHEN: We do indeed, sir.
HUGH: Thought so. I saw these woollen things hanging up in the window, sort of foot-shaped but with a hole where a person's leg could easily come out of, but I wasn't a hundred per cent...
STEPHEN: We sell socks, sir.
HUGH: I'd like one, please.
STEPHEN: Sir?
HUGH: I'd like to buy a sock, please.
STEPHEN: A sock?
HUGH: Yes.
STEPHEN: One sock?
HUGH: Please.
STEPHEN: Yes. Our socks usually come in pairs.
HUGH: Pairs?
STEPHEN: Yes, sir.
HUGH: Twos, you mean?
STEPHEN: Yes, sir.
HUGH: Ah. That's rather thrown my calculations.
STEPHEN: Has it?
HUGH: Are they cheaper in twos?
STEPHEN: Much cheaper, sir. Same price for two as for one.
HUGH: Ah. Buy one, get one free sort of thing.
STEPHEN: Precisely.
HUGH: You ought to put some posters up
STEPHEN: I'm sure we will.
HUGH: Er... you don't...
STEPHEN: What?
HUGH: Bit difficult, this. You don't sell used socks, by any chance, do you?

STEPHEN: Used socks?
HUGH: Yes.
STEPHEN: No
HUGH: That's funny.
STEPHEN: Is it?
HUGH: Yes it is. Immensely funny. Because...

OSTER MILEPIECE

HUGH AND STEPHEN ARE IN A STATION WAITING ROOM. STEPHEN COMES FROM THE SERVICE AREA BEARING A PLATE ON WHICH SIT A PEACH AND A PORK PIE AND JOINS HUGH WHO IS SITTING AT A TABLE STARING SIGHTLESSLY BEFORE HIM. STEPHEN IS DRESSED ROGUISHLY, FOPPISHLY, SOME MIGHT SAY DECADENTLY. HUGH IS NOT. STEPHEN MAKES A START ON HIS PEACH.

STEPHEN: Whenever I eat a peach I seem to hear the whole sorrowful music of humanity playing in the distance.
HUGH: (TOOTHLESS NORTHERNER: YELLING) Oh yes?
STEPHEN: Is not a peach the most tender and yet the most corrupt object you know?
HUGH: Possibly.
STEPHEN: Sometimes when you press a peach with a thumb the full impression is left behind. And yet on other occasions the flesh springs back and no mark remains. Shall we not agree that this is how it is with people?
HUGH: Eh?
STEPHEN: My name is Oster Milepiece. My life is over. I travel North to die.
HUGH: Herbert Twazzock. Sausage pricker for Hawkins and Smell, pork butchers.
STEPHEN: Shall we be friends, Herbert? I feel we shall.
HUGH: Are you going to make a start on that pork pie?

STEPHEN: (LOOKING SADLY DOWN AT IT) I feel I never shall make a start on that pork pie, Herbert, no.
HUGH: I wouldn't dislike a slice.
STEPHEN: (OFFERING IT) Please. You would be rendering me a kindness. Herbert, seldom have I felt so keenly that I have stumbled upon an affinity, a soulmate. I shall write down three words on this sheet of hand-laid vellum.
HUGH: There's never chutney as when you want it.
STEPHEN: (WRITING) No, Herbert. There never is. So, Herbert. My little experiment in affinities is over. Tell me, what is your favourite colour?
HUGH: Me what?
STEPHEN: Your favourite colour. The tint that most inflames your soul?
HUGH: (AFTER THINKING FOR 3.2 SECONDS) Brown.
STEPHEN: Brown.
HUGH: Light brown, mind.
STEPHEN: Your favourite fish.
HUGH: Favourite fish, favourite fish, favourite fish. Squirrel.
STEPHEN: Findus. Mm. Favourite fish, Herbert.
HUGH: Oh. Favourite fish. Haddock.
STEPHEN: My. Your favourite vegetable.
HUGH: (GLARING AROUND THE ROOM AND SAYING LOUDLY) My favourite vegetable is a carrot and I don't mind who knows it.
STEPHEN: Herbert. Listen and look to the words I wrote down just a moment ago. My favourite vegetable is a carrot and I wrote down brown, haddock and carrot. It is impossible to forego our destinies.
HUGH: You wrote down vermilion, turbot and

mange-tout.

STEPHEN: Herbert, I wrote down vermilion, turbot and mange-tout, but inside, Herbert, I was thinking brown, haddock and carrot.

PORTER

HUGH IS SWANKED UP IN TOP HAT AND FROGGED COAT WITH CAPE, SUMMONING TAXIS OUTSIDE A LARGE LONDON HOTEL. STEPHEN EMERGES FROM THE FOYER.

HUGH: Good evening, sir. Taxi?
STEPHEN: Yes, please.
HUGH: Where are you headed, sir? North or south?
STEPHEN: South.
HUGH: South. Hmm. Might be a bit of a wait.
STEPHEN: Long enough for an amusing conversation?
HUGH: Night like this, could well be, sir.
STEPHEN: Oh right.
HUGH: Did you have an enjoyable evening, sir?
STEPHEN: Very enjoyable, thank you.
HUGH: Oh that's good. Wine, women and song eh, sir?
STEPHEN: Er... we had some wine, yes.
HUGH: You had some wine, excellent. But not so much women and song, eh?
STEPHEN: Not so much, no.
HUGH: Not so much, no. Was it red wine you had?
STEPHEN: Sorry?
HUGH: This evening. Did you drink red wine? I mean, don't answer if you think I'm being impertinent. I just...
STEPHEN: We had both, as it happens.
HUGH: Both what?
STEPHEN: Red and white wine. This evening.
HUGH: Red and white wine. Well, well, well. You know how to enjoy yourself, don't you, sir? Red and white wine. Was it a special

	occasion? Birthday? Wedding anniversary? Won the pools?
STEPHEN:	No, we just had a meal. Thought it would be nice.
HUGH:	Well why not, if you can afford it? For goodness' sake, no sense mouldering at home if you can be drinking red and white wine on the same night in there. Lord no, I'd do the same if I was you, sir.
STEPHEN:	Right.
HUGH:	Yup, I'd be in there like a shot. Wild horses wouldn't stop me. Couldn't stop me, not just wouldn't. Couldn't. No, it's always been a bit of a dream of mine.
STEPHEN:	What's that?
HUGH:	Going in there. Ordering a bottle of red and white wine. Bit of women, bit of song. I mean what could be better than that?
STEPHEN:	But you must have been in there, surely?
HUGH:	In there? No. Never have. Never had that good fortune.
STEPHEN:	Not even once?
HUGH:	Not even once. North Africa at sixteen, lied about my age, came back, been out here forty-six years. Calling taxis for gentlemen such as yourself. Who come for a nice meal and a bit of red and white wine.
STEPHEN:	That's amazing. Forty-six years, and you've never set foot inside the hotel?
HUGH:	I have used the toilet, sir.
STEPHEN:	Oh I see.
HUGH:	Coronation day. Got caught short, nipped inside. Beautiful it was. Marble, taps. They still have the taps, do they? Only there was talk of changes...

STEPHEN: No, there are still taps.
HUGH: Oh good. Sometimes I think we like to change things just for the sake of it, don't you, sir?
STEPHEN: Yes, it does...
HUGH: Fashion, they call it. I'm not so sure sometimes. You can't beat a good tap. Mr Marshall was ever so nice about it. 'Tom', he said, 'today is a very special day. On this day we have been blessed with a new sovereign. So I'm going to forget about this incident. It's going to be our little secret.' Then he patted me on the back and out I came. He was a very nice man, Mr Marshall. A very nice man indeed. What's your line of work, if you don't mind my asking, sir?
STEPHEN: Me? I er... commodity broker.
HUGH: Oh yes? Stocks and shares, eh? Shouting on the telephone all day.
STEPHEN: Well not really...
HUGH: Got any tips for me?
STEPHEN: Er...
HUGH: No, don't worry, sir. I don't expect you to tell me anything. I'm not a gambling man, to be honest with you. I once bought some shares, though. Company called Starline. Lost the lot. Turned out, the feller had said Starfine, not Starline. Starfine went up three times in value in a month.
STEPHEN: Oh, that's terrible luck.
HUGH: Not luck at all, sir. My own silly fault. Didn't listen properly. But I tell you what. If I'd gone for Starfine, d'you know what I'd have done with the money?

STEPHEN: No.
HUGH: I'd have gone in there. Jess and me would have gone in there, ordered some red and white wine, we'd have had a high old time.
STEPHEN: Would you?
HUGH: No, not really, sir. But it's a nice thought. On a cold wet night. Wine, women and song...
STEPHEN: Look, I'm sorry. I can't bear this any longer. I have an utterly pointless and futile life, and I have more money than I know what to do with. I want you to take this... (STEPHEN HANDS OVER A BUNDLE OF NOTES)... go in there, the next chance you get, and have dinner. Red wine, white wine, the lot. Order whatever you want.
HUGH: What are you doing, sir? You've gone a bit strange.
STEPHEN: I'm going to walk home. Forget about the taxi. Just go in there, take Jess, have a high old time.

STEPHEN TURNS HIS COLLAR UP AND SETS OFF. HUGH LOOKS DOWN AT THE NOTES.

HUGH: Twit.
(END)

SHOP ASSISTANT

HUGH IS A FLOOR-WALKER. STEPHEN IS BROWSING THROUGH SOME CLOTHES RAILS. HUGH APPROACHES.

HUGH: Do you need any help at all, sir?
STEPHEN: What?
HUGH: Do you need any help at all, sir?
STEPHEN: Help to do what?
HUGH: Do you need any help choosing anything...
STEPHEN: Oh yes, that's incredibly likely, isn't

	it? That I'd want to come in here and let you choose what clothes I ought to buy.
HUGH:	Well, help with looking...
STEPHEN:	Do I need you to help me look? Yes. I seem to have come without my arsing blind dog. Perhaps you could find him for me. His name's 'Bugger Off'.
HUGH:	Well, perhaps you might want help with...
STEPHEN:	With what? What might you be able to help me with?
HUGH:	Sizes?
STEPHEN:	Of what? Brain?
HUGH:	Of the garments.
STEPHEN:	Oh they come in different sizes, do they? I wondered what these numbers meant. I thought perhaps it referred to the year they were made.
HUGH:	No, they come in different...
STEPHEN:	I know that. I know they come in different sizes, and I can read Arabic numerals, thank you so enormously much.
HUGH:	Well, if you need...
STEPHEN:	If I need some maddening little creep to come and interfere while I'm trying to buy a pair of trousers, then yes, I will certainly 'give you a shout'.
HUGH:	Can I say something?
STEPHEN:	What?
HUGH:	You're a very insulting man.
STEPHEN:	I'm a very insulting man. Am I? Am I really very insulting?
HUGH:	Very insulting.
STEPHEN:	Bugger off! Bugger off!

STEPHEN'S ZOO

STEPHEN SAYS HELLO. STEPHEN IS ON SET.

STEPHEN: I don't know if you're anything like me — if you are, you will have a small mole just below the left nipple — but I am very concerned about the fate of London Zoo. London Zoo is, well, I mean, it's just London Zoo, isn't it? There are those who go about the place saying it's wrong to keep animals in captivity. There are those who don't go about the place at all, they just stand still and say that it is wrong to keep animals in captivity, that it is rather unpleasant and undignified. I am one of those who sometimes goes about the place and sometimes stands still and says, 'But look at the research benefits of keeping animals in zoos. Rare species can be bred, our children...' God bless our children, by the way, may I say that here and now? God bless our children. Our children are... well, they're our children, aren't they? I was once our children, I am now one of our grown-ups, but I still remember when I was once our children and it was lovely to be blessed and thought of. Where was I? Rare animals can be bred, our children God bless them, can learn to respect and love them and we can all find out more about this extraordinary world that I, and I must assume, most of you watching, inhabit. But that's such a lovely reason to have zoos that I can't understand why it is confined to animals. Our children, God bless them again, by the way, also need to learn about disappearing tribes, whose habitat is threatened, just like the animals. So why can't we keep rare human beings in cages? If it isn't undignified for animals, why should it be for humans? That's why I have put Hugh Laurie, who comes from a very rare Southern Caledonian tribe, in a cage.

STEPHEN IS WALKING TOWARDS A LARGE CAGE WHERE HUGH IS STANDING LOOKING RATHER PISSED OFF. HE HAS A TYRE TO PLAY WITH AND SOME STRAW.

STEPHEN: The research benefits are tremendous. (PUSHING A BERNARD MATTHEWS GOLDEN TURKEY DRUMMER THROUGH THE BARS) He likes to eat Bernard Matthews Golden Turkey Drummers, by the way.

HUGH GRABS THE GOLDEN DRUMMER.

STEPHEN: And most exciting are the possibilities of breeding.

WE NOTICE THAT BY CLEVER CAMERA TRICKERY THERE IS A FEMALE VERSION OF HUGH (PLAYED BY HUGH) SITTING IN A CORNER, SUCKING HER THUMB AND LOOKING SHY.

STEPHEN: This is Hatty Laurie, I bought her from a collector in Kirkcudbrightshire. Unfortunately I haven't been successful in getting Hugh and Hattie to mate. But who could possibly call this undignified? Who could say it is wrong to keep them locked up in this spacious and generous accommodation when the research benefits are so tangible?

HUGH: I could.

STEPHEN: (IGNORING HIM) Some people will just grab hold of any old trendy cause that comes along and make a fuss.

HUGH: I would like to be let out please to roam at will.

STEPHEN: So I would be very grateful for any

HUGH: contributions to help save and expand my historic and beneficial zoo.
HUGH: I would like my freedom.
HUGH: (AS HATTY) So would I. I would like to be let out so that I could meet a real man. A man that didn't reek of Bernard Matthew's Golden Turkey Drummers.
HUGH: Well at least I don't snore.
HUGH: (AS HATTY) Well excuse me... Mr Windy-Bottom.
STEPHEN: Ha, ha! Um... I am hoping to see if I can get a David Gower and a Bernard Levin next. Anyway... (forge link)

TIDY YOUR ROOM

STEPHEN IS BECARDIGANED, SITTING ON THE BED OF AN ADOLESCENT-LOOKING ROOM, RUMMAGING AROUND IN A CARDBOARD BOX. THE DOOR OPENS AND HUGH, IN YOUTHFUL APPAREL, ENTERS.

HUGH: Father!
STEPHEN: Gavin. Oh dear. Caught me at it.
HUGH: What are you doing in here?
STEPHEN: Doing. What am I doing. Yes. What am I doing? Well, I'm sitting on your bed, Gavin. How's that? Does that satisfy you, as an answer?
HUGH: Well... no.
STEPHEN: Hm. Yes. Pretty lame, I suppose. It was your mother's idea. Not mine. She's... how can I put it? Gone shopping. She's concerned, Gavin.
HUGH: Oh?
STEPHEN: Yes. Very concerned. She was ironing the vacuum cleaner in here and came across some things of yours. Wanted me to have a look.

HUGH: She'd been searching my room...?
STEPHEN: Hoo, searching. Searching's a pretty strong word, old chap. Sure you want to go that far?
HUGH: I think so.
STEPHEN: Alright then, searching it is. Anyway, she was searching your room, and she found one or two things.
HUGH: She doesn't understand, Father...
STEPHEN: That's exactly what I thought, old fellow. I thought hello, a few pictures of busty ladies, where's the harm in that? So I came up here, had a look around, and came across this.

STEPHEN HOLDS UP THE SKULL OF A GOAT WITH KNIVES PLUNGED INTO THE EYE SOCKETS.

HUGH: I'd rather you put that down, Father...
STEPHEN: Gavin, this is not a picture of a busty lady.
HUGH: No.
STEPHEN: No. Not by the very longest of long chalks.
HUGH: Father...
STEPHEN: Now I'm going to ask you something, Gavin, and I'd be obliged if you'd give me as straight an answer as you possibly can. Alright?
HUGH: Alright.
STEPHEN: Are you trying to summon up Satan on a regular basis?
HUGH: Huh, don't be silly, Father...
STEPHEN: Answer me, Gavin. If you please.
HUGH: Of course not.
STEPHEN: Sure?
HUGH: Positive.
STEPHEN: Well, Gavin, I'm pleased to hear it. Your mother and I have done a lot of

	work to this house since we came here. New kitchen. Gas central heating. Car port. Knowing that Satan was in the house would... well, take a bit of the shine off it all, if you follow me.
HUGH:	I know, Father.
STEPHEN:	And make the place a damn sight harder to sell, I wouldn't be surprised. So this little fellow is..?
HUGH:	Lardwayne.
STEPHEN:	Lardwayne?
HUGH:	Lardwayne. He is a god.
STEPHEN:	Is he? Is he really? Of... anything in particular? I mean, does he specialise at all?
HUGH:	Lardwayne is the god of everything and nothing.
STEPHEN:	Ah hah. Bit of an all-rounder, then? Good. And what might Lardwayne be doing under your bed, Gavin, if that's not too probing a question?
HUGH:	I worship Lardwayne, Father.
STEPHEN:	Oh you do. I see. Well, that's sort of cleared things up. Your mother will be very relieved, I know.
HUGH:	Good.
STEPHEN:	Er...why?
HUGH:	Why what?
STEPHEN:	Why do you worship Lardwayne, Gavin? She's bound to ask, you see, and it's probably easier if I can just give her a thumbnail picture...
HUGH:	Because all other systems of political and religious thought are as rotting carcasses in the desert of human folly.
STEPHEN:	Hmm.

HUGH: Only Lardwayne, fount of power and destruction, lord of vengeance, grand priest of the far worlds beyond Trappithew, only he has the answer.
STEPHEN: Rrrrright. Which is?
HUGH: Kill.
STEPHEN: Kill?
HUGH: Kill.
STEPHEN: I've seen one of these before, you see.
HUGH: Have you?
STEPHEN: Oh I know what you think. To you, I'm just a cardiganed old fool who spends his life adjusting the colour balance on the wireless, but I had a life too, you know.
HUGH: Of course you had.
STEPHEN: Not much of a life, but a life nonetheless.
HUGH: Father...
STEPHEN: Thirty-three years trouble-shooting for Her Majesty's Stationery Office. Not many people can say that.
HUGH: That...thing, is for a geography project I'm doing at college.
LONG PAUSE.
STEPHEN: Knew it. I knew there was a perfectly reasonable explanation. So what's the project on?
HUGH: Greater Manchester's Traffic Zoning policy, '81 to '86.
STEPHEN: '81 to '86? Good heavens. Bitten off a fair old chunk, haven't you?
HUGH: I'm calling it 'Contra-Flow. The Way Forward?'
STEPHEN: What an excellent title. One of the best titles I've come across since 'The Thirty-Nine Steps', which happened to be a... so this?

HOLDS UP THE SKULL.
HUGH: Background stuff.
STEPHEN: Background stuff, I see. And this...?
STEPHEN RUMMAGES IN THE BOX AND PRODUCES A LARGE DAGGER WITH A NASTILY TWISTED BLADE.
STEPHEN: This wouldn't be for extracting the organs of young virgins, would it, Gavin? Be honest with me now. I don't mind what you tell me, as long as it's the truth.
HUGH: Honestly, Father, what an idea...

PRIVATISATION
STEPHEN ADDRESSES THE CAMERA.
STEPHEN: Ladies and gentlemen. You know, they say that size isn't important. What I always say is, size isn't important, provided it's very big.
HUGH POPS HIS HEAD INTO FRAME.
HUGH: Sorry to interrupt. You don't know where my toothbrush is, do you?
STEPHEN: Ah. Meant to tell you about that. I had a bit of an accident with some vomit. Belonging to a friend. I'm afraid I had to use your toothbrush. What happened was, Terry got into a bit of a tangle, pubic-wise, so I lent him your toothbrush.
HUGH: That's alright. Where is it now?
STEPHEN: In the cupboard under the sink.
HUGH: Cheers.
HUGH MAKES TO GO.
STEPHEN: Hugh, where are you going?
HUGH: I'm going to live in New Zealand.
STEPHEN: Right. For the weekend, or...?
HUGH: For good. I've had it with this bloody country. I'm leaving this country for good.
STEPHEN: Hm. Any particular reason?

HUGH: A whole raft of reasons, Stephen.
STEPHEN: Give us a for instance.
HUGH: I cannot bear to hear the word 'raft' used to mean anything other than 'raft'.
STEPHEN: Right. Anything else?
HUGH: I said to myself this morning: if I hear one more person talk about identifying core objectives, I shall go ballistic. If I hear one more person say 'I shall go ballistic,' I shall go to New Zealand. It's that simple.
STEPHEN: Hugh, I think I know you well enough to say that there's more to this than meets the eye.
HUGH: I'm leaving for tax reasons.
STEPHEN: Really?
HUGH: The taxes are far too low.

NICENESS POLICE

HUGH IS HAVING A ROW WITH HIS WIFE AT HOME. THEY ARE WATCHING TV, HUGH SWITCHES ONTO THE OTHER SIDE. HIS WIFE STARES AT HIM FOR A MOMENT AND GETS UP TO CHANGE MANUALLY.

WIFE: If you want to watch that kind of thing, you can get a video out when I've gone to bed.
HUGH: (CHANGING BACK) Shut your face, you stupid tart.
WIFE: (changing again) Don't call me a tart, you fat slob.
HUGH: Stick it between your thighs, woman. We're watching this.

SHE TRIES TO CHANGE AGAIN, BUT HE HAS THE REMOTE CONTROL AND IT'S MUCH EASIER FOR HIM. SHE LAUNCHES HERSELF AT HIM. HE ENJOYS THE GAME OF HOLDING IT OUT OF HER REACH.

WIFE: Give me that.
HUGH: Sod off, woman.
WIFE: You bastard! You foul, cruel, mean, disgusting bastard.
HUGH: Temper, temper. You're turning into your mother, that's your trouble.

WE SEE TWO SWEET CHILDREN, A GIRL AND BOY, LIKE THE BROTHER AND SISTER IN MARY POPPINS, STANDING IN THEIR PYJAMAS IN THE DOORWAY, WATCHING THEIR PARENTS ROW.

WIFE: My mother! Don't talk to me about my mother. At least she doesn't drink a pint of gin a day like certain people's mothers. At least she's not a drunken hag of a bitch.
HUGH: Up your flap, you pathetic cow.

THEY CONTINUE TO ROW AND SCREAM AT EACH OTHER, AD LIB. THE CHILDREN LOOK AT EACH OTHER UNHAPPILY. THEY NOD AND MOVE AWAY, A DECISION ARRIVED AT. WE SEE, WITH HUGH AND HIS WIFE STILL SCREAMING INSULTS AT EACH OTHER AND, IN THE BACKGROUND, THE BOY AND GIRL ON THE TELEPHONE. WE DIMLY HEAR 'AND HURRY PLEASE...' OR SOME SUCH PHRASE. THERE IS A SCREECH OF BRAKES. THE NOISE OF THEIR ARGUMENT AND THE NOISE OF STEVEN SEAGAL'S VIOLENCE BECOME INTOLERABLE. AND A RING ON THE DOORBELL.

HUGH: Get the door, cow-bitch.
WIFE: Get it yourself, pig-arse.

THE CHILDREN ANSWER THE DOOR THEMSELVES AND STEPHEN COMES IN, WEARING A MOST UNUSUAL STYLE OF POLICE UNIFORM. POSSIBLY YELLOW OR PINK, BUT OTHERWISE UNMISTAKABLY A POLICE UNIFORM, COMPLETE WITH HELMET. HE WALKS IN SMILING, TOUSLING THE CHILDREN'S HAIR, TOWARDS THE ROWING COUPLE.

STEPHEN: Hello!

THEY STOP.

HUGH:	Who the bag of pus are you?
STEPHEN:	(EXTENDING HAND) Sergeant Derek Hopkiss, Metropolitan.
WIFE:	Police?
STEPHEN:	Niceness police.
HUGH:	You what?
STEPHEN:	Niceness police.
HUGH:	Niceness police?
STEPHEN:	Well, we like people to be nice. We received a call from Mark and Samantha, just now. They told us you weren't being nice. Popped in to see if I could help in any way.
HUGH:	Why can't you mind your own business, for Christ's sake? Bog off out of it, can't you?
WIFE:	Give him a chance, Don. Since he's...
HUGH:	Will you shut your bleeding neck, you daft warthog?
STEPHEN:	Ah. Whoops. There we are already. You're not being nice, and that's a pity. We don't say 'daft warthog', we say, 'my beloved'.
HUGH:	Look...
STEPHEN:	And we don't say 'shut your bleeding neck' we say 'that's a very interesting point.'
HUGH:	If you don't get out of...
STEPHEN:	Let's put those together, can we? 'That's a very interesting point, my beloved.' Go on, try it, old fellow.
HUGH:	I'm not going to...
STEPHEN:	Just to please me.
HUGH:	Why the hell should I...
STEPHEN:	(REPROVINGLY) Uh uh!
HUGH:	And then, you'll go?
STEPHEN:	Certainly I'll leave when you've started being nice to each other.

HUGH: (GRUDGINGLY) That's a very interesting point, my beloved.
STEPHEN: Well now, that didn't sound very sincerely meant, but I'll let it go for the time being. Now. Mark and Samantha tell me it all started with the television, is that right?
WIFE: He wants to watch 'Hard To Kill'.
HUGH: Damned right I do. And I'm going to.
STEPHEN: And you'd like to catch up on 'EastEnders'?
WIFE: That's right Derek. Not much to ask is it?
STEPHEN: Well now. Here's my scheme. Why not simply turn it off?
HUGH: You what?
STEPHEN: Simply turn the silly old thing off, invite Mark and Samantha in and have a jolly game of Spillikins or hunt the slipper. What do you say to that?
HUGH: I say, 'Snot off out of it before I set fire to you, you creepy little turd,' that's what I say.
STEPHEN: No, Don, you don't, actually. You say, 'There's an interesting idea.'

TART
STEPHEN IS WALKING ALONG THE STREET. A TART EMERGES.
TART: Hello darlin'.
STEPHEN: Oh. Hello.
TART: You after a nice time?
STEPHEN: I'm so sorry?
TART: I can give you the best time you've ever had. You look like you need it.
STEPHEN: Can you?
TART: Yeah.
STEPHEN: Well, that would be lovely.
TART: What do you like?

STEPHEN: I'm so very sorry?

HUGH, AS A POLICEMAN IS APPROACHING. TART LOWERS HER VOICE.

TART: Shut up a sec. (RAISING HER VOICE AGAIN) You want the time, yeah?

STEPHEN: A good time, yes please.

TART: The time is twenty-five past four.

HUGH: (CHECKING A LARGE POCKET WATCH) Half past more like.

STEPHEN: Really? I make it twenty to.

TART: Yeah, well.

HUGH: No, no, no, no, no. This watch is never wrong.

STEPHEN: But hers is better.

HUGH: Come again, sir?

STEPHEN: She told me that she could give me the best time.

HUGH: Oh did she indeed.

TART LOOKS DAGGERS AT STEPHEN.

TART: I just meant this watch is accurate, that's all.

HUGH: Oh, that's what you meant is it? Just what exactly did she say to you, sir?

STEPHEN: Well... let me think. She told me she could give me the best time I've ever had. Then she asked how I would like it and I was about to reply in the twenty-four hour clock, because I was in the army and that's how I always thinks of it .. you know 1625 hours that kind of thing. But then you came along and she told me to keep my voice down.

HUGH: I'll bet she did, sir. You come along with me, my girl. Just you leave her to me, sir. We know young Sara, here, down the nick, you can bank on it.

STEPHEN: Oh, but Constable, come now. No harm's been done... surely we can stretch a point here and let her go on her way. She's young, she knows no better and besides...
HUGH: Besides, sir?
STEPHEN: I was about to offer her some money for a good shag.
HUGH: Right ho, sir. Seeing as it's Easter.
(MWAH, FUCKING, MWAH.)

CELEBRITIES TONIGHT

LONDON NIGHT TIME. DRAMATIC MUSIC. TIMPANI. FANFARE. THE TITLE OF THE PROGRAMME 'CELEBRITIES TONIGHT' WRITES ITSELF ACROSS THE SCREEN. CROWDED LONDON STREETS OUTSIDE A CINEMA. HUGH STANDS IN FRONT OF THE CROWD WITH A MICROPHONE. THIS IS EITHER DONE SUPERIMPOSED ON FOOTAGE OF A PAST EVENT OR WE MAKE THE DEEP PLUNGE OF RECORDING THIS DURING A REAL PREMIERE OR SHOWBIZ BASH.

HUGH: Good evening from a packed and exciting scene in the heart of the West End's famous London for our gala celebrity opening. All around me, as you can see, crowds are here, paparazzi, TV crews and ordinary members of the public, jostling for the attention of some of the celebrity stars who are expected this evening. I'm going to try and talk to some of them as they make their way in. Judy is actually inside where she'll be meeting some more celebrities. Judy, are there any celebrities in there at the moment?
STEPHEN: Chris, it's very early. We only expect the B list to come as early as this. I am with producer Larry Mankowitz however, whose evening this is. Larry,

	what exactly is this celebrity opening all about?
LARRY:	Judy, we are very excited about the new celebrity that we are opening tonight.
STEPHEN:	What is his or her name?
LARRY:	Our new celebrity is called Sharon Wade.
STEPHEN:	Sharon Wade.
LARRY:	That's right. Sharon is probably the hottest celebrity in the States right now and we are very proud to be opening her in the States for her European premiere.
STEPHEN:	So all these celebrities have come to see Sharon Wade being opened here tonight.
LARRY:	I can't answer that right now.
HUGH:	The special Royal Celebrity is arriving at eight o'clock, of course. Are people very excited? Is there a feverish amount of anxiety?
STEPHEN:	Well, Chris, let's see. Here's a non-celebrity. Excuse me madam, are you very excited about all the celebrities...?

SUSPICIOUS GIT

AN INDIAN RESTAURANT. HUGH AND STEPHEN ARE WAITING, SEPARATELY, FOR SOME TAKEAWAYS. STEPHEN IS READING A PAPER, HUGH IS SIPPING SOME LAGER. THROUGHOUT THE SKETCH, HUGH TREATS EVERYTHING THAT IS SAID AS IF IT'S SOME KIND OF PRACTICAL JOKE, AND EVERYONE ELSE AS IF THEY'RE MAD. AN INDIAN WAITER ENTERS WITH TWO BAGS OF FOOD (HAVE FAITH, ROG).

WAITER: Smith?

STEPHEN LOOKS ROUND TO SEE IF THERE IS A SMITH PRESENT. HUGH SNIGGERS.

WAITER: Smith?

STEPHEN SHAKES HIS HEAD. THE WAITER EXITS. HUGH SUDDENLY BURSTS OUT LAUGHING.

HUGH:	What did he say?
STEPHEN:	Smith.
HUGH:	Smith?
STEPHEN:	A takeaway for Smith.
HUGH:	(SNIGGERING) What?
STEPHEN:	He wanted to know if either of us was called Smith.
HUGH:	Tscch. Pillock.
STEPHEN:	I beg your pardon?
HUGH:	Smith.
STEPHEN:	Someone called Smith ordered a takeaway, and he wanted to know who it was.
HUGH:	Tscch. Berk.
STEPHEN:	Why is he a berk for wanting to know if someone's called Smith?
HUGH:	I'm not called Smith.
STEPHEN:	No, well he didn't give you the takeaway, did he?
HUGH:	(MIMICKING THE WAITER) Smith?
STEPHEN:	Look, what is wrong with asking if either of us is called Smith?
HUGH:	I'm not called Smith.
STEPHEN:	He didn't know that.
HUGH:	Shut up.
STEPHEN:	What?
HUGH:	You're mad.
STEPHEN:	What do you mean?
HUGH:	You're as bad as him. Talking... Smith?
STEPHEN:	Look, what is the matter with you? All he said was 'Smith'. What is wrong with that?

HUGH JUST SNIGGERS, NERVOUSLY.

STEPHEN:	Don't laugh. Don't sit there laughing like some kind of turd. Tell me! Tell me what is wrong with a waiter asking for someone called Smith!

HUGH: Alright, alright. Tschh. Honestly.
STEPHEN: AAARGGH!!!

SPECTRE

HUGH IS DRIVING A CAR TOWARDS AN AUTOMATIC CAR WASH. HE LOOKS ROUND NERVOUSLY, AS THE FRONT WHEELS ENGAGE IN THE SLOTS. THEN SPEAKS INTO THE MICROPHONE CONTRAPTION ABOVE THE START BUTTON.

HUGH: Mother Goose has unusually fat ankles.

THERE IS A CLICK. THE BRUSHES DESCEND AND THE CAR IS HIDDEN IN FOAM AND WATER. WHEN THE BRUSHES LIFT, THE CAR IS EMPTY. CUT TO: A SPECTRE-LIKE ROOM. A DOZEN MEN IN SUITS SIT ROUND A LARGE TABLE. AT THE END OF THE TABLE ON A PODIUM, SITS A SILHOUETTED FIGURE, STEPHEN, STROKING A STUFFED WHITE CAT. ONE OF THE MEN, NUMBER 12, IS ON HIS FEET, FINISHING A REPORT.

NUMBER 12: The operation was concluded with the loss of only two of our operatives...

A DOOR SWISHES OPEN AND HUGH HURRIES IN AND SLIDES INTO AN EMPTY SEAT.

STEPHEN: You are late, number 7.
HUGH: Sorry. Had to get some cheese... my wife's making a... we didn't have any cheese, basically.
STEPHEN: Proceed, number 12.
NUMBER 12: Overall profit on this operation, including sale of the Journeyman space probe to the Chinese Government, one hundred and fourteen million dollars...
STEPHEN: The result is satisfactory. Number 7. Your report.
HUGH: Right, yes. Er... well, not a bad month, really, considering we had this bug going round and a lot of people... did anyone here have it? I woke up on a Wednesday, felt fine, then at about lunchtime...

STEPHEN:	You report, number 7.
HUGH:	Yes. Right ho. Er... I haven't actually written anything down... at least I did, but Sophie, who's my youngest..
STEPHEN:	Number 7.
HUGH:	Hello?
STEPHEN:	You were assigned the objective of fatally undermining the morale of the British people. What progress has been made?
HUGH:	Well, let's see. Managed to get 'Woman's Hour' moved from two o'clock to ten o'clock in the morning, which got a lot of people quite upset...
STEPHEN:	What else?
HUGH:	What else. All Sunday Papers have those little shiny brochures that fall out onto the kitchen floor when you open the magazine.

SILENCE FROM THE REST.

HUGH:	I mean, that's assuming you open the magazine in your kitchen. If you open it on a bus, the brochures aren't going to find their way back to your kitchen and lie down on the floor... although we're working on that.
STEPHEN:	Number 7.
HUGH:	Yes?
STEPHEN:	You know the price of failure.
HUGH:	Er... it's quite a lot, isn't it?
STEPHEN:	Members of the organisation who...

I'M A SUCKER

STEPHEN SITS AT A HIGH-TECH DESK. A BIG COMPUTER IN FRONT OF HIM.

STEPHEN:	I have to confess I'm an absolute sucker for modern technology. It's absolutely

amazing what you can do these days isn't it. Handwriting recognition is now pretty much old hat, and there's voice recognition too. I mean I can remember when the fax machine was considered pretty impressive, but now, with digitising software and one of these home computers you can actually transmit voice messages. Let me show you what I mean. Hugh is across there, the other side of the studio...

HUGH SITTING AT ANOTHER COMPUTER. HE WAVES GUILTILY. WHY GUILTILY? WELL, HE'S HUGH, ISN'T HE?

STEPHEN: ... but he could actually be the other side of the world for all I care. All I need is one of these, that's a high-speed data modem, a computer, a microphone like so, a digital telephone line, and some software that can digitise my voice. I'll also need a big hard disk, because of course digitised sounds are very greedy on memory. Right. I dial up Hugh's number like so...

HUGH'S PHONE RINGS AND IS ANSWERED, NOT BY HUGH.

STEPHEN: ... Hugh's computer has answered. And as you can see a screen comes up to show that we're 'handshaking' as the jargon has it. Now. I click 'Voice messaging' here and speak into the microphone. 'Hello, Hugh it's Stephen here.'

SHOT OF SCREEN, WE CAN SEE THAT THE SOUND WAVES FORM ON THE SCREEN.

STEPHEN: ... that's being digitised and can now be sent to Hugh's modem.

CUT TO HUGH RECEIVING DATA.

STEPHEN: (OOV) Hugh can now interpret that data with his software... which he's doing and click 'play' and... (HUGH CLICKS A MOUSE

OR WHATEVER. OUT OF HIS COMPUTER COMES, AT THE WRONG PITCH, A VERY SLOW 'HELLO, HUGH, IT'S STEPHEN HERE.') You see! Obviously in a few years prices will come down and for just a few thousand pounds you'll be able to have actual voice messaging conversations with someone thousands of miles away, as long as they've got the software, the computer, the modem and of course...

STEPHEN'S TELEPHONE RINGS. HE ANSWERS.

HUGH: (OOV) Just to let you know that that came through very clearly and well.

TURNPIKE SONG

HUGH SINGS AT THE PIANO.

Six o'clock in the morning,
Everything is quiet,
Nobody is stirring,
Everything is quiet,
New Jersey Turnpike stretched out before me,
New Jersey Turnpike up ahead,
I had a New Jersey Turnpike for breakfast,
I've got a New Jersey Turnpike on my head,
What is a turnpike? (x3)
And whatever it is, what's so special about the one
    in New Jersey?

Got my '57 Chevy,
In the boot of my car,
I'm gonna to take it to the levy,
Hope it's not too far,
I seen a lot of things,
That made me stop and think,
But if I see a Hershey bar,
I'm gonna go in and have a drink...

ONE THING SONG
HUGH STRUMS A PIANO.
One thing, I'll never forget about you,
One thing that will always mean the same.
When I hear that thing, it makes my heart flutter,
Yes I thrill to the sound of your name,
MUSIC GATHERS ITS SKIRTS, AND STEPHEN SHOUTS VERY LOUDLY FROM OFFSTAGE.
STEPHEN: MARJORIE...
HUGH: Marjorie, I can't stop singing it,
Marjorie, it's got such a ring to it,
Though we may be miles apart,
There's one thing engraved on my leg,
And that one thing is...
STEPHEN: MARJORIE...
HUGH: Your name...
The name you have...
You answer to it... Marjorie.

NOTES

THE FIRST BIT
1. Stephen Fry, *Moab Is My Washpot*, Random House, London, 1997.
2. *Friday Night, Saturday Morning*, BBC1 16/11/1979 (unreleased).
3. *Ibid.*
4. Fry, *Moab Is My Washpot*.
5. *Ibid.*
6. *Ibid.*
7. *Ibid.*
8. Stephen Fry, *The Ode Less Travelled*, Hutchinson, London, 2005.
9. Fry, *Moab Is My Washpot*.
10. *Ibid.*
11. *Ibid.*
12. *Ibid.*
13. *Ibid.*
14. *Ibid.*
15. *Ibid.*
16. *Ibid.*
17. *Ibid.*
18. *Ibid.*
19. *Ibid.*
20. Stephen Fry, *The Fry Chronicles*, Michael Joseph, London, 2010.
21. *Ibid.*
22. *Ibid.*
23. *Ibid.*

24 *Ibid.*
25 *Ibid.*
26 *Ibid.*
27 *Comedy Connections*, BBC 2005.
28 Fry, *The Fry Chronicles*.

THE NEXT BIT
1 Stephen Fry, *The Fry Chronicles*, Michael Joseph, London, 2010.
2 *Ibid.*
3 *Ibid.*
4 *Ibid.*
5 *Desert Island Discs*, BBC R4 1996.
6 Fry, *The Fry Chronicles*.
7 *Ibid.*
8 *Ibid.*
9 *Alfresco*, Granada TV, dates unknown 1983–84 (Network DVD, 2009).
10 Fry, *The Fry Chronicles*.
11 *Ibid.*
12 *Ibid.*
13 *Alfresco*, Granada TV, dates unknown 1983–84 (Network DVD, 2009).
14 *The Crystal Cube*, BBC2, 07/07/1983 (unreleased).
15 Fry, *The Fry Chronicles*.
16 *Ibid.*
17 *Ibid.*
18 Stephen Fry, *Paperweight*, Heinemann, London, 1992.
19 Robert Butler, 'The Press as Toilet Paper', *The Independent*, 26 February 1995.
20 *Me & My Girl*, Samuel French Ltd, 1990.
21 *Alfresco*, Granada TV, dates unknown 1983–84 (Network DVD, 2009).
22 Fry, *The Fry Chronicles*.
23 *Ibid.*
24 *Ibid.*
25 *Ibid.*

26 *Saturday Live*, Granada TV, dates unknown (Network DVD, 2009).
27 *Ibid.*
28 Fry, *The Fry Chronicles*.
29 *Ibid.*
30 *Ibid.*

THE MAIN BIT
1 *Saturday Live*, Granada TV, dates unknown (Network DVD, 2009).
2 *Blackadder Rides Again.*
3 *Comedy Connections*, BBC 2005.
4 Stephen Fry, *The Fry Chronicles*, Michael Joseph, London, 2010.
5 Stephen Fry, *More Fool Me*, Michael Joseph, London, 2014.
6 *Ibid.*
7 *Ibid.*
8 *Saturday Night Fry*, BBC Radio 4, 30/04/1988 (BBC Audio, 2009).
9 Stephen Fry, *More Fool Me*, Michael Joseph, London, 2014.
10 *Ibid.*
11 *Jeeves & Wooster*, Granada TV, 22/04/1990 (ITV Studios DVD, 2005).
12 *Comic Relief*, BBC1, 15/03/1991 (unreleased).
13 Stephen Fry, *More Fool Me*, Michael Joseph, London, 2014.
14 *Peter's Friends*, Channel 4 Films, 1994 (Eiv DVD, 2001).
15 *Spitting Image*, Central TV, dates unknown (release unknown).
16 *Christmas Night with the Stars*, BBC2, 27/12/1994.
17 *A Bit of Fry & Laurie*, BBC Radio 4, date unknown (unreleased).
18 BBC Video commercial, *c.* 1993 (unreleased).

THE LAST BIT
1 *Fortysomething*, Carlton TV, 2003 (Strawberry Media, 2012).
2 *Parkinson*, BBC 2007.

INDEX

A Bit of Fry and Laurie (ABOF&L): commissioned 119; pilot 131, 133–4, 135, 139–43, 157, 165; first episode transmission 161; first series 146, 154–61; second series 163–5, 174, 175–80, 182; third series 180, 189–96, 210; fourth series 205–9, 210–19, 221, 223, 227, 230–1, 234, 238; compilations 228, 229, 256; fourth wall 156–7; guide 269–70; lost landscape of 262; move to BBC1 210–11; name of show 211–12, 228; new audience after *House* 256; partnership end 241, 250; radio shows 227–8; songs 219–20; 'Soupy twist!' ending 193–5, 219, 238; targets 122, 190; theme tunes 142, 176, 196; thirtieth anniversary 263, 266; tie-in books 183–4, 187, 196; 'Vox Pops' 157–60, 176, 177, 190, 196, 216, 231; *see also* sketches; songs; unseen archive extracts

A Bit More Fry & Laurie (book) 184

ABOF&L *see A Bit of Fry and Laurie*

Absolute Power 217
Absolutely Fabulous 209, 260
Adams, Douglas 17, 49, 69, 81, 115, 131, 214, 245
Aitken, Maria 180
Alan & Bernard 58, 59, 77, 84
Alas Smith & Jones 105
Alfresco 78–9, 84–6, 88, 89, 90, 94–6, 107, 157
All or Nothing at All 206, 218
Allam, Roger 223
Allen, Keith 66, 143
Allen, Tony 66
Alliance & Leicester adverts 80, 195, 223
Alternative Comedy 66, 70, 73–5, 83, 97, 260
Anderson, Clive 17, 146, 220, 240
Anderson, Lindsay 53
Andreas, Dimitri 179
Aniston, Jennifer 243
Anything More Would Be Greedy 161
Arden, Annabel 52
Arden, Mark 104, 105
Armitage, Reginald 20, 92, 102, 115
Armitage, Richard 21, 60–1, 63–4, 68, 70, 72, 78–9, 92, 102, 115
Armstrong, Alexander 261
Atkinson, Rowan: ABOF&L 179–80; and

Armitage 21; *Blackadder II* 102, 103; *Blackadder the Third* 128, 129, 130; *Blackadder Goes Forth* 165; and *The Cellar Tapes* 60; class register sketch 46; Fringe First award 44; and Fry 69, 93, 116; *Hysteria* shows 138, 167, 186; *Maybe Baby* 244; *Not the Nine O'Clock News* 21; Perrier Award panel 66–7; royalty visit 175; *Saturday Live* 121; *The Thin Blue Line* 242; *Weekend In Wallop* 103
Atkinson-Wood, Helen 120, 186
Aunts Aren't Gentlemen (Wodehouse) 203, 204
Ayckbourn, Alan 58–9, 78, 205

B15 (radio show) 98
Bachelors Anonymous 198
Baddiel, David 211, 261
Bambi (*The Young Ones* episode) 89–90
Banks, Morwenna 67, 98, 192
Barker, Ronnie 105; *see also* The Two Ronnies
Barlow, Patrick 218, 250
Baron Cohen, Sacha 250
Barraclough, John *see* Peter & John

369

Barrymore, Michael 107
Barton, John 54
Bathurst, Robert: *Anything More Would Be Greedy* 161; Cambridge Footlights 18, 20, 52; Cook meeting 68; *Injury Time* 67; *Joking Apart* 74, 218; *Kingdom* 256; *The Nearly Complete and Utter History of Everything* 250; *Saturday Night Fry* 149
BATS drama group, Cambridge 42, 45
BBC: *ABOF&L* 141–3, 210–11; *The Cellar Tapes* 70; *The Crystal Cube* 87, 88; Fry & Laurie pilots 86, 87, 115–16, 141–3; Fry approaches 35–6; radio work 98
BBC Broadcasting House 98
BBC Radio 18, 63, 64; *see also* Radio 1; Radio 4
BBC TV Centre 179, 262
Beatnews 98–9
Before the Act 138
'BEHHH!' 42, 166, 229
Bennett, Alan 28, 43, 72, 102, 242, 245, 246
Bentine, Michael 126
Bergman, Martin 18, 20, 21, 60, 67, 198, 199, 202
Beyond the Footlights 68, 70, 71, 209
Beyond the Fringe 6, 71
Bigger Than Hitler, Better Than Christ (Mayall) 238
Billington, Michael 71
Bird, John 217, 243
The Bishop & The Warlord 137, 191
Bishop, Kevin 163, 190, 191, 192
Blackadder series 163, 191, 246, 264
The Black Adder 86, 102
Blackadder II 102–4, 113
Blackadder the Third 127–31
Blackadder Goes Forth 165–7, 168, 174

Blackadder Back & Forth 250
Blackadder: The Cavalier Years 147
Blackadder's Christmas Carol 161
Blair, Tony 140, 217
The Bleak Old Shop of Stuff 260
Bloody Lucky (anthology) 188
Bones 255
The Bonzo Dog Doo-Dah Band 33, 34
Booker, Jane 217
The Borrowers 243
Botham: The Musical 67
Bottom 238
Bowery, Leigh 115
Boyd, Don 90
Bradbury, Malcolm 161
Bragg, Billy 184
Branagh, Kenneth 121, 198, 199, 201
Bremner, Rory 98
Brett, Jeremy 258
Brett, Simon 98
Briers, Richard 169
Bright Young Things 248
Brigstocke, Marcus 205
Brint, Simon 219, 220
Broadbent, Jim 149
Brown, Gordon 140
Brown, Ian 132
B'Stard, Alan 160
Burstingfoam, Suckmaster 132–3
Burton, Tim 242
Bush, Kate 115, 221
By Jeeves (musical) 205

Callow, Simon 115, 148
Calloway, Cab 172
Cambridge Footlights: *Aladdin* 18–19; Alternative Comedy 66; *The Cellar Tapes* 52, 53, 55–61, 65–8, 70, 72, 198, 261, 269; centenary documentary 102; *Chox* 17; *Cinderella* 50; comedy influence 64, 260–1, 262; Edinburgh Fringe 24; *Electric*

Voodoo 22; *Friday Night, Saturday Morning* 21, 24, 50; Fry and Laurie first meeting 8, 9; Fry at Cambridge 42; Laurie joins 17; *Live From the Lighthouse* 250; May Week Revue 20; *Nightcap* 7, 20, 21, 22, 44; Perrier Award 66–7; *The Snow Queen* 24–5, 48, 50–1, 52; *Tag!* 18
Cambridge Mummers 7, 45
Cambridge University: Boat Race 16, 22–3, 45; Fry at 7, 40, 41–2, 45, 47, 60, 65; Laurie at 7–8, 15, 16, 65; *see also* Cambridge Footlights
Cameron, David 12
Cannon & Ball 74, 105, 139, 197
Canter, Jon: *ABOF&L* 164, 177, 193, 194, 195, 205; Cambridge Footlights 17, 154; *Fortysomething* 252; *I Love Stephen Fry* 249; Jo Green friendship 127; royalty visit 175
The Canterville Ghost 259
Capaldi, Peter 249
Carbide, Hecate 133
Carlton Club 102
Carmichael, Ian 33, 169, 196, 203
Carmichael, Rick 33
Cause Celeb (Fielding) 126
Cell Mates (Gray play) 224, 233, 234–7, 238, 242–3
The Cellar Tapes (Footlights show) 52, 53, 55–61, 65–8, 70, 72, 198, 261, 269
Chance 266
Chance in a Million 115
Chancellor, Anna 249
Channel 4 83, 97, 99, 104
Chariots of Fire 47, 53, 70
Charles, Prince 147, 175, 264
Christmas Night with the Stars (CNWTS) 224–7, 230, 270
Clary, Julian 106

Cleese, John: and Armitage 21; Cambridge Footlights 55, 64; 'Class sketch' 250; corporate comedy 80–1; *A Fish Called Wanda* 125; and Fry 69, 232; *Hysteria* 167; as influence 71, 72; *Secret Policeman's Ball* 114; *Secret Policeman's Third Ball* 124–5; tallness 49; Video Arts 80
Clenchwarton, Gerald 100
Cleobury, Simbold 190
Clituris, Simon 140, 147
Clooney, George 253, 260
Clunes, Martin 215
CNWTS *see Christmas Night with the Stars*
Cold Comfort Farm 222
Colin's Sandwich 217
Colman, Olivia 261, 266
Coltrane, Robbie: *Alfresco* 83, 85, 95, 96; *The Crystal Cube* 87; Samuel Johnson show 127; *Tutti Frutti* 121; *The Young Ones* 89
comedy: Alternative Comedy 66, 70, 73–5, 83, 97, 260; Cambridge Footlights 64, 260–1, 262; corporate comedy 80–1, 105; 'PC humour' 125; satire 139; sketch comedy 44, 72, 116, 155, 158, 256, 262–3
Comedy Connections 209, 240, 258, 270
The Comedy Store 20, 74, 112
Comic Relief 113–14, 127, 146–7, 167, 184–6, 221, 260
Comic Relief Utterly Utterly Live 113
The Comic Strip 83, 89, 104
The Common Pursuit (Gray play) 148, 224
Conan Doyle, Arthur 258–9
Connolly, Billy 103
Control & Tony 154–5, 164, 180, 184, 274–7

Coogan, Steve 201, 226
Cook, Peter: Cambridge Footlights 21, 55; Comic Relief 221; end of Cook & Moore 240; first meets Moore 6; friendship with Fry 232; as influence 71, 72, 209, 223, 232–3, 254; meeting at la Sorpresa 68–9; *Saturday Live* 107; tallness 49; *The Two of Us* 254; *Weekend In Wallop* 103; *Whose Line Is It Anyway?* 146; death of 232
Cook & Moore: 'Bo Dudley' 123; *Derek & Clive* 240; 'Goodbye' song 195; as influence 28–9, 34, 35, 150, 184, 240, 261; *Not Only ... But Also* 28, 147; Pete & Dud, 28, 240
Copper Bottom Band 258
Copper Bottom Blues (Laurie documentary) 258
Corbett, Ronnie 226; *see also* The Two Ronnies
Coren, Alan 189
Cornes, Lee 104
corporate comedy 80–1, 105
Countdown 192–3
Cromie, Anthony 29, 30, 31
Cryer, Barry 101, 126, 132
The Crystal Cube 87–8, 115, 269
Cumberbatch, Benedict 249
Cuminmyear, Peter 162
Cunterblast, Ted 162
Curtis, Richard: *Blackadder II* 102; *Blackadder the Third* 127–8, 129; *Blackadder Goes Forth* 165, 166; *Blackadder Back & Forth* 250; Comic Relief 113, 114, 146, 186; *Four Weddings and a Funeral* 126; Fry & Laurie friendship 64; *Hysteria* shows 167, 186; Oxford Revue 120; *The Tall Guy* 175

Dahl, Roald 197
Dale, Jim 246
Dalliard, Mr 157, 190–1, 216
The Dam Busters 265
'DAMN!' 154, 180
Danger Mouse 260
The Dangerous Brothers 104, 107, 109, 130
Darling, Captain 166
David Frost on Sketch Shows 263
Davies, Alan 248
Davies, Karl 256
Davis, Geena 243
Daws, Robert 183, 203, 218, 230, 238
De Quincy, Dr 76, 97, 103, 107
Deighton, Len 14, 192
Delve Special 99, 115, 131
Denim, Sue *see* Fry, Stephen
Dennis, Hugh 211
Derek & Clive 240; *see also* Cook & Moore
Dexter, Felix 225
'DHT' (Deep Humiliating Troub') 107
Diana, Princess 175
Didn't It Rain? (Laurie album) 258
Dixon, Willie 14
Docherty, Jack 147
Doctor Strangelove 178
Don & George 147
The Dongle of Donald Trefusis 247
Dover Street Jazzomaniacs 203
Down by the River (Laurie documentary) 258
Dracula monologue 57, 93, 116, 134, 135
Dragans of New York 252
Dreyfus, James 250
Dudley, Anne 171, 203
Duvitski, Janine 218, 230
Dwyer, Penny 52, 57, 58, 67, 70

Eastman, Brian 168, 169, 170, 172, 183, 198, 204
Eddington, Paul 179

Edinburgh Fringe:
  Alternative Comedy 66;
  Cambridge Footlights 7,
  20, 22, 24, 24; *The Cellar
  Tapes* 60, 65; Fringe
  First award 44, 47; Fry
  & Laurie meeting 7; Fry
  & Laurie appearance
  153; *Latin!* 47; Perrier
  Award 66
Edis, Steven 59
Edmondson, Ade: *Bottom*
  238; The Dangerous
  Brothers 104, 107,
  109, 130; *Filthy Rich
  & Catflap* 114; *Happy
  Families* 97; music 220;
  Rik & Ade double act
  104, 105, 107, 109, 130,
  197; *The Young Ones* 83
Edwards, Jimmy 17
Elizabeth II, Queen 36, 139
Elliott, Mark 104
Elton, Ben: on advertising
  79, 82; *Alfresco* 79,
  84, 94, 96; *Blackadder
  II* 102–3; *Blackadder
  the Third* 127–8, 129;
  Blackadder Goes Forth
  165, 166; *Blackadder
  Back & Forth* 250;
  Central Weekend 126;
  fame 117; *Filthy Rich &
  Catflap* 114; *Friday Night
  Live* 147; Fry's asthma
  attack 151; *Gasping* 181–
  2; *Happy Families* 96–7;
  on Laurie 244; *Maybe
  Baby* 244; *Saturday Live*
  105, 107, 119, 123;
  as scriptwriter 74, 75,
  76–7; *South of Watford*
  115; and swearing 110;
  *There's Nothing to Worry
  About!* 78; *The Thin Blue
  Line* 242; *Upstart Crow*
  260; *The Young Ones* 74,
  83, 89
Elton, Sir G. E. 84, 168
EMF 221
Enfield, Harry: comedy
  career 260; *Delve Special*
  99; fame 117; *Friday
  Night Live* 147; *Harry*

Enfield and Chums
  215; *Hysteria Hysteria
  Hysteria* 138; Radio 4
  115; *Saturday Live* 107,
  112, 113, 121; *Spitting
  Image* 121; *Television
  Programme* 179
Eton College 11–15
Everett, Kenny 190
The Exorcist 134
Experiment IV (Bush video)
  115
Exton, Clive 169, 170, 171,
  172, 173, 203, 204

Fable game series 259
'The Fabulous Tony'
  (Hawks) 178
The Failiure Press 38
Fascinating Aida 138
The Fast Show 180, 225,
  243
Fat Chance (Gray) 234–5
Fawcett, Richard 34, 35
Ferguson, Craig 186
Ferrell, Will 259
Fielding, Helen 126, 139
50 Not Out! 264
'50 Words for Snow' (Bush
  song) 221
Filthy Rich & Catflap 114
A Fish Called Wanda 125,
  180
Fitzgerald, F. Scott 39
Five Go Mad in Dorset
  (The Comic Strip) 83
Flanders & Swann 194,
  220, 261
Flight of the Phoenix 252
Flituris, Simon 140
Forrest, Timothy 195
Fortysomething 249–50,
  251–2
Forty Years On (Bennett
  play) 102
*Four Weddings and a
  Funeral* 126
Fox, Michael J. 243
Foxprints (McGinley) 198
French, Dawn 99, 105, 115,
  138, 153, 243, 244
French & Saunders 7, 105,
  153, 167, 190, 209, 211,
  219

Freud, Emma 186
Freud, Sigmund 25
Friday Night Live 147
*Friday Night, Saturday
  Morning* (Footlights
  show) 21, 24, 50
Friends 243
Frondo, Mighty Birdlord of
  Thribble 161
Frost, David 18, 157, 263
Frost, Stephen 104, 105
Frost Report 250
Frozen Assets (Wodehouse)
  46
Fry, Alan (father of SF) 25,
  26, 28, 36, 37, 45, 231,
  235, 237
Fry, George (uncle of SF) 25
Fry, Jo (sister of SF) 28, 45,
  145–6, 265
Fry, Marianne (née
  Neumann) (mother of
  SF) 25, 26, 36–8, 41, 45,
  231, 235
Fry, Roger (brother of SF)
  26, 27, 28, 29, 38, 175,
  223
Fry, Stephen
  birth 26
  childhood 26–31, 32–7
  family background 25–6
  education: Chesham
    Prep 26–7, 29; Stouts
    Hill School 29–31;
    Uppingham 31–6,
    60; Paston School 37;
    Norfolk College of
    Arts & Technology 37;
    Norwich City College
    40–1
  criminal behaviour 39–40
  at Cambridge 7, 40, 41–2,
    45, 47, 60, 65
  Cambridge Footlights 8,
    25, 42, 44, 47, 49–52,
    55–61, 65–7
  health and mental health:
    asthma attack 151;
    bipolar disorder 39,
    143, 231, 244–5,
    247; broken nose 26;
    cancer 266; depression
    156, 232, 235–6,
    244–5; developmental

delay diagnosis 36;
disappearances 137,
234–7, 238; drug use
143–4, 205; suicide
attempts 38, 231
interests: acting and drama
38, 41–5, 47, 52, 53–4,
102; black taxi cab 145;
comedy 28–9, 33–6,
44–5, 48, 63; computers
and gadgets 69, 131;
games and panel games
101; internet and social
media 246, 247; language
and speech 27–8, 31–3,
35, 135–6, 149–50, 187,
194; literature 30, 32;
motorbikes 92; musical
(in)ability 34; play
writing 45–6; poetry 38;
and Wilde 47
marriage to Elliott
Spencer 265
as National Treasure 245–6
partnership with Hugh
Laurie: first meeting 7–8,
9, 21, 48; early memories
23, 24, 25, 47; Noel Gay
signing 63–4, 68, 69; as
best man 162; corpsing
191, 250; falling out
137; friendship 205, 255,
266–7; Fry on Laurie
2, 49, 97, 101, 128–30,
144–5, 151–3, 164, 195,
240–2, 244, 255–7, 267;
Fry's disappearance 235,
236–7; as godfather
162, 240; Laurie on
Fry 2, 8, 48–9, 64,
97–8, 101, 130, 135–7,
151–3, 162–4, 200, 240,
245–6, 255, 259, 266–7;
Laurie's Hollywood Star
speech 1–2; last joint
performances 227, 239,
250; end of working
partnership 239–42;
potential reunion 263
as polymath 248
press coverage 125–6, 174
quoted comments: on
America 26, 122–3,
266; on comedy 8,
72–5, 78, 80–2, 97, 106,
109–10, 116–17, 139,
164, 234, 261–3; on
corporate comedy 80–2;
on criticism 140–1; on
family 26; on himself
9, 27–8, 29, 32, 140–1;
on honours 264–5; on
Mayall 73–4; on memory
8–9; on politics 91; on
radio 98; on Sayle 90;
on sketch comedy 263;
on success 261–2; on
swearing 126; on writing
75, 78, 92, 116–17, 132,
151–5, 157–8, 164
relationships and celibacy
32–3, 37–8, 91–2, 162,
243
sexuality 27, 32–3, 37–8,
45, 138
work:
adverts 80–2, 105, 195, 223
audio work and voiceovers:
audiobooks 197, 246,
266; *The Dongle of
Donald Trefusis* 247;
videogames 259; *Words
with Stephen Fry* 265
benefit shows: Comic Relief
114, 146–7, 184–6, 260;
Hysteria 167–8, 184,
186–7; *Live From the
Lighthouse* 250
books: *A Bit of Fry and
Laurie* tie-ins 183–4,
196; guide 270–1;
The Hippopotamus
222–3; *The Liar* 9, 181,
187–8, 198, 223; *Making
History* 247; memoir
144; *Mythos* 266; *The
Ode Less Travelled* 247;
Paperweight 189; *The
Stars' Tennis Balls* 247
films: *Alice in Wonderland*
242; *Bright Young
Things* 248; *Chariots of
Fire* (as extra) 47, 53;
A Fish Called Wanda
125; *Gossip* 90; *The
Hitchhiker's Guide to
the Galaxy* 260; *The
Hobbit* 265; *I.Q.* 221;
Peter's Friends 198–200;
Sabotage! 250; saves
Sense and Sensibility
222; *Sherlock Holmes*
film series 259; unmade
projects 198; *V for
Vendetta* 242; *Wilde*
242–3
live dates 116–17, 124–5,
133–9, 148–9, 153, 197,
257
political speech writing
139–40
print credits 90–2; 'Licking
Thatcher' 139; 'Things I
Do Not Do' 91–2
radio: *Delve Special*
99, 115, 131; Fringe
interview 65; *Fry's
English Delight* 245; *I
Love Stephen Fry* 249;
*I'm Sorry I Haven't a
Clue* 101, 251; *Injury
Time* 67; *In the Chair*
217; *In the Red* 217; *Just
a Minute* 101; *Kingdom*
radio pilot 256; *Loose
Ends* 99–100; *Nineteen-
Ninety-Four* 96; Radio
1 *Beatnews* 98–9; Radio
4 98, 132; *Saturday
Night Fry* 131–3,
149–50; *Whose Line Is It
Anyway?* 146
screenwriting: *A
Confederacy of Dunces*
221; *The Dam Busters*
265; *Long Island Iced
Tea* 221
television: *A Bit of Fry and
Laurie* 131, 139, 175–80,
189–96, 205, 209–19,
221, 223, 227, 230–1,
234, 238, 241; *Absolute
Power* 217; *Alfresco*
78–9, 84–6, 88, 89, 90,
94–6; BAFTAs presenter
248; *Blackadder II* 102–
4; *Blackadder the Third*
129–30; *Blackadder Goes
Forth* 165–7; *Blackadder
Back & Forth* 250; *The
Bleak Old Shop of Stuff*
260; *Bones* 255; *Celebrity*

Mastermind 251;
Central Weekend 126;
Chance in a Million 115;
Christmas Night with
the Stars 224–7, 230;
Cold Comfort Farm 222;
Comedy Connections
209, 240, 258; Comic
Relief 146–7, 184–6, 260;
The Common Pursuit
148; Countdown 193;
The Crystal Cube 87–8,
115, 269; Danger Mouse
260; documentaries 245,
271; 50 Not Out! 264;
Filthy Rich & Catflap
114; Fortysomething
250; Friday Night Live
147; Fry Night 264;
Fry & Laurie Reunited
258; Gadget Man 245;
The Great Indoors 265,
266; guide 269–70;
Happy Families 97; In
Confidence 245; Jeeves
& Wooster 169–74,
182–3, 196–7, 203–5,
262; Kingdom 256–7;
Last Chance to See
245; The Laughing
Prisoner 114; Live From
the Lighthouse 250;
The Nearly Complete
and Utter History of
Everything 250; Ned
Blessing 206; Never Mind
the Buzzcocks 251; The
New Statesman 160–1;
Not the Nine O'Clock
News writing credit
56; Old Flames 148;
Out There 244; panel
games 251; Planet Word
245; QI 248–9, 251;
Rita Rudner show 190,
198; Saturday Live 97,
104–5, 106–13, 119–23;
The Secret Life of the
Manic Depressive 244;
Spitting Image puppet
121, 201–2; Stalag Luft
206; There's Nothing to
Worry About! 77–8; This
Is David Lander 99, 147,
148; This Is Jinsy 260;
24: Live Another Day
265; University Challenge
45; Veep 266; Yonderland
260; The Young Ones
89–90
theatre: Beyond the
Footlights 71; Cell Mates
224, 233, 234–6, 238,
242–3; The Common
Pursuit 148; Latin! or
Tobacco and Boys 22,
46–7, 52, 102; Love's
Labour's Lost 53–4; Me
and My Girl 92–4, 115;
Twelfth Night 257
Fry & Laurie
first meeting 7–8, 9, 21, 48
Cambridge Footlights 50–1,
59, 70, 71
Noel Gay signing 63–4,
68, 69
launched as double act
104–5
adverts and voiceovers
80–2, 105, 195, 223, 259
films: Gossip 90; Peter's
Friends 90, 198–200, 218
live dates 116–17, 124–5,
133–9, 148–9, 153, 197
press coverage 174
sketches see sketches; songs;
unseen archive extracts
slapstick violence 129–30
Strom language 77, 149,
191, 216
last joint performances 227,
239, 250
end of working partnership
239–42
potential reunion 263
television: A Bit of Fry and
Laurie 131, 139–43,
154–61, 163–4, 175–80,
189–96, 205, 209–19,
221, 223, 227, 230–1,
234, 238, 241; Alfresco
78–9, 84–6, 88, 90, 94–6;
Blackadder II 102–4;
Blackadder the Third
127–31; Blackadder Goes
Forth 165–7; Blackadder
Back & Forth 250; The
Cellar Tapes 70; Comedy
Connections 209, 240,
258; Comic Relief 146–7,
184–6; The Crystal Cube
87–8, 115, 269; Filthy
Rich & Catflap 114;
Fortysomething 250;
Friday Night Live 147;
Fry & Laurie Reunited
258; guide 269–70;
Happy Families 97;
Jeeves & Wooster 169–
74, 182–3, 196–7, 203–5,
218, 257, 262, 270; The
Laughing Prisoner 114;
The New Statesman 160–
1; pilots 86, 116; Royal
Variety Performance 139;
Saturday Live 97, 104–5,
106–13, 119–23; There's
Nothing to Worry About!
77–8; The Young Ones
89–90
see also Fry, Stephen;
Laurie, Hugh
Fry & Laurie Reunited
(documentary) 258, 270
Fry Night (BBC Four) 264
Fry's English Delight (Radio
4) 245
'Fry's Turkish Delight' (Viz
comic strip) 202

Gadget Man 245
Galahad (film) 198
Galahad at Blandings
(Wodehouse) 14
games 259, 271
Gardhouse, Ian 99, 100
Gascoigne, Bamber 89
Gasping (Elton play) 181–2
Gay, Noel (Reginald
Armitage) 20, 92, 102,
115
Geldof, Bob 113, 114
George (Blackadder) 127,
128, 129, 166, 250
Gervais, Ricky 81
Giedroyc, Mel 250, 261
Gilbert, Brian 242
Gillies, Fiona 218
Girls On Top 105
'Glass Smash Jack' (EMF
song) 221
Goodall, Howard 126, 220

The Goodies 66, 209
The Goons 70, 175
Gordon & Stuart 59, 110–12, 139, 146, 178, 179, 180, 190
Gormenghast 257
Gossip 90, 198
Gran, Maurice 160
Granada TV 45, 72, 78, 89
Gray, Simon: Cell Mates 233, 234–7; The Common Pursuit 148, 224; Fat Chance 234–5
The Great Indoors 265, 266
Green, Jo (wife of HL) 126–8, 144–5, 154, 161–3, 167, 175, 183, 186–7, 195, 205–6, 253
The Groucho Club 143, 144
Gruffudd, Ioan 243
The Gun Seller (Laurie novel) 247
'Gunge Tank' 147
Gutfright, Gelliant 57, 216

Hailsham, Lord 102
Hale, Gareth 105
Hale & Pace 105, 139, 153
Hamilton, Lorraine 115, 237
Hamm, Jon 256
Happy Families 96–7
Hardie, Sean 21, 73
Hardy, Robin 198
Harris, Kim 43–4, 47–8, 50–1, 59, 65, 68, 91, 187
Harry Enfield and Chums 215
Harry Enfield's Television Programme 179
Harry Potter 246
Hasbeen, Colin 22
Hat Trick 105, 148
Hatch, David 18
Have You Seen the Yellow Book? 47
Havers, Nigel 179, 215
Hawks, Tony 178, 179
Hazlehurst, Ronnie 70
Health and Efficiency 156
Heap, Mark 205
The Hee Bee Gee Bees 24
Hendrie, James 132
Henry, Lenny 106, 107, 127, 220
Hicks, Bill 79
Hiddleston, Tom 266
Higson, Charlie 112, 113, 226
Hills, Julia 149
The Hippopotamus (Fry) 222–3
'Hit it, bitch!' 133
The Hitchhiker's Guide to the Galaxy (Adams) 69, 150, 218, 260
The Hobbit (film) 265
Holland, Jools 103, 114
Holmes, Sherlock 30, 36, 258–9, 266
Holmes and Watson (film) 259
Holness, Bob 134, 185, 186
Hordern, Michael 169
House 230, 249, 252–3, 254, 256, 257, 259
Hugh Laurie's Blues Changes 258
Hunter, Moray 98, 147
Hysteria shows 138, 167–8, 184, 186–7, 201, 250, 270

I Love Stephen Fry (play) 249
Iannucci, Armando 99, 150, 266
Idle, Eric 183
I'm Sorry I Haven't a Clue 101, 251
I'm Sorry, I'll Read That Again (ISIRTA) 140
The Importance of Being Earnest (Wilde) 31, 215
In Confidence 245
In the Red 217
Inchpractice, Tony 191
The Incredible String Band 33
Inglis & Marsh see Gordon & Stuart
Injury Time 24, 67
Innes, Neil 33
Inside the Actor's Studio: Hugh Laurie 137, 270
I.Q. (film) 221
ITV 86, 173
Izzard, Eddie 67, 186

Jackson, Michael (BBC2 controller) 224
Jackson, Paul: British comedy 104; Friday Night Live 147; Happy Families 96, 97; Saturday Live 97, 104, 105, 106; The Young Ones 96
Jackson, Peter 265
James, Clive 122, 261
Jammin' (radio show) 221
Jay, Antony 80
Jeeves & Wooster 169–74, 182–3, 196–7, 203–5, 218, 257, 262, 270
Jeeves in the Offing (Wodehouse) 203
Jencks, John 223
Jennings stories 197
Jensen, David 'Kid' 98
Jerome, Jerome K. 197
Jim'll Fix It 131
John, Elton 198
Johnson, Samuel 127
Joking Apart 74, 218
Jones, Griff Rhys 17, 21, 89, 105, 153, 197, 211, 235
Jongleurs 106
Jordan, Louis 133
Just a Minute 101

Kelly, Katie 19, 23, 48, 50, 51, 65, 98, 112, 127
A Kick Up the Eighties 73, 83
Kilby, John 70, 87
Kingdom 256–7
Kinnock, Neil 139–40
Kit & The Widow 138, 194
Kline, Kevin 125

Labour Party 139–40, 209
Laidlaw, Patricia (mother of HL) see Laurie, Patricia
Lance, James 205
Lander, David 99, 115, 147, 148, 218
Langham, Chris 21, 74
Last Chance to See 245
Late Show 232
Latin! or Tobacco and Boys (Fry play) 22, 46–7, 52, 102

The Laughing Prisoner 114
Laurie, Charles (brother of HL) 14
Laurie, Charles Archibald (Charlie) (son of HL) 145, 156, 161, 162, 175, 206, 212, 253
Laurie, Hugh
  birth 10
  childhood 10–12
  Eton College education 11–15
  family 9, 10, 12, 205–6, 253
  at Cambridge 7–8, 15, 16, 65
  Cambridge Footlights 8, 9, 17, 18–24, 47, 49–53, 55–61, 65–7
  health and mental health: depression 230, 243–4; drug use 144
  honoured with CBE 264
  interests: Hong Kong Police 15; literature 14; motorbikes 15, 69, 92; music 13, 14, 52–3, 59, 257–8; rowing 10, 15, 16–17, 19, 21, 22–3
  invents the spoffle 82
  partnership with Stephen Fry: first meeting 7–8, 9, 21, 48; early memories 23, 24, 25, 47; Noel Gay signing 63–4, 68, 69; corpsing 191, 250; falling out 137; friendship 205, 255, 266–7; Fry on Laurie 2, 49, 97, 101, 128–30, 144–5, 151–3, 164, 195, 240–2, 244, 255–7, 267; Fry's disappearance 235, 236–7; Laurie on Fry 2, 8, 48–9, 64, 97–8, 101, 130, 135–7, 151–3, 162–4, 200, 240, 245–6, 255, 259, 266–7; last joint performances 227, 239, 250; end of working partnership 239–42; potential reunion 263
  press coverage 174
  quoted comments: on America 123, 252, 254–5, 266; on comedy 10–11, 15, 17, 19, 64, 73, 80–2, 116–17, 139, 150–1, 164, 197, 206, 227, 234, 240; on corporate comedy 80–2; on Emma Thompson 18, 19; on himself 9–15, 17, 72, 73, 253; on music 257–8; on sports 22; on Wodehouse 14; on writing 75, 151, 154, 155, 157, 161–2, 164, 188–9
  relationships: Emma Thompson 18–19; Katie Kelly 19, 23, 48, 50–1, 65, 98, 112, 127; Jo Green (wife) 126–8, 144–5, 162–3, 183, 186–7, 205–6, 253
  work:
    adverts 80, 81, 105, 195, 223, 253–4
    audio work and voiceovers 81, 82, 197, 259, 271
    benefit shows: Comic Relief 146–7, 184–6, 221; *Hysteria* 167, 186–7; *Live From the Lighthouse* 250
    books: *A Bit of Fry and Laurie* tie-ins 183–4, 196; *The Gun Seller* 247; *The Paper Soldier* 247
    films: *The Borrowers* 243; *Flight of the Phoenix* 252; *Gossip* 90; *Hollywood* 252; *Holmes and Watson* 259; *Maybe Baby* 244; *101 Dalmatians* 243; *Peter's Friends* 198–200, 218; *A Pin for the Butterfly* 221; *Sense and Sensibility* 222; *Strapless* 150; *Stuart Little* 243; unmade projects 198
    live dates 116–17, 124–5, 133–9, 148–9, 153, 197
    music: *ABOF&L* 219–20, 238; blues music 13, 14, 52–3, 59, 203, 257–8; *Didn't It Rain?* 258; *Let Them Talk* 203, 258; pop promo appearances 115, 221; *The World of Jeeves & Wooster* 203; *see also* songs
    print credits 91
    radio: debut appearance 22; *Hugh Laurie's Blues Changes* 258; *In the Chair* 217; *Nineteen-Ninety-Four* 96; *Nineteen-Ninety-Eight* 98; *The Party Party* 98, 218; *Saturday Night Fry* 132, 149; *So Much Blood* 98; *Whose Line Is It Anyway?* 146
    television: *A Bit of Fry and Laurie* 131, 139, 175–80, 189–96, 205, 209–19, 221, 223, 227, 230–1, 234, 238, 241; accents 255; *Alfresco* 78–9, 84–6, 88, 90, 94–6; *All or Nothing At All* 206, 218; *Blackadder II* 104; *Blackadder the Third* 127–31; *Blackadder Goes Forth* 165–7; *Blackadder Back & Forth* 250; *Chance* 266; *Christmas Night with the Stars* 224–7, 230; *Comedy Connections* 209, 240, 258; *Comic Relief* 146–7, 184–6; *The Crystal Cube* 87–8, 115, 269; documentaries 271; *Dragans of New York* 252; *Filthy Rich & Catflap* 114; first TV appearance 21–2; *Fortysomething* 249–50, 251–2; *Friday Night Live* 147; *Friday Night, Saturday Morning* 21–2; *Friends* 243; *Fry & Laurie Reunited* 258; guide 269–70; *Happy Families* 97; *House* 230, 249, 252–3, 254, 256, 257, 259; *Jeeves & Wooster* 169–74,

182–3, 196–7, 203–5, 262; *The Laughing Prisoner* 114; *Live From the Lighthouse* 250; *The Nearly Complete and Utter History of Everything* 250; *The New Statesman* 160–1; *The Night Manager* 266; *QI* 251; *Red Dwarf* audition 150; *Saturday Live* 97, 104–5, 106–13, 119–23; *South of Watford* 115; *Spitting Image* puppet 121, 201–2; *There's Nothing to Worry About!* 77–8; *Veep* 266; *The Young Ones* 89–90
theatre: *Beyond the Footlights* 71; *Gasping* 181–2; *Love's Labour's Lost* 53–4
Laurie, Patricia (née Laidlaw) (mother of HL) 9–10, 11, 12, 13, 162
Laurie, Rebecca Augusta (daughter of HL) 205, 222, 253
Laurie, William 'Ran' (father of HL) 9–10, 11, 12, 16, 22, 162
Laurie, William (Bill) (son of HL) 183, 195, 206, 253
Law, Jude 243
Law, Phyllida 18, 149, 198, 218, 256
Lawrence, Josie 147
le Carré, John 14, 192, 266
Lee & Herring 261
Legends of Treasure Island 197
Lennon, John 59
Lennox, Annie 221
Leonard, Robert Sean 252
Let Them Talk (Laurie album) 203, 258
Leveson, Mark 146
The Liar (Fry novel) 9, 187–8, 198, 223
'Licking Thatcher' (Fry article) 139
The Life of Brian 21
Lindsay, Robert 94, 96

The Listener 91, 139
Literary Review 189
Little & Large 105
Little Crackers 30
LittleBigPlanet 3 (game) 259
Live Aid 113, 114
Live From the Lighthouse 250, 270
Livingstone, Ken 121
Lloyd, Claudia 225
Lloyd, John: *ABOF&L* 139, 163; *Alfresco* 86; *The Black Adder* 86; *Blackadder II* 102, 103; *Blackadder the Third* 128, 129; *Blackadder Goes Forth* 166; *Blackadder Back & Forth* 250; British comedy 104; Cambridge Footlights 17, 69; *Central Weekend* 126; *Not the Nine O'Clock News* 21, 56; *QI* 248, 251; *South of Watford* 115; *Spitting Image* 86, 121; *Weekend In Wallop* 103
Lloyd Webber, Andrew 205
Loadsamoney 147
Lochhead, Liz 74
Longhair, Professor 14, 142
Loose Ends 99–100
Lowe, Alex 198
Ludwig the Indestructible, Prince 104
Lynam, Chris 167
Lyndhurst, Nicholas 206
Lyttelton, Humphrey 251

Macfadyen, Matthew 205
The Magic Roundabout 18
Main Wilson, Dennis 70, 71
Making History (Fry novel) 247
The Man Behind the Green Door 83
Mandela, Nelson 148
Mangan, Stephen 205
Manning, Bernard 125–6
Mantle, Clive 218
Marchant, Bevis 98–9
Margolyes, Miriam 148, 156, 256

Marks, Laurence 160
Marshall, Andrew 156
The Mary Whitehouse Experience 211, 261
The Mausoleum Club 132
Mayall, Rik: *Bigger Than Hitler, Better Than Christ* 238; *The Black Adder* 103; *Blackadder II* 103; *Bottom* 238; *Cell Mates* 224, 233, 234–5, 236, 237–8; *The Common Pursuit* 148; *The Dangerous Brothers* 104, 107, 109, 130; *Filthy Rich & Catflap* 114; Fry on 73–4; health 238; Kevin Turvey 83, 103; *A Kick Up the Eighties* 73, 83; *The Man Behind the Green Door* 83; *The New Statesman* 160; Rik & Ade double act 104, 105, 107, 109, 130, 197; live dates 197; *Weekend In Wallop* 103; *The Young Ones* 74
Maybe Baby 244
McBurney, Simon 20, 24, 50, 52
McCloud, Kevin 56
McGinley, Patrick 198
McGivern, Geoffrey 17, 177
McGowan, Alistair 201
McGrath, Rory 17, 20, 24, 94
McHale, Joel 265
McInnerny, Tim 79, 120, 127, 128, 165, 166, 223
McIntyre, Phil 116, 137, 138
McKellen, Ian 54, 138
McNally, Kevin 217, 218
'm'colleague' 190, 225
McShane, Mike 184
Me and My Girl 20, 92–4, 96, 102, 115
Meat Loaf 123
Mel & Sue 250, 261
Melchett (Baron/General/Lord) 57, 75, 83, 103–4, 147, 161, 166–7, 250, 257
Melville, Pauline 66

Men Behaving Badly 218
Michael, Ralph 177, 260
Millennium Dome
   Blackadder 250
Miller, Ben 261
Miller, Max 17, 34, 55
Mills, Nick 20
Mitchell, David 260, 261
Mitchell & Webb 260, 261, 263
Mitchinson, John 248
Moir, Jim (TV executive) 86, 116
Moir, Jim (Vic Reeves) 7, 184, 186
Molina, Alfred 74
Monkhouse, Bob 206
Monsters vs Aliens 257
Montgomery, Lucy 261
Monty, Lord 89, 128
Monty Python's Flying Circus 15, 33–5, 66, 114, 139, 151, 157–8, 183, 209, 256
Moore, Dudley 6, 195, 232, 240, 254, 266; *see also* Cook & Moore
Moore, Stephen 218
Morecambe, Eric 105
Morecambe & Wise 7, 72, 105, 150, 152, 184
Morris, Chris 99, 150
Morrison, Steve 78, 169
Mortimer, Bob 7, 184; *see also* Reeves & Mortimer
Mostyn, Peter 80, 107
'Mrs Stephen Fry' 249
Much Obliged, Jeeves (Wodehouse) 204
Muir, Frank 188
Muldoon, Freddie 178, 180
Muldoon, Neddy 193
Mullarkey, Neil 50, 59
Mulville, Jimmy 17, 20, 94, 147
Mummers Club, Cambridge 7, 45
Murchison, Tony *see* Tony & Control
Murdoch, Richard 'Stinker' 17
Murdoch, Rupert 179
Mythos (Fry) 266

The Nearly Complete and Utter History of Everything 250
Ned Blessing 206
Nesbitt, Rab C. 225
Neumann, Marianne (mother of SF) *see* Fry, Marianne
Neumann, Martin (grandfather of SF) 25–6, 28, 29, 223
The New Statesman 160
Newman, Rob 211
Newsnight 99
The Night Manager 266
Nightcap (Footlights show) 7, 20, 21, 22, 44
Nineteen-Ninety-Four 96
Nineteen-Ninety-Eight 98
Niven, David 169
Nobbs, David 206
Noel Gay Organisation 20, 64, 79, 115, 199
Norden, Denis 22
Norman, Barry 22
Norton, Deborah 156, 161, 176
Not Only … But Also 28, 147
Not the Nine O'Clock News 21, 56, 66, 72–3

The Oblivion Boys 105
Ockrent, Mike 92
The Ode Less Travelled (Fry) 247
Oedipus Rex 44
'Oh, Christ, I've left the iron on!' 119, 177
Old Flames 148
Oliver, John 261
On The Hour 99, 150
On the Margin 28
101 Dalmatians 243
Open to Question 109, 114, 126
The Oranges 257
Ordish, Roger 131, 132, 143, 156, 158, 162, 163, 179–80, 189–90
Orton, Joe 47
O.T.T. 89
Out There (Fry documentary) 244

Oxbridge comedy 73, 77, 89, 194, 209, 262
Oxford University 24, 120, 261

Pace, Norman 105; *see also* Hale & Pace
Palin, Michael 245, 248
Palmer, Geoffrey 206
Palmer, James 16, 22
The Paper Soldier (Laurie planned novel) 247
Paperweight (Fry collection) 189
Parkinson, Michael 141, 227
Partridge, Alan 225
The Party Party 98, 218
Patterson, Dan 131, 132, 133, 146
Percy, Lord 127, 129
Perfect Nonsense 205
Perkins, Geoffrey 177
Perkins, Sue 250, 261
Pete & Dud 28, 240; *see also* Cook & Moore
Peter & John 154, 165, 177, 178, 180
Peter's Friends 198–201, 202, 206, 218
Pigmot, Lord, Majestic Prince of Frumpity 161
A Pin for the Butterfly 221
Pinter, Harold 148, 236
Planer, Nigel 249
Planet Word 245
'Please, Mr Music, will you play…?' 133, 239
Plowman, Jon: *ABOF&L* 209, 210–11, 213, 214, 219, 227, 230, 234; on *Alfresco* 96; *Beyond the Footlights* 70; *A Sense of Nonsense* 72; on sketch comedy 262–3; *There's Nothing to Worry About!* 74, 77, 78
plumpening of scripts 128, 129, 161, 166
Pocoyo 257
politics 77, 139–40, 179
Pols, Robert 38
Poor White Trash 220, 222
Pope, Philip 176, 178, 220

Popey, William 156
Posner, Geoff 70, 105, 110, 120, 225
Price, Dennis 169, 196
Punt, Steve 67, 211

QI (Quite Interesting) 248–9, 251
Queens' College, Cambridge 40–3, 45, 48
Quentin, Caroline 206, 218

Radio 1, *Beatnews* 98–9
Radio 4: *ABOF&L* 227–8; debut Laurie appearance 22; *Delve Special* 99, 115, 131; Fry on 98, 132; *I'm Sorry I Haven't a Clue* 101, 251; *Just a Minute* 101; *Loose Ends* 99–100; *Saturday Night Fry* 131–3, 149–50; *Whose Line Is It Anyway?* 146
Radio Times 150, 174, 226
Randi, James 222
Ravens, Jan 22, 48, 50, 59
Raw Sex 219, 220
The Real McCoy 225
Red Dwarf 150
Red Nose Day 114, 146–7, 184, 260
Redmond, Siobhan 74, 84, 95, 96
Reeves, Vic 7, 184, 186
Reeves & Mortimer 7, 184, 197, 205, 211, 225, 260
Reid, Anne 177
Reilly, John C. 259
Reitel, Enn 146
Revenge (The Stars' Tennis Balls) (Fry novel) 247
Richard, Cliff 113
Richardson, Miranda 103, 129
Richardson, Peter 74
Rickman, Alan 222
Rider, Steve 213
Right Said Fred 221
Rik & Ade 104, 105, 109, 130, 197; *see also* Edmondson, Ade; Mayall, Rik
Ritchie, Guy 259

Rivron, Rowland 114, 219, 220, 221
Robinson, Robert 35, 89, 193, 194
Robinson, Tony 99, 165, 245
Ross, Sandy 72, 74, 86
Rowling, J. K. 246
Royal Variety Performance 139
Rudner, Rita 190, 198, 202
Russell-Beale, Simon 52, 102, 250

Sabotage! 250
Sachs, Andrew 205
Sahlins, Bernie 78
Sarchet, Tony 99
Sastry, Sunetra 103, 145, 186
Saturday Live 97, 104, 105–13, 115, 119–23, 130, 220
Saturday Night Fry 131–3, 149–50, 269
Saturday Night Live (US) 260
Saturday Stayback 74
Saunders, Jennifer 97, 105, 153, 209, 260; *see also* French & Saunders
Savident, John 87
Sayle, Alexei 66, 74, 89–90, 114, 212, 225
The Secret Life of the Manic Depressive (Fry documentary) 244
Secret Policeman's Ball 114
Secret Policeman's Third Ball 124–5
Seddon, James 71
Sellers, Peter 175, 178
Selwyn College, Cambridge 7, 10, 15, 16
Sense and Sensibility (film) 222
A Sense of Nonsense 68, 72
Sessions, John 146, 148, 150
Shand, Neil 126
Sharpe, Tom 168, 197
Shaw, Sandie 226
Shearer, Paul 50–1, 53, 56, 65, 69, 77–8, 83, 87, 96, 102

Sheen, Michael 243
Sherlock Holmes films 259
Sherlock Holmes Society 36
Sherman, Peter *see* Peter & John
Sherrin, Ned 99, 100, 131
Shore, David 230, 252
Sinclair, John Gordon 205
Singer, Bryan 252
sketch comedy 44, 72, 116, 155, 158, 256, 262–3
sketches: 'Ballet Masterclass' 133; 'Barber' 157; 'Barman' 219; 'Cakes' 50; 'The Cause' 178, 193; 'Comedy Masterclass' 108–9, 139; *Countdown* 192–3; 'Dancercises' 181; 'difficulty of writing a sketch' sketch 206–8; 'Flowers for Wendy' 216; Fry's memories 241; 'Gannet' 76; 'Get Well Card' 229; 'The Hedge Sketch' 119–20, 124, 184, 250; 'Honour' 135, 136–7, 142; 'Inspector Venice' 157; 'Language' 136; 'The Letter' 57–8; 'Major Donaldson' 178; 'Marmalade' 195; masterclasses 108; 'Merchant Banker' (Python sketch) 114; 'My Darling' 57; 'Operational Criteria' 210; 'Pet Shop' 230; 'Piano Masterclass' 108, 133, 138; 'Pimhole' 260; 'Police PLC' 139; 'Prize Poem' 133–4, 139, 216; 'Prompt' 142; prototype shop sketch 85–6; 'Race Driver' 219; 'Shakespeare Masterclass' 54, 103, 106, 116; 'Sound Name' 229; 'Soup' 157; 'Special Squad' 156; 'Spies' sketches 154, 184, 274–7; 'Tales of the Barely Credible' 84–5;

'Tomorrow' 87–8;
'Troubleshooters' 153–4, 165; 'The Two of Us Again' 215–16; *see also* unseen archive extracts
Slattery, Tony: Cambridge Footlights 52, 58, 59, 60, 67; *The Cellar Tapes* TV recording 70; depression 244; Footlights centenary documentary 102; *Hysteria* shows 184; *Kingdom* 256; *Peter's Friends* 198; *Saturday Stayback* 74; *This Is David Harper* 148
sloblock (anagram) 193
The Smell of Reeves & Mortimer 211
Smith, Liz 177
Smith, Mel 21, 89, 103, 105, 197, 217
Smith & Jones 105, 153, 197, 211
SNF *see Saturday Night Fry*
Snot, Lord 89
The Snow Queen (Footlights pantomime) 24–5, 48, 50–1, 52
So Much Blood 98
Sodom, Colonel 75
songs: *ABOF&L* 219–20; 'America' 137, 221; 'The Ballad of Neddy Muldoon' 193; 'Everybody Hates You' 59; 'Grease My Gristle, Blow My Whistle' 191; 'I Want to Shoot Somebody Famous' 59; IRA song 7–8, 48; 'Little Girl' 219; 'Mardi Gras' 142; 'Minnie The Moocher' 172, 203; 'Mystery' 137; 'One Thing Song' 364; 'Steffi Graf' 219; 'Stick It Out' (Comic Relief) 221; 'Turnpike Song' 363; 'What Would I Do Without You, Jeeves?' 203; 'You You You' 220
'Soupy twist!' 193–5, 219, 238
South of Watford 115

Spanking, Mr 85
Spearing, Tony 100
Spencer, Elliott 265
Spiers, Bob 209, 214, 219
Spitting Image 86, 102, 121, 138, 146, 175, 201–2, 238
spoffle, invention of 82
Sprout Pictures 245
Squeeze 84
Stalag Luft 206
Stanshall, Vivian 33, 34, 69
The Stars' Tennis Balls (Fry novel) 247
Staunton, Imelda 'Snutty' 199, 200, 218, 222, 259
Stavros 112, 138
Steadman, Alison 149
Steen, Steve 192, 206
Stephenson, Pamela 21
Stoneham, Harry 142
'The Stonker' (Comic Relief) 184
Strapless 150
Strom language 77, 149, 191, 216
Stuart Little 243
Suchet, David 54, 169, 250
Super Clyde 254
Swinton, Tilda 51, 52
Symons, Nick: *ABOF&L* 163, 164, 178, 191, 193, 205, 209; Cambridge Footlights 22, 50, 59, 65; *Kingdom* radio pilot 256; living with Fry & Laurie 65, 98, 112; *Nineteen-Ninety-Four* 96; royalty visit 175

Talent, Juliana 59; *see also* Thompson, Emma
Talkback 105
The Tall Guy 175
Tarrant, Major Alan 191, 192
Tarrant, Chris 74, 89
Tavener, Mark 217
Temple, John 94
Terrence Higgins Trust 138
Tewson, Jane 113
Théâtre de Complicité 52
There's Nothing to Worry About! 77–8

The Thick of It 217
The Thin Blue Line 242
'Things I Do Not Do' (Fry article) 91–2
This Is David Harper 148
This Is David Lander 99, 147, 148
This Is Jinsy 260
Thompson, Emma: *Alfresco* 85, 88, 94; *Beyond the Footlights* 71; and Branagh 121, 201; at Cambridge 7, 45, 47–8; Cambridge Footlights 18–20, 22, 25, 47, 50–2, 57, 59; *The Cellar Tapes* 59, 65, 68; *The Crystal Cube* 87, 88; on Elton 75; *Emma Thompson Up for Grabs* 121; *Friday Night, Saturday Morning* 24; and Fry 44, 130; on Fry & Laurie 68; Fry & Laurie pilot 86, 87; *Happy Families* 97; and Harris 187; Hollywood Star 1, 253; and Laurie 18–19; *Maybe Baby* 244; *Me and My Girl* 94, 96–7; *Peter's Friends* 198, 201; *Saturday Live* 121; *Saturday Night Fry* 132, 149; *Sense and Sensibility* 222; *Spitting Image* puppet 201; *There's Nothing to Worry About!* 76, 77; Thompson 121; *Tutti Frutti* 121; *Women's Hour* 48; *The Young Ones* 89
Thompson, Eric 18, 22
Thompson, Sophie 18
Thorpe, Harriet 177
3 Bits Of Fry & Laurie (tie-in book) 196
Thruss, Bennifer 132
Tideyman's Carpets 178
Tiger Aspect 105
Tish & Pish (Ferris book) 249
Toksvig, Sandi 20, 22, 48, 52, 59, 249
Tomorrowland 253

Tony & Control 154–5, 164, 180, 184, 274–7
Treacher, Arthur 169
Trefusis, Professor Donald ix, 100, 188, 247
Trouser, Trouser, Trouser 74
'Trouser trouser trouser!' 142
The Tube 114
Turner, Tina 167
Turvey, Kevin 83, 103
Tutti Frutti 121
Twelfth Night (Shakespeare) 257
24: Live Another Day 265
The Two of Us 254
The Two Ronnies 104, 105, 120, 150, 164, 220, 250

Ullman, Tracey 107, 243
University Challenge 45, 89
unseen archive extracts: 'Attack Dog' 305–7; 'British National' 302–5; 'Celebrities Tonight' 357–8; 'Climb Every Mountain' 326; 'Clive & Clive' 281–4; 'Coffee' 279–81; 'Critical Review' 315–16; 'Curriculum Complaint' 307–12; 'Deed Poll' 291–4; 'Etiquette' 277–9; 'Fan Club' 313–15; 'The Farkling' 329–32; 'Gaslight' 284–6; 'Genital Nonsense' 288–9; 'Hello Julian What Are You Up To?' 300–2; 'I'd Like to Buy' 336–7; 'I'm a Sucker' 361–3; 'Insurance' 289–90; 'Interval' 317–19; 'Lavatory Monologue' 290; 'Niceness Police' 352–5; 'Novels' 294–5; 'Odd' 319–20; 'One Thing Song' 364; 'Oster Milepiece' 338–9; 'Passport' 320–1; 'Penises' 326–7; 'Play for Today' 286–8; 'Porter' 340–3; 'Privatisation' 351–2; 'The Professionals' 316–17; 'Rival Parents' 295–9; 'Sergeant Davies' 327–9; 'The Seven Functioning Arses of Maxwell Furnitt' 288; 'Shop Assistant' 343–4; 'Smoking' 321–4; 'Spectre' 360–1; 'Spies Taxi' 274–7; 'Stage Directions' 312–13; 'Stephen's Zoo' 344–7; 'Strange Studio Link' 324; 'Suspicious Git' 358–9; 'Tart' 355–7; 'Tidy Your Room' 347–51; 'Turnpike Song' 363; 'Two Undergraduates' 273–4; 'Viewing Clothes' 324–5; 'What Do You Think' 325–6; 'Wrestling' 332–5
'Untitled Epic' (Fry poem) 38
Upstart Crow 260
Ure, Midge 114

V for Vendetta 242
Veep 266
Video Arts 80
videogames 259, 271
Vile Bodies (Waugh) 248
'Virtual Fry' app 246
Viz comic 202, 246
Vorderman, Carol 193
'Vox Pops' (*ABOF&L*) 157–60, 176, 177, 190, 196, 216, 231
Vranch, Richard 67

Waistsplendour, Frillidy 132
Ward, Simon 237
Wardle, Irving 71
Waugh, Evelyn 248
Wax, Ruby 244
Webb, Robert 205, 260, 261, 263
Weekend In Wallop 103
Wegman, William 142
Wellington, Duke of 129, 130, 250
Wheeler, Simon 256
Whitehouse, Paul 112, 113, 179, 180, 226, 260
Whiteley, Richard 192, 193
Whiting, Alan 256
Whitrow, Benjamin 157
Who Dares Wins 94, 138
Whose Line Is It Anyway? 146, 148
Wilde (film) 242–3
Wilde, Oscar 31, 32, 47, 206, 242, 259
Wildebeest, Theophilus P. 127
Williams, Kenneth 115
Williams, Mark 243
Wilson, Harold 21
Wilson, Jack 10
Wilton, Robb 34
Wind in the Willows 197
Wodehouse, P. G.: *Aunts Aren't Gentlemen* 203, 204; *Frozen Assets* 46; Fry & Laurie 13–14, 30, 46, 91, 169, 170; *Galahad at Blandings* 14; *Jeeves & Wooster* series 169–74, 182, 183, 196, 197, 203–5; *Jeeves in the Offing* 203; Ritz Hotel 39
Wogan 8, 115, 146, 196, 197, 211
Wogan, Terry 196, 197
Women's Hour 48
Wood, Jo 36
Wood, Victoria 74, 153, 190, 243
Woolf, Virginia 113
Words with Stephen Fry 265
The World of Jeeves & Wooster (LP) 203
The World of Wooster 33, 169
'The Wow Show' 104

Yentob, Alan 210, 227
Yes, Prime Minister 156
Yonderland 260
Young, Robert 171
The Young Ones 74, 83, 89–90, 94, 113, 216

Unbound
Liberating ideas

Unbound is the world's first crowdfunding publisher, established in 2011.

We believe that wonderful things can happen when you clear a path for people who share a passion.

That's why we've built a platform that brings together readers and authors to crowdfund books they believe in – and give fresh ideas that don't fit the traditional mould the chance they deserve.

This book is in your hands because readers made it possible. Everyone who pledged their support is listed below.

Join them by visiting unbound.com and supporting a book today.

Paul Abbott
Sharon Ackland
Heidi Afele
Kevin Aitchison
Annie Aizon Karaan
Susan Allardyce
Beth Allen
David Robert Allen
Marc Allen
Mark Allison
Karen Anderson
Anitha & Sridhar
Teresa Ankin

Rich Ard
Sandra Armor
Evan Armour
Wendy Armstrong
Jon Arnold
Craig Arnush
Michael Arthur
Adrian Ashton
Samantha Atherton
Luke Atkins
Rayna Azuma
James Bachman
Sarah Baggott

Nicholas Baker
Ian Bald
Cliff Bambridge
Karen Banno
Natasha Barrault
Gavin Bartlet
Simon Battersby
Rhoda Baxter
Adam Baylis-West
Paul Beaman
Sean Beattie
Adrian Belcher
Matthew Bell

Gareth Bellamy
Marcus
    Vinicius Benedicto
Cindy & James Bennett
Daniel Benoliel
Julian Benton
Matthew Best
Jo Biddiscombe
Glynn Bird
Kyle Bishop
Suman Biswas
Kim Bjarkman
Carmel & Jason Black
Matt Blackler
Nicholas Blair
Louise Blakelock
Philip Boardman
Günther Boeyens
Rachael Bohn
Tom Boon
E. Tristan Booth
Florus Both
Nezih Bouali
Libby Bounds
Andy Bower
Jules Bowes
Bruce Bowie
Nick Bradbury
Matt Braithwaite
Andrew Brebner
Philip Brennan
James Brew
Neil Brewitt
Christopher Brochon
Diana Broeders
Margaret JC Brown
Julian Browne
Judy Brownsword

Phil Bruce-Moore
Nicola Brunger
Richard Budgey
Niel Bushnell
Margaret Cabourn-
    Smith
Nicola Cadogan
Maria Mar Calleja
David Callier
Sue Campbell
Carla Campero
Andy & Joy Candler
Thomas Canning
Jon Canter
Blu Cantrell
Brittany Carr
Zoë Carroll
Zoé Carty
Chris Carus
Susan T Case
Christian Cawley
David
    Lars Chamberlain
Kayleigh Chan
Jeannine Chang
Chris Chantler
Andy Chapman
Shao Ying Choo
Christine
Julian Christopher
Rob Clark
Jenny Clarke
Paula Clarke Bain
John-Paul Clough
Garrett Coakley
Stuart Coates
Robert Cole
Leo Collett

Joel Collins
Melusine Colwell
Jack Compere
Paul Cooke
Bruce Cooper
Stephanie Cornwell
Jo Cosgriff
Andrew Cotterill
Christelle Couchoux
Simon Coward
Jonathan 'Jake' Cox
Stuart Gordon Craig
Ewan Crawford
Adam Cresser
Richard Croasdale
Kate Crockett
Deborah Crook
Steven Croston
Tony Cullen
Heather Culpin
Ian Cummings
James Cuningham
Stephen Cunningham
Jules Curran
Tanya Curtis
Catherine Daly
Clare Daniels
Carole Davies
Carolyn Davies
Chris Davis
Andy Dawson
John de Jong
Deadmanjones
Nick Dean
Connie Dee
Sandy DeMartini
Dan Deming-Henes
Chris Dewar-English

John Dexter
Matthew Diamond
Regien Dilg
Trevor Dolby
Richard Donlan
Jason Douglas
Claire Douglass
Dan Duffek
Charles Dundas
Simon Dunn
Matthew Durey
Chris Durie
Laura Đurinec
Caius Durling
John Earls
Daniel Earwicker
Barnaby Eaton-Jones
Anne-Marie Edmonds
Brian Edwards
Cian Egan
Josh Egginton
Monika Eidt
Steve and
  Michelle Elgersma
Elizabeth Ellis
Neil Emery
Selvy Emmanuel
Lucelli Enriquez
Carolyn Estes
Chris Evans
Tom Fassnidge
Simon Fathers
Peter Faulkner
Joshua Feasel
Daniel Felice
Madeleine Fenner
Corinne Fernando
Øygunn Fet

Stuart Fewtrell
Paul Fillery
Deborah Fishburn
Andrew Fisher
Annica Flödén
Ron Florax
Connor Flys
Sarah Forbes
Stephen Forcer
Cory Foster
Michele Foulger
Joanna Franks
Catherine Frankton
Samuel Frost
Andrew Fryett
Jan Funchess
Ian Furbank
Michael Fürstenberg
Simon Gale
Joseph Gander
Paco B. Garcia
Matthew Gathercole
Martin Gear
The Gedemondan
Geoffrey Gifford
Pam Gillespie
Richard Gilmore
Fab Giovanetti
Marcus Gipps
Sherri Goldman
Fenneke Gonggrijp
Neil Gooderham
Mark Goodyear
Jo Gostling
Rachel Gough
Charlie Gould
Karen Grant-Bond
Sean Gray

Simon Greenwood
Katrina Griffiths
Mark Griffiths
Mike Griffiths
Davida Grimes
George Grimwood
Matt Grist
Zhongtian Guan
Rebekka Gudehus
Louisa Gummer
Jóhann
  Georg Gunnarsson
Janet Guo
Amelia Hackworth
David Haddock
Mark Hainsworth
Andy Hall
Dani Hall
Katherine Hall
Paul Halligan
Deborah Halpryn
Louise Hamilton
Catherine Hanley
Donna Hanley
Ryan Hanley
Michaele Hannemann
Kate Harbour
Samyogita Hardikar
Estelle Hargraves
Dianne Harmata
Andrea Harms
Simon Harper
Lisa Hart
Simon Hart
P Hartland
Martha Hartman
Dave Harvey
Brogan Hastings

Krister Haugen
Jonny Haw
G.D. Hayes
Richard Hayter
Nik Hayward
Tony Hayward
Hazel Haywood
Jason Hazeley
Alan Hazlie
Chris Head
Jonathan Head
Rachael Headrick
Charlotte Heathcote
Alan Hedgcock
Margot Heesakker
Sally Henderson
Iain Hepburn
Karen Hepworth
Sandy Herbert
Patricia Herterich
Sean Hewitt
G. J. Hick
Mary Hiles
Eleanor Hill
Matthew H. Hill
Ulrike Hillebrand
Ed Hind
Mary R Hinsdale
Ted Hobgood
Claire Hobson
Lauretta Hobson
Amy Hodges
Denise Hoelandt
Dave Hollander
Rob Holloway
Iain Holmes
Janice Holve
Samuel J. Hooper

Stephen Hoppe
Jen Howard
Robert Howcroft
Doug Hudson
Anne Hungerford-Lowell
Richard Hunt
Jane Hunter
Jon Hunter
Nancy Hutchings
Nadine Ingham
Alison Irwin
Stephen Jackson
Oscar Jacques
Cameron James
Scott Jamieson
Laura Jellicoe
Rob Jenkins
Paul Jenner
Tim Jenness
Susanne Jensen
Tone Jensen
Cathy Jesser
Marjorie Johns
Trish Johns
David Johnson
Lauren Johnston
Daniel Jones
Julie Jones
Raymond Wynne Jones
Rebecca Jones
Åsa Anastasia Jonsén
Nynne Smedegaard Jørgensen
Tobias Joss
Erin Justice
Keith Kahn-Harris
Sam Kaislaniemi

Emma Kako
Shashwati Kala
Orange Kana
Jørgen Kann
Yuko Kato
Caroline Kay
Jacqui Kelly
Adam Kennedy
Scott Kennedy
Steven Kennedy
Ida Berglöw Kenneway
Stephen Kent-Taylor
Emily Kenworthy
Sean Keogh
Julian Key
Dan Kieran
Haram Kim
Cathy King
Julian King
Will King
Julie King-Henry
Simon Kingston
Joe 'Ofrty' Kirkham
Adam Kirtland
Doron Klemer
Narell Klingberg
Evay Knecht
Andy 'Pimhole' Knight
Tim Knight
Richard Knowles
Sam Knowles
Barend Köbben
Larissa Kockelkorn
Robin Kok
Raymond Koole
Sven Körner
Marguerite Krause
Nicole Krumm

David Kuchheuser
Roy Lake
Monica Lamont
Alexandra Lanoix
Warren Lapworth
Jordan Lara
Sarah Louise Lashley
Darcy Latremouille
Nicola Lawson
James Le Lacheur
Jørgen Leditzig
Dave Lee
Sanna Lehtonen
Agnes Leijon
Joe Leyare
Peiyuan Li
Katrin Liang
Michael Lloyd-Jones
Isabell Lorenz
James Lowe
Aude Lumiere
Frida M. Lund
Andreas Lundgren
Andre Luth
Jen Lutley
James Lydon
Tom Lynton
Mike Lythgoe
Amy MacDonald
Chris Macdonald
Seonaid Mackenzie
Darrell Maclaine-Jones
Sarah Maidstone-Henriksen
Christopher 'Chris' Man
Katharine Manfè
Chris Mannion

Anthony Maplesden
Milcah Marcelo
Heather Marchant
Georgina Marcisz
Nick Marple
Sarah K. Marr
Mary Rouine Marsh
Charlotte Martyn
Kati Marx
Dan Mason
Reb Mason
Laetitia Mavrel
Patty Mazzocca
Kyle McAbee
Carol McCollough
Ailsa McCullagh
Anne-Marie McElhinney
Molly McEnerney
Daniel McGachey
Ian McGill
Mark McKean
Dhugael McLean
Steven Medcraft
Jonathan Melville
David Merrick
Rob Mesure
John Mitchinson
Fiona Mitford
Jared Mobarak
Meredith Modzelewski
Azhul Mohamed
Ken Monaghan
Ryan Mooney
Mike Moore
Rebecca Moore
Robert Moore
Jade Moores

Pierce Moran
Charles Morgan
Deb Morris
Iain Morrison
Victoria Mostue
Daisy Muir
Duncan Muir
Ella Muir
Helen Muir
Rik Muller
Lauren G L Mulville
Yoshiko Murakami
Andy Murray
Clive Murray
Ewen Murray
Martin Mycock
Judy Myers
Carlo Navato
Chris Neale
Owen Needles
Erik Nell
Antony Nelson
Kara Nelson
Roo Newton
Cindy Nielsen
Cindy Nielsen
Marie-Jose Nieuwkoop
Erika Noguchi
Betty Anne Noir
Martin Nooteboom
Clare Norris
Remembering O
Brian O'Connor
Paul Oakley
Anna-Maja Oléhn
Gregory Olver
Patricia Oppenheim
Robert P

Tim Page
Lev Parikian
Kirsty Parker
Ol Parker
Robin Parker
Christopher Parsons
Damon Parsons
Steve Parsons
Virginia Pasley
Amie Patton
Jo-Anne Pawley
Torrie Payne
Kevin Pazdernik
Noreen Pazderski
Lesley Pearson
Francois Peaudecerf
Aric Pedersen
Nigel Pennington
Alexandra Perelygina
James Perrin
Alexander Peterhans
John Petrie
Hazel Phillips
Laura Phillips
Anita Philpott
Simon Picard
Neville Pitty-Rose
Hannah Platts
Andy Polaine
Justin Pollard
Ashley Porciuncula
Gregg Porter
John Porter
Gudrun Pötzelberger
Neil Pretty
Rhian Heulwen Price
Caroline Priestley
James Priestley

Helen Quigley
Barbara Raekson
Sean Raffey
Duncan Raggett
John Rain
Adam Raven
Lily Redman
Helen Reece
Mark Reed
Gareth Rees
D S Reifferscheid
René Reinholz
Jeannette Remington
Annie Richards
Stephen Richards
Tim Richards
Kieran Rid
Jessica Ridders
Darren Rigby-O'Neill
Matt Riggsby
Amanda Rippon
Rinat Ritchie
Zuza Ritt
Jan Rivers
Alexander Roberts
Jane Roberts
Jon Roberts
Nick Roberts
Anthea Robertson
Kev Roe
Colin 'Dammit Peter' Rogers
Wojciech Rogozinski
Ira Rosenblatt
John Roughton
Jane Rowe
Christina Royal
Benjamin Russell

Gerard Ryan
Stephen Sadler
Dr. Daniella Saltz
Dolores Sams
Steven Schwartz
Colin A Scott
Siobhan Scott
Stewart Scott
Pat Scrimgeour
Jack Seale
Sam Seaver
Chadwick Severn
Alan Shaw
Andy Sheard
Richard Sheppard
Tabitha Siklos
Eileen Silcocks
Uncle Paul Silcox
Neil Simmons
David Simpkin
Matt Simpson
Inbal Sinai
Kim Sirag
SisterRainbow
Denise Skea
Lisette Skyrme
Remco Slager
Nicola Slater
Miss Smee
Derrick Smith
Marc Smith
Richard Smith
Scott Smith
Sharon Smith
Simon Smith
Will Smith
Nicholas Snowdon
Christie Snyder

Jenny Sparks
Duncan Speed
Stephanie Spurr
David Stacey-Gee
Chris Stallard
Mark Stay
David Stelling
Jim Stevens
Kelly Stevens
Martin Štochl
Paul 'Stokesie' Stokes
Chris Storer
Michael Story
Lauren Strauss-Jones
Arielle Sumits
Anja Summa
Scott Sundberg
Robin Suoss
Keith Sutherland
Lindsay Swann
David Swendeman
Keith Talbot
Marjolein Tamis
Neil Xavier Taylor
Richard Taylor
Paul Taylor-Greaves
Elaine Teenan
Andrew Tetreault
Claudia Lovell Tetreault
Ben Thomas
Jayne Thomas
Scott Thomas
Nicholas Thompson
Nick Thompson
Rory Thompson
Bridget Thornton
James Thrift
Danson Thunderbolt

Amanda Thurman
Ben Thurston
Magnus Tjernström
Katherine Tomkins
Graham Tomlinson
Samuel Toogood
Molly Torra
Elizabeth Townsend
Karen Trethewey
Stephen Trudgian
Konchong Tsering
Andy Tubb
David G Tubby
SB Tucker
Olivia Twose
Simcha Udwin
Wilko Ufert
Nikita van 't Rood
George Van Veen
Kim van Zundert
Lieven Vandelanotte
Scott Varnham
Kostyantyn Vasylenko
Kevin Veloso
Jose Vizcaino
Dagmar Viždová
Nicklas von Plenker-Tind
Richard Wainman
Steve Walker
Nick Walpole
Sean Walton
Dean Wanless
Jason Ward
Mo Warden
Bernadine Wasser
Alice Watkins
Gareth Watkins
Mark Watkins

Lilian Weber-Caravia
Matthew Weed
Aletta Welensky
Luke Weston
Paul Whelan
Richard Whitaker
Steve Whitaker
David Whitworth
Wendy Wigger
Andrew Wiggins
Bobby Wilcox
Stuart Wildig
Robin Wilgen
Tony Wilkes
David Williams
Elric Williams
Jenny Williams
Michelle Willis
Eliot Wilson
Stephen Wilson
Suzanne Wilson-Higgins
Carol Wise
Stephen Wise
Ian Wolf
Jia Min Wong
Matthew Wood
Stacey Woods
Steve Woodward
Wendalynn Wordsmith
David Wragg
Chris Wright
Elizabeth Wright
Vivienne Wu
Markus Wuttke
Rupert Wynne
Debbie Wythe
Michael Wyzard
Takako Yamamura

Mary Yang
Akiko Yoshida
Blossom Young
Peter Young
Alena Zaharudin
Liuba Zanardini
Ningshan Zhou
Анна Юдаева